Holiness and Transgression

*Mothers of the Messiah
in the Jewish Myth*

Psychoanalysis and Jewish Life

Series Editor
JESS OLSON (Yeshiva University)

Editorial Board

SUSANNAH HESCHEL, PhD
(Dartmouth College, Hanover)

ARNOLD RICHARDS, MD
(New York University, New York)

MOSHE HALEVI SPERO, PhD
(Bar-Ilan University, Ramat Gan)

KAREN STARR, PsyD
(Long Island University at C.W. Post, Brookville, New York)

Holiness and Transgression
Mothers of the Messiah in the Jewish Myth

Ruth Kara-Ivanov Kaniel

Translated by **Eugene D. Matanky** with
Ruth Kara-Ivanov Kaniel

Boston
2017

Library of Congress Cataloging-in-Publication Data

Names: Kara-Ivanov Kaniel, Ruth, 1979- author.

Title: Holiness and Transgression: Mothers of the Messiah in the Jewish Myth / Ruth Kara-Ivanov Kaniel.

Other titles: Qedeshot u-Qedoshot: Imahot ha-Mashi'ah ba-Mitos haYehudi.

Description: Boston: Academic Studies Press, [2017]

Series: Psychoanalysis and Jewish life | Includes bibliographical references.

Identifiers: LCCN 2016046319 (print) | LCCN 2016046459 (ebook) | ISBN 9781618115607 (hardcover) | ISBN 9781618115614 (e-book)

Subjects: LCSH: Jewish mythology. | Messiah—Judaism. | Mothers in the Bible. | Mothers and sons—Religious aspects—Judaism.

Classification: LCC BM530 .K354 2017 (print) | LCC BM530 (ebook) | DDC 296.3/360852—dc23

LC record available at https://lccn.loc.gov/2016046319

Copyright© 2017, Academic Studies Press
ISBN 978-1-64469-014-7
ISBN 978-1-61811-561-4 (electronic)

Book design by Kryon Publishing
www.kryonpublishing.com
On the cover: *Ruth*, by Ephraim Moshe Lilien. 1911.

Academic Studies Press
28 Montfern Avenue
Brighton, MA 02135, USA
www.academicstudiespress.com
press@academicstudiespress.com

Table of Contents

Acknowledgments	vii
Translator's Note	ix
Introduction	x

PART ONE
Messianic Mothers in the Bible — 01

1. Feminine Genealogy and the Lineage of the House of David — 07
2. The Type-Scene of "The Birth of the Messianic Hero" — 26

PART TWO
The Messianic Mother in Rabbinic Literature—Sororal Love and "Ethics of Redemption" — 71

3. David's Mother(s) in *Yalkut ha-Makhiri* — 73
4. *Gedolah Aveirah Lishmah*—From Rabbinic Literature to the Messianic Teachings of R. Moses Ḥayyim Luzzatto — 86

PART THREE
The Messianic Mother in the Zoharic Literature — 112

5. Lot's Daughters and the Zoharic "*Ṭiqla*" — 124
6. The Burning Face of the *Shekhinah*—Tamar in *Zohar Aḥrei Mot* — 146
7. The *Shekhinah*'s Exile and Redemption in Ruth and Naomi's Journey — 173

CONCLUSION
Gender Reversal and the Poetics of Redemption   210

EPILOGUE
The Messianic Mother in Judaism and Christianity   219

Bibliography   253

Index   272

Acknowledgments

Many people collaborated in the writing of this book, and to them all I give my heartfelt thanks and appreciation.

The book is based on my PhD dissertation written at the Hebrew University of Jerusalem, under the supervision of Marc Hirshman, Yehuda Liebes, and Ilana Pardes, who ventured with me on this journey into the unknown. I am indebted to them for their many insights, instructive comments, as well as their encouragement. I would also like to express my gratitude to the Shalom Hartman Institute and its faculty members for many stimulating conversations and innumerable comments and suggestions, as well as their friendship and support. I owe additional thanks to the Tikvah Center for Law and Jewish Civilization at New York University, the Hadassah-Brandeis Institute, the NYU Postdoctoral Program in Psychotherapy and Psychoanalysis, as well as the Department of Jewish Thought at Ben Gurion University of the Negev. My warmest of thanks to all my colleagues and friends at these institutions who supported, encouraged, and criticized my work throughout the writing process. Unfortunately, I cannot name them all here, but they were personally thanked in the Hebrew edition of this book.

Some of the chapters of this book have already been published as articles. The fourth chapter appeared in the journal *Nashim* 24 (2013), as "*Gedolah Averah Lishmah*: the Development of Messianic Thought from Rabbinic Literature to Luzzatto." Chapter five appeared partially in three journals: in *Jerusalem Studies in Jewish Thought* 22 (2011) as "Seed from Another Place: Transformation of the Account of Lot's Daughters," edited by Rachel Elior, and in *ELN* as "The Enigma of the Term 'Tiqla,'" which was based on the Hebrew version published in *Kabbalah* 23 (2010). Chapter six was published in *Yehuda Liebes Festschrift* (2012), and chapter seven appeared in *Da'at* 72 (2012). The epilogue has also appeared in a condensed form in *JAAR* 82 (2014), entitled

"The Myth of the Messianic Mother in Jewish and Christian Traditions: Psychoanalytic and Gender Perspectives." I am grateful to the journal editors for allowing me to reprint these papers here.

My thanks to Gene Matanky for his careful and precise translation, and to Elizabeth Michel for her meticulous editing and her keen eye. I have greatly enjoyed working with you, and appreciate the generous amount of time and effort that you have invested in this project. A special thanks goes to Daniel Matt and Joel Hecker for assisting me with the English translation of the Zoharic homilies. To Dani and David Kazhdan, as well as to Iris Felix, my thanks for their advice and input, and to Lewis Aron, who encouraged me to publish this book in English.

Last but not least, I would like to thank my family and friends. To my friends, who have supported me in this endeavor, I am honored to have your friendship. To my parents, *refuseniks* who taught me Hebrew during those dangerous years in Soviet Russia, who also instilled in me the love of learning Torah, and who continue to inspire and encourage me at every turn. To my children, Hallel, Talya, Evyatar, and Ro'i, who challenge me daily, both emotionally and intellectually. To my helpmate, Asi, who has been a true source of support and love. I can only say that, if not for them, I would not be able to bear the conflict between motherhood and femininity, between a fractured reality and the desire for redemption.

Translator's Note

In this work I have had to make use of many rabbinic texts and have relied upon different translations. The biblical text in this book has largely been quoted from the *Revised Standard Version of the Bible (RSV)*. The Talmudic sections have made use of *The Soncino Talmud*. Midrash Rabbah translations have been mainly from or based on the *Soncino Midrash Rabbah*. The *Zohar* quotations have been selected from the *Zohar Pritzker Edition*, for the available sections. All italics or emphases in these sources have been added by the author. Lastly, works that have originally appeared in Hebrew and were subsequently translated into English are paginated according to the Hebrew edition. The current translation is of the Hebrew title *Qedeshot u-Qedoshot: Imahot ha-Mashi'ah ba-Mitos ha-Yehudi*. This translation was done with the collaboration of the author.

Introduction

The messianic myth has played a central role in Jewish culture for generations. Eschatological concepts and messianic figures left their mark on grand historical processes and constituted a formative power in the areas of religion, cult, theology, and ritual. Messianic wishes and hopes sprouted within the individual and collective soul, echoed throughout midrashic, apocalyptic, and mystical literature, as well as the folkloric tradition. The roots of the messianic idea lie in the Bible, particularly in the descriptions of the Messiah as an elected son and king, in the visions of the prophets, and in the books of Writings. These messianic ideas also influenced Judeo-Christian discourse and attained surprising interpretations in Christology and the theosophic-kabbalah of the Middle Ages.

This book will illuminate the paradoxical roots of the messianic idea and discuss its evolution from the Bible, through the rabbinic Midrashim, and until the Zoharic literature—all canonized corpuses reflecting foundational notions of Jewish culture. I will focus on the narratives of the biblical foremothers of the Davidic dynasty, which is transformed in the Second Temple literature into the dynasty of "the Messiah son of David." I claim that the mother of the Messiah does not represent a particular figure, but a genealogical continuum of female figures bonded through an entangled, intertextual tale. In contrast to the biblical narrative that portrays the foundations of the messianic myth, rabbinic Midrashim focus on ethical questions, while the *Zohar* reflects mystical interpretations of these antinomian trends. Yet in all these corpuses, the Messiah is perceived as a chosen son through the merit of his foremothers and their extraordinary deeds.

The Davidic dynasty in the Bible presents a recurring pattern: seduction and sexual transgression initiated by the feminine heroines cause the birth of the elected son. Beginning with Lot's daughters' incestuous relations with their father, continuing with Tamar masquerading as a harlot and seducing her father-in-law, and culminating with Ruth going to the threshing floor and seducing Boaz (an act that results in King David's birth), this overall pattern of deviance brings about the Messiah's birth. We may also add here the story of Rachel and Leah, two sisters sharing one husband through ruses and bedtricks, and Bathsheba's story, which begins with illicit relations and ends with the birth of King Solomon (who symbolizes an additional chosen son of the royal dynasty). This feminine continuum is characterized by a unique motherly and seductive "type-scene" that merits divine justification and constructs the House of David. Therefore, I propose that the Davidic redeemer is the Messiah "through the merit of his mothers."

The enigmatic bond between transgression and redemption will be examined from mythical and gender perspectives, using a variety of literary, psychoanalytic, and religious theories. I will discuss the cultural function of the heroines' sins and clarify the manner in which the recurring narratives of harlotry, seductiveness, and forbidden relations were understood throughout generations of Jewish interpretation. The study of the messianic myth will follow Mircea Eliade, C. G. Jung, George Bataille, Michel Foucault, and others who claim that the profane forms the sacred, and that taboo is conditioned upon its violation.[1] These assumptions will be analyzed in conjunction with gender and feminist theory. Questions regarding the tension between motherhood and seductiveness, or feminine freedom and agency in the Davidic dynasty, have been treated separately from the messianic myth. I will discuss the figure of the messianic mother from the ancient period until the Middle Ages from both of these perspectives. In my opinion, Mary's miraculous conception should be analyzed as a reaction to the biblical Davidic stories; in the epilogue I will outline the polemic regarding the mother of the Messiah in Judaism and early Christianity, and its influence on the *Zohar*.

As we shall see, the messianic mothers present a normative-halakhic ideal, imitated by women of the Nasi House in the rabbinic era; they were identified with the figure of the *Shekhinah* in kabbalistic literature, and they commonly served as archetypes of motherhood and fertility in a reality dominated by famine, oppression, and death. These women symbolize the active choice of motherhood, rather than the exploitation of childbearing for patriarchal needs. The Messiah's birth in the Bible, Midrash, and Kabbalah demonstrates

---

1 As Bataille writes: "The transgression does not deny the taboo but transcends it and completes it…Organized transgression together with the taboo make social life what it is." Georges Bataille, *Death and Sensuality: A Study of Eroticism and Taboo* (New York: Walker and Company, 1962), 65.

the centrality of feminine heroines in the founding texts of Jewish culture and their narrow spaces of freedom. The choice to devote a book to the "messianic mother" stems from my personal and intellectual search for figures who contended with the tension between motherhood and femininity without losing their connection to desires of personal and collective redemption. These figures reflect rich and layered worlds in which feminine subjectivity, maternal experience, sin, and fantasy are bound in a polyphonic embrace transcending and traversing the Jewish tradition.

THE LAYOUT OF THE BOOK

The book will present the messianic myth in the Bible, rabbinic Midrash and Zoharic literature. In each section I will discuss the enigmatic relationship between feminine sexual transgression and messianic redemption, and analyze its proposed solutions throughout the generations. The first two chapters will discuss the biblical continuum that develops from the individual story of each heroine and connects to the collective template shared by all the messianic mothers. This continuum mitigates the severity of the feminine sins, sublimating the heroines' transgressions while simultaneously broadening their liberty; it thereby intensifies the tension between biblical narrative and law, and illuminates the relations between God, the father, the mother, and the son of the messianic dynasty.

In the third and fourth chapter I will explore the adoption of the messianic type-scene in *Yalkut ha-Makhiri* and examine the story of David's birth in light of his foremothers' narratives. The sages suggest their own subversive reading based on the biblical myth and propose a unique ethic derived from the Davidic heroines' deeds, which I have termed an "ethics of redemption." In the midrash, the sages deal with these figures as a whole but also explore each story individually: Lot's daughters give birth to Moab and Ammon through "the seed that comes from another place," Tamar seduces Judah at the "entrance of Enaim" and is presented as a holy harlot, and Ruth exposes Boaz's feet and is portrayed as the direct cause of David's birth.

The fifth, sixth, and seventh chapters will deal with the figure of the *Shekhinah* and her link to the messianic mothers in the kabbalistic literature. Lot's daughters, Tamar, and Ruth, are depicted in the *Zohar* as agents of cosmic salvation whose sexual transgressions represent an encounter with demonic forces that must be engaged for the sake of redemption. The actions of the messianic mother reflect in the *sefirotic* realm the human ability to influence divinity and bring about its restoration. Their actions are not only vindicated but also transcend moral and judicial judgments while constructing dynamic connections between heaven and earth. For example, the *Zohar* describes a celestial wheel of souls called *Ṭiqla*, which is propelled initially by the incestuous act of Lot's daughters and continues moving through the power of Tamar and Ruth's harlotry and seduction, transgressions interpreted as reparations for the world of the dead and living. In a different passage discussing Tamar's covered face at the "entrance of Enaim," the *Zohar* focuses on the mystery of feminine sexuality and connects it to Judgment (*Din*) and the destructive and erotic forces of the *Shekhinah*, which must be assuaged. Zoharic passages about Ruth fluctuate between describing her as the *Shekhinah*, rolling in the dust of exile and in need of masculine and divine external salvation, and conceiving of her as a woman who initiates her own redemption. Over the course of these chapters I will discuss central issues in Zoharic literature, such as the editing process of the *Zohar* and the crystallization of kabbalistic views regarding forbidden relations, sexuality, sin, exile, and redemption. Consequently, in the epilogue, I will suggest that the *Shekhinah* in the *Zohar* represents a mixture of Jewish and Christian perceptions of the messianic mother that developed from ancient times until the Middle Ages.

EVOLUTION OF THE MYTH

The Davidic dynasty is well-known for its exceptional stories. It is possible to claim that characteristics of these biblical stories are in line with feminine oral traditions, whereas the weaving of the stories into rabbinic and Zoharic midrashim reflects a transition from the semiotic world and feminine *chōra* to the symbolic language uniting the hermeneutical and exegetical structure of the "father's tongue." Judicial trends that emerge in rabbinic and Zoharic exegesis follow the biblical course and intensify the dominance of the messianic mothers, while at the same time propose a unique narrative for the heroines' multifacetedness.

I define myth as a story interweaving the divine and human across generations. Following the research of Gershom Scholem, Moshe Idel, Yehuda Liebes, and additional scholars who have discussed the messianic myth in Kabbalah, scholars of the "myth of the hero's birth," like Otto Rank, Alan Dundes, and Joseph Campbell, as well as Robert Alter in the biblical context, I seek to construct a scene of the birth of the Davidic Messiah and subsequently discuss the model that characterizes his mothers. The combination of the motifs of transgression and redemption in the redeemer's figure and in his foremother's stories reveals a model of chosenness that stems from sexual deviancy, which receives vindication through *tiqqun* (reparation) and repentance. These motifs characterize King David in biblical and rabbinic literature. They also emerge in descriptions of Jesus. In contrast, in the Synoptic Gospels, the main features of the Davidic mothers are attributed to Mary. Therefore, I will explore the centrality of the messianic mother in both religions and discuss the polemical perspectives and mutual influence between rabbinic Midrashim and Christian traditions, which attest to the existence of a messianic nucleus shared by Judaism and early Christianity.

The central motif in the Davidic myth is the Messiah's foremothers' sexual subversiveness, a subject that I will examine in consideration of the scholarship of David Biale, Daniel Boyarin, Wendy Doniger, Ishay Rosen-Zvi, Charlotte Fonrobert, and additional scholars who have discussed conceptions of corporeality and sexuality in biblical and midrashic literature. Alongside the feminine ruse and dominance, the covenant between the Davidic mothers and God is prominent and reflected in the ambivalent treatment of sexual transgression. In rabbinic literature these actions are called "sin" (*ḥeit*) and "transgression" (*aveirah*)—yet it is precisely these deeds that are ultimately vindicated. Compared to the women, the men are weak and mostly marginal figures, unaware of the feminine schemes. Other aspects of the myth, such as the perception of the elected son, his connection to his mother, and various motivations for the transgression, change from corpus to corpus and will be discussed throughout the study.

MYTH AND GENDER

This book seeks to present a multilayered picture of the messianic mother, her personality and voice. The prevalent division between the mother figure and the sexual women—between Eve and Lilith, the virgin and harlot—will stand at the base of this discussion. Central questions that I will examine include: the possibility of separating motherhood from seduction in the Davidic stories, and whether these figures are exploited and coerced to use their bodies, or whether they act of their own volition, liberty, and agency. The premise in the ancient world is that an abandoned woman would play the role of a seducer and deceiver in order to survive. However, the Davidic mothers are not marginal or vulnerable figures; rather, in each story their independence is highlighted. The question regarding their freedom, therefore, is not so simple and can be interpreted in many ways: as the heroines' autonomous choice to use their bodies to accomplish their goals, as an exploitation of men for the sake of pregnancy, as an expression of the divine plan, or simply as patriarchal oppression. From a psychoanalytic perspective, here is a pattern of oedipal relations between the heroines and actual or symbolic father figures. Thus, the forbidden relation between "father" and "daughter" allows the sacred and messianic link between "mother" and "son." In the dynastic stories, illicit relations, harlotry, and seduction constitute the foundation of civilization and correspondingly establish biblical law upon the violated taboo.

The genealogical sequence of the messianic dynasty reflects a paradoxical stance in which each heroine's story presents a discrete deed, yet the conjoined stories form a deterministic chain of sexual transgression defining the boundaries of the law. The dynastic structure offers a solution for the individual feminine figures as free agents and autonomous subjects. The stories' gradual development, mitigating severe sexual transgression, expanding choice, and assuaging dire circumstances, demonstrates the feminine development within reparation. By situating the feminine genealogy at the Book of Ruth's conclusion, the maternal responsibility of the dynastic heroines regarding their "symbolic daughters" is highlighted, as well as the feminine redemption sprouting forth from the ensemble of Davidic stories.

This book is based on central studies in feminist, gender, and psychoanalytic literature. In my opinion, the figure of the messianic mother represents an axis around which foundational topics in gender theory and feminist criticism should be analyzed. Here I follow Adrienne Rich, who discussed the gap between motherhood as a "patriarchal institution" and motherhood as a "private experience" for women; Simone de Beauvoir, who explored the connection between the degradation of the mother and her adoration as a "goddess," and examined the danger that the mother symbolizes for her son as a reminder to him of his mortality; Julia Kristeva, who examined the characteristics of the mother in Christian myth and the mother's symbolic lure and repulsion in both an individual's psyche and the annals of religion and culture; Hélène Cixous, Jessica Benjamin, and Luce Irigaray, who dealt with the uniqueness of the feminine and maternal voice and analyzed the brutal attempts to repress and silence it; as well as Phyllis Trible, Ilana Pardes, Mieke Bal, Esther Fuchs, and other scholars who illuminated subversive voices and gender critical readings in biblical literature. Following these studies, I seek to depict the messianic mother's figure and discuss her connection to the messianic son, the father, God, and additional women in her world.

Even though the Messiah is the Messiah through the merit of his foremothers, it is impossible to ignore the centrality of the son in the Jewish messianic myth. The perception of the redeemer as an idealized masculine figure fits other cultural myths of the hero's birth in the ancient world. Therefore, besides the emphasis this book places on the motherly figure, I will also examine the son and the means by which his chosenness is anticipated in his foremothers' stories. In many ways, King David represents the pinnacle of the Judean dynasty. Despite his description as the Messiah in the Bible, David is not unequivocally depicted as an eschatological hero, but rather as a chosen king anointed with oil. In rabbinic and Second Temple literature, like Apocrypha, Pseudepigrapha, Qumran Scrolls, and Christian Gospels, the elected status of the Davidic dynasty is developed and the "Scion of David" is presented as both a historical figure as well a transtemporal and eternal mythic symbol. Rabbinic literature hints that David is not only the father of the Messiah, but that he himself will be resurrected in the future and will redeem, as it is written in the Palestinian and Babylonian Talmuds.[2] Additionally, in the continuation of this messianic discussion in Tractate Sanhedrin, it is said that David symbolizes the "viceroy" who, sitting to the right of the emperor, represents God or the future Messiah.[3] David's figure will be analyzed below in light of his birth story in the later Midrash and in connection to his dynastic mothers. The paradox of perceiving him as an actual historical figure—yet also as one who, in the future, will return—signifies a parallel to Jesus' figure. In the epilogue, I will discuss the motif of repentance linked to David and Jesus as well as the hope planted in them both, even before their births. The tense anticipation of the coming of the redeemer is shared by Judaism and Christianity; in both religions it is presented as a paradoxical desire that cannot come to fruition. As Kafka said, "The Messiah will come only when he is no longer necessary; he will come only on the day after his arrival; he will come, not on the last day, but on the very last."[4]

---

2   The quotations are: "If the King Messiah comes from among the living, his name will be David; if from among the dead, his name will be David as well" and "The Holy One, blessed be He, will raise up another David for us." *b. Sanhedrin* 98b; *y. Berakhot* 2:4 [13d]; *Zohar* 1:82b. On the concept of David as the future Messiah, see Yehuda Liebes, "Mazmiah Qeren Yeshu'ah," *Jerusalem Studies in Jewish Thought* 3 (1984): 313-49; Peter Schäfer, *The Jewish Jesus* (Princeton: Princeton University Press, 2012), 79-90.
3   As is written in *b. Hagigah* 14a, "Till thrones were place... one [throne] for Him, and one for David." In contrast, Rashi in *b, Sanhedrin* 98b interprets that the "new" David is acting as the emperor and the "old" David as the viceroy.
4   Franz Kafka, *Parables and Paradoxes* (New York: Schocken, 1971), 81.

By bringing together fields that are generally discussed separately—myth and gender, and more precisely, the research of the messianic myth through a feminine perspective and gender analytic tools—I will analyze the figure of the messianic mother in Jewish culture. By highlighting the antinomian model and sexual transgression of the Davidic heroines, we may illuminate the background from which the Christian messianic myth blooms. I claim that Mary symbolizes a biblical "return of the repressed," which is not only echoed in the Gospels of Mathew and Luke but also in rabbinic traditions alluding to Jesus's genealogy, in later Midrashim, and in the *Zohar*. The link between Mary's model of virginity and the sexual licentiousness of the Davidic mothers is exposed in connection to the figure of the *Shekhinah*, and it stresses the centrality of the redeemer's mother in Judaism and Christianity. Both religions are engaged in the paradoxical encounter between feminine transgression and redemption.

Part One

Messianic Mothers in the Bible

> *For surely I know the plans I have for you,*
> *says the Lord, plans for your welfare and not for harm,*
> *to give you a future with hope (Jeremiah 29:11)*

When we examine the royal dynasty in the Bible, starting from the tribe of Judah and continuing until King David, a surprising connection emerges from the stories of the dynastic mothers: Leah gives birth to Judah while entangled between Rachel and Jacob. Tamar disguises herself as a prostitute and gives birth to Perez and Zerah with Judah, her husbands' father. Ruth seduces Boaz on the threshing floor and gives birth to Obed, the grandfather of David. Bathsheba gives birth to Solomon through an adulterous relation with David. In addition, we include the stories of Lot's daughters, the foremothers of Ruth, who give birth to Moab and Ammon through incestuous relations with their father, and the later Midrashim from *Yalkut ha-Makhiri*, which state that David was born through an extramarital relationship between Jesse, his wife, and his maidservant.

All of these stories are located on the spectrum between forbidden relations (according to its biblical definition, as in the case of Lot's daughters and Bathsheba), licentiousness and prostitution (as in the story of Tamar), and a problematic feminine seductiveness (evident in the stories of Ruth, Rachel and Leah, and David's mother). Although there are essential differences between forbidden sexual relations and acts of seduction or harlotry, it is still possible to say that all the sons of the biblical Davidic dynasty were born through questionable copulation, embodying the paradoxical connection between transgression, messianism, and redemption.[1]

In contrast to claims which marginalize the messianic mother in the Jewish narrative and view her as a myth originating in Christianity, this book wishes to highlight the mother's centrality in the royal and messianic myth of the Bible.

---

1 David Biale, *Eros and the Jews* (New York: Basic Books, 1992), 13-20.

In order to investigate the development of this figure from the ancient world through the rabbinic exegesis and the *Zohar*, I will focus on the provocative stories of the mothers of the House of David: the tales of the daughters of Lot, Tamar, and Ruth. As we will see, the recurring motif in these stories (Genesis Ch. 19, 38, and the Book of Ruth) demonstrates the crucial influence of the mother on transforming her child into "the chosen son" and messianic hero.

RUTH, TAMAR, AND LOT'S DAUGHTERS

The decision to examine the stories of Lot's daughters, Tamar, and Ruth is based on considerations of form and content. Lot's daughters mark the first maternal link of the chain, beginning with Ammon and Moab, whose descendants beget Ruth the Moabite.[2] Tamar gives birth to Perez, the son of Judah, constituting the first point in the Jewish lineage, whereas the Book of Ruth formulates a conclusion to its predecessors and informs us about the birth of King David. Although Lot's daughters are not mentioned in the book, they are, however, present in the background of the seduction on the threshing floor, a scene which recalls the sexual act in the cave of Zoar that resulted in Moab's birth. The stories of these four heroines utilize idiomatic expressions and shared motifs such as disguises, isolated locations, drunkenness, seduction, and concealment, thereby demonstrating the development of the feminine narrative from the Book of Genesis until the era of the kings.

Tamar, Ruth, and Lot's daughters clearly initiate the messianic birth scenes, for the men "did not know when the women lay or arose." Unlike these four heroines, Rachel and Leah are traded by men and passed from their father to Jacob, who is now responsible for their fate. Similarly, Bathsheba is portrayed as a dominating mother who worries for her son's kingship (I Kings 1), yet the portrayal of her being taken by David (II Samuel 11), is utterly dissimilar to her former control.[3] While focusing on the connections between Ruth, Tamar, and Lot's daughters, I will reference Rachel, Leah, and Bathsheba to the extent that they illuminate the feminine and messianic drama in the House of David.

---

[2] Harold Fisch, "Ruth and the Structure of the Covenant History," *Vetus Testament* 32 (1982): 425-437; Arthur B. Brenner, "Onan, the Levirate Marriage and the Genealogy of the Messiah," *Journal of the American Psychoanalytic Association* 10 (1962): 701-21; Yair Zakovitch, "The Threshing-Floor Scene in Ruth," *Shnaton* 3 (1978–1979): 29–33.

[3] In spite of Bathsheba's passivity in II Samuel, 11:4, a later Midrash assigns her both initiative and promiscuity, similar to that of her predecessors. See Louis Ginzberg, *Ginze Schechter* (New York: Jewish Theological Seminary of America, 1928), 1:166.

1. Intertextuality in the Book of Ruth

Within the academic literature, we can outline three trends exploring the connections between Ruth, Tamar, and Lot's daughters. Many scholars have emphasized the intertextual style of the Book of Ruth, which reworks stories of the past. In the terminology of Harold Fisch, Lot's daughters represent the primitive extreme of the story model, Tamar's actions symbolize the middle component, whereas the Book of Ruth represents a sophisticated variation of a heroine who "redeems" her foremothers and grants legitimization to their actions.[4] David Biale highlights the potency of the Judean heroines' "subverting sexuality," where they appear to act in service of the patriarchy, even as they disrupt the order with their erotic initiatives. He claims that the positioning of their stories at the closing of the Book of Ruth attests to the centrality of the Davidic narrative to the biblical canon.[5] Ilana Pardes views the relationship of Ruth and Naomi as an "idyllic writing" of the struggle between Rachel and Leah and an expression of love between two women, uncommon in biblical stories.[6] Nevertheless, other researchers emphasize the concealed tension between Ruth and Naomi and claim that Naomi exploits the 'foreign woman' for her own purposes.[7] Mieke Bal draws attention to Ruth's vulnerability at the end of the Book, when she is without the support of other heroines. For Bal, the compilation of the stories of Rachel and Leah, Tamar, Ruth, and Lot's daughters constructs a succession of "bitter stories" which are reflected in each other, a type of *mise en abyme* characterized by irony.[8] Yair Zakovitch and Avigdor Shinan emphasize the difference between the positive figure of Ruth, on the one hand, and the stories of Tamar and Lot's daughters, on the other hand, which, like the sin of David and Bathsheba, reflect an anti-Judean composition intended to slander the Davidic dynasty.[9] If their portrayal is

---

4 Fisch, "Ruth," 425-37.
5 Biale, *Eros and the Jews*, 11-32; Amy Jill Levine, "Ruth," in *The Women's Bible Commentary*, eds. Carol A. Newsom and Sharon H. Ringe (London: SPCK, 1992), 78-84.
6 Ilana Pardes, *Countertraditions in the Bible—A Feminist Approach* (Cambridge: Harvard University Press, 1992), 60-70, 98-117.
7 Danna Nolan-Fewell and David Gunn, "A Son is Born to Naomi," *JSOT* 40 (1988): 99-108; Michal Ben-Naftali, *Chronicle of Separation: On Deconstruction's Disillusioned Love* (New York: Fordham University Press, 2015), 15-53.
8 Mieke Bal, *Lethal Love: Feminist Literary Readings of Biblical Love Stories* (Bloomington: Indiana University Press, 1987), 68-103, and specifically 83-5.
9 Avigdor Shinan and Yair Zakovitch, *The Story of Judah and Tamar* (Jerusalem: The Hebrew University Press, 1992), 219-28, 240-8. In contrast to "the actual crisis" of Boaz and Ruth, they claim that Lot's daughters use unjustified deceit. Zakovitch, "The Threshing-Floor Scene"; Yair Zakovitch, *Ruth: Introduction and Commentary. Miqra' le-Yisra'el* (Tel Aviv and

meant to be fundamentally negative, why did the author of the Book of Ruth choose to situate these heroines together within the blessing of the elders? This choice attests to the author's fondness for these characters, who unify the split between the positive mother figure (or "the virgin"), and the erotic woman, identified with Tamar and Lot's daughters. A similar rift can be found in the adoration of Mary, mother of Jesus, in the Synoptic Gospels, when compared with the Davidic mothers, an issue that we will return to in the epilogue.

This positive attitude to the stories of Tamar, Ruth, and Lot's daughters is an essential component of the Davidic narrative. The Book of Ruth is designed to complete the missing details regarding the origin of King David, and therefore the linking of these stories is central to understanding his character in the Book of Samuel. Thus, the Book of Ruth constitutes an integral intertextual link in relation to the transmission of the biblical royal dynasty and in relation to its blossoming future. In a structural analysis that focuses on the development of the feminine and messianic model, Ruth assuages the severe sexual transgressions of her ancestors not only in a literary manner, but also on the ethical and moral plane. These stories conduct a challenging dialogue with the biblical law and represent a fertile tension created between the *nomos* and the *narrative* in the tales of the mothers of the House of David.[10]

2. The Feminine Ruse in the Mirror of Feminist Criticism

A prominent trend in feminist theory is the inclination to define the feminine ruse of the biblical heroines as a patriarchal tool for the purpose of reproduction. For instance, Athalya Brenner claims that these heroines represent an example of 'positive foreign women' that have dedicated themselves on behalf of the Israelite people, through denying their own volition.[11] Esther Fuchs claims that the theme of these stories is older men

---

Jerusalem: Am Oved and Magnes Press, 1990), 24-33, 112-8; Yair Zakovitch, *David: From Shepherd to Messiah* (Jerusalem: Ben-Zvi Institute, 1995), 24-35, 181-99.

10 On sublimation of the narrative in the Book of Ruth, see Phyllis Trible, *God and the Rhetoric of Sexuality* (Philadelphia: Fortress Press, 1978), 166-96; Mishael M. Caspi and Rachel S. Havrelock, *Women on the Biblical Road: Ruth, Naomi and the Female Journey* (Lanham: University Press of America, 1996), 175-6; Esther Fuchs, *Sexual Politics in the Biblical Narrative: Reading the Hebrew Bible as a Woman* (Sheffield: Sheffield Academic Press, 2000), 80, finds in the Book of Ruth apotheosis of the 'seduction scene.'

11 Athalya Brenner, *The Israelite Woman: Social Role and Literary Type in Biblical Narrative* (Sheffield: JSOT Press, 1985), Ch. 6, 9; Athalya Brenner, *Ruth and Naomi* (Tel Aviv: Sifriat Poalim, 1988), 29-48, 51-60.

who take advantage of younger women—whether daughters (as with Lot) or daughters-in-law (Judah and Tamar), or relatives (Boaz and Ruth)—for the sake of reproducing sons for the royal house.[12] Similarly, Tikva Frymer-Kensky understands Ruth as "an agent of continuity," who connects the beginning of the royal dynasty to its end. By disregarding sexual conventions, the Davidic mothers wrest sovereignty from the patriarchal monarchy. The Book of Ruth is an allegory of a people who have returned from exile and are grappling with its past; Ruth not only symbolizes an individual, but also the attitude towards foreign women in the days of the return to Zion.[13] Johanna W. H. van Wijk-Bos and Susan Niditch stress that it is only through God's collaboration with the women that their ruse is successful, for they were predetermined to fulfill the divine plan in which they have no will of their own.[14]

In contrast to these readings, I claim that the biblical authors stress the *volition* of Tamar, Ruth, and Lot's daughters, counterpoising them to men who are portrayed as marginal and weak. In distinction to the stories in which heroines are exploited, these tales are depicted by heteroglossia and polyphony; the women here choose their motherhood while struggling with a reality of annihilation, abandonment, and unwillingness to impregnate (as arises particularly in the actions of Er and Onan, the first husbands of Tamar).[15] These figures have political liberty and they disrupt the "patrilineal succession" in order to actualize their goals. Indeed, towards this aim, they use their bodies and sexuality; nonetheless, the stories emphasize the heroines' freedom and volition, in contrast to oppressive circumstances that were widespread in the Ancient Near East. This book wishes to examine through feminist criticism the topics of motherhood and seduction, messianism and gender, while also illuminating points of weakness and strength in current theories, in order to express the myth of the messianic mother, which is revealed through the gender-power relations that arise in every story in their own right.

---

12 Fuchs, *Sexual Politics*, 44-90.
13 Tikva Frymer-Kensky, *Reading the Women of the Bible* (New York: Schocken Books, 2002), 238, 264; Claudia V. Camp, *The Strange Woman and the Making of the Bible* (Sheffield: Sheffield Academic Press, 2000), 13-35, 331-44.
14 Johanna Van Wijk-Bos, "Out of the Shadows: Genesis 38; Judges 4:17-22; Ruth 3," *Semeia* 42 (1988): 37-67; Susan Niditch, "The Wrong Women Righted, Genesis 38," *Harvard Theological Review* 72, no. 1-2 (1979): 143-9; Carol A. Newsom and Sharon H. Ringe, eds. *The Women's Bible Commentary* (London: SPCK, 1992), 11.
15 Robert Alter, *The Art of Biblical Narrative* (New York: Basic Books, 1981), 23-32; Pardes, *Countertraditions*, 1-12, 119-21.

3. Messianism, Motherhood, and Gender

As previously stated, researchers from different disciplines have studied the Davidic stories: biblical literary scholars have clarified the shared motifs of the dynastic mothers, feminist scholars have stressed their weakness and portrayed their dependence on ruses and deception as "the power of the weak," scholars of myth have grappled with the idea that the Messiah is born of sexual transgression, and scholars of biblical law have discussed them in the context of the laws of forbidden relations in the stories of the Judean dynasty.[16] Generally, research of the messianic myth has abstained from the gender perspectives, while gender scholars have mostly ignored the messianic significance of these stories in the biblical, rabbinic and Zoharic perception of the Davidic dynasty.[17] Therefore, in order to enrich the understanding of the connection between female transgression and redemption, this study explores the messianic myth from within a perspective of gender and psychoanalysis. These perspectives, in their conjunction, impart that the Davidic dynasty was transformed into a sacred and elected dynasty not in spite of the actions of its foremothers, but rather *because* of them.

Situated at the foundation of this book is the premise that the Davidic stories are charged with a messianic tension already present in the biblical literature.[18] In contrast to the prevalent trend of focusing on the figure of the "son," the redeemer, and the masculine aspects of the messianic narrative, my book focuses on the messianic mothers, who constitute the elective status of the sons. A type-scene of "the annunciation of the messianic hero" emerges from the parallels between the stories of Ruth, Tamar, and Lot's daughters.[19] In the forthcoming chapters, we will examine the literary content and the characteristics of this scene, the singularity of each heroine, and their common features, as they appear in the genealogical list at the end of the Book of Ruth. We will begin with this list which represents an internal biblical exegesis, portraying David in the background of his mother's stories of seduction and childbirth.

---

16 Fuchs, *Sexual Politics*, 44-90; Israel Knohl, *The Many Faces of Monotheistic Religion* (Tel Aviv: The Broadcasted University, 1995), 28-32; Adin Steinsaltz, *Women in the Bible* (Tel Aviv: The Ministry of Defense, 1983), 53-64; Moshe Idel, *Kabbalah and Eros* (New Haven: Yale University Press, 2005), 59-73.

17 For an exception, see Charlotte E. Fonrobert, "The Handmaid, the Trickster and the Birth of the Messiah," in *Current Trends in the Study of Midrash*, ed. Carol Bakhos (Leiden: Brill, 2006), 245-75.

18 As can be seen in the research of Sigmund Mowinckel, *He That Cometh: The Messianic Concept in the Old Testament and Later Judaism* (Oxford: Basil Blackwell, 1956), 155-86, 304-54; Moshe Idel, *Ben: Sonship and Jewish Mysticism* (London: Continuum, 2007), 1-106; Israel Knohl, *Biblical Beliefs* (Jerusalem: Magnes Press, 2007), 40-62; Yair Lorberbaum, *Disempowered King: Monarchy in Classical Jewish Literature* (London: Continuum, 2011), 13-39.

19 The origin of the term 'type-scene' is in the research of Robert Alter, also see the opening of the second chapter.

CHAPTER 1

Feminine Genealogy and the Lineage of the House of David

> *If we are not be accomplices in the murder of the mother*
> *we also need to assert that there is a genealogy of women.*
> *Each of us has a female family tree: we have a mother,*
> *a grandmother and great-grandmothers, we have daughters.*
> *Because we have been exiled into the house of our husbands,*
> *it is easy to forget the special quality of the female genealogy...*
> *Let us try to situate ourselves within that genealogy*
> *so that we can win and hold on to our identity.*
>
> Luce Irigaray, *Sexes and Genealogies*

The biblical stories of the messianic mothers conclude with a family tree at the end of the Book of Ruth:

> Then all the people who were at the gate, along with the elders, said, 'We are witnesses. May the Lord make the woman who is coming into your house like Rachel and Leah, who together built up the house of Israel. May you produce children in Ephrathah and bestow a name in Bethlehem; and, through the children that the Lord will give you by this young woman, may your house be like the house of Perez, whom Tamar bore to Judah.' So Boaz took Ruth and she became his wife. When they came together, the Lord made her conceive, and she bore a son ... Now these are the descendants of Perez: Perez became the father of Hezron, Hezron of Ram, Ram of Amminadab, Amminadab of Nahshon, Nahshon of Salmon, Salmon of Boaz, Boaz of Obed, Obed of Jesse, and Jesse of David. (Ruth 4: 11-22)

Generally, genealogical lists constitute an instrument for granting rewards or disinheritance and fill in the gaps of the biblical narrative.[1] Most of the genealogical lists symbolize reproductive continuity, whereas in the above case the links of the chain are constructed through deviations from the natural order. The conjunction of names in the Judean dynasty exemplifies a form of unexpected procreation, which demonstrates that transgression and forbidden relations cause the birth of the son, the redeemer. The list clandestinely conceals the feminine narrative, which fluctuates on the spectrum between illicit relations, prostitution, and forbidden sexual acts. It illustrates that breaching limitations defines the biblical conception of the sacred and elected.

Scholars suggest that the Book of Ruth represents a polemic concerning foreign women at the time of the return to Zion. Some clarify the layers of editing in the work, while others claim that the text defames King David's descendants. Overall, the book gestures to a pre-destruction era from the position of a later, post-destruction reality.[2] In addition to these approaches the role of the Book of Ruth in completing David's missing background in the Book of Samuel should be emphasized. The messianic configuration of David, which is developed in the chapters of the Prophets and Psalms, is portrayed for the first time in this genealogical list, which justifies the stories of the dynastic heroines, while simultaneously transforming David into a chosen hero because of his relation to them. The notion of the "Messiah son of David" found in rabbinical exegesis is clarified through the feminine continuum woven into the intertextual ending of the book. In fact, in the Septuagint, the Book of Ruth is situated between the Book of Judges and the Book of Samuel, thereby indicating the direct link between the dynastic mothers and the elected son.

By positioning the Book of Ruth before the Book of Samuel, the Septuagint hints at a radical position: since King David does not have a birth story of his own, his birth scene is embroidered within the story of Naomi and Ruth, Rachel and Leah, Tamar, and Lot's daughters. This exposition portrays David as an outcome of his foremothers and their behavior becomes a clue to understanding his character. Indeed, from the multiple characteristics of David's personality, the Book of Ruth emphasizes his transgressive background, an issue which reappears in the narratives of David's wives and his sin with Bathsheba. Seemingly, the sages

---

[1] Frederic W. Bush, *Ruth*. Word Biblical Commentary (Dallas: Word Books, 1996), 14-5; Gary N. Knoppers, *1 Chronicles 1-9*. Anchor Bible 12 (New York: Doubleday, 2003), 245-65; Fuchs, *Sexual Politics*, 81-90.

[2] Edward F. Campbell, *Ruth*. Anchor Bible 7 (Garden City: Doubleday, 1975), 23-8; Camp, *Wise, Strange, and Holy*, 215-26; Zakovitch, *Ruth* 14-40; Zakovitch, *David*, 24-35; Frymer-Kensky, *Women of the Bible*, 254-5; Brenner, *Ruth and Naomi*, 61-84.

transformed sexual transgression into his unique signature and described David as the Messiah, "the man who elevated the yoke of repentance."[3]

TWO GENEALOGICAL LISTS AT THE CONCLUSION OF THE BOOK OF RUTH

The Davidic lineage connects the sacred and the profane. I claim that the Book of Ruth ends not with one list, but two, one well known and masculine, the second, by contrast, subversive and feminine. The dialectical relation between these two lists is central to understanding the function of the messianic idea, which emerged through overt and covert biblical polemics. As it is stated in the concluding verses of the book:

> Now these are the descendants of Perez: Perez became the father of Hezron, Hezron of Ram, Ram of Amminadab, Amminadab of Nahshon, Nahshon of Salmon, Salmon of Boaz, Boaz of Obed, Obed of Jesse, and Jesse of David (Ruth 4: 18-22)

This is a conventional list, resembling classic biblical and ancient Near East genealogies. It marks the following names: Perez—Hezron—Ram—Amminadab—Nahshon—Salmon—Boaz—Obed—Jesse—David. This line of ten generations focuses on chosen males and disregards others, thereby highlighting the connection between the father and the elected son.[4] It opens with Perez, son of Judah, mentions the present—with the birth of Obed to Boaz—and concludes with the future of the dynasty: the appearance of David, son of Jesse. In the ascending aspect of the genealogy, David is attributed to the "primordial father," Judah, whereas in the descending aspect, the birth of David surpasses the narrative of Ruth and Naomi.[5] According to Frederick Bush's proposal, the name "David" signifies a dramatic character and a "coda of redemption" in the closing of the Book of Ruth, and it is David who bestows a new meaning to the entire plot.[6]

As a result of the list's deviation from the plot of the story, some hypothesized that the text in question was copied from Chronicles or added later. Other

---

3 b. Mo'ed Qatan 16b, b. Avodah Zarah 5a; for the justification of his sexual transgression, b. Sanhedrin 107a; b. Shabbat 56a.
4 Bush, *Ruth*, 15. Judah and David are perceived as the extremes of the dynasty in I Chronicles 28:4.
5 This list is similar to the lineage in Chronicles 6:16-17 and Jesus's relation to Adam and to God in the Gospel of Luke (3:23-38).
6 Bush, *Ruth*, 268; Campbell, *Ruth*, 169.

scholars have even suggested that it constitutes a "masculine" editing of the book which was originally written by a woman.[7] This reading stresses that the concluding list ignores the feminine heroines of the book, and—like most genealogies in the Bible—marks only the masculine association. In this manner, the true aim of the story is exposed, creating a dramatic saga of King David's origins.[8] David provides a justification for all the plots' entanglements and he symbolizes their zenith; however, concomitantly, he overshadows the feminine heroines' initiative that made his birth possible. According to Hannah Naveh, this process parallels the disappearance of Tamar at the conclusion of Genesis 38:

> In this way they promptly erased the actions of Tamar, Naomi, and Ruth ... The stories' structure is directed towards their conclusion, in order to join them to the national story in general and the Davidic dynasty in particular, thus showing the reason they were included in the canon. The feminine dramas were included only because they are conceived as links in the middle, and not as foundational stones within the framework of the male narrative. By being like this they are able to be erased once the men return. In both of these family episodes, the women, who initiated the nationalistic history and solved the family crisis, were drowned out and disappeared behind the family curtain.[9]

This process does not only characterize the house of David. It begins in the Book of Genesis, with the Priestly (P) and Judean (J) genealogy and is completed in Chronicles, where the forefathers are presented as "the primary agents of the

---

7 According to Campbell, the book portrays a unique genre of "Hebrew historical short story," inspired by Genesis and Judges, transmitted orally and written around 700-950 BCE; whereas according to Bush it discusses a post-destruction priestly source, in which the list is part of the original compilation. According to Rofé, the list is an integral section of the book, which was edited in a later era. Zakovitch also proposes that the story and the genealogical list should not be separated. van Dijk-Hemmes, Fokkelien. "Ruth: A Product of Women's Culture?" In *Ruth and Esther: A Feminist Companion to the Bible*, edited by Athalya Brenner, 134-9. Sheffield: Sheffield Academic Press, 1999. Campbell, *Ruth*, 170-3; Bush, *Ruth*, 13-6, 265-8; Alexander Rofé, *Introduction to the Literature of the Hebrew Bible* (Jerusalem: Simor, 2009). 91; Zakovitch, *Ruth*, 14-6, 33-5.
8 Knoppers, *Chronicles*, 249.
9 Hannah Naveh, "Heart of Home, Heart of Light: Representation of the Family in Hebrew Literature," in *The Love of Mothers and the Fear of Fathers*, ed. Aviad Kleinberg (Tel Aviv: Keter and Tel Aviv University, 2004), 131-2. Also, Gen. 38:29-30, "But just then he drew back his hand, and out came his brother; and she said, 'What a breach you have made for yourself!' Therefore he was named Perez. Afterwards his brother came out with the crimson thread on his hand; and he was named Zerah."

divine blessing," while the foremothers—the wives and daughters—are forced out of the official genealogical documentation.[10] According to Esther Fuchs, these masculine lists reflect a consistent denial of the feminine and the attempt to naturalize "the patriarchal construction of generational history."[11] The conjoining of the feminine and masculine lists reinforces the hierarchal relations, while simultaneously, the women are assimilated in the lives of the fathers and sons.

Nissan Rubin connects the exclusion of women in the Bible to their physiological fluctuation between purity and impurity; accordingly they belong and are excluded from a society on a periodic basis. This fluctuation also has legal ramifications, inasmuch a woman belongs to her father's house, then to her husband's, and finally her sons'.[12] This being the case, the laws of menstruation express the unstable status of women in the ancient world. At the time when a woman gives birth she is needed for the communal continuity, but afterwards she is concealed from the lineage's documentation and is narratively marginalized. Another cause for the absence of women from the genealogical lists may result from the men's effort to strengthen their paternity, which could not until recently be proven biologically, while motherhood cannot be disputed and does not require proof.

As we will see, this prevalent claim becomes more complex in the Davidic tales, where the identity of the mother is put into doubt. See, for example, the statement "a son was born to Naomi" (even though Ruth is the son's mother), the declaration that Tamar "is pregnant through prostitution," after she has been portrayed as a bride, a *qedeisha* (cult prostitute) and her identity is not clear, or the conception of the *Yalkut ha-Makhiri* that David is the son of two mothers: Jesse's wife and Jesse's maidservant.

THE FEMININE GENEALOGICAL LIST—EXCLUSION OR REDUNDANCY?

I will now freshly examine the ending of the Book of Ruth and challenge the premise that this genealogical list is the exclusion of the Davidic foremothers. Without deciding the question of list's dating, let us focus on the final edition,

---

10   Pardes, *Countertraditions*, 56; Camp, *Wise, Strange, and Holy*, 191-226; Knoppers, *Chronicles*, 250-3.
11   Fuchs, *Sexual Politics*, 81, 47-9.
12   Nissan Rubin, *The Beginning of Life: Rites of Birth, Circumcision and Redemption of the First-Born in the Talmud and Midrash* (Tel-Aviv: Hakibbutz Hameuchad, 1995), 16-8. On the fear caused by female blood, see Hélène Cixous and Catherine Clément, *The Newly Born Woman*, trans. Betsy Wing (Minneapolis: University of Minnesota Press, 1986), 34-40, 62; Simone de Beauvoir, *The Second Sex* (New York: Vintage Books, 1989), 219.

which clearly includes two different genealogical models, presented alongside each other:

> Then all the people who were at the gate, along with the elders, said, 'We are witnesses. May the Lord make the woman who is coming into your house like **Rachel and Leah**, who together built up the house of Israel. May you produce children in Ephrathah and bestow a name in Bethlehem; and, through the children that the Lord will give you by this young woman, may your house be like the house of Perez, whom **Tamar** bore to Judah.' So Boaz took **Ruth** and she became his wife. When they came together, the Lord made her conceive, and she bore a son. Then the women said to Naomi, 'Blessed be the Lord, who has not left you this day without next-of-kin; and may his name be renowned in Israel! He shall be to you a restorer of life and a nourisher of your old age; for your daughter-in-law who loves you, who is more to you than seven sons, has borne him.' Then Naomi took the child and laid him in her bosom, and became his nurse. The women of the neighborhood gave him a name, saying, 'A son has been born to **Naomi**.' They named him Obed; he became the father of Jesse, the father of **David**.
>
> Now these are the descendants of **Perez**: Perez became the father of **Hezron**, Hezron of **Ram**, Ram of **Amminadab**, Amminadab of **Nahshon**, Nahshon of **Salmon**, Salmon of **Boaz**, Boaz of **Obed**, Obed of **Jesse**, and Jesse of **David**. (Ruth 4: 11-22)

Shortly before the familiar genealogy, which concludes the book (verses 18-22), there appears a feminine list, which focuses on David's foremothers (verses 11-17). This list offers an alternative to the dynastic-historic, masculine-linear writing, focusing on a different temporality, chronoscopic and circular, and recording the "great foremothers" of the tribe. This reading strengthens the idea that the Book of Ruth is a feminine work, which describes an actual or symbolic journey "outside of the patriarchal order."[13] The tension created between the two lists, demonstrates that the author's intention to portray a "peaceful construction of a matrilineal tradition within the

---

13 Michael M. Caspi and Rachel S. Havrelock, *Women on the Biblical Road: Ruth, Naomi and the Female Journey* (Lanham: University Press of America, 1996), 66-9, 53-73, 186-90. According to Fonrobert, the dynastic stories in the Book of Ruth represent a "masculine-scene." Fonrobert, "Birth of the Messiah." On feminine writing from gender perspective see Luce Irigaray, *Je, Tu, Nous: Towards a Culture of Difference* (New York and London: Routledge, 1993), 29-37; and also Cixous, Gilbert and Gubar, Rattok.

framework of a blessing addressed to a would-be-father" did not succeed.[14] The proximity of the lists creates a fertile collision between the masculine and feminine narratives, which influences the dialectical character of the messianic son.

Both of the genealogical lists conclude with the name David, attesting to the contradictory narratives that are found in the book and in the Judean stories. The first list is rooted in the feminine drama and the personal stories of Ruth and Naomi: "The women of the neighborhood gave him a name, saying, 'A son has been born to Naomi.' They named him Obed; he became the father of Jesse, the father of David" (Ruth 4:17). The second list depicts a concise narrative, also ending with the same name: "Obed of Jesse, and Jesse of David" (Ruth 4:22). This duplication of content and style is certainly not accidental. I claim that this structure exemplifies the feminine margins constituting the center, while simultaneously remaining marginal elements, thereby subverting the patriarchal order. In this way the focus is moved from David's birth to his foremothers; nonetheless, doubt is not cast on the importance of the elected son. It appears that the authors of the book wanted to preserve the two voices and document the alien women and sinners who founded the royal family. The tension and supplementation between the feminine and masculine lists thereby form the messianic myth in the Bible.

The Book of Ruth answers Luce Irigaray's proposal calling for women to take their place anew in the genealogical lists of women and daughters, as a reparation of the "exile" which has been forced on them in the patrilineal world.[15] In fact, this feminine list counts Rachel and Leah, Tamar, Naomi and Ruth—even Lot's daughters are hinted at in the book's background, through the seduction scene on the threshing floor. The appearance of these figures together forms a feminine dynasty, which may be termed a "literary genealogy." Models of male kinship are not discussed here, but rather epic and poetic deeds tied together and "bequeathed" from mothers to their symbolic daughters. After all, Lot's daughters are biologically connected only to Ruth, whereas Leah and Tamar symbolize the foremothers of the tribe of Judah, Perez, and Boaz.

The masculine genealogy conceals life episodes hidden behind succinct lists of names, while in the feminine list, the divine plan is concealed within the essence of dynasticism. In each story, the same forbidden acts are repeated and the heroine takes the similar, unexpected road of her own volition. However,

---

14 Pardes, *Countertraditions*, 98
15 Luce Irigaray, *Sexes and Genealogies* (New York: Columbia University Press, 1993), 19. Cited at the head of chapter 1.

when all these figures are joined together, a deterministic chain of "one-time" sexual transgressions and breaching of boundaries is created. Finally, these stories define the boundaries of the sacred and acquire divine justification through the birth of a son. The linking of the feminine list to the masculine "exhibits a sense of movement within history towards a divine goal."[16] Together with the masculine list, the problematic feminine seduction-scene repeated over generations is transformed into a paradoxical reconciliation. If only the masculine list appeared it would be possible to claim that there is no direct connection between the two genealogical lists. The binding of the lists at the conclusion of the book indicates the double origin of the Davidic dynasty and its diverse roots.

It appears that the author or editor wished to veil the discussion of an "alternative" genealogy by weaving it into the story. In contrast to the masculine list, which is summarily "**his**torical," the feminine list is portrayed as "**her**story" and as part of the Boaz and Ruth's wedding scene. This list functions as a connecting link for the formal closing of the book and a disposition to recast forbidden actions into "an expression of blessing" is prominent in it. Absent here is the unforgiving terminology found in the original story: the figure of the *qedeisha* or the prostitute at the entrance of Enaim, the problematic revelation at Boaz's feet, and the hesitation of the redeemer to corrupt his inheritance, the threat of the world's annihilation in the story of Lot's daughters and their abandonment to be raped in the beginning of the story of Sodom, the poverty, calamity, and death that accompany Ruth and Tamar, the clashing of the sisters Rachel and Leah. All of these are transformed into unified harmony in the mouths of the congratulators at the city's gate.

THE BLESSING AT THE GATE

We will examine a few expressions mentioned in the Davidic feminine genealogy:

> Then all the people who were at the gate, along with the elders, said, 'We are witnesses. May the Lord make the woman who is coming into your house like Rachel and Leah, who together built up the house of Israel. May you produce children in Ephrathah and bestow a name in Bethlehem; and, through the children that the Lord will give you by this young woman (Ruth 4: 11-12)

---

16 As quoted in Roddy Braun, *1 Chronicles*. Word Biblical Commentary (Waco: Word Books, 1986), 3.

Firstly, it should be noted that the connection between the ancestral foremothers to Ruth is attributed to "all the people," thus sympathizing with the dynastic heroines without casting doubt on their validity. In this public ritual, which delivers communal and nationalistic messages, the women use the patriarchal institution ("all the people who were at the gate, along with the elders, said, 'We are witnesses'") to reverse the power relations, by emphasizing the feminine dominance in the Judean dynasty.[17]

The men's blessing highlights Ruth's creative initiative in the action of redemption, thus subverting Boaz's words. Initially, Ruth is depicted as an acquisition being transferred to a merchant. At the beginning of the chapter, Boaz recounts how Ruth is to be passed "from Naomi's hand" to the hands of the redeemer, then to his hands, and how he "acquired" her with the entire congregation's testimony: "Then Boaz said to the elders and all the people, 'Today you are witnesses that I have acquired from the hand of Naomi all that belonged to Elimelech and all that belonged to Chilion and Mahlon. I have also acquired Ruth the Moabite, the wife of Mahlon, to be my wife, to maintain the dead man's name on his inheritance ... today you are witnesses" (4: 9-10). But in verse 11, Ruth is no longer an acquisition, rather an active woman "who is coming into your house," just like Rachel and Leah, Tamar, and Lot's daughters.

The hope that Boaz's wife will be considered one of them expresses the acceptance of the foremothers by the leaders and the nation, knowing full well the background of the birth of Perez, Judah, and Obed. The blessing opens (4:11) by referring to Rachel and Leah and the birth of Judah, which echoes to the birth of Perez son of Judah in the masculine genealogy (4: 18).[18] This doubled linguistic form approves the messianic coupling, in which the father, mother, and God are partners and the couple is blessed in the foremothers' names.

LIKE RACHEL AND LIKE LEAH

Even though this book does not focus on the figures of Rachel and Leah, I wish to emphasize their connection to the Judean genealogy. The decision to bless Ruth and Boaz by referencing Rachel and Leah "who together built up the house of Israel," begs interpretation. In Genesis 30-31, the sisters' relationship is fraught with difficulties and fighting. The two represent the rivalry between

---

17 Campbell, *Ruth*, 139-69; Bush, *Ruth*, 238-48; Fuchs, *Sexual Politics*, 76.
18 According to Alexander Rofé the masculine list does not begin with Judah, but rather with Perez as an integral continuation of verse 12. *Introduction* 173-5.

women in the patriarchal world with its low resources and the need to share one husband, transforming them into "agents of oppression" against each other. Consequently, a number of scholars stress the idyllic relationship of Ruth and Naomi in contrast to the confrontational relationship of Rachel and Leah.[19]

However, the blessing at the gate scene does not necessarily attest to the conflict of Rachel and Leah, but rather illuminates the dichotomous nature of the Davidic biblical stories. The fact that Rachel and Leah "both built the house of Israel" demonstrates the foremothers' substantial difficulty and distress embedded in the building of the royal dynasty, the center of the houses of Israel. Ilana Pardes points out that this blessing stresses "the brief moments in which the two matriarchs manage to cooperate."[20] In fact, it is significant that the sisters' background—the pains of infertility and giving birth, of naming their sons while fighting over Jacob's love—are not ignored by the congratulators. The very fact that both sisters are mentioned here, indicates that the feminine narrative is compelled to deviate from reality and biology in favor of mythology. For the sake of repairing the archetypical figure of the messianic mother the narrative of Genesis is rewritten.

The tragedy, embedded within the figure of Rachel, is alleviated at the conclusion of the Book of Ruth. Rachel, the mother of the house of Saul, symbolizes the rejected, absent monarchy that was usurped by the sons of Leah. In the words of Betty Rojtman, "in the Jewish tradition the daughter of Laban remains a figure of exile, daughter of Aram, who was lost to Jacob at the threshold of the land and never returned. *She is a gloomy figure, a murmur of life that was never satisfied.*"[21] If the book had not mentioned Rachel, we would be witnesses to an exclusion focusing only on the successful model of femininity and motherhood. The decision to discuss the sisters' relationship and situate them next to each other, adds to the richness and complexity of the Davidic plot. The absence of Jacob's name (in contrast to Judah and Perez's names, which are mentioned together with their mothers'), suggests that *both* Rachel and Leah were foremothers of the house of David. For if not for Rachel, Jacob would not have been married to Leah, and thus the sister's relationship symbolizes a fracture which repairs the dynasty.

In addition, the Book of Ruth emphasizes the location of the blessing, in Bethlehem (*beit*–house, *leḥem*–bread) of Judah. "House" and "bread" are typical feminine symbols. Alongside the messianic significance, the blessing for Boaz,

---

19 Brenner, *Ruth and Naomi*, 14-24; Pardes, *Countertraditions*, 98-117.
20 Pardes, *Countertraditions*, 101.
21 Betty Rojtman, *The Forgiveness of the Moon* (Jerusalem: Carmel Publishing, 2008), 20, 23.

"May you produce children in Ephrathah and bestow a name in Bethlehem" (Ruth 4:11), returns us to the death of Rachel on the threshold of Benjamin's birth: "So Rachel died, and she was buried on the way to Ephrathah that is, Bethlehem" (Gen. 35:17-20). The place where the story occurs connects Ruth and Naomi with Rachel and Leah. In this place Rachel died in childbirth, and there she is mentioned in the blessing to the new mother. Ruth's progression from the fields of Moab to Bethlehem is relevant not only for Naomi, but also for Rachel, assuaging her tragic death and securing that the Messiah who will come out of Bethlehem will also be her son. Thus, the "Messiah son of Joseph" who comes from Rachel is transformed in Second Temple literature into the herald of the "Messiah son of David," in the same manner that Rachel and Leah together announce the acceptance of Ruth at the city's gate.[22] Not only are the two sisters connected in their lives, but also in their deaths and in their descendants' monarchies, of Saul and David, with their struggles and their mutual reconciliation.

Rachel and Leah shared the sorrow of building the "house of Israel," one through infertility and the other due to the absence of love. Their self-sacrifice is highlighted by comparing it to Ruth's clinging to Naomi and their shared motherhood of Obed, as it is written "a son was born to Naomi." Rachel and Leah, who "together built," and Ruth and Naomi, who "gave birth together," are rooted within a chain of strong women who strode through obstacles and brought redemption. The promise of verse 11 announces that messianic salvation cannot be born through a simple and straightforward way, but rather is achieved through feminine initiative and complex volition. David's grandmother carries within herself facets of Rachel and of Leah together with facets of Tamar, Lot's daughters, and Naomi. These heroines are described as dual figures: as two sisters (Lot's daughters), as partners (Ruth and Naomi), and as a split characterization of a single woman (Tamar the Bride and Tamar the Harlot). Therefore, the dual mentioning of the sisters emphasizes the wish to unify the facet of the beloved woman with the facet of the fertile mother, and to heal the rift between motherhood and seductiveness, in order to construct the complete figure of the messianic mother.

THE MOTHERS OF THE DAVIDIC DYNASTY IN *CHRONICLES*

In the beginning of the Book of Chronicles, there are lengthy genealogies that rewrite the early biblical history, and describe procreation through mul-

---

22 Ephraim E. Urbach, *The Sages: Their Concepts and Beliefs* (Cambridge: Harvard University Press, 1975), 616-20; Schäfer, *Jewish Jesus*, 236-71.

tiple verbs, pointing to the importance of dynastic consciousness and patterns of motherhood and fatherhood in Israelite genealogy.²³ There we find a list parallel to the one at the conclusion of the Book of Ruth:

> These are the sons of Israel: Reuben, Simeon, Levi, Judah ... Perez and Zerah. Judah had five sons in all ... Ram became the father of Amminadab, and Amminadab became the father of Nahshon, prince of the sons of Judah. Nahshon became the father of Salma, Salma of Boaz, Boaz of Obed, Obed of Jesse. Jesse became the father of Eliab his firstborn ... David the seventh (I Chronicles 2: 1-15).

The list of heroes from Judah to David fills about one third of the author's ethnographic introduction, which stresses the electiveness of the Judean tribe.²⁴ As in the Book of Ruth, the chosenness of the dynasty is not determined by the purity of its heroes, rather the opposite.²⁵ The women's sins are added to the men's sins and present an antinomian picture of the dynasty throughout the generations. Perhaps the list in the fourth chapter of Ruth was copied from Chronicles and attached to the book in a later period, or possibly an independent source was placed before two authors.

A surprising adaptation of Genesis 38 includes the names of two feminine heroines, Tamar and Bath-shua.²⁶ "The sons of Judah: Er, Onan, and Shelah; these three **the Canaanite woman Bath-shua** bore to him. Now Er, Judah's firstborn, was wicked in the sight of the Lord, and he put him to death. **His daughter-in-law Tamar** also bore him Perez and Zerah" (Ibid. 2: 2-3). Why does the author emphasize the sin of Er, while ignoring the sin of Onan and his death, and abstaining from mentioning the copulation of Tamar and Judah, which brought about the birth of Perez and Zerah? Yairah Amit claims that these verses reflect a hidden polemic regarding Genesis 38 and clearly sympathize with Judah, who is denounced for taking a foreign wife and daughter-in-law for himself and his sons.²⁷ I propose that these names hint also to a polemic regarding the Davidic dynasty. In the following chapter, in the list of David's wives and children, it is written, "These are the sons of David who were born

---

23 Knoppers, *Chronicles*, 70-100; Braun, *1 Chronicles*, 23-9; Rofé, *Introduction*, 191.
24 Rofé, *Introduction*, 173-5; Sara Japhet, *The Ideology of the Book of Chronicles and its Place in Biblical Thought* (Frankfurt: Peter Lang, 1989).
25 This is in contrast to Knoppers' claim. Knoppers, *Chronicles*, 250-3.
26 S. R. Driver, *The Book of Genesis, with Introduction and Notes* (London: Methuen, 1904), 326-327; Isaac Kalimi, *The Book of Chronicles* (Jerusalem: Bialik Institute, 2000), 205, 217, 303-4.
27 Yaira Amit, *Hidden Polemics in Biblical Narrative* (Leiden: Brill, 2000), 91.

to him in Hebron: the firstborn Amnon, by Ahinoam the Jezreelite; the second Daniel, by Abigail the Carmelite; the third Absalom, son of Maacah ... These were born to him in Jerusalem: Shimea, Shobab, Nathan, and Solomon, four by **Bath-shua, daughter of Ammiel**" (I Chron. 3: 1-5).

The wife of Judah and the wife of David have the same name here: "the Canaanite woman Bath-shua" (Ibid. 2:3) and "Bath-shua, daughter of Ammiel" (Ibid. 3:5). Since in the Vulgate and the Septuagint she appears as Bathsheba, her changed name may reflect a pro-Judean attempt to obscure the scandals of David's court.[28] In retrospect, the distortion creates a connection between the edges of the dynasty: the act of Judah and Tamar, his first marriages, the death of his sons, and the birth of Perez and Zerah, connected to David and Bathsheba, the death of his firstborn son and the birth of Solomon. The intersection between the feminine heroines attests to the foreign foundations and alien women who constructed the house of David: Tamar, a Canaanite or Aramean, the Canaanite Bath-shua, Bathsheba, who appears to have been a Hittite, and Ruth the Moabite, who, though her name is not mentioned here, does appear in the parallel list in the Book of Ruth.[29]

Noting the names of the dynastic mothers is a rare custom in the Bible and ancient Near East and their mention, few or many, is a testament to the uniqueness of the House of David. A comparison of the lists from Chronicles and the Book of Ruth demonstrates the elaborate documentation of the dynastic deeds found in the Book of Ruth. The efforts of the book to balance the feminine and masculine lists are remarkable when compared to the genealogies that only mark male names and therefore indicate that the events were driven by feminine and motherly initiatives.

THE FOREIGN WOMEN OF THE HOUSE OF DAVID

The ability to connect the Davidic heroines through a feminine 'literary genealogy' rather than a male lineage, shows that the authors are aware of the mythological thinking that facilitates it. In addition to their seductiveness, these women are characterized by foreignness and their unique absorption into the ancient Israelite family.[30] Their origins in distant cultures arouse fear,

---

28 Rofé, *Introduction*, 174.
29 Braun, *1 Chronicles*, 14; Frymer-Kensky, *Women*, 278-82.
30 The definition of ancient Israelite nationalism is quite complicated. Nonetheless, Lot's daughters are foreign to Abraham's family and afterwards are incorporated into the national story with Ruth's birth. Athalya Brenner, "Biblical Attitudes toward Foreign Women and Exogamic Marriages," *Beth Miqra* 100 (1984): 179-185; Brenner, *Israelite*, 108.

even as it allows them to breach the social order and give birth to the messianic son, representing in anthropological terms the *communitas* formed through the meeting of structure and antistructure.[31]

These women, going to the threshing floor, to the cave, and to the entrance of Enaim, disguised and hidden, are figures whose essence is flexible and their "unstable" identities are a source of power, allowing them to enlarge circles and create a life outside of the strict tribal boundaries.[32] By not belonging to any place, they belong to every place. In accordance with their identification with "untamed nature," they are depicted as running wild and crafting "culture" anew.[33] This is the way Tamar, Ruth, and Lot's daughters are integrated into the people of Israel, and the messianic heroes are born. From an ethnic perspective, they represent the power of the weak, and their seductive manner reflects—as in other cultural contexts— a vital survival practice against oppressive or life denying forces.[34]

DYNASTICISM, EROS, AND MESSIANISM

As we have seen, the masculine and feminine lists unite to form an impressive genealogical scheme, which doesn't focus on the justification of individual motherhood or fatherhood, but rather the multi-generational genealogy, which exceeds the sum of its parts. Every human structure of lineage reflects the processes of the divine creation and thereby actualizes "God's image" in man.[35] The uniqueness of the genealogical lists here derives from the birth of the messianic son. In the ancient Near East the Messiah was conceived as the "son of God;" this approach also permeates the Bible and particularly the

---

31 The significance of *communitas* is in communal relations of fraternity and solidarity and also as a description of individual liminal circumstances that are due to the fracturing of hierarchies. Victor Turner, *The Ritual Process: Structure and Anti-Structure* (Chicago: Aldine, 1969), 87-143.

32 Adrienne Rich, *Of Woman Born: Motherhood as Experience and Institution* (New York: Norton, 1976), 84-109, 186-217; Cixous and Clément, *The Newly Born Woman*, 110-26; Gloria Anzaldúa, *Borderlands La Frontera: The New Mestiza* (San Francisco: Spinsters, 1987).

33 Sherry B. Ortner, "Is Female to Male as Nature to Culture?" in *Woman, Culture, and Society*, eds. Michelle Zimbalist Rosaldo and Louise Lamphere (Stanford University Press, 1974), 67-87; Raphael Patai, *The Hebrew Goddess* (New York: Ktav Publishing House, 1967).

34 Daniel Boyarin, *Dying for God: Martyrdom and the Making of Christianity and Judaism* (Stanford: Stanford University Press, 1999), 67-92; Joshua Levinson, *The Untold Story: Art of the Expanded Biblical Narrative in Rabbinic Midrash* (Jerusalem: Magnes Press, 2005), 213, 300-4.

35 Yair Lorberbaum, *In God's Image: Myth, Theology, and Law in Classical Judaism* (Cambridge: Cambridge University Press, 2015), 386-435; Daniel Boyarin, *Carnal Israel: Reading Sex in Talmudic Culture* (Berkeley: University of California Press, 1993), 197-225; Idel, *Kabbalah and Eros*.

chapters of the Prophets and Psalms.[36] In all the stories of the House of David there is a recurring pattern in which the biological father "does not know" of the lying down or rising of the mother, a description implying that it is God who actively impregnates the dynastic heroines and transforms the Messiah into a collaborated creation of the supernal and lower realms.

The Judean dynasty deviates from the tribal, familial, and particularistic perspective, replacing it with a model of creation and redemption, past and future, linked together in a circular manner. The birth of the Messiah echoes the creation of the world and simultaneously constructs the prototype of redemption at the end of days.[37] These stories are assessed not only from a biological perspective, seen as ordinary childbirth, but also from an account of God's providence towards the transgressive messianic mothers. Their transgressions are portrayed as part of the divine plan and natural order of the developing universe. Georges Bataille maintains the link between dynastic consciousness, eros, and death, and suggests that sometimes the best way to recognize the extremes of life and death is through areas of licentiousness, which in our context bridge the gaps between bodies and the forbidden and permitted.[38]

Recognition of the end instills in humankind a sense of "continuity," while lineages constitute an opening into understanding human eroticism. Dynasties, similar to the sexual act, conjoin bodies and separated entities, in order to create a continuum that maintains the world. The paradoxical potencies of fertility of the Davidic family symbolizes the "life after death," departing from individual life into the space of the mythic. These lists indicate the manner in which the erotic is bound with birth, seductiveness with motherhood, the sacred with transgression, and life with the peril of death. The Messiah that is born through forbidden relations reinforces the "naturalistic" culture, while simultaneously representing a subversion of the cosmic order and its end.

---

36 Johannes G. Botterweck, *Theological Dictionary of the Old Testament* (Cambridge: Eerdmans, 2003), 43-54; Lorberbaum, *Disempowered King*, 13-39; Israel Knohl, *The Messiah Before Jesus: The Suffering Servant of the Dead Sea Scrolls* (Berkeley: University of California Press 2000); Knohl, *Biblical Beliefs*, 40-62; Michael Schneider, "The Angelomorphic Son of God, Yahoel and the Prince of Peace," *Kabbalah* 21 (2010): 143-254; Martin Hangel, *Whose Child, The Son of God* (Philadelphia: Fortress Press, 1976).

37 Gershom Scholem, *The Messianic Idea in Judaism and Other Essays on Jewish Spirituality* (New York: Schocken Books, 1971); Galit Hasan-Rokem, *Web of Life: Folklore and Midrash in Rabbinic Literature* (Stanford: Stanford University Press, 2000), 165.

38 Bataille, *Death and Sensuality*, 11-13; Ruth Stein, "The Otherness of Sexuality: Excess," *The Journal of the American Psychoanalytic Association* 56 (2008): 43-71.

The Messiah symbolizes the "complete man," incorporating all humankind and personifying their wishes and yearnings, precisely because he is not only an individual figure, but also a symbol.[39] Even King David is presented in the Bible as a "shadowy figure," ambiguously situated between an ideal hero and an actual man.[40] By examining the Judean mothers in this transgressive context, their realness and independence manifest through each personal story and their interwovenness.

The promiscuity that characterizes the Davidic motherhood increases the infrastructural fragmentation and sharpens the relations between reproduction and unraveling. The messianic dynasty is chosen not only due to the redeeming son, but also because of the antinomian sequence woven into its components. We know nothing about David from the Book of Ruth, but we learn much regarding how he came into this world due to his mothers' nature. Consequently, in the Zoharic literature, David is identified with the *sefirah* of *Malkhut*, which is identified as that which "does not have anything of herself" and which projects the potency of the divine measures that overflow her. The dynastic heroines enable the materialization of the Messiah and his "incarnation in the flesh." Finally, the mothers give him the "name" David, the word sealing the Book of Ruth.

FEMININE DOMINANCE AND ANTINOMIANISM IN THE "J" SOURCE

Before we discuss in detail the recurring pattern in the stories of the messianic mothers, let us focus on a biblical research question: Is it possible to ascribe the episodes of Lot's daughters (Gen. 19: 29-38), Tamar (Gen. 38), and the Book of Ruth to one literary document or one literary school? This question arises because of the remarkable antinomian trend common to these stories and the emphasis on the feminine heroines in their center.

Indeed, according to biblical critics, most of the Davidic stories are attributed to one document referred to as the "J source," which probably originated from the Judean kingdom and is characterized by its extensive use of the Tetragrammaton (read as Jahweh, thus being called J). In addition, the "J source" is characterized by dominant feminine figures and an ambiguous outlook.[41] The figure of God in this source is anthropomorphic and the

---

39 Gershom Scholem, *Explications and Implications: Writings on Jewish Heritage and Renaissance*. 2 Vol (Tel Aviv: Am Oved, 1986), 189-90; Moshe Idel, *Messianic Mystics* (New Haven: Yale University Press, 1998), 1-37.
40 Mowinckel, *He That Cometh*, 168, 336-43.
41 Campbell, *Ruth*, 3-41; Ephraim Avigdor Speiser, *Genesis: A New Translation with Introduction and Commentary*. Anchor Bible 1 (New York: Doubleday, 1979), 20-9; Driver, *Genesis*,

expressive poetic aspects serve God's diverse and colorful representation. This document is likewise notable for the number and quality of its stories, in comparison to the other sources (P, E, and D) which are dominated by codes of law and other biblical genres. In our context, it is evident that there is a contradiction between the sins of the Davidic dynasty and the parallel prohibitions in the book of Leviticus. Lot and his daughters, David and Bathsheba, and Jacob's marriage to two sisters demonstrate blatant violations of taboo relations, while the Book of Ruth and Tamar's actions demonstrate a deviation from the laws of levirate marriage (*yibbum*).[42] According to Robert Cover, the tension between the biblical law and stories is solved through a narrative exegesis (*paideia*) that flows from the internal flexibility of the law and its adaptation to reality.[43] In our context, the inner-biblical exegesis of the Davidic stories attests to the paradoxicality of the laws of forbidden relations and the manner of their actualization.

Israel Knohl states that sin functions in these stories in a way similar to the story of the Garden of Eden, in which God needs the snake in order to unleash knowledge and make restitution and progress possible:

> The development of humankind and the development of the monarchy of Judah would not be possible without the intervening of the evil potency, without the instigating of the snake, and the incitement of Satan. The evil is the yeast in the dough—rotting, but also fermenting … only through the potency of the struggle between good and evil can innovations be made … only the intrusion of the potencies of evil can give vitality and the possibility for growth and development.[44]

The figure of God in the J source is not distant, even he sins, and it is apparent that God identifies with his heroes and has a close and supporting relationship with them.[45] His involvement in the deeds of the House of David weaves the theological and psychological foundation that allows for his self-deception; he is, in Susan Niditch's words, "a God of the tricksters" who overcomes the institutions of power. Prominent in the Judean source is his covenant with marginal

---

12-22, 202-5, 326-32.
42 On the status of these laws in the times of the patriarchs: Moshe Idel, "The Interpretations of the Secret of the 'Arayyot in Early Kabbalah," *Kabbalah* 12 (2004): 93-103.
43 Robert M. Cover, "The Supreme Court, 1982 Term—Foreword: Nomos and Narrative," *Harvard Law Review* 97, no. 4 (1983): 4-68.
44 Knohl, *The Many Faces*, 31-2; Knohl, *Beliefs*, 9-23.
45 Speiser, *Genesis*, 27.

figures and heroines like Tamar, Rachel and Leah, for the sake of the founding and continuation of the nation.[46] Harold Bloom went so far as to suggest that the author of "J" was a woman (!), who has God act as a partner and a rebellious "son." This aristocratic author lived parallel to the writer of the Book of Samuel, competed with him, and bested him with her talent of "telling a story." Perhaps she was affiliated with the monarchy and saw its glory and its fall, and cleverly succeeded in documenting reality while emphasizing the subversive characteristic of the Judean narrative, integrating history and myth in dark irony.[47]

Nonetheless, it is not necessary to rely on the theory of a female author in order to prove that the dynastic heroines receive bold attention in the J source, more than in any other biblical source. Bloom himself limits his premise and claims the hypothesis being discussed would be the same also with regards to a male author.[48] In any event, it appears that the Judean author feels affection for his heroines; nevertheless, like all authors in the ancient world, even he sometimes silences their voices in service of oppressive models, by appropriating birth for the patriarchal ideal and portraying the feminine womb as the national or divine womb.[49] Therefore an analysis of the feminine messianic myth must take into account God's sympathy, while simultaneously examining the misogynistic ideologies covertly rooted in these stories. The representation of the women as mediators of the "hidden" divine plan, may hint at the crossing point between the matriarchal period, discussed by J. J. Bachofen, and the patriarchal order, dominant not only in the Bible, but also in the ancient Near East. The Judean stories about fertility and seduction reflect the transference of power from women to men, thus forming a new messianic identity at the meeting point of creation and redemption.[50]

In the figure of King David, whose centrality to the Judean source cannot be ignored, this new identity emerges. David exemplifies the "new man" who surpasses all limitations and therefore (according to Bloom), the author of 'J' conscientiously portrays David as "other" and unusual, in order that he will not dominate the story.[51] This statement provides the conception

---

46 Newsom and Ringe, *The Women's Bible Commentary*, 11, 16.
47 Pardes, *Countertraditions*, 33-6; Fonrobert, "Birth of the Messiah," 259; Harold Bloom and David Rosenberg, *The Book of J* (New York: Grove Weidenfeld, 1990), 12-15.
48 Ibid, 12.
49 Trible, *Rhetoric of Sexuality*, 34-5.
50 Pardes, *Countertraditions*, 33-6; Irigaray, *Je, Tu, Nous*, 17-22; Rich, *Of Woman Born*, 86-91; Cixous and Clément, *The Newly Born Woman*, 131-2.
51 According to Bloom, David invented the Judean God, while the author of J invented David. Bloom and Rosenberg, *The Book of J*, 41-3.

of David as a symbol of shattering stereotypes in the Bible: for example, the dichotomy between masculinity and femininity, strength and weakness, war and poetry, and more. David unifies within himself sensuality and eros, politics and spirituality, female conquests and male fraternity, artistic ability, accomplishments and defeats. More than any other figure, he represents the "feminine" voice born through the meeting between forbidden relations, seductiveness and messianic designation. He himself acts in a similar manner as many of his wives, and continues, in spite of his sin, to be rewarded with the title of "The Messiah-King" who has the assurance of divine protection. It is possible to say that the compilation of Davidic stories in the Book of Ruth was done with the inspiration of the varied figure of David, who represents the ensemble of his promiscuous foremothers and the unification of their many facets in one figure.

CONCLUSION

The feminine dominance situated at the center of the J source and the way that God acts as a partner to the subversive heroines, are interwoven in the Book of Ruth. As we have seen, the book converses with ancient Judean stories and completes David's background that is missing from the Book of Samuel. David is the fruit of his foremother's actions and he is the messianic archetype who actualizes the antinomian characteristic linked to God's covenant. When we discuss the stories of Tamar, Ruth, and Lot's daughters, it is clear that the place of each heroine in the collective memory is dependent on its context, its character, and its narrative. Despite the differences between these figures, in the following chapter we shall discuss the themes that connect them and explore the archetypical model that unites the dynasty into one mythical story.

CHAPTER 2

The Type-Scene of "The Birth of the Messianic Hero"

Robert Alter, who coined the term "type-scene" in its biblical context, defined it as "a series of recurrent narrative episodes attached to the careers of biblical heroes that are analogous to Homeric type-scenes in that they are dependent on the manipulation of a fixed constellation of predetermined motifs."[1] An additional criterion is that these episodes occur "at the crucial junctures in the lives of the heroes, from conception and birth to betrothal to deathbed."[2] Following this, Alter presents six recurring scenes in the Bible: the annunciation of the birth of the hero to his barren mother; the encounter with the future betrothed at a well; the epiphany in the field; the initiatory trial; danger in the desert and the discovery of a well or other source of sustenance; and the testament of the dying hero. He analyzes two of these scenes at length: "the encounter with the future betrothed at a well" and "the annunciation of the birth of the hero to his barren mother."[3] Regarding the latter, Alter concentrated on the mother's infertility and God's intervention in the hero's birth.

I will propose a model of my own, a "type-scene of the birth of the messianic hero." This model is characterized by sexual transgression and fertility, which are both situated in contrast to the motif of feminine barrenness of the "annunciation scene." Here there is no appearance of an angel or a messenger announcing a miraculous birth, like in the stories of Hannah and Sarah; rather, the women themselves initiate the birth and are masters of their own fate. In contrast to the annunciation prior to the barren women's impregnation, in the Davidic stories, the women's vindication arrives *after* the birth and is communicated not only by a divine voice, but also through a congregation of people. In the "type-scene of the birth of the messianic hero" fundamental conflicts recur: the struggle and crisis of the heroine, the ruse that saves her from her

---

1 Alter, *Biblical Narrative*, 51.
2 Ibid.
3 Ibid., 85; Robert Alter, "How Convention Helps Us Read," *Prooftexts* 3 (1983): 115-30.

predicament, and the birth of a son at the story's conclusion. It is crucial to examine the "feminine deception" in each story from the perspectives of gender and myth, for the myth expresses the theological purpose of the story, the birth of a son to the monarchy, whereas the gendered perspective focuses on the liberty of the heroines and the motivation that drives them. One may say that the stories' "structural depth" explores femininity and motherhood, while the "structural width" discusses chosenness, messianism, and dynasticism. The unification of both structures discloses the cultural function of the feminine ruse in the messianic mother's myth.[4] In terms of the Davidic archetype, I shall explore how the nine stages of the type-scene strengthens or weakens the heroines situated at its center.

1. THE BACKGROUND: THE APPEARANCE OF THE FOREIGN WOMAN

Foreignness is the central characteristic shared by the dynastic mothers. They were isolated, widowers, lacking sons, poor, and did not belong to the Israelite nation. The Bible frequently inveighs against marrying foreign women, a prohibition intrinsically embedded in the symbolic danger of God's betrayal and damaging the offspring's purity. The prophets conceived of the Jewish people as an adulterous woman seduced by foreign gods, as seen, for example, in God's words to Hosea: "Go, love a woman who has a lover and is an adulteress, just as the Lord loves the people of Israel, though they turn to other gods and love raisin cakes" (3:1).[5] Yet, the foreignness of Ruth, Tamar, and Lot's daughters is perceived as a "positive foreignness," which is mobilized in order to establish the Judean monarchy.[6] The Book of Ruth describes the journey from foreignness and alienation to being rooted and building a home, not only on the personal level, but also as a national allegory. In Ilana Pardes's opinion, Naomi and Ruth are found at the beginning of the tale "between two lands, in a dual exile" and at its conclusion they are transformed from foreign to familiar.[7] As we will see, this observation is fitting for the array of dynastic heroines.

---

4 Levinson, *The Untold Story*, 108-9. On other definitions of the myth see Lorberbaum, *In God's Image*; Ithamar Gruenwald, "Myths and Historical Truth," in *Myths in Judaism—History, Thought, Literature*, eds. Moshe Idel and Ithamar Gruenwald (Jerusalem: The Zalman Shazar Center, 2004), 15-52; Carl G. Jung, *Memories, Dreams, Reflections* (New York: Vintage, 1965).
5 Halbertal and Margalit, *Idolatry*, 9-36; Biale, *Eros and the Jews*, 20-32.
6 Brenner, "Foreign Women," 182-4; Brenner, *Ruth*, 51-60, 70-71.
7 Pardes, *Countertraditions*, 105-117.

Lot's daughters are portrayed as foreign to Sodom and its leaders and also to Abraham's family, from which Lot has separated. Their father's proposal to abandon them to gang rape testifies that they are even alienated from their own family.[8] After the city's destruction they are left motherless and stranded in the cave of Zoar, in which they seduce their father. Ultimately, they establish the dynasty of two nations which became hostile to Israel, to the point of a complete separation between them, as it is written:

> No Ammonite or Moabite shall be admitted to the assembly of the Lord. Even to the tenth generation, none of their descendants shall be admitted to the assembly of the Lord, because they did not meet you with food and water on your journey out of Egypt, and because they hired against you Balaam son of Beor, from Pethor of Mesopotamia, to curse you (Deut. 23:4-5).

It is almost certain that Lot's daughters, more than the other dynastic heroines, represent marginalized figures eternally disconnected from any place. Their legitimate affiliation to the House of David is cast into doubt until Ruth arrives and "legitimizes" their story.

After the marriage to Bath-shua the Canaanite, appears Tamar, also a foreign woman, who Judah gives to his sons. The Book of Malachi severely depicts the private action of Judah as a national transgression: "Judah has been faithless, and abomination has been committed in Israel and in Jerusalem; for Judah ... has married the daughter of a foreign god" (Malachi 2:11). Judah, the man, becomes a symbol of an adulterous kingdom and only at the story's conclusion, with the statement "She is more righteous than I," is his sin forgiven.[9] Tamar is represented as a woman abandoned by her husbands and by Judah, to a situation of "living widowhood" and sentenced to be burnt. Only with the birth of sons and the tying of the crimson thread the plot resolved, even as Tamar remains other and lonely.[10] Notably, in this story, exclusion and insult are transformed into a driving force, which arouses Tamar to act: "Then Judah said to his daughter-in-law Tamar, 'Remain a widow in your father's house until my son Shelah grows up' ... she put off her widow's garments, put on a veil, wrapped herself up, and sat down at the entrance to Enaim" (38:14).[11]

---

8   Ruth Tsoffar, "The Trauma of Otherness and Hunger: Ruth and Lot's Daughters," *Women in Judaism* 5, no. 1 (2007): 1-13; Fuchs, *Sexual Politics*, 44-90, 209.
9   Shinan and Zakovtich, *Story*, 219-48.
10 As it is written, "And he did not lie with her again" (Gen 38:26).
11 Alter, *Biblical Narrative*, 16

The Book of Ruth, dedicated to the question of foreignness and belonging, exemplifies—on the one hand—the successful absorption of a foreign heroine, and—on the other—a demonstration of her exclusion. From the moment of her appearance in Bethlehem and until the end of the story, she remains "Ruth the Moabite," the other woman, who even the immediate redeemer refuses to marry, for: "I cannot redeem it for myself without damaging my own inheritance."[12] According to a pessimistic reading of the book, it is possible to say that Ruth remains an indistinct character, "A faceless Moabite woman."[13] This uneasy feeling is reinforced when Ruth's son is appropriated and Naomi presented as his mother. The Book of Ruth was also perceived as an allegory of the Return to Zion and the polemic against the expulsion of foreign women in the era of Ezra and Nehemia. As Frymer-Kensky suggests, Boaz represents those who remained in the land during the exile, while Naomi embodies the returning nation demanding ownership of its space, and Ruth the many foreign women who joined Israel.[14] Likewise, Bathsheba, Solomon's mother and David's wife, is not necessarily Judean. Her husband Uriah is a Hittite, and apparently her father is counted among the foreign mercenaries of the king.[15]

According to Athalya Brenner, the idea of the foreign feminine that emerges from these stories, is developed in the motif of sexual transgression and bears upon the definition of gender and national identity:

> In the worldview of the faithful there was a close link between foreign women and various types of fertility cults. Consequently, the women's alienness is bound to seductiveness, harlotry, and sexual licentiousness. Even the 'good' ones, who were assimilated into a Hebrew congregation and transformed into foremothers, heroines, or national heroines in their own right, are described as acting within a framework of sexual promiscuity.[16]

---

12   The redeemer highlights Ruth's foreignness with his statement 'lest I mar mine own inheritance' (Ruth 4:6), while Tamar's husbands waste their seed, and it is written about Onan 'he spilled it on the ground, lest he should give seed to his brother' (Gen. 38:9),
13   Caspi and Havrelock, *Women on the Biblical Road*, 169
14   Frymer-Kensky, *Women of the Bible*, 255; Zakovitch, *Ruth*, 19. On Ruth as an "archetype for converts" in rabbinic literature: see Avi Sagi and Zvi Zohar, *Conversion and Jewish Identity* (Jerusalem: Bialik Institute, 1995), 221-6.
15   II Samuel 23: 34-39
16   Brenner, "Foreign Women," 182.

Utilizing the approaches of Brenner and Esther Fuchs, sexual freedom may be ascribed to the foreign women—for they are not of "our own" and thus it is "permissible for them"—therefore, they may be exploited for the purposes of reproduction, and have their children appropriated by Jewish matriarchs. Nonetheless, one must remember that the Davidic heroines are not portrayed as oppressed and vulnerable figures; instead, they are foreign women who become founders of the monarchy. Their motherhood redeems them from their foreignness, while their initiative and seductions, transform their foreignness into a source of power.[17]

The Davidic dynasty's stories emphasize the tension between the dread of the foreigner and their acceptance. This issue is heightened in the figure of Ruth, who asks Boaz, "Why have I found favor in your sight, that you should take notice of me, **when I am a foreigner,**" and in his answer, which reflects an acceptance of the other and treats her according to her own worth, regardless of her national affiliation: "All that you have done for your mother-in-law since the death of your husband has been fully told me, and how you left your father and mother and your native land and came to a people that you did not know before" (Ruth 2:10). According to Phyllis Trible, Boaz's answer teaches an ethical principle of establishing the nation on the obligation to love the other through the help of marginalized figures.[18] In contrast, there are those who claim that the dynastic mothers are assimilated into the royal family, to the point that their foreignness disappears along with their personalities.[19]

Prominent in these stories, whether according to the approaches that emphasize the integration of the Davidic heroines or those that highlight their flawed origins, is the complex identity which the women bear: Ruth the Moabite, Tamar the Canaanite, and Lot's daughters, the foremothers of the enemies, Ammon and Moab.[20] Their foreignness stands out in relation to the nation and even to their places of origin, to which they will never return.[21] For Ruth belongs to the fields of Moab, as Lot's daughters belong to Sodom, thereby leaving her in an eternal position of liminality. Still, a unique freedom stems from their alterity, which

---

17 Anzaldúa, *Borderlands La Frontera*.
18 Trible, *Rhetoric*, 172.
19 Frymer-Kensky, *Women of the Bible*, 282; Fuchs, *Sexual Politics*, 84-90.
20 Shinan and Zakovitch, *Story*, 207-51; Zakovitch, "The Threshing-Floor Scene."
21 Brenner, *Ruth and Naomi*, 51-60.

allows them to fluctuate between interior and exterior and to create more vibrant identities that exist in multiple worlds, as Julia Kristeva explains:

> Foreignness and incest were thus at the foundation of David's sovereignty. The biblical narrative suggests that being chosen is paid and deserved by the possibility of transgressing strict obedience and taking the risk of deviation—provided the latter is subordinated to a global design. It also assumes a conception of sovereignty based on the rejected, the unworthy, the outlaw… Ruth the foreigner is there to remind those unable to read that the divine revelation often requires a lapse, the acceptance of radical otherness, the recognition of a foreignness that one might have tended at the very first to consider the most degraded… if the one 'outside-the-covenant' accepts the moral rules of the covenant, the latter finds therein its mainspring, its vital momentum, its sovereignty. Perhaps damaged, worried at any rate, that sovereignty opens up through the foreignness that founds it—to the dynamics of a constant, inquisitive, and hospitable questioning, eager for the other and for the self as other.[22]

These heroines situated at the center of the Judean dynasty challenge the nation's and individual's ability to be inclusive and illustrate the essence of the messianic idea: the recognition of foreignness and alterity hiding in the familiar, acceptance of the blackened and foreboding face of law and order, a journey towards the other within the self, and a perception of the foreign woman as a source of the uncanny (*unheimlich*), from which—through her merit—redemption sprouts.[23]

2. THE CRISIS—HUMAN AND COSMIC TRAUMATIZING CIRCUMSTANCES

The trauma set in the background of the tales of the dynastic heroines begins with a universal or national distress and culminates in a personal and feminine crisis.[24] In contrast to the model of infertility, which highlights the

---

22 Kristeva, *Strangers*, 75
23 Sigmund Freud, "The Uncanny," reprinted in *The Standard Edition of the Complete Psychological Works of Sigmund Freud*, 24 Vol, ed. and trans. James Strachey (London: Hogarth Press and Institute of Psychoanalysis, 1955), 17:217-256. See also Bracha L. Ettinger, *The Matrixial Borderspace* (Minnesota: University of Minnesota Press, 2006), 157-61.
24 When compared to Ruth and Naomi's existential crisis, Tamar's physical damage and Lot's daughters' sexual abuse are highlighted. Tsoffar, "Trauma."

miraculous birth and mother's passivity, the type-scene of the Messiah's birth emphasizes the combination of divine rescue and feminine initiative. The most trying circumstance is in the episode of Lot's daughters. In the story's beginning, Lot proposes that the men of the city rape his daughters as a legitimate tactic meant to prevent injury to his guests. The incest in the cave of Zoar should be viewed as a reaction to this proposal: "and [Lot] said, 'I beg you, my brothers, do not act so wickedly. Look, I have two daughters who have not known a man; let me bring them out to you, and do to them as you please; only do nothing to these men'" (Gen. 19: 4-8). For the biblical heroines, the home is not a "safe space," and not only in extreme cases, like of Lot's daughters or the parallel story of the concubine in Judges 19.[25] The seduction of Lot in the cave is a proportional retaliation (*mida ke-neged mida*) for their father's behavior, and evidence that they have internalized the menacing values of Sodom.[26] Both daughters express themselves through sexuality and have been forced into perverted relations due to the influence of Sodom, from which no one could survive unchanged.

The crisis of Lot's daughters dominates all of life's areas, beginning with the destruction of their world and surviving an abusive father, and culminating with the death of their family members and their mother's transformation into a pillar of salt. This surrealistic trauma establishes their identity and is revealed as a "continuous" incest, which is fixed in both sons' names: Ammon and Moab.[27] As it is written, "Thus both the daughters of Lot became pregnant by their father. The firstborn bore a son, and named him Moab (*comes from a father*) ... The younger also bore a son and named him Ben-ammi (*son of my people*)" (Gen. 19:37-38). The firstborn son's name openly proclaims that he was conceived by their father, whereas the younger son gently hints to it. Nevertheless, the story ends in an optimistic tone embedded in the yearning to create life as a reaction to the catastrophe, continued by the appearance of Ruth, David's grandmother, the descendant of the elder daughter of Lot.

---

25 Fuchs, *Sexual Politics*, 44-90, 209; Zakovitch, *Ruth*, 15-6.
26 Dorit Abramovitch, *The King is Naked: Incest in a Feminist Perspective* (Tel Aviv: Babel Publishing House, 2004); Judith L. Herman, *Trauma and Recovery: The Aftermath of Violence-From Domestic Abuse to Political Terror* (New York: Basic Books, 1992).
27 For the definition of sexual trauma, see Jean Laplanche and Bertrand Pontalis, *The Language of Psychoanalysis* (New York: W.W. Norton & Company, 1973), 465-70; Sigmund Freud and Josef Breuer, "On the Psychical Mechanism of Hysterical Phenomena," *International Journal of Psycho-Analysis* 37 (1983): 8-13; and in the biblical context, Tsoffar, "Trauma"; Michal Ben-Naftali, *Childhood, a Book - A Novella* (Tel Aviv: Resling, 2006).

Tamar also acts due to desperation and degradation, which are interwoven in her pursuit of justice. In the beginning of her story, the crisis is not cosmic and chaotic like in Sodom, but rather originates with the male attitude towards Tamar. Judah, who promised to give her his son Shelah, abandoned her and finally sentenced her to death for "playing the whore." Similar to the revenge of Lot's daughters, the seduction of Judah serves as retribution as well, not only for withholding Shelah, but also for Er's and Onan's refusal to live with her in proper matrimony.[28] A misogynistic reading of the story portrays Tamar as a *femme fatale* responsible for the death of her husbands, while other interpretations highlight her vulnerability in a man's world, which stigmatizes her by marking her as a "harlot" and "*qedeshah*."[29] In light of feminist theory that sees heterosexual relations as a product of a system of oppressive power, Tamar's utilization of her body may reflect her last means of survival.

Ruth and Naomi's story is enveloped by anxiety regarding starvation and death, and it echoes the intertextual traumas of Rachel and Leah, Tamar, and Lot's daughters. From the story's beginning, death motivates Ruth, who swears: "Do not press me to leave you or to turn back from following you ... Where you die, I will die—there will I be buried. May the Lord do thus and so to me, and more as well, if even death parts me from you!" (Ruth 1:16-17). In following Naomi, Ruth seeks to heal her memory by establishing the names of the deceased. Despite the crisis in its background, scholars describe the book as ideal and optimistic, one which portrays a solution to conflict and successful feminine journey. As Mieke Bal suggests, a "circle of kindness" triumphs in this story, as Naomi grants Ruth shelter, gaining a replacement for her deceased sons. Boaz, who possesses capital and power, but lacks progeny, establishes a dynasty for himself. Ruth, who has nothing but her own body, is able to bestow her kindness on Naomi and Boaz. Each one receives what s/he lacked and gains support. This circle reflects the hierarchies of gender and ethnic power relations replicated in the story.[30] Until the conclusion of the Book of Ruth,

---

28 In the Bible, Onan is blamed for withholding scion from his brother (and post facto Tamar), while the rabbinic image of "plowing on roofs," means that they refrained from regular intercourse. Esther Menn, *Judah and Tamar (Genesis 38) in Ancient Jewish Exegesis: Studies in Literary Form and Hermeneutics* (Leiden: Brill, 1997), 145, n. 93.

29 Alice Ogden, *Helpmates, Harlots, Heroines —Women's Stories in the Hebrew Bible* (Louisville: Westminster/John Knox, 1994), 8-13. Meanwhile, according to Speiser, Hirah's calling her a *qedeshah* was for societal purpose. Speiser, *Genesis*, 295-300.

30 Bal, *Lethal Love*, 70-3.

it is unclear if the famine will cease, if the redeemer will redeem, if the land will be rescued, and if the child, for whom the story was written, will be born.

In fact, in all of the dynastic stories, death reappears so frequently as to be considered the primary character: the deaths of Lot's wife and the people of Sodom, Tamar's husbands, Ruth's, Naomi's, and Orpah's husbands, and David and Bathsheba's firstborn. Even the names of the former husbands echo themes of mourning, sickness, and death: Mahlon (sickness) and Chilion (annihilation), and alongside them Er (evil) and Onan (mourning), and Lot, whose name suggests a curse in Aramaic or hiding in Hebrew. Destruction, war, famine, abandonment, rape, deception, fighting, exclusion—these are the main forces that drive the Davidic tales. From within these crises flowers the reparation: in their struggle against destruction and annihilation, Lot's daughters give birth to Ammon and Moab, whose descendants are Ruth and Naama the Ammonite. Tamar, neglected and silenced, musters her courage and seduces Judah after he breaks his promises. From the fight between Rachel and Leah blossom the tribes of Israel and the father of the dynasty, Judah is born. The Book of Ruth emphasizes the human acts of kindness, and only in the aftermath of the death of Uriah and her firstborn does Bathsheba give birth to Solomon, who symbolizes the elected son emerging from within circumstances of distress and crisis.

Harold Fisch suggests that the background of the elected son's birth is embedded in the rescuing of the heroine from a judicial crisis. Each story opens with the problem of *agunah* ("chained" women), which is solved through an expansion of the laws of levirate marriage (*yibbum*): through the women's redemption by her father (Lot's daughters), father-in-law (Tamar) or a different male relative (the Book of Ruth).[31] However, a consideration of these women independent of their husbands or sons highlights the heroines' successful, autonomous escape from calamities created through no fault of their own. In this way, the Bible illuminates its sympathy for the courage of these women, who "redeem" themselves and their surroundings.[32] Furthermore, the crises are reflective of the "failures" of the religious system and flawed relations between people and between man and God. For example, the famine in the beginning

---

[31] Brenner claims that the birth of the legitmate son from the proper father is the solution of the crisis. Fisch, "Ruth"; Steinsaltz, *Women*, 53-64; Brenner, "Genealogy of the Messiah," 701-21.

[32] Trible and Van Wijk Bos explore a counter type-scene that creates a surprising and positive reality through the feminine ruse. Trible, *Rhetoric of Sexuality*, 161; Van Wijk-Bos, "Shadows," 37-67. On the dual model, which has oppressive and empowering aspects, see Frymer-Kensky, *Women of the Bible*, 238-77; Phyllis Silverman Kramer, "Biblical Women that Come in Pairs: The Use of Female Pairs as a Literary Device in the Hebrew Bible," in *Genesis: The Feminist Companion to the Bible*, ed. Athalya Brenner (Sheffield: Sheffield Academic Press, 1998), 218-232.

of the Book of Ruth mirrors the dejected state of people. The actual famine thereby symbolizes a spiritual famine as well, which merits, at the conclusion of the book, a response and "nourishment."[33] The traumas of the dynastic mothers demonstrate that flawedness is a condition for redemption. These women have no choice but to struggle with foreignness, alienation, abandonment, and degradation. In the end, God joins their struggle, fills the void, and mends all shortcomings, even granting progeny.

3. THE OBSTACLE—THE SEXUAL PROHIBITION: INCEST, HARLOTRY, AND SEDUCTION

The Bible maps an ample selection of forbidden relations, including relations with a married woman or menstruant, homosexual acts, and inter-familial relations. In addition, in Leviticus 18-20 there are distinctions between harlotry, adultery, and cult prostitution.[34] An examination of sexual transgression in the Davidic dynasty shows striking contradictions between the law and its corresponding story. For example, in the detailed lists of illicit relations the prohibition of incest between a father and daughter is, astonishingly, absent. This matter makes it difficult to interpret and judge the action of Lot's daughters. Indeed, the sages deduced the taboo of incestuous relations between father and daughter through an *a fortiori* argument of the prohibition of relations with a granddaughter, yet the absence of a straightforward law infuses the episode with a radical ambiguity.[35] Indeed, an examination of the tribe of Judah in the entire Book of Genesis reveals tensions pertaining to the foundation of the biblical laws of forbidden relations. The fact that Jacob married two sisters or that Tamar received a death sentence raises questions about the validity of these laws in early biblical times.[36] Furthermore, the only two stories in the Bible in which the root '*y-b-m*' (levir) is mentioned are the Book of Ruth and Tamar's episode, and in both of them the difference between the laws of *yibbum*

---

33 Through the famine, the conclusion of the Book of Ruth can thereby "feed" the lack of the reader. Tsoffar, "Trauma"; Ben-Naftali, *Chronicle,* 132-201.
34 Botterweck and Ringgren, *Theological Dictionary of the Old Testament,* 343-9; Jacob Milgrom, *Leviticus 17-22: A New Translation with Introduction and Commentary.* Anchor Bible 3B (New York: Doubleday, 2000), 1516-71.
35 Milgrom, *Leviticus,* 1528-9.
36 The tension may be resolved by ascribing the stories and laws to different documents. According to the Documentary Hypothesis, the chapters of illicit relations in Leviticus belong to the Holiness Code, in contrast to the J stories in Genesis. Cover, "Nomos and Narrative"; Idel, "Secret of the 'Arayyot.'"

found in Deuteronomy 25 and its literary manifestation is large. In both stories, *yibbum* expands from only the deceased's brother to include additional figures, for example the husbands' father (Judah) and the distant relative (Boaz).[37] The Davidic stories reflect, each in their own way, a judicial reworking of the strict laws of illicit relations.

Even though the Bible contains no explicit prohibition against relations between a father and daughter, the configuration of the tale in Genesis 19 emphasizes the transgression in the act. The seductive means, the cover of night and the cave, the need for Lot's daughters to intoxicate him, the manner in which the elder daughter convinces her younger sister, and the repetition of the phrase, "he did not know when she lay down or when she rose" (Gen. 19: 33, 35), all stress the need for secrecy and deceit in order to conceive. Yet, Lot's earlier suggestion to the men of Sodom that they rape his daughters, and Abraham's separation from him because of his lustful tendencies, confirm the transgressive motif laying in the background of Ammon and Moab's births, and subsequently in the Judean dynasty. Even though Lot's daughters are not directly affiliated to the tribe, the birth of "Moab" provides an opening note which the array of dynastic heroines repeats.

Tamar's story raises a different question: why does Judah sentence her to be burned, for premarital sex—even though perceived unfavorably—is biblically permitted for an unmarried woman? Different solutions have been suggested for this question throughout the ages. According to one theory, Tamar and Judah sinned by violating the prohibition: "If a man lies with his daughter-in-law, both of them shall be put to death; they have committed perversion; their blood is upon them" (Leviticus 20:12). Others derive from the term "*qedeshah*" that Tamar was suspected of cult prostitution, while others ascribed the severe punishment for injuring Judah's honor.[38] In the laws regarding illicit relations, the punishment of being burnt is only mentioned in two cases: having relations with a wife and daughter and a priest's daughter who commits harlotry (Lev. 20:14; 21:9). Therefore, some scholars suggest that since Tamar was a priest's daughter, designated for Shelah and "reserved for levirate marriage,"

---

37 The multiple use of the term "redemption" in the Book of Ruth (3:12-13; 4:1-8) parallels the act of *yibbum*, due to the use of the idiom "to maintain the dead man's name on his inheritance" (Ruth 4:5, 10-11), which appears as well in Deuteronomy 25:6. Campbell, *Ruth*, 130-8.

38 Zakovitch, *David*, 28; Speiser, *Genesis*, 300.

she was sentenced to the pyre.[39] A different interpretation claims that the punishment was not actual burning, but rather only a marking on her brow.[40] Naḥmanides weighs a few of these reasons and in the end reads Tamar's actions in light of the reality of his day:

> It appears to me that since Judah was a chief, an officer, and a ruler of the land, his daughter-in-law who committed harlotry against him was not judged by the same law as other people, but as one who degraded royalty ... In line with the literal interpretation, it is possible that their law was similar to that which is presently customary in some of the countries of Spain, that a married woman who commits a faithless act is turned over to her husband who decrees death or life for her, as he wishes. Now Tamar was designated for his son Shelah, and in the eyes of their laws she was considered a married woman.[41]

Naḥmanides connects Judah's motivations to the medieval Spanish custom, in which the husband decides whether his wife lives or dies. An analysis of the halahkic and gender ramifications of the story, as well as the multiple suggested interpretations for the burning, attest to the judicial problem in Tamar's episode; the multiplicity stresses the impulsive motives of Judah, whereby a death sentence was almost issued. This scene is reversed after her identity is revealed. Judah's words reflect conscious recognition of the sin and the injustice of Tamar's punishment: "Then Judah acknowledged them and said, 'She is more righteous than I, since I did not give her to my son Shelah.' And he did not lie with her again" (Gen. 38:26).[42] It may be that the conclusion "And he did not lie with her again" is a later addition, designed to create harmony between the laws of illicit relations in Leviticus (ascribed to H) and the story attributed to J in Genesis.[43] From the consolidation of these sources it appears that after Judah fulfilled the commandment of *yibbum* with the birth of Perez and Zerah, the taboo returned, and Tamar was again forbidden to Judah.[44]

---

39 Genesis Rabbah 85:10 (24) (ed. Theodor – Albeck, 1044); *Midrash Sekhel Tov*, ed. Buber, Gen. 38:11. Niditch, "Genesis 38," 146-9; Fuchs, *Sexual Politics*, 76-7.
40 As R. Judah he-Hasid suggests; Frymer-Kensky, *Women of the Bible*, 273.
41 Naḥmanides, *Genesis*, 476.
42 Brenner, *The Israelite Woman*, 82-3; Menn, *Judah and Tamar*.
43 Niditch suggests that "And he did not lie with her again" is a priestly addition to the ancient J narrative. Niditch, Genesis 38, 148.
44 As seen from *Sifré* to Numbers 88, "Since he realized that she was his daughter-in-law, he did not again have sexual relations with her."

Despite the approaches that portray the Book of Ruth as a story free of sexuality, in which maximally seduction happens without copulation, the similarity of the threshing floor scene to the meeting at the *entrance of Enaim* and the *cave of Zoar*, cries out for interpretation.[45] The transgression in the episode is implied by Naomi's advice for Ruth to go to the threshing floor while Boaz sleeps, and her emphasis on Ruth needing to veil herself, change her clothes, primp, and wait until he is pleased. Even though we do not know what happened that night, it is evident that the ambiguity of the scene allows Ruth to perfect the feminine template in the messianic myth. The inferred transgression here repeats and is reminiscent of additional biblical scenes, as David Biale writes:

> In the charged scene of Ruth accosting the drunken, sleeping Boaz on the threshing floor, the text repeatedly uses words like 'to lie down' and 'to know,' both of which have clear sexual connotations. Ruth uncovers Boaz's legs, an occasional biblical euphemism for the genitals ... To 'uncover the genitals' is the technical term in biblical law for a sexual violation, and Ruth's act alludes suggestively to the sin of Noah's son Ham.[46]

These actions have already appeared in the episode of Lot's daughter, a story that represents the first sexual deviance of the dynasty, similar to the illicit relations of David and Bathsheba, which signify, in the Bible, its conclusion.

The Spurned Women

In the margins of the stories, I wish to illuminate the emotional perspective of the rejected woman. Lot's daughters are offered by their father to be raped, and Tamar is unwanted by her husbands—who are either unwilling to impregnate her or in the case of the third son, Shelah, are simply too young. Even Judah, as we saw according to some interpretations, did not stay with her afterwards. Ruth is unwanted by the redeemer who fears the destruction of his scion, and Boaz initially limits his responsiveness to the redemptive act, albeit in a subtler way than his predecessors: "But now, though it is true that I am a near kinsman, there is another kinsman more closely related than I. Remain this night, and in the morning, if he will act as a redeemer for you, good; let him do so.

---

45 Zakovitch, *Ruth*; Rachel Adelman, "Seduction and Recognition in the Story of Judah and Tamar and the Book of Ruth," *Nashim* 23 (2012): 98.
46 Biale, *Eros and the Jews*, 14-5.

If he is not willing to act as a redeemer for you, then, as the Lord lives, I will act as a redeemer for you. Lie down until the morning" (Ruth 3: 12-13). To this list we may add Leah, the mother of Judah, who was spurned by Jacob for the beloved Rachel. Similarly, the later tradition regarding David's birth portrays his mother as an unwanted woman. This Midrash develops the biblical type-scene and describes David as being born through an entangled threesome between Jesse, his wife, and his handmaiden, an issue which David hints at in Psalms, by writing, "Indeed, I was born guilty, a sinner when my mother conceived me" (Psalm 51:7).

What connects these spurned women to the transgressions which bring about the birth of the elected sons? The type-scene's configuration suggests that these women are rejected because of the taboo that they must violate, and simultaneously they are rejected in order to bypass every hindrance, and so give birth to the redeemer against all the odds and prohibitions. Harsh judgment of their behavior eases over the generations: the story of Lot's daughters prompts discussion of a father who abused his daughter, Tamar's husbands are depicted as neglectful, and in the Book of Ruth there is a redeemer who rejects his role. In this manner, the foundation of the Davidic dynasty demonstrates the process of restoration as a condition of redemption. Sexual transgressions (and the accompanying trauma) are mitigated, whether incestuous relations between a father and his daughters, an act of harlotry between father-in-law and daughter-in-law, or the implied seduction on a Bethlehem threshing floor. As we saw, the Book of Ruth links these actions within a genealogical framework sketching a model of dynastic redemption.

Lot's daughters, lacking all alternatives, are forced to act in a perishing world. Tamar fights for an unrealized promise against the men on whom her life depends. Naomi and Ruth form a reciprocal sorority. The similar design of the seduction scenes—despite the differences in severity of the transgressions—preserves the mysterious and contradictory nature of these stories. The desecration of the sacred and the forbidden sexual relations cause damage to God himself, yet these stories exhibit that God justifies the dynastic mothers' transgressions and even acts as a partner to them in their tales.[47]

---

[47] From the Davidic stories emerges a subversive voice of "deterministic debauchery" that forms the sacred, similar to the relations between God and Israel, in Ezekiel 16 and Hosea 2. See Halbertal and Margalit, *Idolatry*.

4. THE MESSIANIC FATHERS—THE SYMBOLISM OF THE FATHER FIGURE

Notably, the men depicted in these stories are not only partners, but also father figures. Even though their precise ages are not mentioned in the Bible, each story involves copulation with an older man who represents an actual or symbolic "father" figure. Lot's daughters seduce their actual father, Tamar seduces her father-in-law, Bathsheba is taken by the king, who represents the "father of the people," and lastly, Boaz—the judge who sits at the gate—attests to his own senescence when he tells Ruth that "this last instance of your loyalty is better than the first; you have not gone after young men, whether poor or rich" (Ruth 3:10). The Midrash radicalizes this theme by claiming that Rachel was three years old when she married Jacob, who was much older than her. If we focus this model on the Judean dynasty, we suggest that Ruth, Tamar, and Lot's daughters deliberately seduce father-figures and thereby create a messianic rectification through oedipal perversion. In other words, the forbidden sexual relation between "father" and "daughter" produces the sacred relation between mother and elected son.

This aspect of the messianic scene is combined with the men's passivity, which is striking in contrast to the dynastic mothers' dominance. While Judah, Boaz, Lot, and Jacob are not characteristically passive figures, in each seduction scene, the man serves as a silent background for the woman's actions. The men's temporary weakness contributes to the son's chosenness, and thus the heroines conceive in the moments when the men are asleep and lack control. Furthermore, the weakness of the father figures reinforces the women's relationship in regards to the divine father. From a psychoanalytic perspective, the father represents God. Thus, the messianic son is transformed into a product of intercourse, between a woman of flesh and blood and a heavenly entity.[48] This relationship symbolizes the sublimation of forbidden relations (as described by Jung), to incestuous fantasies and the desire to return to the motherly womb—here, the myth of *hieros gamos* is grounded in the violation of taboo relations.[49] Lacking

---

48 Brenner, "Genealogy of the Messiah"; Fuchs, *Sexual Politics*, 66. More on the father as a symbol of God, see Julia Kristeva, *Tales of Love* (New York: Columbia University Press, 1987), 234-63.

49 Carl G. Jung, *The Psychology of the Transference* (New York: Routledge, 1983), 37-49; Ruth Netzer, *Journey to the Self: The Alchemy of the Mind – Symbols and Myths* (Ben Shemen: Modan, 2004), 328-31. As well as the discussion of incest in Chapter Five.

the divine impregnation with which the myths of Christianity begin, the Davidic dynasty nevertheless minimizes the roles of the corporeal fathers and emphasizes the transformation of the female figure into the messianic mother.

Mother and Son

In the Judean type-scene, the weak fathers highlight the son's centrality and his link to his mother. The son becomes chosen due to the space that his father relinquishes for him and on account of his mother's preference for him. The primary relationship between mother and son forms a sort of mythical aggregate as can be seen in Leah's happiness on the occasion of Judah's birth ("This time I will praise the Lord" Gen. 29:35), Tamar's midwife's proclamation at Perez's birth, Bathsheba's favoring of Solomon, and Obed's reception in the city's gate.[50]

Effectively, the fathers are exploited in these stories for the purpose of childbirth, while women desire to seduce and give birth. According to this reading, the messianic son is born through a miraculous conception and connection between God and the mother, while the elderly father is seduced, asleep, and deceived. Through acts of seduction and childbirth that are liberating and redemptory *for the mothers,* the bond between the son and his mother is reinforced and the child becomes the "son of God." Here as in many ancient cultures, the mythical figure of "Great Mother"

> ...acknowledged no individual husband, only sons who become consorts ... Spiritualized into a divine being, she was the source of vegetation, fruition, fertility of every kind ... In biological motherhood, as in these other activities ... she was a transformer.[51]

Additionally, it is possible to connect the dynastic heroines' stories of copulation with the slumbering and weakened father figures to the rabbinic idea that the Messiah comes only through absentmindedness (as it states in the Babylonian Talmud: "Three come unawares: Messiah, a found article and a scorpion," Sanhedrin 97a). The father's intoxication, sleep, and unawareness

---

50 Erich Neumann, *The Great Mother: An Analysis of the Archetype* (Princeton: Princeton University Press, 1963), 18-23; Brenner, *Ruth and Naomi,* 20-1; Irigaray, *Je, Tu, Nous,* 37-44.
51 Rich, *Of Woman Born,* 100-101.

allows for the miraculous birth to occur. The Messiah cannot be born in a normal manner and therefore it is necessary to seek him in an "otherly place" and with the assistance of a father figure who represents the Infinite.

5. THE SECRET AND SEDUCTIVE MEANS—WINE, MASQUERADING, AND CONCEALMENT

In this section we will discuss the aspects of concealment, objects, locations, and mediums that assist the Davidic mothers in seducing men and birthing the messianic son. We will also analyze the uniqueness of the feminine scene, its sexual symbols and the dynastic heroines' dress. Finally, we will examine the conception of secrecy and its connotation in these stories, from two perspectives: the mythic and gender.

The story of Lot's daughters occurs at night and under the influence of wine, which contributes to the successful seduction. The hidden location, the cave of Zoar, which isolates the heroines from the external world, appears differently in other stories. Tamar, at the "Entrance of *Enaim* (eyes)," exposes her body as prostitutes did in the ancient world, while veiling her face, so that Judah will not recognize her.[52] Ruth's seduction on the threshing floor, immersed in the darkness of the field, is a secluded location far from the trials of hunger and poverty.

Tamar's seduction of Judah at the "entrance of Enaim" emphasizes the erotic tone of the place's name, and her decisive actions contrast notably with her earlier passivity: she casts off her widow's garb, disguises herself audaciously, and sits at the crossroad (the gate) between two springs, in a symbolic place referred to as "Enaim" (eyes).[53] Tamar is assisted in her seduction by many objects—a widow's garb, a veil, a signet, cord, and staff, a goat and pyre, and lastly, the crimson thread tied on Zerah's hand—which signifies an intersection between life and death, revealing her concealed desires. The signet, cord, and staff are known throughout the ancient world as identity markers.[54] Judah's own willingness to relinquish his identity attests to his desire to forfeit any object in order to have Tamar. Each story's hero collaborates in the divine

---

52 Menachem Horowitz, *Encyclopaedia Hebraica*, s.v. "Zenut" (Jerusalem: Encyclopedia Publishing Company, 1965), 916; John R. Huddlestun, "Unveiling the Versions: The Tactics of Tamar in Genesis 38:15," *Journal of the Hebrew Scriptures* 3 (2001): 325-343.
53 For the erotic meaning of the eye, see Jacob Nacht, *Simlei 'Ishah* (Tel Aviv: Private Production, 1959), 183; Shinan and Zakovitch, *Story*, 99-100.
54 Speiser, *Genesis*, 295-300.

cycle of giving: the transfer of objects between women and men, the woman's transfer between men, the sending of the goats to the Adullamite friend, and finally, the passing of the twins and tying of the thread. Tamar and Judah's meeting is packed with erotic symbolism in a place rooted between concealment and disclosure.

In the third story, Ruth acts according to a similar model of concealment. At night, she heads to the threshing floor, washes and switches her garments, and even changes her identity. Boaz, presumably intoxicated (in accordance with the agricultural and fertile atmosphere of the story: "When Boaz had eaten and drunk, and he was in a contented mood" [Ruth 3:7]), does not initially recognize Ruth and therefore asks "Who are you?" (Ruth 3:9). The motif of the men's intoxication is echoed in the stories of Lot, in the cave of Zoar, and Judah ("when Judah's time of mourning was over, he went up to Timnah to his sheep-shearers" [Gen. 38:12]).[55] Though we do not know if the seduction was successful and if they copulated that very night, Ruth's journey is clearly linked to the actions of Tamar and Lot's daughters. For example, here again we find similar objects: the cloth which hides Ruth when she returns from the threshing floor parallels the veil that conceals Tamar (Gen. 38:14, Ruth 3:15-16), the barley that Boaz measures out for her parallels Judah's gifts and belongings that he left by Tamar (Gen. 38:18-20; Ruth 3:15). Clothes and fabrics repeatedly function here as "signifiers of desire" connecting the links of the feminine dynasty.[56]

The transition from the cave to the "entrance of Enaim" and then to the threshing floor in the fields suggests the symbolic development of these sites of messianic occurrences. According to Fisch, these places reflect social development in the ancient world: Lot's daughters represent a cave-dweller society, Judah and Tamar a pastoral society, and the Book of Ruth an agrarian society. In each case, laws are legislated and anchored in the developing civilization.[57] Following the biblical intertextuality, the sages sought to discuss the stories' connections, emphasizing the symbolism of the locations and objects in the dynastic stories. For instance, the sages describe how Tamar lost Judah's

---

55   The shearing festival had a bacchanalic quality. In the *Testaments of the Twelve Patriarchs* (*Testament of Judah* 11:2; 12:3) Judah is depicted as intoxicated when he marries Bathshua as well as at the sheep shearing and the episode with Tamar, a factor leading to his fall through both women. James L. Kugel, *Traditions of the Bible: A Guide to the Bible as It was at the Start of the Common Era* (Cambridge: Harvard University Press, 1998), 497-9; Adelman, "Seduction and Recognition"; Fisch, "Ruth."
56   Kristeva, *Tales of Love*, 234-63
57   Fisch, "Ruth." On feminine judicial innovations in the Book of Ruth, see Ariella Deem, *Zot ha-Pa`am* (Tel Aviv: Reuven Mas, 1986), 268-71.

belongings and God delivered new ones in their place, similar to his creation of a womb for Ruth, who was barren.[58]

Disguises and Concealments

The seductive feminine cloak is overtly present in the description of Tamar's veil, Ruth's cloth, and hinted at in the description of Lot's daughters. The disguises hide more than they reveal and expose the unseen "persona" hidden behind the mask. However, a differentiation should be made between the disguises which change the disguised, and costumes which disguise superficially, while the character retains a clear identity.[59] Tamar knows what she wants, so in a sense her authentic self is revealed through her veiling, even as it is deceptive: she is not as Judah thought. Nevertheless, a certain change occurs in Tamar after the seduction scene: she becomes a more active, daring character, capable of sending to Judah his belongings and cannily demanding that he "Take note, please" without actually exposing him.[60] Here we notice that Tamar's feminine disguise does not necessarily indicate her *vulnerability*, as suggested by some scholars; rather, it helps release her concealed strength.

In contrast, Ruth's disguises specifically attest to her vulnerability and effacement. Pnina Galpaz-Feller's claim that "through her gown Ruth changes her destiny from being a foreign Moabite woman to being a redeemed woman and earning an official position as a part of the society," ignores the manner in which Ruth is led by others.[61] As we will see in the seventh chapter, the exegetes reinforce the biblical motif of mystery and uncertainty regarding what occurs

---

58 Genesis Rabbah 85:11 (ed. Theodor – Albeck, 1044); Ruth Rabbah 7:14. Also Chapter Seven, footnote 39. Menn, *Judah and Tamar*, 226. The locution "and go down to the threshing-floor" (Ruth 3:3) alludes to a hidden and lowly place like the cave of Zoar, in which people hid wine, like in Genesis Rabbah 51:8 (ed. Theodor – Albeck, 537), also compare it to the idiom "a foretaste of the World to Come" in Ruth Rabbah 2:10 (ed. Vilna).

59 An example of a costume forming a "third self" can be found in Jacob and Esau's story. This disguise causes a new figure to be created, which symbolizes the hybridization of the brothers: a man with the hands of Esau and voice of Jacob, dualistically realizing the blessing "the elder shall serve the younger." On the exchanging of faces and masquerade, see Johan Huizinga, *Homo Ludens: A Study of the Play Element in Culture* (London: Routledge & Kegan Paul, 1949), 35-75; Van Wijk-Bos, "Out of the Shadows"; Zakovitch, *Ruth*, 24-8; Shinan and Zakovitch, *Story*, 224-6.

60 Driver, *Genesis*, 326-32; Alter, *Biblical Narrative*, 20-33; Adelman, "Seduction and Recognition."

61 Pnina Galpaz-Feller, *The Sound of Garments: Garments in the Bible: Do the Clothes Make the Man?* (Jerusalem: Carmel Publishing, 2008), 77.

on the threshing floor. Over the course of this scene, the characters—Naomi, Ruth, and Boaz—exchange expressions indicating their reciprocal façades. For example, the idiom of spreading one's cloak passes from Boaz's blessing for Ruth in the field ("and may you have a full reward from the Lord... under whose cloak you have come for refuge" [Ruth 2:12]) to Ruth's request of Boaz ("spread your cloak over your servant, for you are a redeemer" [Ruth 3:9]). These exchanges unveil the complex disguises, even resulting at times in a loss of identity. Likewise, upon Ruth's return, Naomi asks her, "Who are you, my daughter?" (Ruth 3:16) as if she does not recognize her, echoing Boaz's questions, "Who are you?" (Ruth 3:9) and, in the field, "To whom does this young woman belong?" (Ruth 2:5). The multiple repetitions of the phrase "Who are you?" turn the question into a literary indicator of Ruth's enigmatic figure. This question exposes the disharmonious differences in the Book of Ruth and the concealed facets of the foreign heroine who is unrecognizable.

In Ruth and Naomi's relationship, the feeling that they are exchanging roles under the cover of night is intensified, or perhaps Naomi is exploiting Ruth for her own purposes. In a certain sense, Naomi is the one who walks to the threshing floor that night, as is revealed in the gap between the *Qere* (below, in braces) and *Ketiv* (in bold) in the threshing floor scene:

> Now wash and anoint yourself, and put on your best clothes **and I will go down** [and go down] to the threshing-floor; but do not make yourself known to the man until he has finished eating and drinking. When he lies down, observe the place where he lies; then, go and uncover his feet **and I will lie down** [and lie down]; and he will tell you what to do.' She said to her, 'All that you tell me I will do.' (Ruth 3:3-4)

The use of first-person pronoun ("and I will go down," "and I will lie down") expose Naomi's desires, harmoniously camouflaged in the Book of Ruth.[62] These desires should be examined in light of the book's beginning. There the phrase "have a husband [tonight]" is repeated four times by Naomi: "Do I still have sons in my womb that they may become your husbands... for I am too old to have a husband. Even if I thought there was hope for me, even if I should *have a husband* tonight and bear sons" (Ruth 1:11). Therefore, it is probable

---

62 Zakovitch suggests that the grammatical first person may be an archaic form of female second person, while Ilana Pardes stresses Naomi's identification with Ruth, in contrast to the rift between Rachel and Leah, an interpretation hinted at as well in Ruth Rabbah 5:12 "My merits will descend with you." Zakovitch, *Ruth*, 17, 89; Pardes, *Countertraditions*, 105-7.

that it is Naomi who masquerades on the threshing floor, as a young woman who she can no longer be, through Ruth's veiled body.

In an optimal situation, the feminine disguise is connected to the erotic interplay of concealment and disclosure. In tribal societies, the mask allows for sexual freedom and a carnivalistic breaching of boundaries unobtainable in the everyday. However, in the Book of Ruth, as with the stories of Tamar and Lot's daughters, it is difficult to speak about the donning of a veil as an act of delight. Indeed, the heroines of these stories are forced into their disguises so that their true identities will not be revealed. Had Tamar not disguised herself, it is unlikely that she would have merited Judah's progeny. Had Lot's daughters spoken to their father directly instead of seducing him when he was drunk, there might not have been Ammon and Moab, and, from them, Ruth and King David. Had Ruth turned to Boaz candidly, it is unlikely that he would have been ready to exchange roles with the first redeemer. Furthermore, it would have prevented Naomi's psychological masquerading, which we discussed earlier. In each case, cunning female acts were a condition for their stories' success.

Following Bakhtin, I claim that, just as the carnival blurs hierarchal boundaries and serves the marginalized of society—who become equals to their social superiors when they cannot be identified—so too biblical heroines profit greatly by disguising and covering themselves . In light of the inflexible system of modesty laws then standard in the ancient Near East and the Bible, we understand that the female disguise is not only an expression of concealment and hiding, but also the opposite effort of the body's exposure, in accordance with the woman's volition. In each of the Judean stories, the masquerading allows for seduction and childbirth to occur. Thus, this motif strengthens the heroines' "dual identity," as figures who are coerced, but who also choose to act; who are rescued, but also proactive.

Bed Tricks

The seductive act in the cave of Zoar is described twice, by both of Lot's daughters (Gen. 19:23, 25). Significantly the author intentionally emphasizes this scene instead of skipping this duplication. A similar duplication is prominent in a parallel story regarding a feminine ruse of elder and younger sisters: the mandrake episode in Genesis 30:15-16, in which Leah buys a night with Jacob in exchange for the mandrakes that she gives to Rachel. This symbolic act deals with exchanges and fertility and is an example of the entangled struggle of two sisters.⁶³ Here we find a bedtrick, as Wendy Doniger terms the use of a sexual deception in pursuit of an aim. In all the Davidic tales, the men (Jacob, Lot, Judah, and Boaz) are deceived, whereas the women (Rachel and Leah, Lot's daughters, Tamar, and Ruth and Naomi) initiate the action.⁶⁴

As Lot's treatment in the cave of Zoar is a proportional retaliation for his behavior in Sodom, the mandrake episode repeats the technique that was used on Rachel and Leah by their father on the bridal night.

> So Laban gathered together all the people of the place, and made a feast. But in the evening he took his daughter Leah and brought her to Jacob; and he went in to her. (Laban gave his maid Zilpah to his daughter Leah to be her maid.) When morning came, it was Leah! And Jacob said to Laban, 'What is this you have done to me? Did I not serve with you for Rachel? Why then have you deceived me?' (Gen. 29:22-25)

Ruses are portrayed here as a tool of the powerful men. In this story, the father functions as an omnipotent patriarch, who serves wine to distract his partners, at whim switches women, and capriciously transfers them from one place to another. The linking of events implies both the objectification of women and their exchangeability according to social rank: first Leah is transferred from her father to her husband, and afterwards Zilpah is transferred from her master to his daughter, who as a married woman is someone of economical standing.

Thus, the way in which Rachel and Leah exchange the mandrakes for Jacob implies proportional retribution against the masculine system, similar to Lot's daughters' retaliation for their father's suggestion that they be raped. We have a recurring pattern in which the women jointly seduce and exchange masculine figures who neither see nor are aware "when they lay down or when they rose." The sages emphasize this theme of sororal love in the bridal night, as an alternative to the conflict between the sisters in the Bible. A known Midrash in Lamentations Rabbah describes how Rachel hid under the bed and gave Leah the signs in order not to embarrass her.⁶⁵ Even if the sisters collaborate begrudgingly, they—like Ruth and Naomi and Lot's two daughters—nonetheless

---

63 Fuchs, *Sexual Politics*; Fonrobert, "Birth of the Messiah."
64 Wendy Doniger, *The Bedtrick: Tales of Sex and Masquerade* (Chicago: University of Chicago Press, 2000), 253-9; Van Wijk-Bos, "Out of the Shadows"; Levinson, *The Untold Story*, 205-14.
65 *Lamentations Rabbah*, (ed. Buber) 1:24; Hasan-Rokem, *Web of Life*, 136-40.

demonstrate how, through collaborated deception, female characters withstand oppression and realize their goals.[66]

Secrecy and Concealment

An array of deceptive tools, illusions, and masquerades combine to create and perpetuate the Davidic dynasty. The necessity to please and to seduce, to act in secrecy, at night, under a veil or bed, is on the one hand evidence of female vulnerability, and on the other hand reflects an extraordinary power that brings about the birth of the messianic son. Secrecy is designed to conceal the hierarchical systems, just as it allows for actions that subvert that hierarchy. These heroines are unable to act directly and overtly, rather they are forced to act stealthily because of their gendered and social marginality. As Abramovitch writes, "In the place where there is a deviation from the fantasy, a deviation from the origin myth, there the secret is formed. In the place where it is likely that the terrible price of control will be revealed for everyone to see, there the need to conceal, to hide, to be removed from sight is born."[67] Women who were abandoned and threatened with rape, who suffer from hunger and danger, have few options other than to exploit their bodies.[68] The repetition of sexual deviancies in the Davidic dynasty, generation after generation, by foreign women, may indicate a sophisticated reversal of sexuality as "an instrument of power on the way to messianism"—or, as a number of scholars have claimed, perhaps the heroines' seemingly "liberated" sexual practices are only an illusion of freedom.[69] Actually, they are manipulated by the patriarchal system, while their otherness fits sociological theories, which demonstrate that "isolation or loneliness is the main characteristic of families that have incestuous relations."[70] Interpretations along this line tend to stress the messianic mothers' passivity and the negative aspects of concealment in their stories.

---

66 As Levinson says, "There is more than a hint of feminine subversion when men are the objects being transferred between hands, or better yet between beds." Levinson, *Untold*, 212.
67 Abramovitch, *The King is Naked*, 53.
68 Rich, *Of Woman Born*, 256-80; Andrea Dworkin, *Intercourse* (New York: Free Press, 1987); Jessica Benjamin, *The Bonds of Love: Psychoanalysis, Feminism, and the Problem of Domination* (New York: Pantheon, 1988), 51-84.
69 Avraham Elqayam, "To Know the Messiah: The Dialectic of Sexual Discourse in the Messianic Thought of Nathan of Gaza," *Tarbiz* 65, no. 4 (1996): 649.
70 Yehuda Rimerman, *Forbidden Relations in the Family: Sociology and Psychology of Incest* (Tel Aviv: Shercover, 1985), 12-3.

A different way to understand the sexual secrecy in the Davidic dynasty is by reading it in mythical and anthropological terms that demonstrate the embedded power of hidden and enshrouded places. This complexity allows for subtle sensitivity not found in the unveiled, simple and illuminated space. Here, secrecy is located at the outset as a liberating instrument, as in the words of the *Zohar*: "The world endures only by virtue of the secret."[71] In the kabbalistic conception the acts of seduction and copulation, when done with the correct intentions, may affect the supernal realm, despite and because of the fact that they entail a degree of transgressing of boundaries. The secret of sexual relations in the *Zohar* is built upon the principle "that which is forbidden below, is permitted above" and therefore, inasmuch as in the supernal family incestuous couplings are permitted, this is true also in regards to the birth of the messianic hero and his exceptional family. The hierarchal relations of powers become secondary in the mythic prism, which draws its potency mainly from the place of darkness and liminality which entails transgression and redemption. Likewise, Anzaldúa presents a unique gender and psychoanalytic perspective, claiming that the ambiguity inherent in secrecy may serve a reversal of power relations. Thus, allowing for objection to the existing order creates a new state of relations, a "hybrid," and so enables restoration and redemption.[72]

It is therefore worthwhile to differentiate between the oppressive secret of the first type—which is connected to hiding, fear, and control—and the archetypical secrecy which allows for the dialectic of the messianic borderland. Indeed, kabbalistic thinking distinguishes between the "concealed," connoting the positive qualities of secrecy symbolized by a "Dark Light," and the much more negative "concealment," in which one forcefully uses a secret to dominate another.[73]

As Mary Douglas brilliantly illuminated, the body's margins signify the margins of society and in studying these margins it is possible to learn about the entire system.[74] The Davidic heroines illustrate the dangerous areas of the ancient Israelite. Additionally, the aura of the secret stems from the mystery of the *anima* and the feminine and sexual symbolism, blocked from exterior

---

71 *Zohar* III: 128a
72 Anzaldúa, *Borderlands La Frontera*; Turner, *Ritual*, 101-2, 135-43.
73 Melilla Hellner-Eshed, *A River Flows from Eden: The Language of Mystical Experience in the Zohar* (Stanford: Stanford University, 2009), 103, 174-6, 313-6.
74 Mary Douglas, *Purity and Danger: An Analysis of Concepts of Pollution and Taboo* (London: Routledge, 1966), 115-29.

view.[75] This secrecy is revealed at moments of birth and conception, through seduction and delight, in human eroticism and in the gift of feminine fertility, as it is written in the Talmud, "because blessing is not to be found in anything that has been already weighed or measured or numbered, but only in a thing hidden from sight" (Babylonian Talmud, Tractate Ta'anit 8b). This blessing expresses the motherly body from which sprouts life, the semiotic and impulsive qualities, which symbolize fear, mystery, and danger.[76] A mythic reading thereby illuminates the intensified force in the Davidic dynasty's secrets, overcoming prohibitions for the sake of the redeemer's birth. Acts of feminine deception are transformed into the unique distinction of the dynasty, in which the private becomes the public, the personal becomes the political, and Judean politics undermine the accepted social order and biblical law and even affixes a genealogical seal. Through the power of the secret, these dynastic mothers succeed in constructing a model of redemption which blossoms within crisis and filth, and which constitutes a mirror image of the fantasy of a simple, clean, and straightforward redemption—which may be impossible and no redemption at all.

6. THE DANGER—THE MEN'S UNAWARENESS AND THE WOMAN'S ENDANGERMENT POST-SEDUCTION

The feminine initiative in the moments of seduction highlights the males' passivity and the heroines' vulnerability before and after the action. Prominent in each of the stories is the tension between the docile state of the father figures during the ruse and their activeness that is awakened after the act. Masculine pragmatism comes to compensate for the *coup d'état* and to fill the void that is formed in the moments of unawareness. From a literary perspective, the drama is not only at the moment of the seduction, but also in its consequences, as the women face mortal danger. In these moments, the women are dependent on the divine intervention that allows the son's birth even as they muster the strength and creative bravery to rescue themselves from the crisis. We will first examine the motif of male unawareness at the time of seduction and afterwards the type of danger that the heroines withstand.

---

75 Jung, *The Psychology of the Transference*.
76 Julia Kristeva, *Powers of Horror: An Essay on Abjection* (New York: Columbia University Press, 1982), 1-31; Freud, "Uncanny." Meltzer's "aesthetic conflict" engages this topic as well, which I wish to expand upon at a different time.

And He Did Not Know

Through the phrase "and He did not know" which is repeated in the Davidic stories (Gen. 19:33-35 [Lot]; 38:15-16 [Judah]; Ruth 3:3-14 [Boaz]), we are able to identify an interesting evolutionary process occurring across eras and generations. Lot's unawareness is total and relates to the very act of consummation. Once sober, Lot is unaware of what happened. He certainly does not comprehend that he lay with his daughters. Judah's unawareness, in contrast, pertains only to Tamar's identity. It appears, however, that Judah is in the midst of clarifying his own identity, making it possible for him to declare at the end of the story, "She is more righteous than I" in response to Tamar's request, "Discern, please." In the last story, Boaz's unawareness quickly turns into a clear understanding that it is necessary to conceal Ruth's presence until the issue has been resolved. Displayed across these three stories is an arousing and sobering process—from the phrase "He did not know" to the implied secret of "It shall not be known." Rachel Adelman shows how the stories transit from carnal knowledge to emotional recognition. In concluding with the public redemption by the Gates of the Law, the Book of Ruth demonstrates how the process ends with the assumption of judicial responsibility and establishment of an identity of mutual recognition.[77]

In the gender and psychoanalytic context, it is possible to interpret the unawareness of the father figures as pseudo-passivity or as a partial numbing of the rationalistic-realistic. In Jungian terms, in these moments a yielding of the *animus* for the activeness of the *anima* may be identified, which aids the men's comfort, acts on behalf of their unseeing and unseen aspects, and completes the paradoxical messianic picture.[78] Seemingly, this *anima* is prepared to perform roles which the men are prevented from doing in the stories. Judah, Lot, and Boaz are found benefiting from the unawareness and the same slumber (actual or symbolic), while the women become initiators and transgressors of boundaries. Once again, the question of feminine freedom is raised, for not only does the denial of sexuality indicate oppression, but so does the exaggerated intensification of the transgression. As we will see in the epilogue, both of the extremes—virginity and harlotry—signify different aspects of exploitation. Therefore, the licentious behavior of the dynastic heroines attests not only to

---

77 However, the "recognition" in the Book of Ruth does not entail sexual knowledge. Adelman, Seduction and Recognition, 96-102.
78 Tamar Kron, *Us, Adam and Eve: Myths and Psychology of Couple Relationship* (Tel Aviv: Hakibbutz Hameuchad, 2004), 9-35.

their freedom, but also to their vulnerability and destitution. In contrast to the nocturnal and oneiric spaces in which the seductive women dominate, in the scenes of normative reality, amid the rule of law, these women are oppressed. Tamar is on the pyre, Lot's daughters are almost raped by the men of Sodom, Naomi and Ruth hunger for bread and are dependent on the kindness of men for the sake of their redemption. Through the threshing night, the night of the cave, and the meeting at the "entrance of Enaim," female characters are exploited in a hostile patriarchal world.

From one perspective, the Davidic stories may be interpreted by theories of sexuality, which stress the dissonance between a reality with an ethical code and clear boundaries, and an erotic and chaotic existence which merges suffering and pleasure. As Ruth Stein illustrates (following Bersani and Laplanche), the drawing of boundaries of the self and the development of subjectivity occur because of the tension between the sexual deviation and the ego's ability to bear it.[79] Indeed, prominent in the messianic dynasty is the tension between the men's lack of awareness and the women's alertness and initiative, both of which are immediately reversed after the seductive act. The women's breaching of the boundary is interpreted as "kindness" (ḥesed) (also interpreted as illicit relations, as it is written in Leviticus 20:17), and symbolizes the knowledge acquired through suffering interwoven with pleasure. The women understand the consequences of their actions and allow the men to repent, as in the case of Judah, who states that Tamar "is more righteous than I," or Boaz, who says, "I have also acquired Ruth the Moabite, the wife of Mahlon, to be my wife" because of Ruth's words on the threshing floor.

The ambivalently erotic space—wrapped in concealment which is disclosure, in awareness divided and one-sided or exchanged between men and women, between day and night, between the law and its violation—is where the messianic seed blooms. In a paradoxical manner, these acts of harlotry and female nakedness, sexual excess, and the endangerment of life all unite to establish the pillar of the monarchy. The laws of *yibbum*, the conception of family sanctity, and even the prohibitions of illicit relations are founded upon overt sexual violation repeated for generations. In this way, the dynastic stories unite motherhood and sexuality and challenge the ancient (and modern) world, which tends to divides these two aspects.[80]

---

79 Stein, "Sexuality," 53-4.
80 On the split between sexuality and motherhood, see Rich, *Of Woman Born*, ix-xxxv, 110-115; Astela, Welldon, *Mother, Madonna, Whore: The Idealization and Denigration of Motherhood* (London: Karnac, 1988).

The Danger and Price of Seduction

In each story, the moment in which the power relations are reversed and the heroines' states are weakened is an unmistakable time of danger. This issue is quite noticeable in Tamar's episode, in the suddenness with which she is sentenced to be burned and doomed to the pyre, precisely at her most vulnerable hour: pregnant, abandoned by her family, and without any guaranteed protection. Judah, the person who is supposed to protect her, is responsible for her endangerment and is even described as repeating the harmful pattern of his sons.[81] Only at the conclusion of the incident, through Tamar's ingenuity, courage, and divine providence, is the danger reversed and the "harlotrous" pregnancy transformed into the birth of twins.

In the story of Lot's daughters, the threat is visibly embedded in the sons' names—Ammon and Moab—bearing eternal witness to a dishonorable transgression that cannot be concealed. Ammon and Moab are condemned in their shame, which is transformed into a sweeping hatred and collective blame of the two nations descended from them. The unavoidable collision with these nations is described in Israel's travels in the desert and there the Bible equates their status with bastardry: "Those born of an illicit union shall not be admitted to the assembly of the Lord. Even to the tenth generation, none of their descendants shall be admitted to the assembly of the Lord. No Ammonite or Moabite shall be admitted to the assembly of the Lord. Even to the tenth generation, none of their descendants shall be admitted to the assembly of the Lord" (Deuteronomy 23:3-4).[82] In contrast to Tamar's actions, Lot does not respond actively, nor are his daughters endangered in the wake of their incestuous actions. However, Lot's proposal to the townsmen to rape his daughters in the beginning of the episode may hint at the "cycle of danger" and its emergence earlier or later in the feminine tales.

In Ruth's story, a slight moment of unawareness and threat of abandonment briefly appears, beginning with Boaz's refusal to redeem Ruth and culminating with the reflection of the first redeemer, who is concerned that he may lose his inheritance. Indeed there are no extreme situations here, yet the words of the redeemer delay the story's resolution and remind us that Ruth is an alien, a Moabite, and widow; she is poor, hungry—and dependent on a man to save her. Ruth's vulnerability is symbolized in the act of ḥaliṣa at the

---

81 Frymer-Kensky, *Women in the Bible*, 267.
82 Zakovitch, *Ruth*, 25; Shinan and Zakovitch, *Story*, 224, Tsoffar, "Trauma."

conclusion of the book: "Now this was the custom in former times in Israel concerning redeeming and exchanging: to confirm a transaction, one party took off a sandal and gave it to the other ... So when the redeemer said to Boaz, 'Acquire it for yourself,' he took off his sandal" (Ruth 4:7-8). Ḥaliṣa symbolizes the sexual mimetic act of dissolving the union, in which the foot represents the powerful male who has the ability to get rid of women and transfer them, while the sandal symbolizes the woman's promiscuous sexuality.[83]

Feminine Danger—The Absent Mother Figure

The difference between Ruth, Tamar, and Lot's daughters is expressed not only through the mitigation of sexual transgression throughout the generations, but also by the gap between heroines who lack motherly protection and a woman who has a protective parental figure. Due to Naomi's support and the strength of the relationship built between them, Ruth is able to refine her ancestor's actions. The rare connection between the two women takes on a different character throughout the Book of Ruth, like the erotic shade and the confusion of identities in the threshing floor scene or the parental shelter that Naomi gives to Ruth in the beginning of the book, where she acts as both a mother and a "father" in relation to her adopted daughter.[84] Therefore we will explore the mother-daughter relationship in these stories and their development.

In the story of Lot's daughters, as can be seen in mythological tales, we are witnesses to incest caused by the absence of a protective mother, as in many cases of incest nowadays.[85] It appears that the mother's horrific death and the prohibition to even glance back at her are what particularly push the daughters to perform such an extreme and self-destructive act. Lot's hesitation to flee the overthrown city and their mother's spontaneous disappearance from their lives constitute two factors which transform Lot's daughters into abandoned women, who, with no choice, are forced to be mothers for themselves and their father, while making their absent mother present in their own bodies.[86] Their mother's death acts as a catalyst for their own self-destruction and a factor that creates a feminine, victimized, and masochistic consciousness that is ultimately expressed through incestuous relations with their father.

---

83 Eryl W. Davies, "Ruth 4:5 and the Duties of the Goel," *Vetus Testamentum* 33, no. 2 (1983): 231-34. Campbell, *Ruth*, 160.
84 For the perception of Naomi as a "father figure," see Caspi and Havrelock, *Women on the Biblical Road*, 73-4; Frymer-Kensky, *Women of the Bible*, 240; Bal, *Lethal Love*, 85.
85 Kron, *Us, Adam and Eve*, 36-66; Abramovitch, *The King is Naked*.
86 Tsoffar, "Trauma," 7; Ben-Naftali, *Childhood*, 35-59.

Even Tamar is an isolated woman, imprisoned in a world of men who exert their will on her: Er, Onan, Hirah, Shelah, her father, and Judah. In all likelihood Tamar was purposely untended, and if she had a mother figure, she was not mentioned in the story and is not present in order to protect her, as is seen from the scene of her being sent to her "father's house" after the death of her first two husbands:

> Then Judah said to his daughter-in-law Tamar, 'Remain a widow in *your father's house* until my son Shelah grows up'—for he feared that he too would die, like his brothers. So Tamar went to live in *her father's house*. In course of time the wife of Judah, Shua's daughter, died; when Judah's time of mourning was over, he went up to Timnah to his sheep-shearers, he and his friend Hirah the Adullamite (Gen. 38:11-12).

The sequence of the verses stresses that Tamar lacks a "mother's house" to return to—in contrast to Ruth and Orpah; Naomi tells her daughters-in-law: "Go back each of you to *your mother's house*" (Ruth 1:8). Moreover, Judah's wife, the only female figure who in the story's background, dies, so reinforcing Tamar's maternal void. Tamar's solitude may suggest an explanation for her specific request for Judah's signet, cord, and staff before he comes to her, for she demands not economically valuable objects, but rather *identity signifiers*, which attest to her need to root herself and be anchored in a strange and chaotic world. Contrary to a longstanding tendency to describe Tamar as manipulative and scheming, Alter suggests that she is "fiercely resolved [and] steel-nerved."[87] To this we might add *multifaceted*: she is a vulnerable young woman escaping a world of men who acquire her, abandon her, and transfer her from hand to hand. Only at the story's conclusion, at the birth of the twins, does a protective maternal figure appear: the midwife not only assists Tamar with the physical birth, but also by marking the difference between the sons, and thus actively establishes the Davidic dynasty: "While she was in labor, one put out a hand; and the midwife took and bound on his hand a crimson thread, saying, 'This one came out first.' But just then he drew back his hand, and out came his brother; and she said, 'What a breach you have made for yourself!' Therefore he was named Perez. Afterwards his brother came out with the crimson thread on his hand; and he was named Zerah" (Gen. 38:28-30). Supporting

---

[87] Alter, *Biblical Narrative*, 22. In contrast to Shinan and Zakovitch's interpretation, who see Tamar as a manipulative woman, who subjugates the weakened Judah. Shinan and Zakovitch, *Story*, 219-20.

Zerah's hand, the son not chosen to lead the dynasty until the time of David, repeats and evokes the support and outstretched hand that Tamar needed in her time of need. This solidarity of the two women, Tamar and the midwife, is transformed in the Book of Ruth into a deep maternal partnership, allowing the declaration, "A son has been born to Naomi" (Ruth 4:17).

Ruth and Naomi's relationship has received many interpretations in scholarly literature. For example, Phyllis Trible is inclined to describe Naomi's motherly generosity and her infinite devotion to the foreign woman accompanying her, while Ariella Deem highlights Naomi's reach into the area of the "law of the father," and her innovation in the laws of *yibbum* as her greatest contribution on Ruth's behalf, and Athalya Brenner and Esther Fuchs explicitly illuminate Ruth's concession and self-annulment in comparison to Naomi's implied (or open) exploitation.[88] Even if the ideal relationship is not the topic here, it is important to emphasize that we have a clear example of a development that occurred in a messianic and feminine model. As opposed to Tamar and Lot's daughters who are abandoned at the beginning of their story, Ruth is supported by Naomi from the beginning of her journey: as Ilana Pardes writes, "Ruth chooses to 'cling' to her mother-in-law and go wherever she goes ... 'to cling' in this case means to recapture a primal unity, to return to a time when man and woman were literally 'one flesh.'"[89] Against the stories of maternal absence, the link between the two women is configured as a restoration for the entire dynasty. The "type-scene of the Messiah's birth," as seen in the Book of Ruth, relies on the idea that feminine companionship allows for the delivery of redemption. The book also represents the literary peak in the dynastic tales, and without a doubt the appearance of a protective maternal figure who mends the "maternal failure" that is continued throughout the generations has a decisive influence on this achievement.

Thus, the messianic son has many mothers who support one another between generations. The mitigation of the Davidic dynasty is built on two principles that are developed from within each other: first, the men's unawareness and passiveness at the time of their seductions, which progresses to a partial awareness, then recognition, and then gradual resumption of responsibility in Boaz and Ruth's case. Second is the endangerment of the heroine, isolated

---

88 Trible, *Rhetoric of Sexuality*, 166-96; Bal, *Lethal Love*, 68-88; Ben-Naftali, *Chronicle of Separation*, 15-53; Deem, *Zot ha-Pa'am*, 268-72.
89 Pardes, *Countertraditions*, 102

in a time of crisis, lacking a female figure to offer her shelter, and continuing through the stories to an eventual symbiosis with a protective maternal figure, as in Ruth and Naomi's episode. In this manner the heroines unify the passive and active facets of their soul in each generation and become rounded characters incorporating one another.

7. THE BIRTH—FROM VIRGINITY TO MOTHERHOOD

Motherhood is transformed into a main characteristic of the Davidic heroines' identity. As is well-known, in the ancient world the woman's status is dependent on her fecundity, for which greater value was awarded to those who gave birth to sons.[90] Likewise, it is possible to examine biblical motherhood from different angles, in connection to popular myths of creation and birth in the ancient Near East, Egypt, and Mesopotamia. The fruitful mother's resemblance to the mythological fertility goddesses emphasizes the link between the divine creative act and the mother who bestows life.[91] The first approach focuses on the gender ramifications of the ancient world's conception of motherhood, whereas the second presents her mythological aspects.[92] In our context, I seek to combine the two positions and to illuminate the mothers' centrality in the Judean dynasty by discussing the motivation to conceive which drives the heroines, and the manner in which it is realized in their stories.

An examination of the moment of birth in the Davidic type-scene reveals a few distinctive characteristics of this dynasty. The unique and oedipal connection between the mother and the son derives from the fact that in each of the dynastic stories the heroines give birth to sons. Additionally, in each case the women have no previous children, and therefore the elected sons are presented as "firstborns" and incomparable in their primacy. Significantly, the Bible stresses that there were no fetuses prior to the births of Perez and Zerah, Ammon and Moab, and Obed. In this way, the image of fertility documents the heroines' transformation into mothers, and the fact that the wombs of Ruth,

---

90 Fuchs, *Sexual Politics*, 44-9, 83-90.
91 As Patai, Graves, Rich, Renan and others have shown in the mythological and gender context.
92 According to Simone de Beauvoir, the adoration of the Great Mother is similar to the disdain for her, for both attitudes stem from the same fear of real motherhood. Beauvoir, *The Second Sex*, 33-60. For cultural, gender and psychoanalytic reading see Ettinger, *The Matrixial Borderspace*; Dorit Ashur's discussion of Welldon and Chodorow attitudes, "To Read and Write as If Your Life Depended on It" (PhD diss., Hebrew University, 2005) 120-99, 196-238.

Tamar, and Lot's daughters were sealed until the bursting forth of the elected sons becomes critical information in the messianic dynasty's design.

The sages radicalized this biblical process through Midrashim that describe how these women became pregnant proactively, emphasizing how the Davidic heroines chose their motherhood.[93] Lot's daughters are virgins according to the plain-meaning of the text, Ruth has no children to accompany her from the fields of Moab, and Tamar is presumably a virgin, for her husbands refused to consummate their marriages. Ascribing defloration techniques to the Judean dynastic mothers presumably developed through the impact of the dialogue with Christianity and as a response to the narrative presented in the Gospels of Matthew and Luke, in which Mary is impregnated by the Holy Spirit, while her son is linked to the House of David.[94] Despite the clear disparity between Mary and the biblical Judean heroines, the similarity between the two models stands out. In both of them, motherhood is recognized by boundary markings of the feminine body, whose origin is sealed and closed: both virginity, on the one hand, and promiscuity, on the other, represent opposing extremes and supplements to motherhood and sexuality. In spite of the differences, in both cases the mother and son are turned into a mythic aggregate, which stands in the center of the messianic tradition of both religions.

The idea that the Messiah's mother is a virgin impregnated through divine intervention (as in Christianity), or by physical intervention via natural methods (as in rabbinic Midrashim), reflects the desire to see her as the "Great Mother," who is at the same time both fertile like a goddess, but also immaculate. In both cultures, a parallel is formed between "birth pangs" and "pangs of the Messiah," leading to the conclusion that, much like motherhood, messianism is not a momentary random flicker, but rather a process which requires effort and a breach of the established order.

The polemic against the Christian myth, which expresses the maternal abstention and feminine passivity, emerges throughout the rabbinic exegesis. The Davidic stories, as portrayed by the authors and exegetes, demonstrate the active and physical choosing of motherhood independent of God, man, or son, and resulting from feminine autonomy. The subjective feminine voice arising

---

93 This reading is based on the gynecological premise accepted in the ancient world, according to which, "no woman conceives from the first contact." b. Yevamot 34a; Genesis Rabbah 51:9, 45:4 (ed. Theodor-Albeck, 449, 538); Pes. R. 42 (176a). Ron Barkai, *Science, Magic and Mythology in the Middle Ages* (Jerusalem: Van Leer Institute, 1987), 37-55.

94 For more on the topic of defloration in the House of David, in Judaism and Christianity, see David Malkiel, "Manipulating Virginity: Digital Defloration in Midrash and History," *JSQ* 13 (2006): 105-127.

from these stories is the heroines' voice of amazement at the discovery that they—the dependent, foreign, and abandoned women—are transformed into mothers: firstly, as mothers to their own sons and lastly, as the "Great Mothers" of the messianic dynasty, which they built with their own hands.

The ability to feed, nurse, and procreate is not evident from the context of these women's lives. As Mieke Bal states, Ruth, who flees crisis and famine, becomes a symbol of generosity and benevolence, in contrast to the Moabites who did not meet the Israelites with "bread and water."[95] Throughout the book, Ruth mends the trauma of starvation and the characteristic frugalness of Moab, embedded in them for generations. She treats a wound that cannot heal by itself, and her words signify a "speech act" which makes clear the rupture in which the House of Moab has been from its very beginning.[96] It is precisely Ruth, poor and alone, who is transformed into the nourishing mother, bestowing goodness on all her surroundings. Similarly, Tamar gives birth to twins, attesting to a double fertility and miraculous abundance, while Lot's daughters choose to give birth as a response to cosmic destruction and the universe's annihilation. The sages describe their giving birth as "the seed that comes from a different source" (Gen. Rabbah 51:8), a depiction which we will discuss in the following chapters. The two are conceived as goddesses generating a messianic reality out of Sodom. The impression, left behind by these stories for future generations, hides within it the astonishment and elation of the seduction's success and the feminine childbearing ability.

8. THE HUMAN CONDEMNATION—BREAKING OF TIES: THE DISAPPEARANCE OF MOTHER AND FATHER FIGURES

One of the fascinating details of this type-scene's design pertains to the powerful, fated, and unique meeting of the messianic parents. In each dynastic story, we are witnesses to the moment in which the scene is quickly constructed and just as quickly falls apart, returning to the chaos and confusion that preceded it. At the climax of each story occurs the seduction initiated by the woman and in its wake, the elected son's birth. Immediately afterwards the couple separates, and one of the sides disappears from the plot.

In the episode of Lot's daughters is the extreme action of dual incestuous relations, which presumably was not repeated after the night in the cave.

---

95 Bal, *Lethal Love*, 80. Also Deuteronomy 23:2-4.
96 Tsoffar, "Trauma," 10.

In Tamar's case, the rift is emphasized by the phrase "And he did not lie with her again" (Gen. 38:26), which marks the end of the drama that happened on the threshold of death, survival, and rescue. The disconnection between Judah and Tamar is woven into the pyre scene, immediately following Judah's admittance of guilt and his statement, "She is more righteous than I." The exegetes felt uncomfortable with the string of events and therefore proposed a reversed reading of the words, "And he did not lie with her again," by saying: "Having once known her, *he did not separate from her* again."[97] In the Book of Ruth, immediately after the birth, Ruth disappears from the tale and she is not mentioned until its end.[98] Naomi is situated in the center of the final scene and the feminine chorus assigns the born son to her. From the masculine viewpoint, the Midrash proclaims Boaz's death immediately after the wedding night: "They said, 'he died that very night he came unto her.'"[99] Based on the implications of Boaz's advanced age as a city elder and inspired by the stories of Tamar and Lot's daughters, the Midrash adds this detail in order to emphasize that the "messianic type-scene" is aimed at dissolving relationships immediately after the act.

Esther Fuchs claims that the Bible tends to erase women from the biblical tales immediately after giving birth, since they are no longer needed. In her opinion, the "seduction type-scene" to which Tamar, Ruth, and Lot's daughters belong is designed to exploit the foreign women, appropriate their sons, after which they disappear.[100] Alongside Fuchs' important criticism, I find in the House of David a different model, in which different potencies, divine and human, collaborate in the redeemer's birth. The rift between the father and mother emphasizes the moment of connection, which is only aimed at one goal: the birth of a son. Therefore, the relationship's dissolution is equally purposeful: Lot's daughters slip out of the cave, Judah does not come to Tamar, and Ruth disappears from the text. Thus in these stories, the Bible shows far more interest in the maternal subject, and the son's figure, than in the marital relations.

---

97 b. Sotah 10b.

98 Caspi and Havrelock, *Women on the Biblical Road*, 187-8; Nolan-Fewell and Gunn, "A Son is Born"; Pardes, *Countertraditions*, 103-7.

99 *Ruth Zuta* 4:13 (ed. Buber); Tobiah b. Eliezer, *Midrash Leqaḥ Ṭov*, Ruth 4:17. Louis Ginzberg, *The Legends of the Jews*, 2 vols. (Philadelphia: Jewish Publication Society, 2003), 2: 864.

100 Fuchs, *Sexual Politics*, 72-3, 84-90. According to her the "annunciation type-scene" is no different than the Davidic seduction scene, for in both cases the womb is commandeered for patriarchal needs.

The seduction scene's description and the parents' immediate separation are designed to heighten the fated partnership between the men, women, and God in the moment of the messianic conception. In this way, the copulation's transgressive setting and its intended aim are highlighted. This reading is stressed in the mysterious formulation, "And he did not lie with her again," an idiom which draws our attention, through the word "again," to the very same forbidden copulation at the "entrance to Enaim," which brought about Tamar's pregnancy. The fear caused by the extreme encounter and crossing of boundaries, spurs the collapse of the relationship immediately following its actualization. In this way, the heroic and dramatic conclusion of the mortal story heightens the divine dramatic redemption.

9. THE DIVINE VINDICATION—THE "PROVIDENTIAL TYPE-SCENE" AND GENEALOGICAL SEAL

The elected sons' births and the seductive actions of his foremothers are repeated in every link of the dynasty. From the divine perspective this is the redeemer's birth scene and therefore where and how the divine voice is revealed in these stories must be examined. So far we have proposed that the Davidic heroines' vindication is not only attributed to the birth of sons, but also the sexual violations committed by each one. At the conclusion to the Book of Ruth, we have seen that motherhood and seduction are conjoined and become seals of the messianic covenant, which not only refers to the birth, but also to the circumstances preceding it. At this point we will identify the "justification formula" repeated in the stories and attesting to moments of divine intervention in the Davidic tales. Essentially this is a sub-type-scene, concealed within the larger type-scene of "the messianic hero's birth," and pertaining to the divine providence woven into the feminine narrative.

Determinism, Providence, and Free Will

In order to discuss the divine intervention in the dynastic tales, it is necessary to explore the collaboration of human and divine forces that jointly result in the messiah's birth. This paradoxical circle has two faces, one deterministic and the other elective. On the one hand, the royal dynasty shows an introspective divine vindication for each of the women's stories. On the other hand, the son becomes a chosen following his foremothers' transgression and sin. From this perspective, each story stands on its own and attests to the unfolding drama for the sake of childbirth. The end is never foreknown, and each heroine's mode of operation decisively influences God's attitude towards the act. In the circle of "dual causality" there is an apparent tautology: the vindication is dependent on the success of the feminine action, while the success of the act is dependent on the divine vindication. From the stories' development and the persistence of the ensemble of dynastic heroines we learn that divine intervention developed along with the strengthening of the feminine initiative. God supports the effort invested on behalf of the messianic son's birth, even though this effort entails a blatant violation of the divine law.

Before we can identify the template of divine justification, we must challenge the common assumption that God is not present as an independent figure in the dynastic stories. As Tikva Frymer-Kensky writes, "God never acts in the book of Ruth. Nevertheless, God is very present in the characters' minds and they perceive God's Providence in the working out of their destiny."[101] This description is characteristically fitting for J, for which, as we saw, the stories of Lot's daughters and Tamar in the Book of Genesis are both attributed, as well as the Book of Ruth, which summarizes the Judean tales.

We may ask: in the Davidic dynasty, are we are in fact speaking of a "lowered" and worldly God who is disclosed through the activities of the human characters, or of an elevated God who remotely navigates the human characters? Is God a literary hero or a type of whimsical and rebellious demon (as he is presented by Bloom, who believes that J has a feminine author)? Where is the divine voice in these stories which portray psychological and sexual drama and earthly events that are bound by time and statically-designed narrative routes? A foreign woman emerges from a state of crisis, is hurled into another crisis, seduces a father figure, endangers her life, employs methods of concealment, disguise, intoxication to be impregnated by a father figure, and finally gives birth to a male child who joins the messianic dynasty. Where does God appear here?

If we claim that events in each stage of the story were only made possible through divine providence, we will contribute nothing to the story's understanding and the motivations of its characters. Similarly, if we claim that the

---

101 Frymer-Kensky, *Women of the Bible*, 242.

events were decided entirely by the heroine and those at her side, then we miss the radical development of the messianic idea from within transgression. Myth occurs at the point of encounter between heaven and earth: in the words of Yehuda Liebes, in "the direct reference to the divine entity itself, which is available on the same plane of awareness and meaning as are all other observable phenomena."[102] Where does God speak with the messianic mothers and where is his voice heard through them, in the same plane of awareness, which is both human and divine?

The Divine Type-Scene: God Slays, Revives, and Bestows a Name

Within the expanded type-scene, four fixtures are repeated and document God's link to the Davidic stories. In the first three, providence is interwoven in the actions of the dynastic mothers, whereas in the fourth, God intervenes by bestowing a name of mythical significance to the messianic son. Below are the stages:

1. In the beginning of each story, God openly slays those who are destined for death.
2. The women, survivors of the deaths, devise their scheme of seduction.
3. God is revealed covertly and acts through the motherly wombs to enable pregnancy and birth.
4. God collaborates (openly or secretly) by bestowing a unique name to the newborn.

God is revealed in the liminal areas of the stories of the Messiah son of David. This pattern touches upon extremely desperate circumstances and at moments of life and death. It demonstrates that God is able to kill alone, but in order to create life, and specifically in order to birth the messianic figure, he needs female and motherly help from Lot's daughters, Tamar, and Ruth, as well as Rachel, Leah, and Bathsheba. God's character emerges in the literary margins, at moments of danger and peril or salvation and blessing. God is a partner to both good and evil and therefore the Messiah's birth cannot happen without him.

---

102 Yehuda Liebes, "Myth vs. Symbol in the *Zohar* and Lurianic Kabbalah," in *Essential Papers on Kabbalah*, ed. Lawrence Fine (New York: New York University, 1995), 213.

The Episode of Lot's Daughters: "To this Day"

In this story, God is active only in the beginning, while in the cave itself only human characters overtly act, night after night. The seduction may occur through simple human initiative. However, a woman's ability to bring life is a divine gift, especially in traumatic contexts like the destruction of Sodom. Amidst overt destruction and death, God is revealed here as the creator of new life, in a graceful and concealed manner:

> So they made their father drink wine that night ... *Thus both the daughters of Lot became pregnant by their father.* The firstborn bore a son, and named him Moab; he is the ancestor of the Moabites *to this day*. The younger also bore a son and named him Ben-ammi; he is the ancestor of the Ammonites *to this day* (Gen. 19:33-38).

The immediate pregnancies and births attest to a scene of election (and even annunciation, though in the opposite order) led by an invisible hand.[103] The balance and doubling between the first and second night, the elder daughter and younger, and finally the first and second newborns, reinforce the blessedness of the act. The etiological formula "to this day," exists not to expose a textual anachronism or evidence for later editing, but rather to stress the divine intervention which allows these two daughters to conceive there in such a precise and intentional manner.[104] The names of the firstborn son, Moab ("comes from a father"), and of the younger son, Ammon ("son of my people"), reflect the essence of the messianic dynasty, which is built upon relations of incest, harlotry, and seduction.

"Ammon" and "Moab" hint at more than the condemnation of Lot lying drunk in the cave: they suggest the impregnation of Lot's daughters by God, the supernal father. As we will see in the following chapters, the sages interpreted that the Messiah is born from a divine "other seed" purposely embedded in the cave of Zoar. The divine signature seals the episode of Lot's daughters with the justification of the miraculous and transgressive significance of the son's names, from whom, in the future, will emerge Ruth the Moabite and Naama the Ammonite, who are directly linked to Judean dynasty.

---

103 For a critical reading see Fuchs, *Sexual Politics*, 66-9.
104 Speiser, *Genesis*, 142-6; Driver, *Genesis*, 202-5.

The Episode of Tamar: "It Is from Me That All These Things Happened"

Similar to the story of Lot's daughters, in Tamar's story we again encounter the divine presence as a fatal punishment for those deserving. In the story's beginning we encounter the deaths of Er and Onan; both sons' deaths, like Sodom's upheaval, constitute a sign of divine intervention in the messianic type-scene. Afterwards God disappears until the end of the tale. Tamar is occupied in her agony and devises her scheme for Judah. However, the way in which Tamar is saved from the flames attests to the supernatural means: instead of her being put on the pyre, we have a scene of confession and public vindication. In this case the miracle is not only the quick conception, although the sages also interpreted it in that way, but the reversal of a scene of death into one of birth, and Tamar's portrayal as an idealized mother who gives birth to sons for the royal tribe.[105] God, who slayed both of Tamar's husbands, saves her from death and expresses his providence explicitly through the birth of twins.

The redundancy of the phrases ("Your daughter-in-law has played the harlot," "She is pregnant as a result of harlotry," "When the time of her delivery came," and "While she was in labor," Gen. 38:24-30), reflects the urgency of the events crafted for the elected son's birth. The quick turning around of events stresses the incredible rescue and Judah's public apology. Judah's words "She is more righteous than I" stand out from the rest of the Bible. Significantly, Judah admits his error to a widowed, foreign, and vulnerable woman. The sages emphasize this moment of miraculous divine intervention: "And Judah acknowledged them, and said: She is right; it is from Me. The Holy Spirit crying out and saying, It is from Me that all these things happened."[106]

The naming moment is highlighted at the story's conclusion similarly to the episode of Lot's daughters. The tying of the crimson thread is designed to mark the difference between the twins and discern the elected son from his brother; however, it also attests to the rescuing of the two fetuses from death. The names of the infants have symbolic meaning, so Zerah (*shone*), like other firstborns, loses his elected status to his younger brother, Perez (*breach*), who surpasses his brother. Perez, due to his name and the manner of his birth, is

---

[105] b. Yevamot 34a.
[106] Ecclesiastes Rabbah, 10:17; Genesis Rabbah 85:12 (ed. Theodor-Albeck, 1042-44): "What is *mimmeni* (than I)? R. Jeremiah said in the name of R. Isaac: The Holy One, blessed be He, said, 'You will attest to that which is revealed, and I will attest to that which is secret.'" Also, Menn, *Judah and Tamar*, 214-85.

transformed into an archetypical symbol of breaching boundaries and sexual transgressions in the Judean dynasty. The divine imprint is hinted at in the mysterious formula "he was named," without indicating the namer, joining the phrase of "to this day" of Lot's daughters, and demonstrating the vindication of events and their immortalization.

The Book of Ruth: "The Lord Made Her Conceive"

The Book of Ruth begins with the deaths of the husbands, continues with the feminine seduction, and culminates with pregnancy and birth, like the stories of Tamar and Lot's daughters. The book adds to this template a naming ceremony for the chosen offspring, as part of the public blessing. Alongside the name bestowing for Obed, the book's conclusion emphasizes the "deciphering name" David, the receiver of the unique divine blessing thanks to his foremothers' initiatives.

The conclusion of the book reveals the direct divine intervention in Ruth's pregnancy: "So Boaz took Ruth and she became his wife. When they came together, *the Lord made her conceive*, and she bore a son" (Ruth 4:13).[107] Each pregnancy in the Bible obviously originates with God and therefore this description is conspicuously unlike other biblical stories. The phrase "the Lord made her conceive" interrupts the verse's sequence and highlights God's active partnership in the scene. God made Ruth conceive, in the same covert and concealed manner in which he made Lot's daughters and Tamar conceive, an intervention that demonstrates the successful process of constructing the entire dynasty. The naming of Obed is spread out among multiple verses and receives a unique emphasis in the blessing scene at the gate:

> So Boaz took Ruth and she became his wife. When they came together, the Lord made her conceive, and she bore a son ... The women of the neighborhood gave him a name, saying, 'A son has been born to Naomi.' *They named him Obed; he became the father of Jesse, the father of David* (Ruth 4:13-17).

---

[107] This verse and the verse "the Lord had had consideration for his people and given them food" (Ruth 1:6) are the only two places that God directly acts in the story. According to Campbell, God's intervention is expressed through the kind relations between the figures. For a discussion of the symbolic meaning of the verse (Ruth 4:13) as alluding to divine and miraculous conception, see the Epilogue. Campbell, *Ruth*, 29, 80.

Again, the phrase "he was named," hints at God's involvement in the birth of the messianic son, who is conceived symbolically as "the son of God." The motif of redemption appears in the book in connection to land and a woman, husband and son, as it is written, "who has not left you this day without a redeemer" (4:14). Here I disagree with Jonathan Cohen's claim that in the stories of Lot's daughters, Ruth, and Tamar, feminine ruses and initiative work *against* divine providence (in contrast to the annunciation scene of the infertile mothers like Sarah, Manoah's wife, and Hannah, which demonstrates a supportive divine intervention in the events). Boaz not only redeems Ruth, but also her son, as does God, who directly collaborates in this childbirth.[108]

In the Davidic type-scene, God intercedes through his concealed covenant with the women, which is revealed in the narrative framework: in the deaths at the stories' beginnings, at the moments of birth at their endings, and in the seductions in between. Without God's help and his control of events, the heroines would not have been saved from the dire circumstances thrust upon them. God's overt presence in the stories' beginnings highlights that he is the guiding factor of the crises driving the women to act. Afterwards, he saves them and enables their personal redemptions through their giving birth; finally, his voice is intensified with the imprinting of the messianic dynasty's genealogical seal. The naming moment, in which issues of power and authority are intertwined, is presented in these stories as a theological and mythic act, for Moab, Perez, Obed, and especially David are described not only as their *parents'* sons, but also as *God's* sons. God is the one who names them ("and his name was called," "to this day"), alongside the mothers who imprint through their actions the significance embedded in these names.

THE MOTIF OF DOUBLENESS

The motif of doubleness is emphasized in the type-scene of the "birth of the messianic hero," and reflects the paradoxical relation of transgression and redemption in these tales. Biblical stories are rich with paired female characters who complete one another, struggle with one another, or reflect different facets of one another, like the figures of Ruth and Naomi, Rachel and Leah, Hannah and Peninnah. Lot's daughters, who are nameless, give birth to two sons with symbolic and incestuous names following two nights in the cave, in which they

---

108 Jonathan Cohen, "The Traditions of Jesus' Birth against the Background of the Birth Stories in the Bible and Jewish Tradition" (PhD diss., Hebrew University, 1989), 13-4.

said identical words. Lot's name has a twofold meaning, on the one hand symbolizing concealment, lies, and even a curse (in Aramaic), and on the other hand, encoding the concealed quality of the House of David. In Tamar's story there are two husbands whose names symbolize mourning and evil, and she gives birth to twin boys who receive meaningful names of chosenness: Perez, the Breacher and Overtaker of his brother, and Zerah, marked by the crimson thread. Tamar, whose name hints at the androgyny of the palm tree, is referred to as a "bride" and "harlot"; like a bride she is passive and obedient, whereas like a harlot she is proactive and transgressive.[109]

The Book of Ruth opens with two husbands and two wives and continues with a counter reflection, when Orpah returns home and Ruth clings to Naomi. This motif is repeated in the conflicting figures of the two redeemers: the closer redeemer and the further redeemer.[110] The blessings at the city gate are also twofold and befit a book structured in pairs. This duality is seen in the connection of Er and Onan to Mahlon and Chilion—in the models in which one man rejects the woman and the second draws her near (Boaz and the closer redeemer, Judah and his sons), or conversely, in two women facing one man (Rachel and Leah facing Jacob, Ruth and Naomi facing Boaz, Lot's daughters facing their father). The root of the word "y.b.m" (levir) is repeated in the Book of Ruth and the episode of Tamar. The names of Bathsheba and Bath-shua are the same in Chronicles, likewise David's words "I have sinned against the Lord," following the Bathsheba incident (II Samuel 12:13), are parallel to Judah's words "She is more righteous than I" following the Tamar incident (Gen. 38:26).

The doubleness is found in the content and form of the Judean dynasty and compensates for the absence that motivates the dynastic mothers to act. From a different perspective, the excess in the stories grants depth to the language, characters, and symbols, as well as a complex and layered perspective. The mythic quality of the secret encircling the messianic type-scene bestows upon it a cloak of doubleness, loaded and multifaceted. In this way, contradictory motifs of power and vulnerability, fullness and emptiness, and feminine passiveness and activeness are integrated. Models of doubled women—Ruth and Naomi, Lot's daughters, the elder and younger, Tamar the abandoned and Tamar the initiator—join to create the whole and personal face of the messi-

---

109 Kramer, "Biblical Women that Come in Pairs." On the androgyny of the palm tree, see Chapter six, footnote 10.
110 As Zakovitch, *Ruth*, 8 states: "The story's plot needs two sons in order to have two widows, and this is in order to contrast Ruth, the central character of the two, with the secondary character, Orpah... for the positiveness of one figure is even more noticeable when cast against another positive figure, rather than a negative one." Zakovitch, *David*, 24-35.

anic mother. As we will see in the coming chapter, this multifaceted figure will continue and echo the type-scene in the later Midrash discussing David's birth.

SEXUALITY AND MESSIANISM

The mysteriousness in the messianic myth indicates that the deviant union is a potency that allows redemption. During the discussion of the type-scene, I suggested a dual perspective of sexuality: firstly, as it is, and then followed by an examination in light of its messianic aspects. The sexuality's uniqueness derives from the fact that it allows the rescuing of the "alterity" of man, that which he can only understand through the other.[111] Coupling discloses that which cannot be known in singularity, a knowledge only available through the body's clinging, which reflects the image of God.

The unique model of sexuality that arises from the messianic type-scene demonstrates that we are not only discussing pleasure or a structure intended for birthing and reproduction, but rather a complex sexuality, incorporating the darker side of seduction and concealment, rejection and crisis, while also grasping the aspect of illumination and visibleness, which establish the royal canon. The "optimistic" ending characterizing the array of stories, which is bound to the messianic annunciation and son's birth, is in stark contrast to the beginning of the tales, in which the heroines appear amidst bereavement, injury, and loss. These female figures, driven by deep conviction and devotion to their goals, experience a sequence of events: they give birth to a child, by a man who is forbidden to them in most cases, and remain, despite the birth, foreign. These descriptions, interweaving coverage and seduction, concealment and disclosure, vulnerability and power, suggest that the dialectical manner and antinomian conditions from which the Messiah is born are what transform him into the "Messiah." The figures of his foremothers and their subversive ways of acting are what transform the son into the redeemer.

THE DEVELOPMENT AND TEMPERING OF THE TYPE-SCENE—WHAT DO THE FOREMOTHERS BEQUEATH TO THEIR DAUGHTERS?

The Davidic stories create an archetypical model and a powerful myth. "The birth of the messianic hero type-scene" is configured as a source of cyclical

---

111 Bataille, *Death and Sensuality*; Ruth Stein, "The Enigmatic Dimension of Sexual Experience: The 'Otherness' of Sexuality and Primal Seduction," *Psychoanalytical Quarterly* 67 (1998): 594–625.

seduction and illicit relations, in which a sequence of predetermined actions, are deterministically repeated. As Freud states, compulsive repetition stems from the attempt to heal trauma, which is compelled to be reproduced again and again, without the possibility of being saved from it.[112] Seemingly, the episode of Lot's daughters creates an opening for a traumatic chain of sexually deviant episodes, which are repeated generation after generation. Therefore, to conclude the chapter, I will ask, is this pattern of illicit relations destined to repeat itself? And if, from the perspective of gender, this dynasty represents an ongoing example of female oppression and lack of choice, a legacy bequeathed by mothers to their daughters?

A close examination of the Davidic stories reveals that there is gradual transition from the extreme incestuous actions of Lot's daughters, to Tamar's resourceful harlotry, and finally an implied seduction on the threshing floor in the Book of Ruth. This type-scene reflects a model of reparation and healing, fighting against patterns of traumatic stagnation that repeat themselves. Generation after generation, the mothers and daughters of the House of David alleviate the actions of their predecessors, and simultaneously cause the birth of the messianic redeemer, while representing the possibility of mitigating and sublimating the sexual trauma at the dynasty's foundation. We see that in each generation, the extent of female volition increases. Lot's daughters face annihilation and the loss of their mother, Tamar is threatened with execution and abandoned by her husbands, and Ruth chooses to follow Naomi, to join her people, and go at night to the threshing floor.

Similarly, even the masculine figures represent a developing range of choice, from a drunken Lot in the cave, to Judah at the entrance of Enaim, and culminating with Boaz, the redeemer at the city's gate. As we saw, Boaz and Ruth are much more aware than Tamar and Judah, and the birth of Ammon and Moab is not identical to the birth of Perez or David. Nonetheless, the Bible reflects a heightened perception of the female crisis, suggesting that there are things that are inherited, genes that repeat themselves, and mythical actions that are "doomed to occur" in the complicated relations of mothers and daughters. Thus, beside their differences, the "type-scene" of the Davidic foremothers is formed.

---

112 Freud, "Beyond the Pleasure Principle." According to Freud, the source of compulsive repetition is in the death instinct. Yet, it seeks to heal the trauma by hoping for reparation which act a according to the life instinct, as is seen from Winnicott's, Bion's, and Kohut's teachings. Devorah Gamilieli, *Psychoanalysis and Kabbalah: The Masculine and Feminine in Lurianic Kabbalah* (Los Angeles: Cherub Press, 2006), 329-31.

Part Two

The Messianic Mother in Rabbinic Literature— Sororal Love and "Ethics of Redemption"

> *Perhaps [transgression] is like a flash of lightning in the night which, from the beginning of time, gives a dense and black intensity to the night it denies, which lights up the night from the inside, from top to bottom, yet owes to the dark the stark clarity of its manifestation, its harrowing and poised singularity.*
>
> Michel Foucault, *Preface to Transgression*

The "birth of the messianic hero" type-scene sharpens the paradox in the heart of the Davidic stories. An examination of the stories in relation to each other underscores their dialectical ambiguity and complexity. On the one hand, they portray transgressions and the breaching of clear sexual and ethnic boundaries. On the other hand, they are about an elected and sacred dynasty and the founding of a monarchy that becomes messianic. This book examines three corpuses: the Bible, rabbinic literature, and Zoharic interpretations. The active demand of the text to have its contradictions deciphered and interpreted is characteristic of the three corpuses that this book examines: the Bible, rabbinic literature, and Zoharic interpretations. The question therefore arises regarding the unifying signature of the rabbinic literature in its relation to the seductive and transgressive actions of the Judean mothers. In the next two chapters, I will propose that this literature establishes a unique feminine and messianic ethic, which situates at its center a mythical aggregate of the mother and her son the redeemer.

The third chapter will discuss the construction of David's mother's figure in the late Midrash and the way the sages internalized the sequence of the biblical literary precedent. This later writing is not only designed to fill in the biblical textual gaps, but also to bestow a renewed meaning to the seductive, transgressive, and redemptive pattern of the Davidic dynasty. The aggadah of *Yalkut ha-Makhiri* folkloristically continues the narrative of the Judean typescene while portraying the Bible as a mythical anchor in which the messianic idea blooms. As is known, different groups in the Second Temple era viewed David as an elected hero and sought to present themselves as his dynastic heirs.[1] Therefore, David's birth story illuminates the biblical stories and imparts a messianic hue and dramatic vindication of his foremothers. In this way the "return of the biblical repressed" occurs as the obvious foundation of the later messianic stories.[2]

The fourth chapter will discuss the Talmudic statment "*Gedolah aveirah lishmah me-mitzvah she-lo lishmah*": greater is a transgression performed with good intent than a commandment performed without good intent. This bold statement—that redemption will be achieved not only through suffering, but through *transgression*—reflects the unique ethical role that the sages envisaged for the messianic mothers. To the extent that a categorical imperative was established, the transition from narrative to the field of law indicates the centrality of the Davidic stories to the development of the messianic idea. According to Gershom Scholem, the kabbalistic literature of the Middle Ages saw a powerful, dualistic, and gnostic outbreak of mysticism and a reliance on the subversive essence of myth.[3] An examination of the following Midrashim demonstrates that the paradoxical connection between transgression and redemption was already present in ancient times. Rabbinic literature institutionalized the sacred attitude towards the Davidic mothers while exploring ethical and theological questions which have implications for the understanding of the role of foreign woman, the essence of redemption, and the characteristics of the redeemer.

---

1 This phenomenon is prominent in apocryphal, qumranic, early Christian , and rabbinic literature: Mowinckel, *He That Cometh*, 155-86, 305-45; Schäfer, *The Jewish Jesus*, 81, 224; Ephraim E. Urbach, *The World of the Sages: Collected Studies* (Jerusalem: Magnes Press, 1988), 306-29.
2 Daniel Boyarin, *Intertextuality and the Reading of Midrash* (Bloomington: Indiana University Press, 1990), 93-104.
3 Gershom Scholem, *On the Kabbalah and Its Symbolism* (New York: Schocken 1965), 87-117.

CHAPTER 3

David's Mother(s) in *Yalkut ha-Makhiri*

In light of the impressive feminine genealogy of the Davidic dynasty throughout the Bible—including the unusual genealogical lists and detailed stories of seduction and childbirth—the absence of myth regarding the birth of the central hero, King David, is especially prominent. King David's figure appears to lack all of the features of the "birth of the hero" type-scene.[1] His character begins with a spontaneous appearance and election and ends with an eternal convenant with his offspring. David, the artist, the judge and victor, the sinner and repentant, is an orphan without a past.[2] Nonetheless, it appears that the later traditions try to complete David with a mythic parameter: his mother is revealed as a figure suspected of illegitimate relations, while his father abandons him after birth.

NOW HE WAS A REDHEAD AND HAD BEAUTIFUL EYES—DAVID'S MOTHER IN *YALKUT HA-MAKHIRI*

The verse "Indeed, I was born guilty, a sinner when my mother conceived me" (Ps. 51:7), is placed not only in the Church Father's readings of original sin, but also in the late exegesis which explores David's birth. According to this Midrash, the outcast son merits greatness and royalty, and appears as a son of man and as "son of God." However, an additional feminine figure is added to this birth story, Jesse's handmaiden:

> 'The stone that the builders rejected has become the chief cornerstone' (Psalms 118:22). Midrash: 'Indeed, I was born guilty, a sinner when my mother conceived me' (Psalms 51:7). 'Guilty' (*be'avon*), [is spelled with]

---
1 Otto Rank, *The Myth of the Birth of the Hero, and Other Writings* (New York: Vintage Books, 1959), 65-6.
2 Kron, *Us, Adam and Eve*, 178-9.

a double letter 'vav.' Two Amoraim in the West [Palestine] had a disagreement how to interpret this verse. One said, David was the son of the beloved wife, but the other said, David was the son of the hated wife. How so? Jesse abstained from sexual relations with his wife for three years, and after three years he acquired a beautiful handmaid and lusted after her. He said to her: 'My daughter, prepare yourself for tonight so you can come to me and thus you will be emancipated. The handmaid went and told her mistress: 'Deliver you, my soul, and my master from hell!' The mistress answered her 'What is the reason?' So the handmaid told her everything. Said the mistress 'my daughter, what can I do, seeing that today he has not touched me in three years?' The handmaid answered: I will give you advice 'Go and prepare yourself, as will I, and tonight, when he says to close the door, you will enter and I will leave.' And so that is what they did. At night, the handmaid stood and extinguished the light. She then went to close the door, and her mistress entered as she left. The mistress was with him all night and conceived David. Because of Jesse's love [lust] for the handmaid, David's 'redness' stood out among his brothers. After nine months had passed, when they saw he was a redhead, her sons wished to kill her and her son David. Jesse said to them, "Leave him and he will be a servant and shepherd for us … Samuel asked Jesse: 'Are these all the boys you have?' He replied 'There is still the youngest. He is tending the flock … Since he arrived, the oil has begun to bubble and rise. The Lord said: 'Rise and anoint him, for this is the one' … Jesse and his sons trembled with fear, as they said 'Samuel is coming to degrade us and to inform Israel that we have an illegitimate son. And David's mother was inwardly happy and outwardly sad. When Samuel took the cup of salvation, they were all happy. Samuel stood up and kissed him [David] on his head and said 'The Lord said to me, 'You are my son; today I have begotten you' (Psalms 2:7). At that moment his mother said 'The stone that the builders rejected, [has become the chief cornerstone].' It is not written—*habonim* (builders) but rather—*habanim* (the sons). The son who was rejected by his brothers, has become the chief cornerstone and surpassed them all. His sons said to him, "This is the Lord's doing," and therefore "This is the day that the Lord has made; let us rejoice and be glad in it."[3]

---

3 Yalkut ha-Makhiri on Psalms 118: 28 (ed. Buber, 214). The translation of this Midrash is based on Fonrobert's version, with changes according to the Hebrew text in Buber edition. Fonrobert, "Birth of the Messiah," 251-52. See also, Ginzberg, *Legends*, 5:51, 167.

The Midrash states that David was born through a feminine ruse and "bedtrick" between the rejected wife and Jesse's desired handmaiden. The story begins with sexual trickery, continues with the hero's birth and endangerment, and it climaxes with the rescuing and miraculous choosing of David. This Midrash fits the Davidic type-scene and thereby transforms sexual deviancy into messianic election. The words of the handmaiden to her mistress: "Deliver you, my soul, and my master from hell," attest to the severity of Jesse's action, although there are several options regarding his sin: not fulfilling the commandment of "*onah*" (intercourse) with his wife, his desire for his foreign handmaiden, or the very fact that he attempted to permit his handmaiden with a "bill of emancipation," an act which, according to the *halakha*, permits her for Israelite marriage, but creates tension between the women.

Following Ḥayyim Yoseph David Azulai (Ḥida), Charlotte Fonrobert claims that Jesse, being descended from a Moabite, was concerned with his "illegitimate status" and therefore refrained from having intercourse with his wife.[4] According to this approach, Boaz and Ruth violated the biblical prohibition of "No Ammonite or Moabite shall be admitted to the assembly of the Lord." It was for this reason that Jesse preferred the handmaiden's sons—who were legitimized through a bill of emancipation and conversion—over the invalid sons of his wife. In Fonrobert's opinion, the portrayal of the Davidic women as tricksters and seducers reflects a solution for the tension between the sages' perception of the *beit ha-midrash* as "a womanless world" and their obligation to procreate. By directing the birth through circumstances of feminine deception and compulsion, the sages incidentally justify Jesse's behavior, and adapt the oedipal drama, as viewed by Jesse wanting to kill David.[5]

This critical reading focuses on the patriarchal goal of procreation and on the masculine narrative situated between the lines of the Midrash. I would rather suggest that *Yalkut ha-Makhiri* adds an additional link to the Judean type-scene, which portrays dominant women and controlled men. Indeed, the Midrash does not explicitly mention why Jesse refrained from his wife for years, however in the background the critical tone against the head of the Sanhedrin is noticeable. The doubling of the *vav* in the word "*avon*" (guilt)—in Ps. 51:7: "Indeed, I was born *guilty*," attests to his sins in the past and in the present. Furthermore, the end of the verse, which deals with the maternal transgression

---

4 In *Ma'amar Hiqur Din* §3:10, there is an adaptation of this motif by R. Menahem Azariah Fano.
5 Fonrobert, "Birth of the Messiah," 272-3.

("a sinner when my mother conceived me"), is absent from the Midrash. The feminine figures are presented as potencies of life and salvation, in contrast to the masculine abandonment and murderousness. Similar to Jesse, his sons also wish to take the lives of David and his mother. The conclusion of the Midrash stresses the transgression in which Jesse is immersed, despite the success of the feminine ruse—which is not only intended for giving birth.

Akin to the biblical Davidic heroines, who actively choose their motherhood and perform transgressions which are not just a submission to the patriarchal order, Jesse's wife and handmaiden share sororal love and rescue their independent pride. Jesse joins the biblical model of passive masculine figures, while the women seduce, masquerade, and establish their domain. The Midrash does not favor a conservative justification of Jesse and strengthen his relationship with his "legal wife," nor does it indulge in a "masculine fantasy" of Jesse copulating with his handmaiden. Rather, it offers a subverting alternative for these models, by engaging feminine narrative and friendship. The author of *Yalkut ha-Makhiri* intends to guide the perception of procreation and sexuality in a different direction, linked to the antinomianism of the messianic idea. The success of the feminine ruse sharpens my claim that in contrast to the known systems of power, the heroine in these stories is an active and desiring subject who establishes her reality.

Yalkut ha-Makhiri, is a collection of Midrashim that were edited by R. Machir ben Abba Mari in Provence in the 14th century, and it includes, among other things, earlier traditions, which only arrived to us in their later versions. Due to the mixed style of the legend of David's birth, Avraham Grossman reasons that it was written around the 7th-8th century and places its writing in the historical reality of Babylon, as a critique against the institution of the Exilarch, who would marry a number of women.[6]

Yair Zakovitch, in contrast, highlights the midrashic slander against David and his mother (and not Jesse), which is similar to the condemnation of Lot's daughters and Tamar.[7] He claims that this Midrash camouflages the possibility that David was born as a bastard to Jesse's handmaiden, and therefore his brothers hated him, or a more severe possibility, according to which David's red hair attests to his mother adulterating with a foreign man. In both cases,

---

[6] Abraham Grossman, "David—The Loathsome and the Repulsive: A Controversial Midrash of the Middle Ages," in *Studies in Bible and Exegesis*, ed. M. Garsiel, et al. (Ramat Gan: Bar Ilan University Press, 2000), 347-9. Grossman claims that the focus of the legend is the tension between David and his brothers.

[7] Zakovitch, *David*, 30-5; Shinan and Zakovich, *Story*, 219-28.

the Midrash does not only validate the son but also hints at the transgression that is concealed in his past. The third option echoes Mary's virginal birth in the Gospels of Mathew and Luke. In Zakovitch's view, the mother standing in the center of the legend is a rejected figure, whose husband desires another and thus reconstructs the biblical theme regarding women fighting over one husband, like Hannah and Peninah, or Rachel and Leah.

In fact, like Jacob assuming it is Rachel, but she is revealed to be Leah, or Judah who views Tamar as a cult prostitute, the Midrash's heroines perform sexual trickery and deception, objecting to the power relations and raising, as Doniger suggests, the question of "who is who."[8] However, in contrast to women who struggle with each other, here we see an act of kindness between two heroines. The Midrash implies that because of their partnership, David is not the son of one woman. Rather, he is the son of *"two mothers,"* just as Obed was born symbolically to both Ruth and Naomi. The theme of dual motherhood is developed from the Book of Ruth, to the Midrash on Rachel giving her 'signs' to Leah, and continues in the *Yalkut ha-Makhiri* tale. David as the Messiah thereby unifies within himself Rachel and Leah; Jesse's foreign handmaiden and the legal wife.

SON OF THE HATED AND SON OF THE LOVED—THE HOLY DECEPTION

In Genesis, Rachel and Leah are defined respectively as the hated wife and the loved wife, a definition unto which the division between motherhood and infertility is joined: "When the Lord saw that Leah was hated, he opened her womb; but Rachel was barren" (Gen. 29:31). In contrast to Rachel and Leah, who define themselves according to the masculine perspective, *Yalkut ha-Makhiri* suggests that David embodies both of these feminine figures. At first glance, Jesse's wife is identified with Leah, "the proper wife" of most of Jacob's children, whereas Jesse's handmaiden is identified with Rachel. However, the blurring of the borders between the hated and the loved figure transforms the rejected woman into the cherished one.

Each of the heroines in the Midrash is hated in her own way: one due to her foreignness and the other because of her husband's abandonment. Nevertheless, the Midrash replaces their voices by using the linguistic terminology characteristic of the two foremothers. For example, the wife's words to the

---

8 Doniger, *Bedtrick*, 253-9.

handmaiden, "what can I do, seeing that *today* he has not touched me in three years," hinting at the relationship of Jacob's wives (as it is written "But in the evening" and afterwards "When morning came, it was Leah" [(Gen. 29:23-25]), and the reference in the blessing in the Book of Ruth, "Then the women said to Naomi, 'Blessed be the Lord, who has not left you *this day* without a redeemer'" (Ruth 4:14), and also by Leah giving birth to Judah, which states *"This time I will praise the Lord"* (Gen. 29:35), similar to Ps. 118:24, quoted in the Midrash *"This is the day* that the Lord has made; let us rejoice and be glad in it."

The Midrash arranges a rectification not only for Leah, as a hated wife who is transformed into "the joyous mother of children," but also for Rachel, reconfigured here as a resilient handmaiden who gives the husband his mistress, without complaint or struggle, and thereby is granted a ruddy son similar to her. The passivity of Jesse's wife and the activeness of the handmaiden interweave the figures of Rachel and Leah.⁹ This sororal love comes as a response to the lack of husbandly love, creating a safe feminine space spurring fertility.¹⁰ The sadness of Jesse's wife is seen from the fondness of the handmaiden and her actions, "At night, the handmaid stood and extinguished the light." The same night which was designed to rectify the bitter wedding night of the two sisters, the climax of which is the switching of the figures and their reflections of each other, in David's own body and likeness.

David is portrayed in I Samuel 16:12: "Now he was a redhead, and had beautiful eyes, and was handsome." This description incorporates both of his foremothers: from one perspective, Rachel who was "graceful and beautiful," and from another perspective, Leah whose "eyes were lovely." David's beautiful eyes imply that Jacob only saw appearance, while God's and David's vision goes to the heart. This feminine rectification draws inspiration from the blessing in the Book of Ruth: "May the Lord make the woman who is coming into your house like Rachel and Leah, **who together built up** the house of Israel"

---

9 Rachel is viewed as an active figure already in the early Midrash: Levinson, *The Untold Story*, 209-10.
10 Like Rachel's outcry "Give me children, or I shall die" (Gen. 30:1), Philo interprets the tension between the sisters in light of the law in Deut. 21:16 and suggests an allegorical reading of the moral virtues they symbolize "The opening of the womb is man's proper function. But mortal kind is prone of itself to hate virtue, and accordingly God has bestowed honor upon it and vouchsafes to her that is hated to bear the first-born... for first of all and most perfect of all are the offspring of the hated virtue, while the offspring of the well-loved pleasure are last of all." (*Allegorical Interpretation of the Law II*, 48), Philo, 10 vols, trans. F. H. Colson and G. H. Whitaker. Loeb Classical Library (Cambridge: Harvard University Press, 1929-1962), 1: 255. As well as, Philo, *On the Changes of Names*, 255.

(Ruth 4:11). This process is developed in the kabbalistic literature, in which David is born from Leah's offspring and the tribe of Judah, identified unexpectedly with the figure of Rachel, who is *Shekhinah*, the *sefirah* of *Malkhut*.

Yalkut ha-Makhiri interprets the meaning of the repeated phrase "he did not know," and explains that the feminine covenant conceals the doubled faced women—Rachel and Leah—who conceived through it. Jesse, presented in the beginning of the Midrash in a critical light, is the one who saves David's life in the end: "Jesse said to them, 'Leave him,'" thus understanding the process of divine providence. In this manner David is created, as the son of the loved one who concedes her position, and the son of the hated one who is transformed in to the loved one, and therefore she says at the end of the Midrash: "The stone that the builders rejected" as describing not only her son, but also herself.

Furthermore, this Midrash challenges the gendered conception of foreign thought in rabbinic literature. As opposed to the inclination to ascribe the "changing of the embryo's face" to the woman's transgression, as according to the Midrash, "the Holy One, blessed be He, transforms the features of the child into those of the adulterer,"[11] *Yalkut ha-Makhiri* attributes the sinful thought to Jesse, and places the responsibility for transforming David into a redhead on him. In the aforementioned Midrash, the face that God "places on the embryo," is actually a face of kindness, which saves the mother and her son from the deceit's exposure, until the moment that David is chosen for kingship. In contrast to the misogynistic trend to harm the woman through her children, the Midrash shows that David was a redhead like his desired mother, in spite of his father's transgressive sexual thoughts. According to Fonrobert and Zakovitch, in the background of this description is "the classic expression of anxiety over fatherhood." Yet the aggadah emphasizes that the son's otherness and redness are dependent on the mother, and not the father! Thus, here is "an expression of anxiety over motherhood," and in a certain way, the desired redheaded handmaiden becomes the object of Jesse's wife's foreign thoughts and not Jesse's. In this manner the exegetes accomplish a twofold achievement: while criticizing the man who is with his wife but desires another woman, they suggest an empowering feminine reading that transforms David into the son of his mother but also of the woman "mistaken for another."[12]

---

11 Numbers Rabbah 9:1; Leviticus Rabbah 23:12 (ed. Margolioth, 545); Gwynn Kessler, *Conceiving Israel: The Fetus in Rabbinic Narrative* (Philadelphia: University of Pennsylvania Press, 2009), 69-71.

12 b. *Nedarim* 20b; Boyarin, *Carnal Israel*, 107-13.

In the claim that David had two mothers, the Midrash is appropriate for the Judean model, but also advances it in a new direction. In contrast to Fonrobert's claim, that the story propagates gender roles under the guise of subversion, I claim that by adding David's mother to the list of heroines mentioned at the end of the Book of Ruth, *Yalkut ha-Makhiri* strengthens the messianic narrative and concealed femininity, which begins in the Bible and develops in rabbinic exegesis, while guiding the seductiveness and feminine trickery not only for the need of procreation and men's sake, but rather for the purpose of collaboration between women and in terms of their subjective volition and liberty.[13]

THE ABSENT MOTHER AND THE EXCESSIVE MOTHER

Psychoanalysts and scholars of myth asserted the complexity of the relation with the mother—since for the infant the mother is the whole world, while she also represents the source of danger and the limitation of his independence. By being "the great other," her womb, which the newborn has left, symbolizes a chaotic primal source which might subsume him. Erich Neumann compares this relationship to the *ouroboros*, whose tail is found in its mouth, as the embryo imprisoned in the womb, unable to free itself. Whereas Simone de Beauvoir, Julia Kristeva, and others have stressed the complicated relationship between sons and their mothers, due to the identification of the mother and feminine body with blood and death.[14] The feminine potencies—pregnancy and birth, procreation and impregnation, are bound to the cosmic cycles of nature that engulf the newborn.

In contrast to these models of a threatening motherly presence, David's birth-myth opens with the figure of the absent mother. Is the absence designed to protect from archetypical danger, or to construct David as a messianic hero, without a feminine figure overshadowing him? It appears that there is a con-

---

13 Fonrobert suggests that the legend does not mark who might have been the hated wife in order to present Jesse in a positive light, as a righteous man careful of sin. However, Jesse's separation from his wife and his chasing after the maidservant raise criticism against the entire rabbinic institution. Fonrobert presents the women as vulnerable and use Jesse's desires "against him," although in this context it appears that he is a passive hero just like the heroes of the Davidic dynasty. Fonrobert claims that "In these stories women act and trick only to preserve and enforce their function as mothers, and more than that, as mothers of sons," while I find in these stories a "female agency" which suggests a subversive plot of its own. Fonrobert, "Birth of the Messiah," 253-4, 270-2; Doniger, *Bedtrick*.

14 Neumann, *Mystical*; de Beauvoir, *The Second Sex*, 33-60; Kristeva, *Power*, 158; Rich, *Of Woman Born*, 105-7.

nection between the feminine dominance which precedes David's appearance and the mother's absence, while emphasizing the divine figure's role in the story. The biblical David is stamped with the seal of lacking, which he wishes to fill through supernatural means. The biographical absence constitutes raw material out of which the messianic figure evolves. Like David's missing biological mother, the text is lacking a "literary" mother and for the Midrash of *Yalkut ha-Makhiri* there is no *urtext* able to be identified. The legend of David's birth is based on her absence in I Samuel 16, and seeks to be filled in variegated forms. Furthermore, the Bible implies that God is David's mother, whereas the Midrash of *Yalkut ha-Makhiri* offers a different answer for the absence, by transforming the feminine figure into a dual faced and transgressive mother.

The biblical Davidic stories are characterized by the remarkable sexual deviancy of the dynastic mothers, which strengthens the expectation to encounter an additional figure that fits the model and play the role of David's mother. Since this figure is missing, the reader of the Book of Samuel is required to stitch together the scene by activating a "poly-systemic filling of gaps."[15] The guided skipping in the story allows the active and primed reader, but also creates uncomfortableness and disruption of the biblical template. This lack is rectified through "excess" which doubles the motherly figure, an idea that also continues the Judean pattern implied in the Book of Ruth. The ability to construct two mothers for David attests to the exegetical liberty, as well as the crisis that creates the genealogical and psychological void. Interweaving two figures in the feminine dynasty exhibits an exegetical abundance, while simultaneously creating a "polyphonic harmony that will be shattered."[16]

CONNECTED MIDRASHIM BETWEEN DAVIDIC MOTHERS

The Midrash of David's birth reconstructs the pattern of female rivalry and brings it to reconcilement. Through the connection to the stories of Rachel and Leah, Ruth and Naomi, Lot's two daughters, and Tamar this late Midrash hints at a dual conception of the messianic mother, sacred and profane, and the

---

15   Menahem Perry and Meir Sternberg, "The King through Ironic Eyes: Biblical Narrative and the Literary Reading Process," *Poetics Today* 7 (1986): 275–322.
16   Wolfgang Iser, *The Act of Reading: A Theory of Aesthetic Response* (London: Routledge, 1978), 184-92. In Ingarden's words, "But if the work is to come together in a polyphonic whole, there must be limits to the tolerable level of indeterminacy, and if these limits are exceeded, the polyphonic harmony will be shattered." Ibid, 172. The work's aesthetic value and metaphysical character are what allow the reader to bestow meaning upon it.

unification of the two parts of one soul.[17] Likewise it appears that the aggadah implies that excess and duality are at the essence of the maternal experience, and in the feminine potency that allows her to conceive, give birth, and bestow meaning to the "not-me within me," like the mythological mother, "who nourishes, and who stands up against separation; a force that will not be cut off."[18]

Despite the impression that David is the hero of this Midrash, we learn that actually the feminine figure, who brought upon his birth, is situated at the center of the text. David's electedness as the Messiah is rooted in his foreignness and originates in the deception and trickery of his foremothers. *Yalkut ha-Makhiri* uses an exegetical story that fits the biblical model and is structured on the familiar pattern, while simultaneously intensifies the dialecticalness of the messianic idea and the subversion of the Davidic heroines' actions.[19]

The exegesis concerning David's mother, hinted at in the the early Midrash and the Talmud, shows a thematic consecutiveness focusing on the Davidic feminine genealogy.[20] From this development, the "sublimative" manner, through which the sages establish the myth of the mother and the redeemer son, becomes evident by transforming the biblical stories into a model to be imitated by the Midrashim written in their wake. The use of the Bible as a familiar foundation, to vindicate the dynastic heroines appears in additional "connected Midrashim," relating to the array of the stories of the Davidic foremothers.

For instance, Tamar's, Lot's daughter's, and David and Bathsheba's episodes, are portrayed as stories that raise doubt regarding the legitimacy of translating them to Aramaic ("to be read and not translated"), whereas Ruth Rabbah concludes with a summary of all the invalid marriages of the Davidic dynasty in order to justify and praise the problematic lineage of the elected king.[21] In a short additional fragment found in the genizah, and copied next to the *Midrash Eshet Ḥayil*, it is written:

---

17 As Kristeva writes, "The theme of the two-faced mother is perhaps the representation of the baleful power of women to bestow mortal life," *Powers*, 158; Kron, *Us, Adam and Eve*, 89-104. On Rachel and Leah as twins, *Sedor Olam Rabbah* 2.
18 Hélène Cixous, "The Laugh of the Medusa," *Signs*, 1, no. 4 (Summer 1976): 875-93, 882.
19 Levinson, *The Untold Story*, 2, 13.
20 In *b. Bava Batra* 91a, David's mother is named "Niztevet, the daughter of Adael," while Leviticus Rabbah 14:5 (Margolioth ed., 308-9), discusses the sin of David's parents at the time of his conception, themes which I will expand upon in the future.
21 *Tosefta Megillah* 3:13; Ishay Rosen-Zvi, *The Mishnaic Sotah Ritual: Temple, Gender, and Midrash* (Leiden: Brill, 2012), 216, fn. 152; Niditch, "Genesis 38." Ruth Rabbah 8:1 (ed. Lerner, 204-11).

> Ten women were created in the world: three cause their husbands death, and three save their husband from death. **Three fornicate and the world subsists through them**, and three intend to fornicate and the world does not subsist.²²

This fragment parallels "*Ma'amar Sheteim Esreh ha-Nashim*" which discusses the righteous biblical heroines that protect the world:

> Twelve women were in the world. Three caused their husbands' deaths and they were: Eve, Delilah, Jezebel. And three who saved their husbands from death, and they are: On's wife, Mihal daughter of Saul, and Serah daughter of Asher. **And three who fornicated and the world subsists through them, and they are: Tamar and Lot's daughters**. And three who intended to fornicate and the world does [not] subsist through them, and they are: Rahab, Yael, and Potiphar's wife.

In a different version of the same Midrash, the three figures are turned into four: "Three who fornicated for the sake of heaven, Lot's daughters, Tamar, and Ruth the Moabite."²³ In these Midrashim, the justification of the Davidic foremothers' actions as "fornication for the sake of heaven," stems from the birth of King David, but also is due to their positive intentions. God is presented in these Midrashim not only as a covenantal partner, but also as establishing the human drama, as is hinted at in Genesis Rabbah 85:1:

> "*For I know the thoughts that I think toward you, says the Lord*" (Jer. 24:11). The tribal ancestors were engaged in selling Joseph ... while the Holy One, blessed be He, [was busy] **creating the light/yeast (*she'oro/she'iro*) of Messiah**.²⁴

---

22 Myron B. Lerner, "A New Fragment of *Midrash Eshet Ḥayil* and the Opening Section of a Work Dealing with Twelve Women," in *Studies in Talmudic and Midrashic Literature: In Memory of Tirzah Lifshitz*, eds. M. Bar-Asher, A Edrei, J. Levinson, and B. Lifshitz (Jerusalem: Bialik Institute, 2005), 274-5; according to Adler's collection of manuscripts, 1269, 13b; Lerner supplements this fragment "Tamar and Lot's daughters fornicated and the world subsists through them" according to a parallel from *Midrash ha-Gadol* on *Parashat Koraḥ* (ed. Z.M. Rabinowitz, 278). Lerner claims that *Ma'amar Sheteim Esreh* is an entirely separate work from *Midrash Eshet Ḥayil*, but was attached by one of the copyists due to the shared topic of biblical women (ibid, 280).

23 According to the version in *Pirqe de-Rabbenu ha-Qodesh*, 3:62 (ed. Schönblum, 30b).

24 Genesis Rabbah 85:1 (ed. Theodor-Albeck, 1030). In the manuscripts there appears different version of this term, in MS. Vatican 60: "He was busy making the yeast of King Messiah, whereas in MS. Munich, Paris, and London "He created King Messiah's light."

Initially this is an ironic Midrash about people discussing their worries, while God works to mend existence. The author describes the processes of disintegration that happen to Jacob's family and configures a tragic scene woven with criticism against the father who did not save his son. Within human devastation, God is presented as a hero who creates the messianic light. Similar to the myth of David's birth, the symbolic birth of the Messiah is dependent on human absence, leaving space for God to bring redemption. Here the Messiah, who is fist created in thought, is portrayed as a remedy for a disease.[25] The messianic connotation of the phrase "creating the light of Messiah" is strengthened in *Pesiqta Rabbati*, there the Messiah is described as a 'light hidden away,' which the Assembly of Israel has been anticipating since the creation of the world:

> Which light does the Assembly of Israel anticipate? This is the light of the Messiah ... it teaches that the Holy One blessed be He awaited the Messiah and his actions before the world was created [and hid it away] for the Messiah and his generation under his Throne of Glory.[26]

Based on the manuscript variations, it is possible to offer a different explanation, hinting at the antinomian character of the Davidic dynasty. According to Saul Lieberman, the phrases "The Holy One blessed be He was busy creating the light (*oro*) of the Messiah," should be read as "that he is creating the yeast (*se'oro*) of the Messiah."[27] Whereby the image situated at the source of the Midrash is the preparation of the yeast (*se'or*) and its fermentation, or the process of arranging and separating the grain from the chaff. These variances attest to an exegetical direction that implies the collaboration of evil forces in the process of the redeemer's birth. The Messiah is perceived according to this interpretation as the "yeast in the dough," which is the vibrant part, leavening the dough and allowing it to rise.[28] The version "creating the yeast," teaches that

---

25 As written in Genesis Rabbah 85:1 (ed. Theodor-Albeck, 1029-30): "Before the last who shall enslave [Israel] was born, the first redeemer was born," b. Megillah 13b.
26 *Pesiqta Rabbati* (ed. Ish Shalom) 36; *Pirqe de-Rabbi Eliezer* (ed. Higger), Horeb 31. For parallel traditions and their development in kabbalistic literature, see Oded Yisraeli, *Temple Portals: Studies in Aggadah and Midrash in the Zohar* (Magnes Press, Jerusalem, 2013), 39-58.
27 According to MS Vatican 30. Lieberman derives this by virtue of the later version kept by Martini, Saul Lieberman, *Sheki'in: Some Thoughts on Jewish Legends, Customs and Literary Sources Found in Karaite and Christian Works* (Jerusalem: Wahrmann Books, 1970), 74; *Tosefta Pesaḥim*, 485. See also *Tanḥuma* (ed. Buber) *Parashat va-Yeshev* 11, "Judah went down to prepare the last redeemer, King Messiah."
28 b. Berakhot 17a; Knohl, *The Many Faces*, 28-32; Steinsaltz, *Women*, 59.

God does not only create the foundation from which the Messiah will emerge from in the future, but also guides the evil forces to give birth to the elected son.

It is not insignificant that this Midrash begins with the story of Judah and Tamar and projects onto the ensemble of dynastic stories that arose for Judah's descendants. The exegetes begin the discussion of Tamar's action with the affinity that is between heaven and earth, opening facing opening. Alongside the statement in Gen. Rabbah 85:2, that Tamar divined that she would give birth to a son from this family, the sages recount that God "creates," together with the women, the messianic yeast and light, and is an active partner in giving birth to the sons, while the men are "working and busy" and do not understand the event. We will now discuss the rabbinic gendered distinction between the dynastic mothers and fathers and the conception of sexual transgression as a sin that "leavens the dough."

CHAPTER 4

Gedolah Aveirah Lishmah— From Rabbinic Literature to the Messianic Teachings of R. Moses Ḥayyim Luzzatto

The unique and radical statement *Gedolah averah lishmah me-mitzvah she-lo lishmah* appears in the Babylonian Talmud just twice, in *Nazir* and in a parallel text in *Horayot*. Scholars and commentators have suggested different interpretations of the enigmatic term *averah lishmah*. Legal readings tend to explicate it as "permission to perform a transgression out of a positive motive," "rejection of one norm in favor of a loftier one," or "violation of the law in order to preserve it." Another reading of the term, in the spirit of Rashi and the Tosafists, takes it as a "transgression committed for the sake of a commandment" or "for the sake of God." I will suggest that the precise meaning of the term is "transgression with good intention," or "a sin done for its own sake," an interpretation that takes into consideration the direct literary and gender context of this Talmudic statement.

In rabbinic literature and in the thought of R. Moses Ḥayyim Luzzatto, the concept of *averah lishmah* pertains to a single matter: a seductive act bordering on sexual transgression performed for the sake of the people of Israel—a role in the drama of national salvation which is assigned to women only. By examining evolving interpretations of this passage in the Talmud, we can observe the development of one type of Jewish messianic thought from its inception in rabbinic sources through its subsequent unfolding in kabbalistic literature, where the perception of male and female roles are underscored in a highly developed myth of national redemption.

The statement *Gedolah averah lishmah me-mitzvah she-lo lishmah* (Greater is a transgression performed with good intention, than a commandment performed with no intent) is remarkable in its daring and simplicity. This statement by R. Naḥman b. Yiṣḥaq belongs to a *sugiyah* (pericope) that appears twice in the Babylonian Talmud: in *Horayot* (10b–11a), in a discussion of the bullock offering for a high priest or king who has transgressed inadvertently, and in *Nazir* (23a–b), in the context of vows and their annulment, and the relationship between intention, action and consequence.[1] This *sugiyah*, one of the most radical Midrashim in the Babylonian Talmud and in rabbinic literature as a whole, has been expounded upon in halakhic literature and in the Jewish hermeneutic tradition throughout the ages. But scholarly attention to the above statement has been devoted mainly to discussions of it in kabbalistic, Sabbatean, and hasidic literature, leaving its treatment in rabbinic thought unexplored.[2] Jewish legal writings view it as representing the notion of "the end justifies the means," while it figures in halakhic debates on antinomianism, among other rabbinic expressions such as *hora'at sha'ah* (an emergency ruling) and *mitzvah haba'ah be-aveirah* (a mitzvah attained from a transgression), and maxims like *be-khol derakheikha da'ehu ... afilu le-devar aveirah* (In all your ways acknowledge him ... even through a transgression), and *et la-asot la-shem heferu toratekha* (It is time to act for God, for Thy law has been broken).[3]

I would like to suggest an alternative reading of the above statement, in which it serves to justify a specific type of transgression, namely, feminine sexual transgression committed with good intentions before both God and law. My understanding follows the messianic reading of R. Moses Ḥayyim Luzzatto (Ramḥal) and his interpretation of gender roles in this *sugiyah*.

In Responsa literature and in other exegetical interpretations, the term *aveirah lishmah* (a transgression committed with good intention) was applied

---

1 Questions pertaining to the source of this *sugiyah* and its philological layers are beyond the scope of the present discussion. It may originally have been located in *Horayot* and been copied to *Nazir* as Epstein suggests, or both these sources may have shared an earlier version of the text. Jacob N. Epstein, *Introduction to Amoraic Literature* (Jerusalem: Magnes Press, 1962), 77.
2 Scholem, *Messianic Idea*, 78–141; Yehuda Liebes, *On Sabbateanism and Its Kabbalah: Collected Essays* (Jerusalem: Bialik Institute, 1995), 53–69, 98; Idel, *Kabbalah and Eros*, 169–84; Tsippi Kauffman, *In all Your Ways Know Him: The Concept of God and Avodah Be-Gashmiyut in the Early Stages of Hasidism* (Ramat Gan: Bar Ilan University Press, 2009), 523–71; Ada Rapoport-Albert, *Women and the Messianic Heresy of Sabbatai Zevi, 1666–1816* (Oxford: Littman Library of Jewish Civilization, 2011), 163–79, 201–15.
3 Urbach, *Sages*, 341, 398; Aaron Lichtenstein, "Does Jewish Tradition Recognize an Ethic Independent of Halakha?" in *Modern Jewish Ethics* (Columbus: Ohio State University Press, 1975), 107; Aaron Lichtenstein, "Aveirah Lishmah in Halakha and Thought," in *The Other: Between Man and Himself and His Fellow* (Tel Aviv: Yedioth Aharonoth, 2001), 99–125; Jeremy Kalmanofsky, "Sins for the Sake of God," *Conservative Judaism* 54, no. 2 (2002): 3-24; Nahum Rakover, *Ends that Justify the Means* (Jerusalem: Library of Jewish Law, 2000), 15–45.

only to Yael's seduction of Sisera (Judg. 4:17–22, 5:24–27), which is mentioned immediately after the statement in which this term first appears. Commentators have mistakenly compared the rabbinic understanding of Yael's sexual act—committed for the salvation of Israel—with the description elsewhere (in *b. Megillah* 13b and *Sanhedrin* 74b) of Esther as *qarqa olam* (inactive "soil"), since both, in their view, demonstrate passivity in the commission of a transgressive sexual act.[4] I will present a different understanding of the *sugiyah*, based on its broad, circular structure, which includes four additional biblical heroines: Ruth, Tamar, and Lot's two daughters. I will argue that in rabbinic literature these four heroines, who become the foremothers of the Davidic dynasty, represent a unique ethic under which they are permitted to engage in prohibited sexual acts.

As scholars have argued, the birth of the Jewish Messiah derives from a concatenation of female sexual transgressions, including incest, prostitution, and seduction. While this notion is rooted in the biblical narratives as a mythic pattern and "type-scene" weaving together the tales of Ruth, Tamar, and Lot's daughters, only in the era of the Second Temple did the sages situate this genealogy within the messianic concept and the idea of "redemption through sin."

The sages consistently interpreted the biblical stories about the foremothers of the Davidic dynasty in a positive light, in which their actions were seen as not merely transgressive but transformative. Ruth, Tamar, and Lot's daughters appear in the Bible as positive and courageous heroines. Unlike Esther, whom the sages describe as a powerless figure used roughly by the men around her, these female characters are presented as active, decisive heroines who influence the future by controlling men. In using the enigmatic term *aveirah lishmah*, the rabbis emphasized female sexual initiatives and God's support for them.

Our *sugiyah* presents heroines—all of them foreign, and four of the five single or widowed—who attempt to save themselves through deliberate seductions that inadvertently become acts of redemption. As previous scholars have suggested, this *sugiyah* also suggests that the foundation of the ethnic and national identity of the Jewish people is based, paradoxically, upon the "other," the threatening and desired foreign woman.[5] None other than Israel's monarchy and its victory over its enemies were facilitated by the subversive, sexually

---

4 *Qarqa olam* is an agricultural term used to denote tilled soil, which the sages use metaphorically to emphasize women's passivity in the sexual act. According to the sages, Esther was Mordecai's wife when she was summoned to Ahasuerus's palace. By characterizing her as *qarqa olam*, they justify her forbidden intercourse. See the commentaries of Rashi and the Tosafists to *b. Sanhedrin* 74b and the glosses of R. Moses Isserles to *Shulḥan Arukh, Yoreh de'ah* 157a.

5 Kristeva, *Strangers*, 75; Doniger, *Bedtrick*, 265; Brenner, *The Israelite Woman*.

transgressive behavior of gentile women. By means of the apparently inscrutable term *aveirah lishmah*, the sages were giving a clear message: The women's seductive actions were righteous.

THE STRUCTURE OF THE *SUGIYAH*

The *sugiyah* in *Nazir* 23a–b turns on an argument between two Babylonian sages, R. Yoḥanan and Resh Laqish, on the relationship between intention and action, in light of the enigmatic verse, "Whoever is wise, let him understand these things; whoever is discerning, let him know them; for the ways of the Lord are right, and the upright walk in them, but transgressors stumble in them" (Hosea 14:10). Adducing cases that demonstrate the gap between intention and action, the rabbis search for an example of "one path" that includes both. The riddle of "two paths that are one" and the disagreement between R. Yoḥanan and Resh Laqish are resolved by invoking the idea of sexual union in general, using the women's stories as examples.

In light of R. Yoḥanan's stance that intention is more important than action, and opposing Resh Laqish's opinion that action takes precedence over intention, the *sugiyah* suggests another solution: intention, action, and consequence are contained in one another. Good and evil are revealed as a unitary concept in the stories of the biblical heroines and their seductions. Contrary to the first two examples adduced in the discussion—two men eating the paschal offering with, respectively, the right or the wrong intention ("one eats it with the intention of fulfilling the precept and the other ... with the intention of having an ordinary meal"), or inadvertently copulating with the right or the wrong woman ("one chances upon his wife and the other chances upon his sister")—the third example, of Lot's daughters, provides an opportunity to discuss consequences through the intention of a single act.[6] The disagreement is resolved, as all parties admit that this "path" includes intention and action, man and woman.

According to the sages, sexual union expresses simultaneously the physical and the mental, desire and its realization, thus constituting a crucial juncture for reflecting man in God's image. Conspicuously, the rabbis praise the five biblical heroines, in stark contrast to the harsh criticism leveled at the sinning men in the *sugiyah*, whose transgressions are, significantly, by and large sexual. The decision by the *sugiyah*'s editors to weave together references to

---

6 The good intentions of those heroines can be discerned from the consequences of their deeds, including the birth of the Messiah and the salvation of Israel.

these heroines by sages from different eras, made in different contexts, offers a key to the meaning of the unique phrase *gedolah aveirah lishmah* and exposes hidden links between the stories.

In terms of its literary structure, the *sugiyah* is organized in concentric circles.[7] The inner circle includes Yael's act and R. Naḥman's bold ruling. The second broader circle mentions Tamar and Ruth, who perform a similar function, from both literary and conceptual perspectives, as the seductive foremothers of the Davidic dynasty's Messiah. In the third and broadest circle, we find a twofold reading of the story of Lot's daughters. The central idea around which all these circles are oriented is that of "transgression with good intention."

Lot's Daughters

These heroines receive the most extensive treatment in the *sugiyah*, appearing in both its opening and its conclusion. Lot's daughters, who transgress the prohibition of incest to seduce their father in the cave of Zoar (Gen. 19:30–38), appear at a critical and liminal stage in the formation of the Israelite nation's identity. They represent the complex relations of Israel with the Ammonites and the Moabites, and with gentile nations in general.

> Rabbah b. Bar Hana, quoting R. Yoḥanan, said: the verse, "For the ways of the Lord are right, and the just do walk in them, but transgressors do stumble therein," may be illustrated by the following example … Rather is it illustrated by Lot when his two daughters were with him. To these [the daughters], whose intention it was to do right, [applies], "the just do walk in them," whereas to him [Lot] whose intention it was to commit the transgression, [applies] "but transgressors do stumble therein" (*b. Nazir* 23a).

---

7 This structure allows the sages to present the stories chronologically, in order of *sublimation*: the primal sexual sin of incest between Lot and his daughters is followed by a lesser perversion, Tamar's copulation with her father-in-law, then by Yael—an uncertainly married woman—bedding another man, and, lastly and least sinfully, by a single woman (Ruth) subtly seducing a man on a threshing floor in Bethlehem. In comparing Yael to the Matriarchs—the "women in the tent" the sages imply that Yael does not have her own home and "tent" and so is perhaps unmarried (cf., e.g., Genesis *rabbah* 48:15). They may also have seen an ambiguity in the expression "a woman of the Kenite troupe" (*eshet Ḥever haKeini*, Judg. 4:17, 5:24). Ogden, *Helpmates, Harlots, Heroines*, 119–23.

Even as they justify the daughters' transgressions, the rabbis emphasize Lot's many sins: his decision to reside in Sodom, city of lechery, his copulation with his younger daughter, though he must then have been aware of his actions, and the quarrels he brought upon Abraham and his family, due to his parting with Abraham, and the birth of Ammon and Moab.[8] This leveling of heavy accusations against Lot is prevalent in Second Temple literature, which invariably describes him as greedy, arrogant, and incestuous, thus reflecting the rabbinic approach to the threatening foreigner.[9]

> R. Yoḥanan has said: The whole of the following verse ['Lot looked about him' Gen. 13:10] indicates his lustful character ... But [maybe Lot] was the victim of compulsion? [then] he should not have drunk wine the next evening. (*ibid.*)

The distinction between evil men and righteous women in this *sugiyah* derives from the tannaitic prohibition: "An Ammonite or a Moabite [man] is forbidden [in marriage to Israelite women] and forbidden for all time, but their women are permitted [to Israelite men] forthwith."[10] The rabbis' bifurcated solution will become a recurring model in our *sugiyah*: men are condemned as sinners, while women, despite having committed similar acts, are justified. Thus, we read at the end of the *sugiyah*:[11]

> R. Ḥiyya b. Abin said ... A man should always be as alert as possible to perform a commandment [*devar mitzvah*], for as reward for preceding the younger by one night, the elder daughter [of Lot] was privileged to appear [in the genealogical record] of the royal house of Israel, four generations earlier [i.e., as the ancestress of Ruth]. (*ibid.*, 23b–24a)

Lot's daughters represent the paradoxical "Other," who defines the Judean kingship and the messianic dynasty through adultery, carnal sin, and the breaking of boundaries. Despite their foreignness, they have undeniable affinities with Israel, thanks to their Abrahamic descent and their impact on the future of the Israelite nation: One daughter will generate Ruth the

---

8 Genesis *rabbah* 51:8–9; 52:2 (ed. Theodor-Albeck, 537–9, 542); *Aggadat Bereshit*, 25:1.
9 For examples see Kugel, *Traditions of the Bible*, 328–336.
10 *m. Yevamot* 8:3; *Pesiqta Rabbati* 42.
11 For expansion on the psychoanalytical aspects of this story, see Tsoffar, "Trauma."

Moabite, King David's grandmother, and the other Naamah the Ammonite, wife of King Solomon.[12]

Tamar

As described in Genesis 38, Tamar conceives twins by her father-in-law, Judah, yet the *sugiyah*'s authors and editors justify her actions. Though they bluntly characterize her as having "committed adultery" (*zintah*), they emphasize the sinful aspects of her behavior only to employ them in her justification.

> Ulla said: Both Tamar and Zimri committed adultery. Tamar committed adultery and gave birth to kings and prophets. Zimri committed adultery and on his account many tens of thousands of Israel perished. R. Naḥman b. Isaac said: *Greater is a transgression performed with good intention than a commandment performed without intent.* (*ibid.*, 23b)

Tamar's anticipation of Judah with a veiled face is described revealingly in other Midrashim, such as Genesis Rabbah 85:7: "She sat at '*Petaḥ Einayim*' and told him 'I am pure and available.'"[13]

In contrast to Tamar, the *sugiyah* harshly criticizes Zimri, the Israelite man who sinned with a Midianite woman (Num. 25:6–15), thereby underscoring the complexity of Israel's relations with Moab (whose women are also named in Numbers 25 as the objects of Israel's sexual transgressions) and revealing an enduring preoccupation with the formation of the Davidic line: Zimri sinned with the seductive women of Moab and Midian, whereas Tamar is a metaphorical descendant of Lot's daughters. As a key figure in the formation of the Davidic genealogy, Tamar repeats the actions of her mothers for the sake of her private and national salvation.

Yael

As her story emerges in the Song of Deborah, Yael's wayward acts earn divine justification. In our *sugiyah*, the riddle of the path, which opens the *sugiyah*, is teamed with the image of the "way" in which Sisera was seduced and killed.[14]

---

12 Also, Genesis *rabbah* 41:4 (ed. Theodor-Albeck, 391).
13 Genesis *rabbah* 85:7 (ed. Theodore-Albeck, 1039–1041).
14 "Ways" and "paths" appear in Judg. 5:6 in connection with Yael and in Prov. 30:18–20 in connection with an adulterous woman. See also Van Wijk-Bos, "Out of the Shadows."

Yael is described here as greater than the national mothers, those "tent-dwelling women" who yearned for children for their own sake and enjoyed their sexual union with their husbands.

> As it is written, "Blessed above women shall Yael be. ... Above women in the tent shall she be blessed" [Judg. 5:24]. Who are the "women in the tent"? Sarah, Rebecca, Rachel and Leah are meant. R. Yoḥanan said: That wicked wretch [Sisera] had sevenfold intercourse [with Yael] at that time, as it says. "He sank, he fell, he lay still at her feet ..." [Judg. 5:27].
>
> But [maybe] she derived pleasure from his intercourse? R. Yoḥanan said: All the favors of the wicked are evil to the righteous ... Thus it may properly be inferred that the good of such a one is an evil. (*ibid.*)

According to Rashi and other commentators, Yael's sexual suffering transforms the act of seduction into an act of "good intention," thereby justifying it. I wish to challenge this reading, which posits women's suffering as an ideal that exonerates their actions.[15] In this *sugiyah*, the association of Yael with the mothers of the Davidic dynasty, although she is not herself a mother, indicates that another commonality amongst the women was the decisive element in the sages' decision to thread these acts together.

As with the other Davidic heroines, Yael actively initiates seduction; and like them she is a foreign woman who took part in establishing the national identity. The *sugiyah* weaves together cases of brave figures who gained their reputation in the moment of setting up a temporary 'tent,' in a single act of seduction.[16] Lot's daughters, as well as Ruth and Tamar, are abandoned women facing the possibility of death, poverty or humiliation within their masculine environment. Similarly, Yael is in a liminal stage in which the tent is a "homeless home," an unprotected location, into which Sisera breaks; and there, of all places, Yael subdues him.[17] Once again, an act that takes place in the private sphere emerges as the locus of the national-political arena.[18]

---

15 For a discussion of cultural attitudes toward female suffering, see Julia Kristeva, *Black Sun: Depression and Melancholia* (New York: Columbia University Press, 1989); Elaine Scarry, *The Body in Pain* (Oxford: Oxford University Press, 2006), 3–27, 161–80; Benjamin, *The Bonds of Love*, 51-84.
16 Genesis *rabbah* 38:16 (ed. Theodore-Albeck, 493).
17 Cf. Freud's notion of the *unheimlich*, see Freud, "Uncanny."
18 Fuchs, *Sexual Politics*, 11–33.

Ruth

Ruth, descended from Lot's daughters, is the proof of our opening statement, since her tender mercies led to the birth of King David, her great-grandson. While David himself does not appear here—the sages seem to have avoided mentioning his name in the context of their condemnation of men accused of carnal transgressions—his messianic birth is implicit in the *sugiyah*, which takes care to describe Ruth's royal descent:

> The above text [states]: Rav Yehuda, citing Rav, said: A man should always occupy himself with the Torah and [its] precepts, even though it be for some ulterior motive, for the result will be that he will eventually do them without ulterior motive. For as reward for the forty-two sacrifices which the wicked Balak offered [Numbers 22–24], he was privileged to be the progenitor of Ruth. For R. Jose son of R. Hanina has said that Ruth was descended from Eglon [the grandson of Balak], king of Moab [Judg. 3:12–30]. R. Hiyya b. Abba, citing R. Yoḥanan, said: How do we know that the Holy One, blessed be He, does not withhold the reward even for a decorous expression [*siḥah na'ah*]? ... (*ibid.*, 23b)

Here the *sugiyah* makes clear that King David, who epitomized Jewish sovereignty, actually was descended and derived his power from a foreign royal dynasty.[19] We find here an example of the unique sexual ethics of royal families in ancient myths, in which the transgression of incest is normative.[20]

Seduction, temptation, and prohibited pairings repeat in a pattern, generation after generation, resulting in the founding of the noblest and most important Jewish dynasty. This pattern extends even beyond the foreign, marginal mothers of the dynasty to King David himself, whose sexual relationship with a married woman, Bathsheba, will result in the birth of King Solomon, builder of the Temple. The messianic mother, it seems, is not a private figure but a feminine archetype, reinforced by a collection of stories of transgressive heroines who are simultaneously *qedeshot* (harlots) and *qedoshot* (holy). At the end of the Book of Ruth (4:11–17), all these "obscene" women are acknowledged as the mothers of King David and hailed as worthy and righteous.

---

19 Ruth Zuṭa 2: 9.
20 See introduction to Ch. 5.

The example of Ruth, allegedly adduced as proof of R. Yehuda's saying, "A man should always occupy himself with the Torah and [its] precepts, even though it be for some ulterior motive," (*b. Nazir* 23a) in fact sides with R. Naḥman's daring statement, *gedolah aveirah lishmah*, thus reinforcing the feminine line constructed in the *sugiyah*. The links between the women, combined with the complex relations of Israel with Ammon and Moab from the nation's earliest days through the establishment of the kingdom, place the *sugiyah*'s heroines within a broad historical and political spectrum.

The notions of "performing a commandment" (*devar mitzvah*) and "decorous expression" (*siḥah na'ah*), which appear in the Midrash on Lot's daughters, may be applied to all of the women in our *sugiyah*. All these stories of seduction serve as examples of rabbinic justification of the very same "path." Again and again, the sages fault the male party, for both intention and action, while judging the female party as justified in her intent and act. In each of these cases the male figure is high-ranking, and the *sugiyah* condemns him harshly: Lot, father of the nations, Zimri, head of a leading Shimeonite family, Sisera, the army general, and Eglon and Balak, Moabite kings. Meanwhile, the women, invariably portrayed as foreign, break boundaries and obfuscate the meaning of the terms "transgression" and "commandment."

THE BACKGROUND OF THE *SUGIYAH*—ḤERUTA'S STORY AND "THE REVOLUTION OF INTENTION"

There is one more story which, though not biblical, nonetheless sheds light on our understanding of the biblical women's roles in the Talmud. The story of Ḥeruta in *b. Qiddushin* has parallels to our *sugiyah* and thus may help us decipher the gendered nature of the term *aveirah lishmah*.

The discussion in which the *sugiyah* of *gedolah aveirah lishmah* appears in *b. Nazir*, concerning intention and action, vows and their annulment, begins with a gender distinction.[21] The opening Mishnah states the case of a woman who has made a Nazirite vow and subsequently broken it by drinking wine and letting herself be exposed to a corpse. Unbeknownst to her, however, her husband had annulled her vow (*Nazir* 23a: the authority of a woman's father or husband to annul her vows is set down in Numbers 30). Should she be punished, since her intention was to sin? According to the first opinion stated in

---

21 In *b. Horayot* 10a–b, this *sugiyah* is found in the context of a discussion of a king who inadvertently sins, implying the idea of the sinner Messiah.

the Mishnah, she is not to be flogged, because her sinful deed was voided by her husband's annulment. According to R. Yehuda, however, she is to be beaten by the court because of her intention to sin, which still requires God's forgiveness. A *baraita* cites Num. 30:13—"Her husband has annulled them, and the Lord will forgive her"—declaring that this verse refers to the instance described in the Mishnah. Every time R. Akiva came to this verse, the narrative continues, he would weep, since her intention was to sin.[22]

The *sugiyah* goes on to present cases of irreconcilable gaps between good intentions and transgressions, as described in Lev. 5:17: "If any of you sin *without knowing it*, doing any of the things that by the Lord's commandments ought not to be done, you have incurred guilt, and are subject to punishment." The Talmudic debate emphasizes the fear of sin, which underlies R. Akiva's sorrow and the requirement to atone even for bad thoughts or evil intentions.[23] Unlike the Mishnah, which is preoccupied with consequences, the Talmud emphasizes intentions and atonement, the psychological aspect of the person's action. Thus, we see the development from the Mishnah and the *baraita* to the Talmud in emphasizing intention over action, in a process referred to as "a revolution of intention."[24]

The explicitly gendered nature of the Mishnah distinguishes between the woman who makes the vow and the husband who annuls it, the woman who is accused of sinning and the male sages who debate whether to punish or excuse her actions. This distinction becomes stronger in the descriptions of the heroines of the Davidic dynasty and of Yael, women who transgress with clearly positive (*lishmah*) intentions, alongside men who, acting similarly, are found guilty because they lack worthy intentions. The women here represent *intention with its accompanying action*, whereas the men represent *action without intention*.

What are these "intentions," which become a moral criterion for judging men negatively and women positively? I would suggest that, according to the sages, an action that is punishable by death for a man—most sexual transgressions fall under the rubric of *yehareg ve'al ya'avor*, "let him be killed rather than transgress"—may be permissible for a woman in a time of great need or for personal or national salvation.[25] Women's acts of seduction and

---

22 For parallels, see *Tosefta Nazir* 3:14; b. *Qiddushin* 81b; y. *Nazir* 4:3, 53a.
23 Hirshman, "Clarification of the Term Sin-Fearing," *Tribute to Sarah* (Jerusalem: Magnes, 1999), 155-164.
24 Urbach, *Halakhah*, 130-8.
25 On this category, see b. *Yoma* 82a and the commentary of Rashi *ad loc*. Of course, the case of Ḥeruta doesn't fall directly under the rubric of *yehareg ve-al ya'avor*. According to the sages,

sexual trickery are given exegetical and midrashic encouragement in cases where the sages consider them to be a matter of salvation and *tiqqun*, as opposed to men's sexual transgressions, which are considered irreparably damaging and dangerous.[26]

The case of Ḥeruta sheds light on our discussion by emphasizing the differences between male and female intentions and their corresponding consequences. Ḥeruta's story concludes by citing the same verse, Num. 30:13, as that cited in our *baraita*. Here, too, in a parallel hitherto not discussed by scholars, we have a female character who acts in a seductive manner to save herself, with the sages passing contradictory halakhic judgments upon the man and the woman, based on their intentions:

> R. Hiyya bar Ashi, each time he fell upon his face [in supplicatory prayers], would say: May the Merciful One rescue me from the *yeṣer hara* [the evil inclination]. One day his wife overheard him. She said to herself: But for so many years he has abstained from me! How come he says that? One day he was studying in his garden. She adorned herself and walked by him. He said to her: Who are you? She said: I am Ḥeruta [a well known prostitute], I have just returned today. He claimed her. She said to him: Go bring me that pomegranate from the treetop. He jumped up and brought it to her. When he came home, his wife was adding kindling to the oven. He climbed inside the oven and sat there. She said to him: What is this? He said to her: Such and such is what happened. She said to him: It was I! He paid no heed to her until she gave him proof. He said to her: But nevertheless, my intention was evil. All his life that righteous man fasted until he died thereof. Even as it was taught: "Her husband has annulled them, and the Lord shall forgive her." (*b. Qiddushin* 81b)

In Ḥeruta's case, too, there is an essential, gendered distinction between the ways in which the husband and the wife negotiate sexuality, and the sages emphasize its moral aspect. The disguise was Ḥeruta's attempt to bring *tiqqun* to her home. Therefore, she can confess and say "It was I" and hope that this will settle the matter both for her and for her husband. By contrast, the situation

---

it is forbidden for a married woman to prostitute herself, but since Ḥeruta knew that the man she was seducing was her husband, she is considered blameless.

26 On the philosophical and psychoanalytic aspects of the term "transgression" see Foucault, Bataille, and Stein.

ends tragically for R. Hiyya.[27] His retort, "nevertheless, my intention was evil," derives neither from a negative attitude toward his wife nor from a rejection of her. Rather, these words reflect his dichotomous view of the world—permitted and forbidden, good and bad—and his difficulty in reconciling the two. In his own eyes, his negative intention damns his action. Both attitudes and judgments hinge upon intention: R Hiyya intended to commit a transgression, whereas "Ḥeruta" intended to bring about *tiqqun*.[28]

Both Ḥeruta's story and our *sugiyah* portray their heroines as capable of combining sexual seduction and *tiqqun*: They accept their sexuality and know how to use it. In a similar vein, Shlomo Naeh draws the meaning of Ḥeruta's story from the double meaning of her name, which refers both to abstinence and to sexual promiscuity.[29] All these women are described as pushing boundaries, using wine and sinning, yet their motivations still justify their behavior. The sages show that women are capable of managing *fluid identities*, disguises and transgressions while maintaining their covenant with God. Men, by contrast, are portrayed as rigid sinners who meet a tragic end.[30] This is true of R. Hiyya, who cannot bear the transgression, as well as of the other censured men: Lot, Zimri, Sisera, Balak, and Eglon. They are joined in the wider context by the husband who annuls his wife's vows and the weeping R. Akiva, whose uncompromising understandings of reality ultimately negate the unity of intention and action.

The end of Ḥeruta's tale and her vindication, which is signified by the quotation of the verse "and the Lord will forgive her" (Num. 30:13)—as in the similar justifications of Yael, Tamar, Ruth and Lot's daughters—therefore

---

27 Shlomo Naeh suggests that this is a late addition, which counters the Christian model by emphasizing the failure of ascetic life. Following his seduction by his wife, R. Hiyya b. Ashi's asceticism deteriorates and ends in prostitution ("Ḥeruta: A Talmudic Reflection on Freedom and Celibacy," in *Issues in Talmudic Research: Conference Commemorating the Fifth Anniversary of the Passing of Ephraim E. Urbach* (Jerusalem: Israel Academy of Sciences and Humanities, 2001), 11–13, 26–7). I suggest, however, that Ḥeruta's act demonstrates that only women may have good intentions motivating their seductive actions, unlike men, who ultimately are destroyed by their sexual drive. Referring to Doniger's "two distinct genders of the mythology of the bedtrick," we might say that this story shows again the repressive hierarchy of this pattern, since even "when a woman does turn a bedtrick... [it] is [with] her own husband, who has been sleeping with another woman." Doniger, *Bedtrick*, 196.

28 Rosen-Zvi points out that although R. Hiyya tries to avoid the *yeṣer hara* as much as possible, he is continuously engrossed with it, Ishai Rosen-Zvi, "The Evil Impulse, Sexuality and Yichud: A Chapter of Talmudic Anthropology," *Theory and Criticism* 14 (1999): 55-84. For more on the story, Ruth Calderon, *The Market, The Home, The Heart* (Jerusalem: Keter, 2001), 49–57.

29 Naeh, "Ḥeruta," 16, 22–3. On the connections between Ḥeruta and Tamar, see Rosen-Zvi, "The Evil Impulse," 81; Doniger, *Bedtrick*, 267.

30 Urbach, *Sages*, 437–58.

reflects a revolutionary opinion. The sages justify active, seductive women based on their intentions, whereas they criticize men for actions that have no deeper meaning or link between action and intention. This gender and moral distinction is rooted in the mishnaic scene of the woman who is responsible for her actions before God, even though her husband had annulled her vow. In contrast to the punishment and guilt emphasized in the Mishnah, however, the Talmudic debate chooses to emphasize the power of intentions.

AVEIRAH LISHMAH AND *DEVAR MITZVAH*

Before proposing solutions to the enigmatic meaning of *aveirah lishmah* based on late kabbalistic thought, let us examine a conceptual and linguistic parallel that the sages present at the conclusion of the *sugiyah*, in stating that Lot's daughters seduced him for the sake of "performing a commandment" (*devar mitzvah*).[31] This expression is even more daring than *aveirah lishmah*, since *devar mitzvah* is devoid of transgressive connotations. As I have noted, Yael's appearance in conjunction with the mothers of the Davidic dynasty suggests that motherhood is not the only measure of the justification of their deeds: The very act of seduction is equated with a commandment! The consequences—the birth of the Messiah and national deliverance—justify female intent.

By joining the idea of *devar mitzvah* with that of *aveirah lishmah*, the *sugiyah*'s editors indicate their approval of female sexual liberties performed with good intentions. These unique, superficially paradoxical terms reflect the sages' exegetical courage. Had the expression *aveirah lishmah* appeared by itself, its meaning and conceptual validity might have been restricted. But its reinforcement with the invocation of *devar mitzvah* at the conclusion indicates the careful considerations that lie behind the editing of our *sugiyah*. These bold statements do not arise out of permissiveness. In both of the *sugiyah*'s appearances, they are accompanied by strong emotional reactions: in *b. Nazir* (23a), by R. Akiva's weeping and the statement "let them grieve that are fain to grieve," and in *b. Horayot* (10b) by R. Yoḥanan b. Zakkai's expression of joy. These suggest how significant and weighty is the ruling "greater is a transgression

---

31 The term *devar mitzvah* (religious deed) and the words for speech (*mesaper, medaber*) are all used by the sages as euphemisms for sexual activity; e.g., *b. Eruvin* 100b, *Nedarim* 20a, *Ketubot* 13a, *Leviticus Rabbah* 26:8 (ed. Margaliot, 611), *Lamentations rabbah* 24 (ed. Buber, 28), etc. The end of our *sugiyah* also appears at the beginning of a *sugiyah* in *b. Bava Qamma* 38b concerning relationships with the gentiles; Marc Hirshman, *Torah for the Entire World: A Universalist School of Rabbinic Thought* (Tel Aviv: Hakibbutz Hameuchad, 1999), 54; Urbach, *Sages*, 524–54.

with good intention," and how radical is the description of the women's seductive acts as the "performance of a commandment."

Transgression with Good Intent: Kabbalistic versus Halakhic Literature

Scholars and commentators have suggested different definitions of the phrase *aveirah lishmah*. In legal readings, they tend to describe it as signifying "permission to perform a transgression out of a positive motive," or "rejection of one norm in favor of a loftier one."[32] English translations such as Jeremy Kalmanofsky's "sin for the sake of God" or Nahum Rakover's "violation of the law in order to preserve it" retain the term's general meaning without elucidating its direct context.[33]

Rashi and the Tosafists, commenting on our *sugiyah*, read *aveirah lishmah* to mean "a transgression for the sake of a commandment" or "for the sake of heaven." This interpretation moderates the Midrash's radical overtones and overlooks the *sugiyah*'s literary and thematic context, teaching that the transgression turns out to be a commandment on account of its intentional and consequential strata.[34] It ignores the explosiveness of the sin latent in the term, as well as the implications arising from the depiction of women as sinners who nonetheless are justified. Tamar "committed adultery," Lot's daughters are described in another Midrash as having "intended to commit adultery," and Yael is suspected of having enjoyed copulating with Sisera.[35] All these examples, I suggest, should be construed as belonging to a single dialectical archetype: the seductive act of sexual transgression performed for the sake of salvation.

Contrary to the legal and halakhic pragmatism whereby the transgression with good intention is perceived as an act whose end sanctifies the means, kabbalistic and hasidic readings emphasize the term's inherent paradox, exposing the tension between good and evil and the link between holiness and

---

32 Rakover, *Ends that Justify the Means*, 15–26; Eliav Shochetman, "Ma'aseh haba'ah be-aveirah," *Israel Law Review* 17, no. 3 (1982): 383-387. However, it does not have a halakhic status. According to Lichtenstein: "As a prescriptive category, the currently popular notion of *aveirah lishmah* has no halakhic standing whatsoever." Lichtenstein, "Ehic," 107.
33 Kalmanofsky, "Sins."
34 See the commentary of Obadiah Seforno on Gen. 19:18, and the comments of Rashi and the Tosafists to our *sugiyah* in b. *Nazir* and *Horayot*.
35 See the opinion of R. Simon in Genesis *rabbah* 51:9 (ed. Theodor-Albeck, 538); According to *Pesiqta rabbati* 42, "the daughters of Lot were not thinking proper thoughts," but still God who knows "hearts" forgave them. In *Aggadat Bereshit* 25:1 the sages use a harsher expression, saying that they deserved to be "burned by fire" for committing incest with their father.

transgression. This concept has been studied in depth in light of its meanings and ramifications in the messianic Sabbatean movement in the seventeenth and eighteenth centuries. The Sabbateans understood *aveirah lishmah* as "transgression for the sake of transgressing," or "a sin done for its own sake"—that is, for the sake of breaking down the existing order and rabbinic concepts were deployed in the creation of Sabbatean ideas: the sanctification of transgression and the justification of sin were tied to a new messianic doctrine, in which the breaking of boundaries became the main tool for separating the divine sparks (*niṣoṣot*) from the husks (*qelippot*) that confined them.[36] In certain strains of the more radical Frankist doctrine of redemption of the late eighteenth and nineteenth centuries, deliberate sexual transgression reflected the position that "to nullify the Torah is to uphold it."[37] Hasidic teachings on the notion of "transgression with good intention" focus on repentance and *tiqqun*.[38] Our *sugiyah*'s representation of the seductive acts of Yael and the heroines of the Davidic dynasty laid the foundations for these constructions. It created an inspiring dialectical model that left a mark on posterity.

AVEIRAH LISHMAH ACCORDING TO R. MOSES ḤAYYIM LUZZATTO

In *Sefer Qinea'at H' Ṣeva'ot*, R. Moses Ḥayyim Luzzatto begins his discussion of *aveirah lishmah* by expressing the following concerns:

> Know that this is a secret in the category of *emergency rulings* [*hora'ot sha'ah*] ... And Yael's act was a *transgression with good intention*. And truly, these matters are secrets of the King for whose exposure one must risk his heart, and were it not that we had to extract this great stumbling block from our midst, my heart would not allow me to utter a word about this matter. (ibid., 95)

---

36 Gershom Scholem, *Sabbatai Ṣevi: The Mystical Messiah, 1626–1676* (Princeton: Princeton University Press, 1973), 683–774; Isaiah Tishby, *The Wisdom of the Zohar: An Anthology of Texts* (Oxford: Littman Library of Jewish Civilization, 1989), 1:26–30; Liebes, *On Sabbateanism*, 53–76; Idel, *Messianic Mystics*, 183–211; Elliot R. Wolfson, *Venturing Beyond: Law and Morality in Kabbalistic Mysticism* (New York: Oxford University Press, 2006), 232–85.
37 Scholem, *Messianic Idea*.
38 Kauffman, *In all Your Ways*, 523–71. Surprisingly, the expression *aveirah lishmah* never explicitly appears in the *Zohar*, but the concept is implied in the dramatic opening of the *Idra Rabbah* (*Zohar*, III: 127b), in its quotation of the verse "It is time to act for God, for thy law has been broken" (*et la-asot lashem heferu toratekha*, Ps. 119:126). Since the purpose of violating the law is to preserve it, Elliot Wolfson suggests that we classify the concept as "hypernomian" rather than antinomian; see Wolfson, *Venturing*, 186.

Luzzatto's concern lest the secrets be misused is directed at the Sabbateans. Despite accusations that he was himself a Sabbatean, Luzzatto's book formally rejected Sabbateanism; at the same time, however, he presented ideas which could be interpreted as dangerously subversive and related to that movement.[39] Luzzatto's most striking statement sheds new light on our *sugiyah*:

> About these passages Scripture says that "the ways of the Lord are right" (Hosea 14:10). Know that the corruption began upon the Serpent's intercourse with Eve, when he deposited filth in her. And because of this she descended into the husks [*qelippot*] as was mentioned above. And this damage cannot be rectified except by way of what is written: "and the women shall be ravished" (Zech. 14:2)... And how immense is the grief of the holy women, the women of Israel, who will need to endure this great evil. And see that this corruption began when "the women of Zion were abused" (Lam. 5:11). Therefore, this purification will end when "the women will be ravished." But know that even this grief will only occur at the very end, when the *tiqqun* is about to be completed. (Ibid., 96–97)

Discerning the overtly gendered character of the notion of *aveirah lishmah* in the Talmud, Luzzatto constructs upon it a theosophical, sociological and eschatological commentary. As a kabbalist and exegete, he develops the rabbinic expression into a messianic and mystical statement while drawing conclusions regarding the feminine role in the redemptive process.[40] In this interpretation, *tiqqun* has been and will forever be brought into the world by women alone, in order to appease the *Sitra aḥra* (the demonic Other Side) and distance it from holiness, while drawing the *Shekhinah* up from the *qelippot*, sweetening and mending her. In the kabbalistic perception, the toughest battle takes place at the dangerous and sensitive connecting point between heaven and earth, the *Shekhinah*.

---

39 Isaiah Tishby, *Studies in Kabbalah and Its Branches* (Jerusalem: Magnes Press, 1993), III: 729–808.

40 Ibid, 729–808; Tishby, *Paths*, 169–85. For more on Luzzatto's tendency to rely on Talmudic and Zoharic sources, see Rubin, *Luzzatto*. For an analysis of Luzzatto's thoughts on gender, Elliot R. Wolfson, "*Tiqqun ha-Shekhinah*: Redemption and the Overcoming of Gender Dimorphism in the Messianic Kabbalah of Moses Hayyim Luzzatto," *History of Religions* 36 (1997): 289–332. According to Wolfson, in Luzzatto's thought "Redemption in its ultimate sense does not signify the perpetual paring of male and female, but the reconstitution of androgyny in the Godhead in which the gender dimorphism is superseded" (ibid, 291), an idea that I will try to challenge later (Part 3, fn 3, 84).

Luzzatto sheds light on the link between the feminine figures and their sexual acts: Eve and her copulation with the serpent, the heroines of our *sugiyah*, and all future women.[41] "The women of Israel who will need to endure this great evil" are identified with the *sefirah* of *Malkhut* (represented by Eve), which is entangled with the *qelippot* and captured by the evil power. The *sugiyah*'s heroines symbolize the mythical process that will determine the results of the battle against the *Sitra aḥra*, but only once the fighting passes through the danger zone of the *Shekhinah* and its corporeal parallel, the woman's womb.[42] The meaning of *aveirah lishmah* is thus discerned and elucidated both in mystical terms and as a gendered distinction between the masculine and feminine roles in the redemptive process:

> And all of this which we have said pertains only to women, because they are *qarqa olam*, who actualize *tiqqun* this way [by the use of their bodies—RK]. But this is irrelevant to men, for whom illicit relations and adultery do not facilitate *tiqqun* at all. ... And even all the commandments which are less important than illicit relations should not be transgressed, Heaven forbid (*Sefer Qinea'at H' Ṣeva'ot*, 98).

The expression *qarqa olam* alludes to a statement attributed to Abaye in *b. Sanhedrin* 74b, according to which Esther, because she was *qarqa olam*, was not required to die for her sexual transgressions, despite their public nature. Men, however, are fully accountable for their carnal misbehavior.[43] The Tosafists, commenting on Abaye's statement, again ask why Yael's act is not comparable to Esther's. In my understanding, the sages consciously refrain from identifying Yael and the Davidic maternal line as *qarqa olam*, because they are perceived as heroines *who chose to take responsibility over their actions*, and not as passive women who were violated.[44] Rather than exempting the women as rape victims, the sages perceive in their behavior

---

41 Genesis *rabbah* 20:20 (ed. Theodor-Albeck, 195). Parallel sources are discussed by Urbach, *Sages*, 169; Boyarin, *Carnal Israel*, 77-106.
42 Idel, *Kabbalah and Eros*; Yehuda Liebes, *Studies in Jewish Myth and Jewish Messianism* (Albany: SUNY Press, 1993).1-64; Daniel Abrams, *The Female Body of God in Kabbalistic Literature: Embodied Forms of Love and Sexuality in the Divine Feminine* (Jerusalem: Magnes Press, 2004), 91–104.
43 Above, fn. 4, 28; Aaron Lichtenstein, "Aveirah Lishmah in Halakha and Thought," *The Other: Between Man and Himself and His Fellow*, eds. Haim Deutsch and Menachem Ben-Sasson (Tel Aviv: Yedioth Aharonoth, 2001), 106–9.
44 Rakover, *Ends that Justify the Means*, 40–2.

voluntary acts of "transgression" with a purpose—"transgression with good intention."

Luzzatto connects these two concepts, *qarqa olam* and *aveirah lishmah*, creating a fascinating synthesis. On the one hand, he distinguishes between Esther's act and Yael's, between rape and "transgression with good intention." On the other hand, by referring to the female community at large as *qarqa olam*, he emphasizes women's unique ability to redeem the *sefirah* of *Malkhut* from the grip of the *Sitra aḥra* through a sexual act. His kabbalistic position extracts a new meaning from these seemingly contradictory halakhic terms. Though he perceives womankind as *qarqa olam* (by including in this notion both the voluntary acts of seduction and the abuse of Zion's women), still certain women are justified in using their bodies and sexuality for deliverance by means of proactive and volitional acts.[45]

Luzzatto's text emphasizes the original meaning of the term *aveirah lishmah* as it was understood by the sages: women are able to save lives and bring about redemption through sexual seduction. To be sure, according to Luzzatto, this can take place only at an extraordinary moment, "when the *tiqqun* is about to be completed," and only as a singular act that follows a *hora'at sha'ah* (emergency ruling). But the editing of the stories in our *sugiyah* already extracts the act from its private and specific context, turning the astonishing acts of individuals into an archetypical pattern. Stories of personal struggles are transformed into a narrative of "great mothers" of salvation, who throughout the generations seduce and perform transgressions "with good intention."

I would like to dispute Isaiah Tishby's claim that Luzzatto's interpretation is based upon Sabbatean notions and to argue that the meaning he attaches to the expression *aveirah lishmah* in fact lies at the root of the rabbinic approach to the editing of our *sugiyah*.[46] The term *aveirah lishmah* implies a worthy act performed in the women's name (*lishman*), beginning with the first woman, continuing with the heroines in the *sugiyah*, and

---

45 Jonathan Garb suggested that the historical context of this description is the mass rape of Jewish women in the Khmelnytsky pogroms in 1648. In Garb's reading, Luzzatto presents a parallel process by which men, too, must suffer like the Messiah in order to bring about salvation through sexual sins and "husks." I argue, however, that Luzzatto's reading of the Talmud distinguishes between male and female roles in the redemptive process. Jonathan Garb, "Gender and Sexuality in the Luzzatto Controversy in Early 18th-century Italy" (presentation, Stanford University, 2011).

46 Isaiah Tishby, *Paths of Faith and Heresy* (Ramat Gan: Masada Publishing, 1964), 184–5.

ending with posterity. Moshe Halbertal, discussing what he calls the "principle of charity," has described midrashic activity as follows:

> Commentators write different chapters in the same story in succession, as each author attempts to pick up from the chapter his predecessor had composed, so that the completed story would be presented in the best way possible aesthetically.... Many times midrash complements the biblical story with an additional account, which interprets the remaining parts of the story in the best way possible.[47]

On the mythopoeic level, we see how this principle operates in the emergence of generations of interpretations, from the daring rabbinic exegeses of the story of the biblical women to the way in which Luzzatto sheds positive light upon it. This is not merely an aesthetic reading; Luzzatto's text cultivates a new meaning that grows out of the language and moral values of the earlier story and enhances it both conceptually and mythically. The aesthetic refinement becomes an antinomian ethic. Alongside the justification of the *sugiyah*'s heroines, the entire commentary process is justified, as well as the paradoxical axial perspective that expands into mystical meanings joining the biblical, rabbinic, and kabbalistic worlds.

According to the sages, the five biblical women were *able* to use sexual deception to bring salvation. Luzzatto, by contrast, asserts that all women will be *obligated* to act in this deviant manner to bring redemption. Here, of course, Luzzatto extends the paradoxical nature of the origins of the Davidic line. He does not limit his evaluation to female biblical heroines of the past but applies his interpretation *to the present and future as well*. In so doing, he weakens the position of women: All of them are *qarqa olam*, and all are supposed to be raped to bring about redemption.[48] At the same time, by vastly extending the subversive readings of the sages, he expands the preexisting antinomian idea of redemption.

---

47 Moshe Halbertal, *Interpretative Revolutions in the Making* (Jerusalem: Magnes, 1997), 190.
48 Elliot Wolfson states: "Redemption signifies the restoration of the feminine to the masculine." Wolfson, *Venturing Beyond*, 276. Luzzatto's description of the rape of the women shows that this "restoration" of the women and their hierarchical negation to the masculine, happens *before* the phase of salvation and the *Tiqqun*. It is an inevitable and tragic component of ḥevlei mashiaḥ (the "birth-pangs" of the Messiah), before his arrival. Thus, I would suggest that Luzzatto, like many other kabbalists, sees in the ascension of the *Shekhinah* and her independence from and equality with the masculine a manifestation of the achievement of the ultimate redemption.

WOMEN AS THE OTHER: GENDER, LANGUAGE, AND POLITICS

Why do the sages describe the women in our *sugiyah* as seductresses and sinners, who use their sins to bring about redemption? This question echoes the paradoxical concept of a "transgression with good intention." The rabbinic myth amplified and developed in Luzzatto's thought may be interpreted in different ways. I shall endeavor to fill gaps and expose new facets of the literary, conceptual and gendered riddle with which I opened this chapter by offering three different, somewhat contradictory explanations.

The Essentialist Solution—Woman as "Vessel" and "Cocoon"[49]

The identification of women with matter, passivity, and subjugation derives from the assumption that they can impact reality only through the use of their bodies.[50] In the symbolic world of the sages, women are the "oven" and the "bread," the "tent" and the "house" (*debeithu*).[51] For the most part, they operate in the private sphere, within the narrow confines of their homes. This approach interprets women's seductive acts as intended to pleasure the seduced men, and it perceives feminine sexuality as a tool in the service of the patriarchal world, used for the purpose of fertility. In this reading, the Davidic mothers and Yael are seductive by their very "nature" and "essence," and therefore they are presented as righteous seductresses. Behind the seemingly daring praises, this reading observes the oppressive paternalistic pattern, which lacks an independent female subject.[52]

An opposing but equally essentialist viewpoint emphasizes the feminine empowerment inherent in a depiction of the women as possessed by their

---

49 b. *Sanhedrin* 22b: "R. Samuel b. Unya said in the name of Rav: A woman [before marriage] is a cocoon, and concludes a covenant only with him who transforms her [into] a [useful] vessel."

50 On Aristotle's matter–form, nature–culture, women–men dichotomies, see Ortner, "Nature to Culture"; Barkai, *Science, Magic and Mythology*, 37–55; Charles Mopsik, *Sex of the Soul: The Vicissitudes of Sexual Difference in Kabbalah*, ed. Daniel Abrams (Los Angeles: Cherub Press, 2005), 5–52.

51 Marc Hirshman, "Changing Foci of Holiness: Honi and His Grandsons," *Tura* 1 (1989): 109–118.; Charlotte E. Fonrobert, *Menstrual Purity: Rabbinic and Christian Reconstruction of Biblical Gender* (Stanford: Stanford University Press, 2000), 40–67.

52 As Ishai Rosen-Zvi argues, "The woman is not included in the group of those seduced by the evil inclination.... She, in a certain sense, is the evil inclination incarnate.... The attraction is in a single direction from the seducing woman to the attracted man." Rosen-Zvi, "The Evil Impulse," 65–6.

bodies, due to their proximity to God. In kabbalistic terminology, the women are described as close to the spirit of "the Tree of Knowledge," in which good and evil are intertwined, a state allowing them to move from harlotry to sanctity. According to this perception, it is actually the body that is the vehicle for the *tiqqun*, on both the personal and the national-messianic levels. The human body reflects God's image, and therefore acts of sexual union performed with worthy intent resolve the apparent paradox of "transgression with good intention." The women, who are in charge of giving birth, correspond with God's spirit of creation, and hence their seductive acts constitute the "soil" (*qarqa olam*) from which the *tiqqun* of the created world will emerge.

Feminine Seduction—An Ethnic-Political Perspective

A characterization of women that focuses on seduction reflects the ethno-political reality within which the sages operated. Behind the praises and fears encapsulated in the notion of "transgression with good intention" hides their identification with the foreign women. Viewed from the perspective of seductive determinism, the female body resembles the Jews, who are forced by their weakness to seduce both God and gentiles.[53] The choice to tell and retell a myth of heroines who repeatedly perform the same seductive act reinforces the text's subversive streak, alongside its authors' weakness. Time and again the sages tell of their attempts to overcome their detractors and use "the power of the weak." As James Scott has observed, "In this respect, subordinate groups are complicitous in contributing to a sanitized official transcript, for that is one way they cover their tracks."[54] Elaborating on Scott's reading, Daniel Boyarin shows how seduction is meant to bridge cultural tensions, including the intolerable tension of difference and otherness.

The seductive acts are projected onto *foreign* women, a representation that liberates men from the dread of desire and plays on the stereotype of the "gentile prostitute." Fear of seduction reflects yearning for collaboration with the foreign and the conqueror, the wish to be like him and be released from isolating strictures. That these foreign women generate a Jewish monarchy reinforces Boyarin's idea that "the approved [rabbinic] practice for Jews is gendered feminine, while the behavior of the Romans is gendered masculine."[55]

---

53 For example: *Pesiqta de-Rab Kahana*, 23:4 (ed. Mandelbaum, 337).
54 James Scott, *Domination and the Arts of Resistance: Hidden Transcripts* (New Haven: Yale University Press, 1990), 2:87; quoted in Boyarin, *Dying for God*, 45.
55 Ibid., 71.

This observation also applies to the Ammonites and Moabites. Foreign rule and power, like foreign women and sexual desire, are all "seductive and dangerous." The sages, who perceive their people as being like a weak woman, undermine their conquerors by using seduction (and the image of *qarqa olam*), thereby overcoming the sense of difference, contempt and alienation.

The punishment of the men in our *sugiyah* could represent a response to the wildness of the body, jailed inside the soul. Applying a Foucauldian reading, we may say that the *sugiyah* teaches us something grim about the triumph of the spirit:

> The man described for us, whom we are invited to free, is already in himself the effect of a subjection much more profound than himself. A "soul" inhabits him and brings him to existence, which is itself a factor in the mastery that power exercises over the body. The soul is the effect and instrument of a political anatomy; *the soul is the prison of the body*.[56]

Paradoxically, women's sexuality saves their lives, yet by transforming them from subject to object, it retrospectively weakens the very device used in their actions. Their source of power is in itself is a source of weakness. The *sugiyah* curbs all things threatening and wild in the woman's body and contends with her unbridled sexuality by transforming her into a "righteous" and "redemptive" figure. Sexuality becomes a domesticated force, meant "for good intention."

These feminine heroines play an important role in the imagined and creative sphere of the exegetes. The seductive woman is an object onto which fantasies may be projected and to which daring acts may be attributed—especially when she is not Jewish and thus can be made to disappear from the story later on.[57]

Gender and Language

The development of the singular expression *aveirah lishmah* testifies to creative rabbinic efforts to reflect through language an experience that unites opposites and resolves complexities. An existing language that is insufficient to contain the wealth of ideas within it requires the invention of new terminologies. The paradoxical idiom we have been studying concerns female sexuality and seductive

---

[56] Michel Foucault, *Discipline and Punishment: The Birth of the Prison* (New York: Vintage Books, 1979), 30.
[57] Fuchs, *Sexual Politics*, 7–33.

behavior, and its subsequent justification or condemnation by rabbinic interpreters. Rare coinages such as *aveirah lishmah*, *devar mitzvah* and *siḥah na'ah* suggest an attempt by the sages to engage in a general discourse on sexuality, in which, as Elliot Wolfson puts it, "Boundaries of law arise in response to transgression, but transgression is not possible without boundaries of law."[58]

The justification and encouragement of female sexuality offers a glimpse into the sages' anxiety about their own sexuality and their stubborn battle against desire.[59] This preoccupation exposes a masculine interest in women's "otherness," which does not require a struggle against desire but permits paradoxes and complexities.[60] In projecting "transgression with good intention" onto women, the sages create a new language to describe women's complex relationship with their own bodies, as well as the powers of seduction and of human fertility.

In feminist writings, sexuality and language mutually reflect one another. Thus, for example, Luce Irigaray, Hélène Cixous, and Bracha Ettinger describe the experience of the female body as interwoven with the language used to describe it, so that a woman continuously encounters the Other within herself, entailing constant hiding and seduction.[61] Our *sugiyah* moves from the question of permission and prohibition to the paradox of *aveirah lishmah*, reflecting the contradiction inherent in feminine seduction through four recurrent stories in which the sexual acts are described as "performance of a commandment." All of these descriptions move away from an ethical discourse toward a metaphorical and erotic language. *Aveirah lishmah* can imply both female empowerment and oppression: It identifies a woman with her body, jails her inside it, and forces her to redeem herself physically. The sages witnessed, contended with, and attempted to decipher this gendered difference. From their discussions emerge expressions of appreciation, wonderment, fear and even jealousy—they understand that there is a different, feminine, wayward path, one that is foreign to them and yet meaningful.

The seemingly binary distinction underlying the *sugiyah* turns out to be a rich axis of characteristics that can be traversed, even if only within the exegetical realm. Men and women, good and evil, permitted and forbidden,

---

58 Wolfson, *Venturing Beyond*, 268.
59 Urbach, *World*, 437–458; Urbach, *Sages*, 471–83; Boyarin, *Carnal*, 107-33.
60 Admiel Kosman, *Femininity in the Spiritual World of the Talmudic Story* (Tel Aviv: Hakibbutz Hameuchad, 2008), 32–51.
61 Irigaray, *Speculum*, 65–79; Cixous and Clement, *Newly*, 105–48; Ettinger, *The Matrixial Borderspace*.

voluntary seduction alongside passivity and oppression—in joining together these apparently binary terms, the rabbis posit a spectrum of movements that reflect the diversity of the term "transgression with good intention" and challenge the oppositional interpretation of the concept. The *sugiyah* expands the definition of the "good and worthy" and can also contain paradoxical concepts: good is not necessarily tied to evil, but it is part of an elaborate scheme that transcends the nomic and binary fields.

Thus, we have encountered the perception of sin as the force motivating *tiqqun* in Luzzatto's messianic commentary on the *sugiyah* in the Talmud. The seductive acts of the Davidic mothers and of Yael earn emphatic rabbinic justification. The sages' courage is evident in their elucidation of the biblical stories, through the extraction of a hermeneutic position with an antinomian aspect. In my reading, only through rabbinic identification with women and curiosity about the Other could such a rich new language have evolved.

CONCLUSION

In this chapter we examined the antinomian linguistic and literary element underlying the sages' perception of Yael and of the Davidic maternal dynasty of Ruth, Tamar and Lot's daughters, leading them to propose the daring statement: "Greater is a transgression performed with good intention than a commandment performed with no intent." The Midrashim in this *sugiyah* not only justify such transgressions, but glorify the acts as well, and thus suggest a subversive feminine empowerment. Focusing on the expressions *aveirah lishmah* and *devar mitzvah*, I have argued that, in the Babylonian Talmud, the Rabbis sympathize with and seek to empower expressions of feminine sexuality and seduction, even as they condemn, by contrast, the men who commit similar transgressions.[62]

Indeed, I suggest that there is a separate moral system for women in rabbinic literature, an "Ethics of Redemption." Women are not required to be put to death for transgressions that are considered to fall within the category of *yehareg ve-al ya-avor*. This principle does not characterize female sexual sins, not only because women are perceived as passive during the sexual act, that is as *qarqa olam* (as the Tosafists imply in their discussion in b. *Sanhedrin* 74b), but also because their proactive and volitional acts could bring redemption. Deliverance can be made possible thanks to feminine choice of a contrivance

---

62 Boyarin, *Carnal Israel*, 107-34; Rosen-Zvi, "The Evil Impulse," 63–8.

and the use of their body, whereas the men who fail in these transgressions do so on pain of death.[63]

The revolutionary implications of *aveirah lishmah* touch upon issues of ethics and messianic theology as well. Contrary to an interpretation that struggles against a threatening gentile world, the *sugiyah*'s dialectical model indicates that the gentile world in general, and seductive gentile women in particular, may be a source of redemption, a motivating and fermenting power. A positive perception of non-Jewish women underlies the *sugiyah*'s justificatory Midrashim. They are seen, symbolically, as catalysts, like the "leavening in the bread" (*se'or sheba-isah*), or like the *yeṣer hara*, the "evil inclination," which—according to the sages—can be a positive force (*b. Berakhot* 17a; *Genesis Rabbah* 9:7).

The notion of aveirah *lishmah* sets a "moral criterion" arising from "an act of choosing between two hermeneutic options" that are presented side by side in our *sugiyah*.[64] On the one hand, it seeks to offer a solution in the halakhic-moral realm, in light of the tension between intention and its consequential act. On the other, it rises up to pose a mythical challenge and suggest a paradoxical concept of redemption, given the generations of sexual sin from which the figure of the Davidic Messiah emerged. These revolutionary, divergent attitudes towards the foreign or "Other," and the expansion of existing definitions of identity, are made possible by the separation of act from intent, and the distinctions between worthy and unworthy intentions, women and men.

---

63 Fonrobert, *Menstrual Purity*, 40–67; Ogden, *Helpmates, Harlots, Heroines*, 14–29, 229–41; Pardes, *Countertraditions*, 104–43; Boyarin, *Dying for God*, 67–92.
64 Halbertal, *Interpretative*, 15–20, 173–203.

Part Three

The Messianic Mother in the Zoharic Literature

In the Zoharic literature, the myth of the messianic mother reflects the *Shekhinah*'s journey of exile and redemption. Even though the messianic idea stands in the center of kabbalah scholarship, the role of the Davidic mother in the mystical *tiqqun* (reparation) has not received adequate scholarly attention.[1] The feminine dominance, which we have identified in previous chapters, and the conception that the redeemer's birth is made possible due to transgression and seduction, are situated at the core of kabbalistic thought. The redemption may be realized only through the encounter with the *sitra aḥra* (other side/demonic realm), and to this end, as more than one kabbalist has emphasized, it is necessary to know how to seduce the demonic realm and transmute it into a force of rectification. This role, first and foremost, falls on the *Shekhinah*, which constitutes the primary link between the worlds: supernal and mundane, good and evil, feminine and masculine. Therefore, the discussion of the maternal and messianic narrative of the House of David is aided by illuminating the connection between the terrestrial woman and the feminine divine, a topic on which the following chapters will focus.

Stories of the Davidic heroines will be presented chronologically, while analyzing their influences on the image of the *Shekhinah* and discussing the process of continuity and change that the exegesis undergoes from rabbinic literature to the *Zohar*. The fifth chapter will explore the illicit relations of Lot and his daughters through the exegesis on "*Ṭiqla*," a cosmic wheel of souls, which includes erotic and maternal facets, aspects of judgment (*din*) and kindness (*ḥesed*), righteousness and justice. I reveal this scene's roots in rabbinic

---

1 On the messianic idea in the *Zohar*, see Scholem, *Explications*, 155-90; Yehuda Liebes, *Studies in the Zohar* (Albany: SUNY Press, 1993), 1-84; Idel, *Messianic Mystics*, 58-109; Idel, *Ben*, 377-425; Haviva Pedaya, *Vision and Speech: Models of Prophecy in Jewish Mysticism* (Los Angeles: Cherub Press, 2002), 208-36; Pedaya, "The Sixth Millenium: Millenarism and Messianism in the *Zohar*," *Da'at* 72 (2012): 51-98; Hellner-Eshed, *A River Flows*, 41-76, 105-29.

Midrash and illuminate the relations between deficiency and reparation in the Judean dynasty.

The sixth chapter will discuss the idea of feminine sexuality in the *Zohar*, as a (re)productive and destructive potency, acting within the human and divine realms. Through the figure of Tamar, I will discuss the destructive powers entailed in the process of redemption in mystical literature, and analyze the bond between the *Shekhinah* and Lilith. In the seventh chapter, I will examine the figure of Ruth and the development of the threshing floor scene from rabbinic literature to the different strata of the *Zohar*: *Midrash ha-Ne'elam Ruth*, *Tiqqunei Zohar* and the *Zohar*. I propose that these different representations of the *Shekhinah* help clarify the question of the *Zohar*'s compilation.

Yehuda Liebes, Moshe Idel, Charles Mospik, and other scholars laid the foundation for the conceptualization of eros in kabbalistic literature.[2] These studies, as well as theories on gender and body, will serve as a background to my exploration of the messianic mothers in the *Zohar*. According to Elliot Wolfson, who has dedicated many studies to the topic of gender, kabbalistic literature is based on an androcentric model, in which the eschatological reparation represents the assimilation of the feminine in the masculine, and the transformation of the *Shekhinah* into the phallic corona (*ateret ha-yesod*). A similar process occurs in his view with the description of the *Binah*, which in the *Zohar* represents the "world-to-come," the Supernal Mother, and is even termed "the world of the masculine" (*alma di-dekhura*).[3]

I will examine these conceptions through the stories of the Davidic heroines, and propose an additional model of "gender reversal" linked to the messianic idea, according to which the messianic mother in the *Zohar* represents the active nature of the *sefirah* of *Yesod*, while the son portrays the passive feminine quality associated with *Shekhinah*. The two are not subsumed within one another, but rather are in a perpetual process of separation and reintegration,

---

2 Yehuda Liebes, "*Zohar* and Eros," *Alpayyim* 9 (1994): 67-119; Idel, *Kabbalah and Eros*, 153-78, 202-50; Mopsik, *Sex of the Soul*; Biale, *Eros and the Jews*.

3 Wolfson, *Language, Eros, Being*, 82, 331-71; Wolfson, *Circle in the Square*, 80-93, 98-106. For example, "One would do better therefore to refer to the creative and maternal element of the female as the transvaluation of the feminine into the masculine... the divine Mother is described in the same or proximate terms used to describe the phallus indicates that the female who gives birth is valorized as a male" (99, 103); Elliot R. Wolfson, "Patriarchy and the Motherhood of God in Zoharic Kabbalah and Meister Eckhart," in *Envisioning Judaism: Studies in Honor of Peter Schäfer on the Occasion of his Seventieth Birthday*, eds. R. Boustan, et al. (Tübingen: Mohr Siebeck, 2013), 1059; Wolfson, "Gender and Heresy in Kabbalah Scholarship," *Kabbalah* 6 (2002): 231-262.

similar to the relation of *Binah* and *Hokhmah*, which for the sake of redemption exchange their roles. The "Great Mother"—representing *Binah*, and *Shekhinah*, who imitates her role in the lower world—are transformed in the messianic myth into "the masculine world" due to their ability to contain the "other sex," rather then to be assimilated into it.

In this analysis, I wish to expand the idea of the "maternal matrix," which Haviva Pedaya, following Bracha Ettinger and Victor Turner, constructs as an alternative to the masculine order and the dominant father-son relations in the "ritual process," and also to expand Charles Mospik's suggestion that Tamar and Ruth in the *Zohar* represent a model of "masculine women" due to their initiation of *yibbum*.[4] Yet, their masculinity does not represent a process of assimilation or subordination to the male or the father, but supremacy and dominance over the male figures and other sefirotic qualities.

Additionally, the discussion of the messianic mother in the Zoharic literature is based on the research of Bracha Sack, Melila Hellner-Eshed, Shifra Asulin, Biti Roi, and Iris Felix, who have dealt with the status of the *Shekhinah* in the *Idra Rabba* literature, *Tiqqunei Zohar*, the writings of Joseph of Shushan, and Cordoverean kabbalah, and stressed the independent stature of the *Shekhinah* in the Zoharic literature and subsequently in Safedian kabbalah.[5] Daniel Abrams has introduced psychoanalytic and gender readings, such as the kabbalistic conception of the "phallic mother" in light of the Oedipus complex, as well as the development of the conception of the feminine as "lacking" in the thought of Freud, Lacan, and the criticism of Luce Irigaray.[6] I wish to expand

---

4   Haviva Pedaya, *Expanses: An Essay on the Theological and Political Unconscious* (Tel Aviv: Hakibbutz Hameuchad, 2011), 126-37; Bynum, *Fragmentatation*, 27-51; Mospik, *Sex*, 42-4.
5   R. Moshe Cordovero, *Ma'ayan Ein Ya'aqov*, ed. Beracha Sack (Beer Sheva: Ben Gurion University Press, 2009); Melila Hellner-Eshed, "On Love and Creativity: Drops from Sea of Myths of Cordovero on the Shekhinah," Hellner-Eshed, 161-188; Asulin, "The Stature of the Shekhina" *Spiritual Authority*, ed. H. Kriesel, (Beer Sheva, 2009), 103-83; Biti Roi, "The Myth of the *Shekhina* in *Tiqqunei ha-Zohar*: Poetic, Hermeneutic and Mystical Aspects" (PhD diss., Bar-Ilan University, 1993); Iris Felix, "Theurgy, Magic and Mysticism in the Kabbalah of R. Joseph of Shushan" (PhD diss., Hebrew University, 2005). On the rise of the *Shekhinah* in 16th century kabbalah, see Jonathan Garb, "Gender and Power in Kabbalah: A Theoretical Investigation," *Kabbalah* 13 (2005): 79-107.
6   Abrams, *The Female Body of God*. This work focuses on the characteristics of the *Shekhinah*, including in the context of motherhood. For the relation between *Binah* and *Shekhinah*, Gershom Scholem, *On the Mystical Shape of the Godhead* (New York: Schocken Books, 1991), 170-96; Asulin, "The Stature of the Shekhina"; Haviva Pedaya, "The Great Mother: The Struggle Between Nahmanides and the *Zohar* Circle," in *Temps i Espais de la Girona Jueva* (Girona: Patronat Call de Girona, 2011), 311-328; Roi, "Shekhina," 68-9.

this direction, adding additional theories designed to enrich the understanding of the feminine messianic myth, in relation to the image of the *Shekhinah*.

By portraying the messianic mother as a mythical figure developed through the biblical, rabbinic, and Zoharic corpora, I join those who view the Zoharic literature as a midrashic renaissance.[7] The authors of the *Zohar* are aware of the Davidic type-scene, and following the sages are aware of the validation and feminine dominance of the dynastic mothers in the messianic myth. In addition to the kabbalists, reliance on rabbinic exegesis, we witness in the *Zohar* techniques of protest, polemic, and ironic dialogue with the ancient Midrash. The *Zohar* situates a divine ethics as a challenge to human-centered rabbinic ethics, and associates the relations of the Davidic family to the drama of the *Shekhinah* in the supernal world. These stories are associated in the *Zohar* to the topos, which Oded Yisraeli terms, "mythic-realistic." This model, he proposes, connects the human to the divine, and demonstrates the theurgic impact of man's actions on the supernal realm. Nonetheless, I claim that sometimes the messianic mother is to be associated with the "mythic-symbolic" and even the "psychological-existential" models.[8] In order to examine continuity and innovation between rabbinic and Zoharic literature, we will preface our discussion of the feminine *tiqqun* with an introduction to the basic characteristics of the Zoharic text and the fundamentals of the messianic idea in kabbalah.

THE MYSTERY OF THE COMPOSITION OF THE *ZOHAR* AND ITS CHARACTER

Scholarly attitudes concerning the compilation of the Book of the *Zohar* oscillate between viewing the *Zohar* as a creation of a group of kabbalists or it

---

7   Yehuda Liebes, "The *Zohar* as Renaissance," *Da'at* 46 (2001): 5–11; Yisraeli, *Temple Portals*; Oded Yisraeli, *The Interpretation of Secrets and the Secret of Interpretation: Midrashic and Hermeneutic Strategies in Sabba de-Mishpatim of the Zohar* (Los Angeles: Cherub Press, 2005); Daniel C. Matt, "*Matnita Dilan*: A Technique of Innovation in the *Zohar*," *Jerusalem Studies in Jewish Thought* 8 (1989): 123–145.

8   Yisraeli, *Temple*, 19-22. Note in Yisraeli's work, the examples that represent the trends of moderation, intensification, and explication of rabbinic Midrashim are only male figures (like Adam, Abraham, Isaac, Esau, Moses, Elijah, Enoch, Aaron's sons, Balaam). In this context, the discussion of Lot's daughters, Tamar, Ruth, and their link to the *Shekhinah*, is complementary to the masculine analysis of the development of rabbinic Midrashim and the relation to the biblical heroine in the *Zohar*. For a discussion of Mary and her connection to the *Shekhnah* in light of the Judeo-Christian polemic, see Daniel Abrams, "The Virgin Mary as the Moon that Lacks the Sun: A Zoharic Polemic Against the Veneration of Mary," *Kabbalah* 21 (2010): 7-56.

being the work of a single author; between attributing it to Castile in the 13th century or viewing it as a composition taking shape over hundreds of years in Byzantine, the Middle East, Ashkenaz, and Spain.[9] The hypothesis supported by Gershom Scholem—that the *Zohar* was written by one author, R. Moses de Léon—was challenged by Yehuda Liebes, who suggested changing the question of "when was it composed?" to the question of "how was the Book of the *Zohar* compiled?" by presenting a fraternity of figures who collaborated in the *Zohar*'s compilation, such as R. David ben Judah he-Hasid, Joseph of Shushan, Joseph Gikatilla, and others.[10] The gaps between the independent creations of the Castilian kabbalists and the *Zohar*, highlight the mythic and poetic power of the Zoharic compilation and its heteroglossic quality.

Boaz Huss has explored the reception of the *Zohar* and its authority, beginning with the development of the "idea of the Book of the *Zohar*" from the 13th century and until its printing in the 16th century.[11] Daniel Abrams suggests that the *Zohar* should be treated as an "open corpus" or a palimpsest similar to the Bible and Talmud, whose authorship is not a subject of inquiry. In light of the liberty taken by copyists, proofreaders, and publishers in dealing with manuscripts in the Middle Ages, he believes that they all left their marks on the Zoharic work until its consolidation as a printed book.[12] Likewise, due to the existing differences between the manuscripts and printed versions of the *Zohar* and its heterogeneous sources, Ronit Meroz concludes that the composition of the *Zohar* was produced by a literary process that occurred over many generation and even many centuries.[13]

---

9   Tishby, *Zohar*, xxviii-cx; Boaz Huss, *Like the Radiance of the Sky: Chapters in the Reception History of the Zohar and the Construction of Its Symbolic Value* (Jerusalem: Bialik Institute, 2008), 1-139; on Zoharic manuscripts and their sources, ibid, 102-10; Yehuda Liebes, "The Zohar and the Tiqqunim: From Renaissance to Revolution," in *New Developments in Zohar Studies*, ed. Ronit Meroz, Te'uda 21/22 (2007): 251-302; Israel M. Ta-Shma, *The Revealed in the Hidden* (Tel Aviv: Hakibbutz Hameuhad, 1995); Ronit Meroz, "The Middle Eastern Origins of Kabbalah," *Journal for the Study of Sephardic and Mizrahi Jewry* 1 (2007): 39-56.

10 Gershom Scholem, *Major Trends in Jewish Mysticism* (New York: Schocken Books, 1941), 156-204; Liebes, *Studies*, 85-138.

11 Huss, *Radiance of the Sky*, 43-139.

12 Daniel Abrams, *Kabbalistic Manuscripts and Textual Theory: Methodologies of Textual Scholarship and Editorial Practice in the Study of Jewish Mysticism* (Jerusalem: Magnes Press, 2010), 224-428.

13 Ronit Meroz, "Zoharic Narratives and Their Adaptations," *Hispania Judaica Bulletin* 3 (2000): 3-63; Meroz, "The Weaving of a Myth: An Analysis of Two Stories in the *Zohar*," in *Study and Knowledge in Jewish Thought*, vol. 2, ed. Howard Kreisel (Beer-Sheva: Ben Gurion University Press, 2006), 167-205. In her opinion, contradictory strands, which reflect groups of authors with opposing ideologies, can be found in the *Zohar*, and therefore she suggests to

The mystery of the *Zohar*'s compilation and the identity of its authors pertain to additional issues concerning the historical setting in which it was written, its reflection of mystical experience, and its relation to *halakha*. Due to its pseudepigraphical character, Moshe Idel and Boaz Huss have demonstrated that the *Zohar* exposes tensions between social layers, such as the rabbinic elite against the secondary kabbalistic elite; while Haviva Pedaya, Moshe Halbertal, and other have shown the relations between the Zoharic innovativeness and the esotericism of Naḥmanides.[14] Meanwhile, Israel Ta-Shma, Moshe Hallamish, and others have discussed the Ashkenazic influence on the *Zohar* and on the Zoharic *halakha*.[15] Elliot Wolfson has investigated the complicated relation between *nomos* and *antinomos* in the *Zohar*, whereby he suggests the term "hypernomian," to describe kabbalistic literature in contrast to the emphasis on the antinomian trend which Gershom Scholem exposed in the Zoharic literature.[16]

Many studies in the last generation have been dedicated to the discussion of "the Zoharic mythopoesis" and the connection between the narrative frame about R. Shimon bar Yoḥai (Rashbi) and his students, and the theosophic and mystical features of the Zoharic literature. Perceiving the *Zohar* as "literature" assists in understanding the self-consciousness of the kabbalists and the ways that the content and poetic form of these compositions are interwoven, as has been shown in the studies of Yehuda Liebes, Melila Hellner-Eshed, Pinchas Giller, Michal Oron, Jonatan Benarroch, and many of the previously mentioned scholars.[17] In the following chapters, I will extend this trend and

---

distinguish between the "epic unit" and the other parts of the *Zohar* that don't have developed narrative frameworks.

14 Boaz Huss, "A Sage is Preferable than a Prophet: Rabbi Shim'on Bar Yohai and Moses in the *Zohar*," *Kabbalah* 4 (1999): 103-139; Moshe Idel, "The Kabbalah's 'Window of Opportunities,' 1270- 1290," in *Me'ah She'arim: Studies in Medieval Jewish Spiritual Life in Memory of Isadore Twersky*, eds. G. Blidstein, E. Fleischer, C. Horowitz, and B. Septimus (Jerusalem: Magnes Press, 2001), 5-32; Haviva Pedaya, *Nahmanides: Cyclical Time and Holy Text* (Tel Aviv: Am Oved, 2003), 439-58; Pedaya, "The Sixth Millenium"; Moshe Halbertal, *By Way of Truth: Nahmanides and the Creation of Tradition* (Jerusalem: Shalom Hartman Institute, 2006), 297-333.

15 Ta-Shma, *Revealed in the Hidden*; Moshe Hallamish, *The Kabbalah in Liturgy, Halakhah, and Custom* (Ramat Gan: Bar-Ilan University Press, 2000); Jacob Katz, *Halakhah and Kabbalah: Studies in the History of Judaism* (Jerusalem: Magnes Press, 1984); Yehuda Liebes, "The *Zohar* as a Halakhic Book," *Tarbiz* 64 (1995): 581-605; Tzahi Weiss, "Who is a Beautiful Maiden without Eyes? The Metamorphosis of a *Zohar* Midrashic Image from a Christian Allegory to a Kabbalistic Metaphor," *The Journal of Religion* 93, no. 1 (2013): 60-76.

16 Wolfson, *Venturing Beyond*, specifically 232-4, 269; Scholem, *Symbolism*, 9-35.

17 Liebes, *Studies*, 18-24 ;Liebes, *"Eros"*; Michal Oron, "Artistic Elements in the Homiletics of the *Zohar*," *Jerusalem Studies in Jewish Thought* 8 (1989): 299-310; Hellner-Eshed, *A River*

demonstrate the centrality of the messianic mother in the Zoharic narratives and exegesis, as well as examine the kabbalists' attitude towards conceptions of sexuality, femininity and motherhood.[18] Despite the difficulty in recreating a uniformed narrative that identifies the messianic mother with the *Shekhinah*, I will present this figure as she emerges from different strata of the Zoharic compilation, highlighting the singularity of each passage in itself as well as the unifying topos intertwining them.

Whether it is a work formed by one kabbalist or a fraternity of authors, it is important to emphasize that contemporaneous kabbalists and their successors related to the *Zohar* as a "book." R. Isaac of Acre mentions in his testimony, which is quoted by Abraham Zacuto, "this Book of the *Zohar*," also termed by R. Moses de Léon as "the ancient book of Rashbi," or, as the author of *Tiqqunei Zohar* states: "this compilation of yours, which is the Book of the *Zohar*."[19] Although the printing of the *Zohar* happened only around 300 years after its revelation, at the end of the 13th century and the beginning of the 14th century, kabbalists viewed the *Zohar* as an independent text and stressed its unique authority. Even if the copyists, proofreaders, and publishers contributed to the continued consolidation of the Zoharic work, from the moment of its revelation the *Zohar* was perceived as a sacred composition, whose tannaitic source is undoubted and therefore it may be interpreted and clarified.[20] The *Zohar*'s authority is based on an ancient and indisputable tradition, as the kabbalist R. Joseph Angelet said when he encountered a contradiction between the *Zohar* and other kabbalists: "So it appears to be the method of the *Midrash ha-Ne'elam*, in

---

Flows; Giller, *Zohar*, 35-86; Pedaya, *Vision and Speech*; Oded Yisraeli, *The Interpretation of Secrets*; Jonatan Benarroch, "'Yanuqa' and 'Sabba' - Two that are One: Allegory, Symbol and Myth in Zoharic Literature" (PhD diss., Hebrew University, 2011).

18 Research regarding the *Shekhinah*, like the research of messianism, have mostly neglected the female figures of the Davidic dynasty.

19 *Zohar* III: 124b; Tishby, *Zohar*, xxviii-xxx; Huss, *Radiance of the Sky*, 67-8; Roi, "Shekhina," 174-8, 323.

20 See Iris Felix and Ruth Kara-Kaniel, "Fire that Bears Fire: The Literary Development of the *Zohar* and the Flourish of Zoharic Exegesis at the Beginning of the 14th Century: Menahem Recanati and Joseph Angelet," *Jerusalem Studies in Jewish Thought* 24 (2015): 157-200. In contrast to this view, Boaz Huss stresses the connection between the mid-16th century phenomenon of Zoharic interpretation and the canonization and printing of the Zoharic composition. Also according to Abrams, Cordovero's *Or Yaqar* constitutes a turning point in the conception of the *Zohar* as a distinct corpus, Abrams, *Kabbalistic Manuscripts and Textual Theory*, 245-56. Also for the perception of the *Zohar* as a "continuity of textual phenomenon," ibid, 370-8, 228-30. Huss, *Radiance of the Sky*, 179-190.

the *Idra*, even though Naḥmanides, may his memory be blessed, did not write as such, nor the rest of the kabbalists. But we only hold by the words of the *Tannaim*, the pillars of the universe."[21]

THE MESSIANIC IDEA IN THE ZOHARIC LITERATURE

The messianic idea is the heart of the kabbalistic literature and there is almost no passage in the *Zohar* which is not grounded in the yearning for redemption. In each layer of the Zoharic work: in the mystical passages, narrative frame, analogous and allegoric passages, development of rabbinic Midrash, and biblical exegesis, we can find expressions of longing for salvation. Alongside clear messianic readings—like the myth of the doe and redeemer's birth from its womb—the passage of "the bird's nest," and the apocalyptic account of the messianic days, or the *Idra* literature, which is imbued, as Yehuda Liebes has shown, with messianic conceptions—the kabbalists' sensitivity to transformational states of "personal redemption," is shown, alongside other redemptive patterns.[22]

Even the process of writing is described in the *Zohar* as an erotic-poetic redemptive act, as the author of the later stratum, *Ra'ya Meheimna* writes: "in merit of your compilation, which is the Book of the *Zohar* ... [Israel] went out from exile through mercy."[23] Similarly, the author of *Tiqqunei Zohar* describes the quill, with which he writes the exegesis, as an instrument of future salvation, and associates it with the staff of Moses, used in the first redemption.[24] As Amos Goldreich has suggested, these phrases attest to the use of mystical and magical techniques of *"shem ha-kotev"* (a magical application of the divine name) in the layers of the *Tiqqunei Zohar*, and it is likely that a similar technique

---

21 Angelet, commentary on *Sha'are Orah*, Ms. London-Montefiore, 321, 33b; Huss, *Radiance of the Sky*, 141.
22 On the doe myth: *Zohar* II: 52b; Yehuda Liebes, "'Two Young Roes of a Doe': The Secret Sermon of Isaac Luria Before his Death," *Jerusalem Studies in Jewish Thought* 10 (1992): 113-169; Ruth Kara-Kaniel, "Eve, the Gazelle, and the Serpent: Narratives of Creation and Redemption, Myth and Gender," *Kabbalah* 21 (2010): 255–310. On the bird's nest, see *Zohar* II: 7-9; Pedaya, *Vision and Speech*, 226-30. For the messianic aspects of the *Idra* literature: Liebes, *Studies*, 1-84. For different models of redemption in kabbalistic literature, Moshe Idel, "Patterns of Redemptive Activity in the Middle Ages," in *Messianism and Eschatology*, ed. Zvi Baras (Jerusalem: Zalman Shazar Center, 1983), 253-280.
23 See above, footnote 21.
24 *Tiqqun* 21, 43a. Liebes, "The *Zohar* and the Tiqqunim." On the phallic aspect of writing, see Gilbert and Gubar.

was used by the authors of the *Zohar*.[25] In spite of the differences between the *Zohar* and the *Tiqqunim*, the possibility that both works contain automatic writing expands the revelatory and redemptive dimension of the Zoharic literature as well as the collaboration of the supernal entities in its writing, such as Elijah the Prophet, Rashbi, and other fellows recalled in the prologue of *Tiqqunei Zohar*.[26] The writing narrative appears in fragmented narratives in the *Zohar*, like *Rav Metivta*, the *Introduction to the Zohar*, *Zohar Ḥadash Ki-Tavo*, and *Zohar Shir ha-Shirim*. These sermons conceal the key task of writing in the *Zohar*, and expose the way in which the Zoharic compilation was itself written. Reconstructing the writing theme from the narrative frame of the *Zohar* reveals the cyclical connection between redemption and creation myths. The depiction of engraving, carving, and sealing appearing in many of the passages dealing with the mystery of emanation and creation, hint at the scribe's quill and writing process involved in the messianic *tiqqun* of the *Zohar*.[27]

In order to analyze the role of the messianic mother in the myth of creation and redemption, I will begin with a short discussion of the development of the messianic idea in the Book of the *Zohar*. The pioneer of the field, Gershom Scholem, viewed the Spanish expulsion as an event which resulted in national, apocalyptic, and mystical elements becoming a systematic messianic doctrine developed in Safedian kabbalah of the 16th century. The catastrophic aspect of the biblical and rabbinic redemptive vision connected the Spanish expulsion with a historic crisis, and the two created an experience of the messianic birth-pangs, which caused the kabbalist, for the first time, to come out into "public space" and vigorously act for the sake of bringing redemption. Lurianic kabbalah also begins with a systematic doctrine which situates exile and redemption as key idioms in the processes of cosmic fractures happening within the divine.[28]

Nonetheless, in the Zoharic literature and synchronous works, Scholem reveals a tendency to escape history, "to the primal days of Creation." As far as

---

25 Amos Goldreich, *Automatic Writing in Zoharic Literature and Modernism* (Los Angeles: Cherub Press, 2010), 43-53, 54-94; while Liebes emphasizes the differences between the writing methods employed for the *Zohar* and *Tiqqunim*.

26 "*The enlightened will shine*... Rabbi Shimon and his companions, *will shine* when they gathered together, they were permitted an audience with Elijah... secrets hidden until the advent of the Messiah." *Tiqqunei Zohar* 1a, translated by Pinchas Giller. Also Tishby, *Zohar*, xxxiv; Huss, *Radiance of the Sky*, 57-66; Elliot R. Wolfson, *Through a Speculum That Shines* (Princeton: Princeton University Press, 1994), 391.

27 For an exploration of writing and revelation, see Pedaya, *Nahmanides*, 54-68; Pedaya, "The Sixth Millenium."

28 Scholem, *Sabbatai*, 7-52; Scholem, *Explications*, 194-8.

he is concerned, the Zoharic kabbalists' spiritual movement is perceived as a return to the "inward home" and the mysteries of the emanation and *merkavah* (chariot), without any attempt to progress and operate with full force to hasten the coming of the redeemer.[29] Yehuda Liebes objected to these conclusions and claimed that alongside the personal and restorative messianism in the *Zohar* there are notions of national and historical redemption. In his opinion, the *Idra* literature expresses the intention of the cohort of kabbalists to create a *tiqqun* in divine and mundane realms, while positioning Rashbi as the heroic messianic figure at its core.[30] Alongside these discussions are others that pertain to additional literary aspects of the work, connected to the figure of Rashbi in the *Zohar* and the redeemer mold as it is portrayed in the *ḥevraya*'s (companions) relationship in the narrative frames, *Saba de-Mishpatim, Yenuqa, Idra Zuṭa,* and *Rav Metivta*.[31]

Gershom Scholem's distinction between the restorative messianism in the kabbalah of the Middle Ages and the active messianism of the Lurianic kabbalah has been challenged from other directions.[32] Moshe Idel has shown models of active messianism in the 13th and 14th centuries, and ascribed the difference to the messianic figure's individual nature and cultural and religious influences, rather than historical and political circumstances.[33] Idel claims that the traumatic mindset emphasized by Scholem is characteristic of popular and binary perceptions of redemption.[34] Nonetheless, according to him the *Zohar* integrates different messianic conceptions: the struggle between good and evil, which is highlighted in the kabbalah of the Cohen brothers (termed by Scholem the "Gnostic Circle") and in the Manichaean sources, join the *Zohar* in the desire for creation of harmony in the supernal realms, while formulating the theurgic-theosophic approach. Additionally, as

---

29   Scholem, *Idea*, 39; Scholem, *Sabbatai*, 13-7; Tishby, *Zohar*, xl. It is interesting to note that this anthology does not include an exploration of the messianic idea in the *Zohar*.
30   Liebes, *Studies*, 1-84; Liebes, *Studies in Jewish Myth*, 1-64; Idel, *Messianic Mystics*. Liebes, "Doe" objects to Scholem's view that the personal messianic figure is not important in Lurianic kabbalah.
31   Liebes, "Zohar and Eros"; Yisraeli, *The Interpretation of Secrets*; Benarroch, "'Yanuqa' and 'Sabba'". Even the transference of secrets between Rashbi and his students reflects an act of bringing the redemption, Hellner-Eshed, *A River Flows*, 187-221.
32   Scholem, *Explications*, 199; Also, see Haviva Pedaya's critique, "Defect and Restoration of the Deity in the Works of Isaac the Blind," *Jerusalem Studies in Jewish Thought* 6 (1987): 157-285.
33   Idel, *Messianic Mystics*, 1-37; Idel, "Patterns."
34   Also Castilian kabbalah is deemed according to this analysis as "traumatic kabbalah," see Idel, *Messianic Mystics*, 103-4.

Haviva Pedaya has illuminated, the perception of redemption in the *Zohar* is based on conceptions of rupture and restoration in the origins of kabbalah and in the school of Isaac the Blind. Following her analysis of the personal and active aspects of Zoharic messianism, we can identify a combination of the extroverted and introverted models of the mystical experience.[35] In the *Zohar* the messianic figure represents a combination of opposites, reflecting the dialectical forces existing in the souls of the *Zohar*'s authors.[36] This redeemer is portrayed as a timeless figure, "existing before existence," but also unrealized and not yet revealed; as a figure that includes feminine and masculine facets, aspects of *Ḥesed* (grace) and *Din* (judgement). The active aspects of the redeemer are bound with the Messiah's identification with *Yesod* and *Ṣaddiq* (righteous one) on whose actions the rectification (*tiqqun*) depends, whereas the passive aspect is identified with *Malkhut*, which is represented as the passive dimension in the divine.[37]

Despite the Zoharic Rashbi being the masculine hero, it is his feminine quality and identification with the *Shekhinah* that is hinted at in certain messianic passages. The Davidic heroines complete this picture, by their actively bringing the redemption, as it were "masculinely," while creating a gender reversal appropriate to the paradoxical character of the messianic idea.[38] In my opinion, these heroines should not be excluded from the other messianic figures in the *Zohar*, and their seductive actions are to be viewed as examples of "redemptive behavior." These women fit the "substitution" model, which Idel contrasts with the "individualistic" and ecstatic model of Abulafian kabbalah. In his view, the "substituting" Messiah gathers within him the forces of evil and sin, and guides them towards reparation through his entering into the demonic

---

35 Pedaya, *Vision and Speech*, 208-36; Idel, *Messianic Mystics*, 106.
36 Liebes, *Studies*, 1-84. On the authors' self-perception as mystics, Pedaya, *Vision and Speech*, 5-29, 117-36; Hellner-Eshed, *A River Flows*, 131-221, 297-441; Idel, *Kabbalah: New Perspectives* (New Haven: Yale University, 1988), xi-16. However, Boaz Huss opposes the use of the term "mysticism" in kabbalah scholarship, *The Question About the Existence of Jewish Mysticism* (Jerusalem and Tel Aviv: Van Leer Institute, 2016).
37 Liebes, *Studies*, 5-15; Idel, *Messianic Mystics*, 104-7. For another perspective of the passive redeemer, Haviva Pedaya, "Sabbath, Sabbatai, and the Diminution of Moon—The Holy Conjunction: Sign and Image," *Eshel Beer-Sheva* 4 (1996):143- 191. On David as a messianic figure, see Hellner-Eshed, *A River Flows*, 199-203, 313-6; Yisraeli, *The Interpretation of Secrets*, 85, 116-24.
38 Wolfson, "Gender and Heresy." In my opinion, David is identified with *Malkhut* and presents the passive aspect in the messianic myth, due to his foremothers portraying the activeness of *Yesod*, as we will see in the forthcoming chapters.

realm.³⁹ Similarly, beginning in the biblical type-scene, the Davidic mothers are configured as substituting figures who bring the redemption. However, in contrast to the passive suffering of Jesus and his mother in the Christian myth, they do this through intensified and transgressive sexuality, actions which enable the birth of the good hidden within the bad. It is possible to say that the Messiah's mothers in the *Zohar* reflect a "hypostasis" and even "incarnation" of the divine and its materialization in corporeal figures.⁴⁰ It is not a coincidence that they are the ones responsible for giving birth to the messianic son, who is perceived as an actual part of divinity, identified with *Malkhut*.

The *Zohar* presents a complex picture of the messianic idea, stemming from contradictions between creation and redemption, feminine and masculine. The mindset of the authors of the *Zohar* is oriented towards "casting an open eye" and a promise to be "full of eyes" in relation to the Torah and its meanings, and through this create a reparation in the celestial realms.⁴¹ According to the *Zohar* the acts of man in the mundane realm can repair the supernal realm, thus the transgressive acts of Tamar, Ruth, and Lot's daughters signify a theurgical process of breaking the law in order to create a utopian space and new world.⁴²

---

39 In contrast to the perfection of the individual found in Abulafia, here collective responsibility is emphasized, Idel, *Messianic Mystics*, 33-110, Idel, *Messianism*, 24-9.
40 In relation to the figures of the 'Old Man' (*Saba*) and 'Youth' (*Yenuqa*) in the Zoharic narrative framework: Liebes, *Studies in Jewish Myth*, 1-64; Benarroch, "'Yanuqa' and 'Sabba'," 189-219.
41 Wolfson, *Through a Speculum*, 384-6; Hellner-Eshed, *A River Flows*, 264-7; Daniel Abrams, "Knowing the Maiden without Eyes: Reading the Sexual Reconstruction of the Jewish Mystic in a Zoharic Parable," *Da'at* 50-52 (2003): 487-511; as well as chapter five.
42 Scholem, *Explications*, 189-90.

CHAPTER 5

Lot's Daughters and the Zoharic "Ṭiqla"

"Ṭiqla" is a unique Aramaic term which appears in the *Zohar* in various passages and contexts. In the existing research, the term *Ṭiqla* was generally interpreted as a scale on the one hand (deriving from the root *t.q.l*), or as a potter's wheels or a water-meter on the other hand. Scholars usually interpret the two meanings, as well as other definitions of the term in the Zoharic literature, as related. I will argue that this term is only used in a few Zoharic passages as a distinctive expression of seduction committed by the Davidic mothers, in order to bring forth redemption and the birth of the Messiah. While discussing the story of Lot's daughters in the *Zohar*, I will suggest that there are different layers hidden in the mystical meaning of the *Ṭiqla*, identify its early source in rabbinic literature and ancient agricultural techniques, and uncover the link between its messianic and feminine connotations.

THE PARADOXICALITY OF INCESTUOUS RELATIONS IN CULTURAL STUDIES, GENDER THEORIES AND PSYCHOANALYSIS

The Judean monarchy blossoms from a violation of severe sexual prohibitions, and embodies the paradoxical encounter between transgression and reparation.[1] While in the Bible, illicit relations (*gilui*—revealing, *arayyot*—nakedness) attest to the sacredness of sexuality as an expression of the divine image, as it emerges from the beginning of the section regarding prohibited relations in Leviticus: "You shall be holy, for I the Lord your God am holy" (19:2), in the kabbalistic literature the *sefirotic* paradigm is constructed upon incestuous relations, between parents and children, sisters and brothers. In the divine *familia*, the principle that "in the world above there is no nakedness (*ervah*)" rules and that which is forbidden in the lower realm is permissible and even desirable in

---

1 See in ch. 1 discussion of Bataille, Foucault, Douglas, and others.

the supernal realm.² The complex relations interwoven between the taboo of incest and its violation forms a tension that allows for the establishment of societal life and the beginning of culture. The story of Lot's daughters reveals the cultural function of incestuous relations in Jewish myth and the link between the "sacred" and "profane" in the Davidic dynasty.

It is known that in tribal societies, the taboo of incest characterizes the beginning of the transition from nature to civilization.³ Theories that discussed the phenomenon from anthropological, psychological, and sociological perspectives revealed the centrality of incest in the stories of the gods and kings, and mythical and fantastic domains.⁴ Psychoanalytic theory shows that "that which threatens is desired" and hence the severe prohibition attests to the yearning to breach it. Freud emphasized the place of the Oedipus complex in the individual's psyche as well as the tribal totem, founded on the forbidden desire for the mother and guilt for wishing to kill the father.⁵

The duality of incest is reflected in Freud's writings: "The meaning of 'taboo,' as we see it, diverges in two contrary directions. To us it means, on the one hand, 'sacred,' 'consecrated,' and on the other 'uncanny,' 'dangerous,' 'forbidden,' 'unclean.'"⁶ In contrast, Erich Fromm stresses the emotional quest embedded in incestual desires, whereas Jung views incest as a desire of the fractured psyche to return to a primal unity.⁷ In a symbolic sense, incestuous relations anticipate individualization and sublimation, and Jung finds in them an echo of primordial myths of *hieros gamos*, leading to the messianic birth.⁸ Malinowski claimed that incest is the foundation of all sexual relations, while Claude Lévi-Strauss sees the taboo of incest as a cultural necessity, which stems

---

2 *Tiqqunei Zohar*, Tiqqun 34, 76b; Tiqqun 56, 89b; Tiqqun 69, 90b, 99a; Zohar III: 74a-79b, etc. More radical depictions of the incestuous relations in the divine family can be found in the writings of R. Joseph of Shushan. For example, "The mystery of incest is a very grand and wondrous mystery… An explanation of '**pouring from one vessel into another, this way the *sefirot* pour one onto the other**'" (Ms. Paris 841, 166b-167a). Felix, "R. Joseph of Shushan," 158; Moshe Idel, "Additional Fragments from the Writings of R. Joseph of Hamadan," *Da'at* 21 (1988): 47-55.

3 Eliade, Turner, Lévi-Strauss and others explore cultures with incestuous origins. See also Idel, "Secret of the 'Arayyot,'" 89-90.

4 Claude Lévi-Strauss, *The Elementary Structures of Kinship* (Boston: Beacon Press, 1969), 67-80; Rank, *Birth of the Hero*, 95-6; Turner, *Ritual Process*, 87-115.

5 Freud, "Totem and Taboo"; Freud, "Moses and Monotheism"; Freud, "Female Sexuality."

6 Freud, "Totem and Taboo," 16.

7 Erich Fromm, *Psychoanalysis and Religion* (New Haven: Yale University Press, 1972), 77-8. Jung, *The Psychology of the Transference*, 52-76, 240-5, 265-318.

8 Neumann, *Mother*, 18-23; Netzer, *Journey*, 328-31; Kron, *Us, Adam and Eve*, 176.

from the transition to exogamic relations, in which men do not marry women from their tribe; rather they exchange women with other families and tribes.[9]

The tendency to divide between biological, psychological, and cultural perspectives causes Strauss to search for a "dynamic synthesis" that will offer a new outlook regarding the question of incest from a multidisciplinary perspective.[10] In my view, incestual relations are situated intentionally at the meeting point between the divine and human world in kabbalistic literature, serving as an example of a productive synthesis, or, in Jungian terms, *"prima materia,"* in which transgression symbolizes redemption.

From the gender perspective, Julia Kristeva has shown the creative power concealed in the yearnings for incest, which represent the seam between the semiotic and symbolic worlds. The sublimation of incestuous relations signifies the ability of symbolization, for language, speech, and writing stemming from the confrontation with the feminine and encounter with the maternal.[11] According to her, incestuous relations symbolize a semiotic quality (*chōra*), which is rejected with the appearance of the "Law of the Father," and within which it undermines. Noticeable in the sociological and gender reality is an imbalance stemming from the exploitation of incest as an instrument of gender oppression. According to feminist critics, such as Catherine McKinnon who discusses judicial aspects, or Esther Fuchs who explores the biblical context, the fact that most cases of incest occur between fathers and daughters attests that mankind has not surrendered the incestual desire, and that the "Law of the Father," which is meant to establish civilization and its order, exploits the vulnerability of women in order to reproduce the patriarchal power structure.

As Dorit Abramovitch and Tikva Frymer-Kensky illuminate, just like in ancient cultures, so too in modern ones there is an interest in preserving the incestuous relations between a father and his daughters, for they serve the androcentric structure and reinforce the father's rule.[12] The symbolic connection between God and the father contributes to the idealization of oedipal relations and the conception of fathers as omnipotent, in contrast to the rejection of the

---

9 Bronislaw Malinowski, *Sex and Repression in Savage Society* (London: Routledge, 1927), 145.
10 Lévi-Strauss, *Elementary*, 12-51; Rimerman, *Forbidden Relations*, 13-21.
11 Kristeva, *Powers of Horror*, 58-9.
12 This is in spite of incestuous relations seemingly symbolizing the dissolution of cultural foundations: Rich, *Of Woman Born*, 104-6, 186-97; Yael Renan, *Goddess and Heroes: On the Limits of Power* (Tel Aviv: Am Oved, 2001), 107-18.

mother, who is identified with weakness and inferiority.[13] Similarly, Simone de Beauvoir claims that the taboo of incest is designed to protect men and preserve the rift between a wife and mother, which threaten the man by reminding him of his mortality.[14] Whereas, according to Catherine Clément, Strauss's theories of exogamy locate women at the center of the discussion, establishing women as a wild and undomesticated function, and harming their chances at meriting protection in the shelter of civilization.[15]

It should be noted that the story of Lot's daughters deviates from these basic premises, and raises new questions pertaining to the gender and cultural meaning of incest. Contrary to the norm, Lot's daughters are not trafficked by men, rather they 'exchange' their father. Similar to Leah who says to Jacob, "I have hired you," Ruth and Naomi stage the threshing floor scene and Tamar initiates the seduction at the "entrance of Enaim." These heroines use the violation of the incest prohibition and sexual devices for the purpose of establishing civilization rather than to dismantle it. Lot "does not know" when they lay or rose, for the women are dependent on this arrangement more so than the men. In contrast to the exchange model, there are no "other women" to transfer in this story, and even the mother disappears together with the destruction of Sodom. Furthermore, as we demonstrated in the second chapter, in the detailed list of prohibitions in Leviticus 18 and 20, the absence of an explicit ban on incestual relations between father and daughter is conspicuous. Whether it is an intentional omission or learned through *a fortiori* argument from the prohibition regarding a granddaughter (Lev. 18:10), the episode involving Lot's daughters intensifies the tension between the biblical law and narrative, raising the question of whether it is solely a prohibition or possibly a sacred deed as well. In Genesis, the incestual relations between the father and his daughters likely represents the connection between the sacred and profane, from which civilization sprouts. In Bergsonian terminology, this is a story of "open morality," which is revealed in the stitching between the law's origin and the world prior

---

13 Julia Kristeva, *In the Beginning Was Love: Psychoanalysis and Faith* (New York: Columbia University Press, 1987); Nancy Chodorow, "Gender, Relation, and Difference in Psychoanalytic Perspective," in *Essential Papers on the Psychology of Women*, ed. C. Zanardi (New York: New York University, 1980), 420-436; Klein, *Writings*, 94-121. Whereas, according to Welldon, incestuous relations between a mother and infant son are particularly common, and are not adequately addressed.
14 Beauvoir, *The Second Sex*, 169.
15 For a critique of Strauss' model, Cixous and Clément, *The Newly Born Woman*, 78-101, especially 61-3.

to its appearance.[16] Similar to other ancient civilizations whose beginnings are in myths of incest—due to their evolution within one nuclear family—so too the Davidic heroines "return the branch to its root" an image used by kabbalists to describe the incestuous episode.[17]

THE PRIMAL STORY AND "PRIMAL SCENE"

The incestual relations of Lot's daughters occur in light of Sodom's destruction and symbolize the primal trauma of the messianic biography. This story reflects in a psychoanalytical sense a "primal scene," in which the child discovers details about his conception, when he contemplates on the actual or symbolic threatening union of his parents.[18] Indeed, in Sodom, the most extreme act in the range of illicit relations in the Davidic stories happens. In contrast to the partial prohibitions and seductive tales of Tamar and Ruth, in Genesis 19 Lot's daughters choose to be impregnated by their father in light of the overturned city, their abandonment to rape, the angels' visit, the hurried rescue, their mother's transformation into a pillar of salt, the smoke, and fire. From these chaotic foundations, the Davidic dynasty begins. Like the individual's "primal scene," here as well, the horror creates an opening of hope and reparation.

Sodom echoes the story of the flood, for in both cases the destruction is presented by the same verb and God wants to annihilate the world and return it to chaos: "For in seven days I will send rain on the earth for forty days and forty nights; and every living thing that I have made I will blot out from the face of the ground" (Gen. 7:4). Similarly, it is written about Sodom: "Then the Lord rained on Sodom and Gomorrah sulfur and fire from the Lord out of heaven; and he overthrew those cities, and all the Plain, and all the inhabitants of the cities, and what grew on the ground" (Gen. 19:24-25). The sages, as well as Josephus, Origen, and others, derive from this that the generation anticipated another disaster after the flood, this time in the form of fire which will end with total annihilation.[19] In this way, the exegetes

---

16 Turner, *Ritual Process*, 100, 113; Gamilieli, *Psychoanalysis and Kabbalah*, 342-8.
17 For the model of returning the branch to its root, Idel, "Secret of the 'Arayyot,'" 96-7; Tishby, *Zohar*, 2: 621-4.
18 Freud, "Female Sexuality"; Freud, "The Interpretation of Dreams"; Melanie Klein, *Love, Guilt and Reparation and Other Works 1921-1945* (London: Hogarth Press, 1975), 210-218; Lewis Aron, "The Internalized Primal Scene," *Psychoanalytic Dialogues* 5 (2005): 195-237; Donald Meltzer and Meg Harris Williams, *The Apprehension of Beauty: The Role of Aesthetic Conflict in Development, Art and Violence* (Perthshire: Clunie Press, 1988), specifically chapters 4-6, 8-10.
19 Flavius states that Lot's daughters thought the world had been destroyed, yet they copulated

justify Lot's daughters as acting from the survival impulse, as the sages wrote: "They thought that the whole world was destroyed, as in the generation of the Flood."[20]

Illicit relations are situated at the beginning of the messianic dynasty and also its end; from Sodom to King David's sin with Bathsheba, these two limits represent a transgressive cycle in the Judean dynasty. In both stories, an extreme breaching of boundaries occurs and the principle of "returning to origins," which begins with the annunciation of David's birth in the Prophets and Writings, in the spirit of Micah's words: "But you, O Bethlehem of Ephrathah, who are one of the little clans of Judah, from you shall come forth for me one who is to rule in Israel, whose origin is from of old, from ancient days," is revealed.[21] The sages sought to highlight the connection between King David and Lot's daughters, and sympathetically present the redeemer's origin in the story of Sodom:

> "Arise, take your wife, and your two daughters that are found" (Gen. 19:15): two 'finds', Ruth and Naamah. R. Isaac commented: "I have found my servant David." (Ps. 89:21): **where did I find him? In Sodom.**[22]

Based on the verse from Psalm 89, "I have found my servant David; with my holy oil I have anointed him," the Midrash demonstrates David's link to Lot's daughters. In Sodom, King David is "found," as well as Ruth the Moabite and Naamah the Ammonite who integrated into the royal family—the first as David's grandmother and the second as Rehoboam's mother and Solomon's wife (I Kings 14:21). Thus, the vindication of Lot's daughters is reinforced, strengthening the sacredness of the feminine genealogy in the messianic myth.

---

with their father covertly, *Ant.* 1:205; Ginzberg, *Legends*, 1:34. For an allegorical vindication of Lot's daughters, who represent the "good hindrance" neutralizing Lot's destructive force, see Origen, *Genesis*, 112-20, as well as Philo, *Questions*, 4:5, 336-7, while the act is directly condemned in Jub. 16:7-9.

20 Genesis Rabbah 51:8 (ed. Theodor-Albeck, 537). Church Fathers like Ephrem the Assyrian, Jerome, and Irenaeus, like the sages, condemn Lot and openly vindicate his daughters; Kugel, *Traditions of the Bible*, 339; Ginzberg, *Legends*, 1:215, fn. 188.

21 Micah 5:1. Also Lamentations 5:21, etc. On the cyclical link between the beginning and end in the messianic myth, see Scholem, *Messianic Idea*, 78-141; Yehuda Liebes, *God's Story: Collected Essays on the Jewish Myth* (Jerusalem: Carmel Publishing, 2009); Pedaya, "Sabbath, Sabbatai, and the Diminution of Moon," 160-9.

22 Genesis Rabbah 41:4 (ed. Theodor-Albeck, 391); As well as Gensis Rabbah 50:10; b. *Yevamot*, 17a.

Moreover, the sages attest to God's active collaboration in the birth of Ammon and Moab, and hint at the conception of the Messiah as the son of God:

> "Come, let us make our father drink wine"... It is not written, that we may preserve a child of our father, but, "so that we may preserve seed through our father": **the seed that comes from a different source**, which is the King Messiah.²³

According to this subversive Midrash, the name "Moab" indicates that he was born from the divine "father," who acts as the partner instead of Lot, who the simple understanding of the story seemingly discusses. The beginning and pinnacle of the dynasty are called here "seed that comes from a different source," and the miraculous birthing process is implied not only regarding David (who said after his parents' sin, "If my father and mother forsake me, the Lord will take me up"), but also in regards to his forefathers, who were born in the cave of Zoar. As we saw in the third chapter, the Messiah is conceived in the Bible as the "son of God," similar to the kings in the ancient Near East.²⁴ Inspired by these Midrashim it is possible to suggest that the Davidic tales, in the eyes of the sages, played the theomachic and theogenic function of the gods in ancient civilizations. Like the gods, the Messiah is born, fights, and dies. His recurring appearance in the dynastic stories symbolizes a sort of "resurrection," and strengthens the messianic template of his foremothers. The sages stress that this family is built upon the repetition of transgressive acts, which merit divine vindication, beginning with the first birth, starting in Sodom. In this fashion the cyclical awareness of the messianic narrative is formed, existing in the heterotopic space, at the edges of space and time.²⁵

---

23 Genesis Rabbah 51:8 (ed. Theodor-Albeck, 537). A parallel Midrash is written about Seth, Genesis Rabbah 23:5 (ed. Theodor-Albeck, 226. Following the verse in Gen. 4:25). According to Albeck, Lot's daughters' story is the source of the Midrash, whereas according to Lerner the source is Seth's birth and then it was copied for the Midrash on Lot's daughters in Genesis Rabbah 51 and Ruth Rabbah (7:16; 8:1). See also *Ruth Zuṭa* (ed. Buber) 4:12; Myron B. Lerner, "The Book of Ruth in Aggadic Literature and Midrash Ruth Rabba'" 2 vols. (PhD diss., Hebrew University, 1971), 83-4. For an interpretation of this Midrash as evidence of a Judeo-Christian polemic and discourse, see Epilogue. For the link of Ruth and Naomi to the messianic dynasty, see Ginzberg, *Legends*, 2:758, 867.

24 On the Messiah as a son of God, see ch. 1 fn. 36.

25 Wolfson, *Venturing Beyond*; Pedaya, *Vision and Speech*, 209-36; Netzer, *Journey*, 328-31.

AMMON AND MOAB—SPLIT ATTITUDES

The primal story of Sodom occurs in an "otherly place" and deals with the "different manner" in which the messianic seed is created, thanks to the initiative of Lot's daughters. The two foreign women, mothers of the hostile and accursed nations, form the mythical template upon which the monarchy is built. This seed is called in *Aggadat Bereshit* "seed of *terumah*," a term signifying the act of grace that allows the world to subsist.[26] The ethnic struggle between Israel and Ammon and Moab starts with the separation of Lot from Abraham, and his choosing Sodom as his dwelling place.[27] The negative stance regarding the two nations is intensified during the time of the desert wandering, due to the sexual transgressions in which Israel stumbled in the plains of Moab, leading to the eternal prohibition of marrying them (Deut. 23:4-5).

The sages' sympathy for Lot's daughters stands in contrast to their charged attitude toward Ammon and Moab, yet gendered distinction helps to modulate the ambivalent attitude towards both nations through an emotional split and directing sympathy towards the women only, as emerges from the Talmudic principle: "An Ammonite, but not an Ammonitess; a Moabite, but not a Moabitess."[28] This principle reflects an absolute difference between the native women and men of both nations. Indeed, in the Midrashim, a certain distinction exists between Lot's daughters, the Moabite women at Shittim, and Ruth the Moabite (Genesis Rabbah 51:10). Nevertheless, the trend of completely justifying the women is prominent, compared to the sweeping condemnation of the men. It could be argued that the vindication reflects the nationalization of the Moabite womb and exploitation of the foreign women for genealogical purposes. However, from paralleling subjects like "greater is a transgression performed with good intent," it emerges that women who do not give birth to sons for the Israelite nation are also vindicated in these Midrashim.

Therefore, according to my claim, the condemnation of the men—in contrast to the sympathy towards the women—is similar to the child's reaction to the "primal scene" and struggling with the mystery connected to his parents' relations. The vindication of the mother and the conflict with the father characterize the oedipal model that constitutes a defense mechanism for the primal

---

26 Teugels, *Aggadat*, 81.
27 Genesis Rabbah, 51:7 (ed. Theodor-Albeck, 393); *b. Nazir*, 23a; *Midrash Tanḥuma, VaYera* 12.
28 *b. Yevamot* 69a; 76b-78b; *m. Yevamot* 8:3. According to *Pesiqta de-Rab Kahana* 16:1; Ruth Rabbah 4:1-2, this law was innovated in Boaz's time. For the development of this dividing principle in kabbalistic literature, see Cordovero, *'Or Yaqar*, 4:201; 5:67.

threat. A similar mechanism is actuated in relation to the chaotic story rooted in Sodom, and from there the twofold attitude regarding Moab and Ammon is founded, which is explained as bringing the women closer and distancing the men and fathers. This split model is designed to strengthen the concealed covenant between God and the Messiah's mother, recurring in each dynastic story. Thus, the otherness of the "the seed that comes from a different source" is transformed into an archetype of the "uncanny" (*unheimliche*) experience, and the Messiah represents the unrealizable desire of being foreign and familiar simultaneously.[29]

THE FIRST APPEARANCE OF THE *TIQLA:* SPAIN OF THE THIRTEENTH CENTURY

With the appearance of the *Zohar* at the end of the thirteenth century, the language of mystical experience attained new levels of religious, poetical, and spiritual expression. During the twelfth century there existed mystical circles, such as Hasidei Ashkenaz or the circle of the *Sefer ha-Bahir* in Provence. But it is only with the appearance of the *Zohar* and its literary circle that we encounter a full exposition of the divine world and an explicit program to insure the possibility of human influence upon it.[30] Thus, it is not surprising that the term *Tiqla* emerges in the literary and spiritual context of the *Zohar*, emphasizing the idea of redemption and its transformative aspects. The first citation of the term *Tiqla* in the Davidic context appears in *Parashat va-Yera* (*Zohar* 1:109b–110a) in the discussion of the daughters of Lot, the foremothers of the dynasty, and Ruth the Moabite, the maternal ancestor of King David. *Tiqla* appears for the second time in messianic context context in the section *Saba de-Mishpatim* (*Zohar* 2:95b), which discusses the transmigration of souls, the mystery of *yibbum*, and the accounts of the messianic genealogy.

Surprisingly, the term does not appear in most of the writings of the Spanish mystics associated with the "Zoharic Circle," who were active in Castile at the end of the thirteenth century. However, the *Dictionary of Foreign Words in the Zohar*, mistakenly attributed to Rabbi David Ben Yehuda he-Hasid

---

29 Freud, "Uncanny"; Freud, *Totem*. Seemingly not only is the future redeemer identified with the threat of the foreign-familiar, but also his alien foremothers and excessive repression bound to the savage and incestuous cultures they represent.

30 The innovative idea of the "Zoharic Circle" was presented first by Liebes, *Studies*, 85-138. For a later development of this theory and other hypotheses on the subject see Huss, *Radiance of the Sky*; Meroz, "Origins"; Meroz, "Zoharic Narratives."

describes the *Tiqla* as a rotating wheel, or "Torno," in the vernacular.³¹ Indeed in the *Book of Mirrors*, Rabbi David Ben Yehuda he-Hasid notes that the realm of *Malkhut*, which is called the "the source of the law" and "the mystery of the possible," is identified with the *Tiqla*.³²

Examining this rare term in its direct literary and conceptual context in the *Zohar* shows most clearly its uniqueness in comparison with other mystical contemporaries. In the *Zohar Lexicon*, Yehuda Liebes proposes the web of associations that I will seek to develop here, one that connects seduction and sexual transgression with the myth of the birth of the Messiah. In general, he interprets the idiom as: 1) potter's wheels, 2) scales, 3) weighted scales, 4) a water-meter, 5) the surveyor's rod, 6) a plumb line, and other building tools in the process of creation and redemption.³³ These different meanings are based on the diverse appearances of the term in the *Zohar*, and on the connection between the root "t.q.l" to the word *Tiqla*.³⁴ Moshe Idel describes the *Tiqla* as the paradisiacal pillar and eschatological "middle bolt," which raises the righteous from the earth to the higher realms and adjudicates justice for all humans. He suggests that the Zoharic *Tiqla* is related to the dualistic Manichean pillar of light, in which the struggle between good and evil generates redemption.³⁵ Haviva Pedaya designates the connection between the divine water-wheel and the wheel of souls, with the mystics' visions through the "eye-wheel" (*galgal ha-ayin*). While analyzing passages on the Zoharic *Galgala*, Pedaya points to the synergetic aspects of the *Tiqla*: liturgical, musical, colorful, and juridical qualities that create its theosophical, mystical, and redemptive meanings.³⁶ Other messianic aspects of the *Tiqla* were discussed by Oded Yisraeli, who emphasized the fundamental question of theodicy in the section of *Saba de-Mishpatim*.³⁷ Since the appearance of the term *Tiqla* in the section *Saba*

---

31 According to Boaz Huss, "A Dictionary of Foreign Words in the *Zohar*—A Critical Edition," *Kabbalah* 1 (1996): 178, the dictionary was composed after the Spanish expulsion, seemingly by the teacher of R. Simeon Ibn Lavi.

32 "*Malkhut* is identified as the *Tiqla* on which all souls revolve," *Sefer Mar'ot ha-Zove'ot* [ed. Matt, 29]. On the "mystery of the possible" see Matt, 53, 77. The *Tiqla* appears later in kabbalistic works such as "*Megaleh Amuqot*" and "*Emeq ha-Melekh*," from the sixteenth and seventeenth centuries.

33 Yehuda Liebes, "Sections of the *Zohar* Lexicon" (PhD diss., Hebrew University, 1976), 327–35.

34 See also Matt, *Pritzker*, 2:158 fn. 320; Vol. 5, 7–8; Gershom Scholem, *Gershom Scholem's Annotated Zohar (Jozefoui 1873)* (Jerusalem: Magnes Press, 1992), 1:445; 3:1455–6.

35 Moshe Idel, *Ascensions on High in Jewish Mysticism: Pillars, Lines, Ladders* (Budapest: Central European University Press, 2005), 113–4.

36 Pedaya, *Vision and Speech*, 128–33.

37 Yisraeli, *The Interpretation of Secrets*, 11–31, 129, 185; Liebes, *On Sabbateanism*, 87–88;

de-Mishpatim has garnered extensive research, in this chapter I wish to shed light on the parallel use of the term in *Zohar va-Yera*, which has yet to be fully examined.[38]

ZOHAR PARASHAT VA-YERA—THE STORY OF LOT'S DAUGHTERS

The idiomatic expression *Ṭiqla* is at the heart of the *Zohar*'s passage on the daughters of Lot, who ran away from the ruins of Sodom, slept with their father, and gave birth to Ammon and Moab (Gen. 19: 29–38). The act of incest between Lot and his daughters is the first story in the genealogy of the Davidic dynasty—which is characterized by a list of sexual transgressions committed by its maternal figures.

By using similar verbs and repetitive expressions in these episodes, the *Zohar* points to the continuity between the stories of Lot's daughters and Ruth's seduction of Boaz upon the threshing floor. Expressions such as, "Then she *came softly,* and *uncovered his feet,* and *lay down*" in the Book of Ruth, echo the portrayal of the cave in Zoar, where the two daughters seduce their father.[39] By using the term *Ṭiqla*, the *Zohar* demonstrates how these female sexual sins transform into tools of divine empowerment and repair (*tiqqun*):

> "Lot went up from Zoar and settled in the hills with his two daughters..." (Gen. 19:30). Rabbi Yiṣḥaq opened, "He revolves wheels by His devices, according to their deeds, whatever He commands them on the face of the inhabited earth" (Job 37:12). He revolves wheels—The blessed Holy One spins revolutions in the world, bringing cloaked dazzlers to carry out His acts, then turning and transforming them.... "According to their deeds"—on account of human deeds: As they act, so He transforms them, because of human acts He rotates those wheels, the turn of events, in all that He commands them ... Rabbi El'azar said "He revolves wheels"— The blessed Holy One spins revolutions, bringing about enduring phenomena in the world, but when people suppose that those phenomena will endure, the blessed Holy One transforms them.

Oron, "Artistic Elements," 299–310.

38 See Yisraeli and Oron (above). More on the poetical, mystical, and gender aspects of this section: Tishby, *Zohar*, 270–71; Liebes, "*Zohar* and Eros"; Giller, *Zohar*, 35-68; Idel, *Kabbalah*, 226–30; Wolfson, "Beautiful Maiden"; Abrams, "Knowing the Maiden"; Hellner-Eshed, *A River Flows*, 190–95; Benarroch, "'Yanuqa' and 'Sabba.'"

39 Ruth 3:7. Also chapters 1–2.

[Read] (*Be-taḥbulotav*), *By His devices* spelled (*be-taḥbulato*), *by His device*. "*By His devices*"—Like an artisan fashioning pottery: as long as that kick-wheel [*Ṭiqla*] keeps spinning in front of him, he can fashion as he imagines—this way or that, turning one vessel into another—since the wheel [*Ṭiqla*] is spinning before him. So the Blessed Holy One Transforms *His* activity—"*by His device*," Who is that? Lower Court of Justice, a potter's wheel [that is the "*Ṭiqla*"] spinning in front of Him, so He transforms vessels, turning one into another... The blessed Holy One revolves the turn of events in the world, to arrange everything fittingly, all issuing from a supernal source and root... Come and see: From Lot and his daughters issued two separate nations, linked to the side befitting them. So the blessed Holy One revolves revolutions, rotates rotations in the world, so that all will turn out fittingly, all linked to its site... Come and see, First it is written: "*He was unaware of her lying down or her rising* (Genesis 19, 33)," ["*or her rising*"]—spelled with [the letter] *vav* dotted above, [because] supernal assistance attending that act, from which King Messiah was destined to issue, so here *vav* is included.[40]

In the story of Lot and his daughters, the *Zohar* finds evidence of the enigmatic connection between sin and redemption. The passage ends by noting that in Genesis 19:33, while describing the night of the conception of Lot's daughters (the predecessors of Ruth the Moabite), the word "rising" (*u-bequma*) is dotted above, because of God's miraculous participation and involvement in the future birth of the Messiah. Therefore, the Messiah, "Son of David," is born thanks to the incest committed by the daughters and their father. By demonstrating the righteousness of Lot's daughters, the paradoxical trends of kabbalistic thought gain new meaning.[41]

The *Zohar*'s passage on the story of Sodom is exceptional in its clarity and forthrightness, and not only because it contains innovative ideas and justifications that had not previously been voiced. Its uniqueness consists in the refinement and integration of rabbinic pronouncements with the mythic process. For example, whereas for the sages the dotted word (*u-bequma*) is an evidence of the blemish of Lot's sin, the *Zohar* uses it to symbolize the opposite concept of divine intervention, which enabled Lot's daughters to give birth

---

40 *Zohar* I: 109b–110a; Matt, *Pritzker*, 2:157–60. The added comments in the brackets are mine.
41 In this passage, the name "Moab" reflects not only the sin of incest ("*from my father*"), but is also evidence for God's participation in the birth of the Messiah (as in Genesis Rabbah 51, 8).

to the Messiah.[42] The ethical judgment that is suited in the center of the rabbinic Midrashim is transformed in the *Zohar* to express the antinomian idea of "redemption through sin."[43]

Here, *Tiqla* serves as a multilayered term and a "dynamic symbol" reflecting the paths of divine providence. According to the *Zohar*, through the seduction of their father and the subsequent birth of their sons, Lot's daughters set the *Tiqla*'s wheels in motion. By their acts of transgression, they alter the swaying of the *Tiqla* from the side of Judgment (*Din*) to the side of Grace (*Ḥesed*), bringing about the messianic salvation. Thus, the idiom *Tiqla* expresses the dialectical relationship between the worlds; just as the lower reality derives from the divine world, human beings also have the capacity to influence and modify what is done in the higher realms.

The creative composition of the Zoharic passage reveals the "Ritual Process" and the duet between divinity and mankind. Human deeds—female seduction in particular—have mystical implications for divinity, while the use of sin and "demonic powers" for theurgic purposes creates bonds between good and bad, heaven and earth.[44]

While discussing the meaning of the term, Yehuda Liebes describes the *Tiqla* as a scale on the one hand, and on the other as a wheel; he points out the contradiction between the two images. To resolve this contradiction, I suggest that the root of the idiom is found in the Greek word "*Antiliya*," which appears in rabbinic sources and is defined as a wheel with two sides that whirl in opposite directions. In fact, the agricultural *Antiliya* combines the image of the wheel with the image of the scales.

THE ORIGINS OF THE *TIQLA* IN THE GREEK WATER-WHEEL OF "*ANTILIYA*"

The Aramaic term *Tiqla* resembles the Greek term *Antiliya* in tone and phonetics, as well as conceptual contexts. The words *Tiqla* and *Antiliya* both have an "onomatopoeic" quality that resembles the sound of water. In addition, they both derive from the foremothers of the Davidic dynasty, which inspired the interpreters to set in motion the wheels of upper and earthly reality, from

---

42 As it is said in *b. Nazir* 23a; *b. Horayot* 10b.
43 Scholem, *Messianic Idea*, 78–141.
44 For a discussion of the theurgical aspects of the Zoharic literature, see Idel, *Kabbalah*, 173–99.

the aspect of law to the plane of compassion, as written in *Midrash Ruth Rabbah*:

> Her mother in law [Naomi] asked her "where did you glean today?" (Ruth 2:19) ... More than the land owner did for the poor, the poor did for the land owner. So Ruth said to Naomi, "the name of the man for whom I did something this day" and she did not say "that *he* did so for me". Rather, that *I did for him*, namely, many things and many good deeds I did for him so that he would feed me this small portion. Rabbi Yossi answered: "I will not reject or spurn them" (Lev. 26:43), *ya'an* is the poor one (*ani*) ... Rabbi Gamliel said "because of this thing" (Deut. 15:10) like a wheel that continually revolves in this world, all reality seems like an **Antilya** wheel, what is full becomes empty and what is empty becomes full. Bar Qapra says: there is no man who does not come to this, and if not him then it befalls his son, and if not his son, then his grandson.[45]

The sages choose the singular term *Antiliya*, which does not appear in other passages, in order to discuss the issues of wealth and poverty and the value of compassion. Since the wheel is in motion in the world, and man does not know what awaits him in the future, he must behave generously to his fellow human beings. *Midrash Ruth Rabba* bases the Midrash about *Antiliya* on Ruth's grace towards Boaz, though at first glance, in light of Ruth's poverty, it seems that Boaz is the one who acts compassionately towards her. The Midrash transforms the provision of a "small portion" of wheat for Ruth in the field into Boaz's spiritual nourishment via the generation of the Messianic seed and the birth of his future progeny.

The Book of Ruth, as noted in the academic literature, delves into agriculture and fertility as symbols of spiritual fruitfulness, in light of the link between the human and divine seed.[46] Wealth and poverty are expressions of divine providence, much like the Midrash about Lot's daughters and the Zoharic *Ṭiqla*. Ruth the Moabite conveys a measure of compassion, which echoes the sexual transgression committed generations earlier by her ancestors. In fact, the act of incest is presented in Leviticus (20:17) as compassion or grace (*Ḥesed*), thus shedding a surprising light on the story of Lot's daughters.

In a capricious world, the wheels of *Ṭiqla* and *Antiliya* turn tempestuously. At the same time, as *Midrash Ruth Rabba* instructs, "what is full [can] become

---

45 *Ruth Rabbah* 5:9.
46 Biale, *Eros and the Jews*, 11–32; Pardes, *Countertraditions*, 98–119.

empty and what is empty [can] become full." Human deeds influence reality and affect the generations to come. An act of charity (*Ṣedaqah*) can save a life, and if not his life, "then it befalls his son, and if not his son, then his grandson."

This midrashic description of Ruth's compassion toward Boaz is fascinating in its link between the image of the wheel and the scales, related both to the *Antiliya* and the *Ṭiqla* wheels. Sokolof and Kraus describe the *Antiliya* as an agricultural tool in which two (or more) buckets rotate on a shared plane holding the water, each feeding the other, to irrigate the fields.[47] The agricultural drawing helps us to gain insight into the many facets connoted by the *Ṭiqla*: feminine and erotic images of plenty and fertility, and ethical images of wealth and poverty, bounty and scarcity. Also recalled are artistic and creative images of movement and playfulness as well as eschatological images to be found in the rebounding motion of divine will and its human fulfillment.

Returning to the end of the passage on the *Ṭiqla*, the *Zohar* summarizes the narrative of the messianic dynasty, beginning with the birth of the Messiah in Sodom through Ruth the Moabite, the grandmother of King David. By stressing the connection between the Hebrew verbs "rising" (*u-be-qumah*), and "salvation" (*tequmah*), the *Zohar* concludes by linking the deeds of the Davidic foremothers with the program of the Creator, whose providence guides their acts. The verb "rising" is attributed in the Bible both to Ruth and to Lot's daughters after they conceive their sons, while the promise of "*tequmah*" is God's contribution to the mutual process of redemption portrayed in these stories:

> Come and see, first it is written: "He was unaware of her lying down or her rising" supernal assistance attending that act, from which King Messiah was destined to issue, so here *vav* is included. Rabbi Shim'on said: "He was unaware … of her rising" as is written: "She rose before one person could recognize another (Ruth 3:14)." That day, she really rose [***tequmah***]—for Boaz united with her "to raise the name of the dead upon his inheritance (Ruth 4:10)," so from her were raised all those kings and the eminence of Israel. "He was unaware of her lying down," as is written: "She lay at his feet until dawn (Ruth 3:14)." Or her rising [***u-be-qumah***], as is written: "She rose [***va-taqam***] before one person could recognize another" (Ruth 3:14). Therefore, *ube-qumah*, "or her rising," contains a dotted *vav*.[48]

---

47 Michael Sokoloff, *A Dictionary of Jewish Palestinian Aramaic of the Byzantine Period* (Jerusalem: Bar Ilan University Press, 1992), 65.
48 *Zohar* I: 109b–110a; Matt, *Pritzker*, 2:161.

The story of Lot's daughters is described as a complex theurgic deed that is powered by good intentions carried out by means of a sin. When the human deed encounters divine will and a higher plan, repair transpires above and below. On the one hand, human acts establish their own reality and obstruct the movement of the wheel, and on the other hand, the divine strategy and program govern all deeds and their outcomes.

In the *Zohar*, the process of redemption is transformed into a mystery linked to the cosmic wheels, moving between *Ḥesed* and *Din*, shifting from the scales of justice to the scales of deceit. The astounding word *Ṭiqla* at the heart of the *Zohar*'s passage reflects the supervision of the entire world and its joyful and paradoxical movement. The daughters of Lot symbolize the paths of God's providence of the world, via the individual who represents the broad universe. As I have shown above, the Zoharic accent on the word "rising" changes the emphasis from the human sphere and moralistic questions, to the *sefirot* and the relationship between upper and lower realms. The Zoharic passage reveals a mystical, transformative act mingled with God's Name, since the dotted letter *"vav"* symbolizes the divine essence and *Tif'eret*. The use of ancient rabbinic Midrashim about the compassion between Ruth and Boaz alongside the Midrash about the dotted *vav* of Lot's daughters, enables the mystics of the *Zohar* to transform the ancient tool, *Antiliya*, to a new and surprising form: *Ṭiqla*.[49]

ṬIQLA IN THE *ZOHAR*—FIVE AXES OF MEANING

In exploring the development of the unique term *Ṭiqla*, we realize the inadequacy of our language to describe an idiom of such rich texture and multiple meanings. "*Ṭiqla*" is defined as "the mystery of the possible," thus affirming the need to reflect complex mystical reality with a "new language." I suggest that *Ṭiqla* represents the convergence of five paths of conceptual and linguistic meaning: (a) art and creativity, (b) gender and psychoanalysis, (c) sexuality and transgression, (d) ethics and norms, and lastly, (e) messianic ideas and eschatology.

Ṭiqla is a dynamic symbol whose aspects and meanings are merged in the following passages. The sexual seductions of the Davidic heroines and the correlation between motherhood and transgression (b, c, d), the messianic and eschatological perspectives, which indicate that the messiah is born out of darkness and

---

[49] On the development of "old" ideas in the *Zohar* see: Daniel C. Matt, "New-Ancient Words: the Aura of Secrecy in the *Zohar*," in *Gershom Scholem's Major Trends in Jewish Mysticism 50 Years After*, ed. Peter Schäfer and Joseph Dan (Tübingen: J. C. B. Mohr, 1993), 181-207; Liebes, *Studies in Jewish Myth*, 1-64.

evil (e), the artistic perspective, which describes the human being in his creative process as a reflection of God's image (a). Finally, the *Tiqla* links between heaven and earth, and dependent on the existence of all these aspects together.

I will now briefly shed light on the five meanings of the *Tiqla*, starting with the image of the artisan fashioning pottery on the kick-wheel, through the messianic and feminine aspects of the Zoharic passage, and ending with its juridical, moralistic, and even antinomian meanings.

A: From an artistic perspective, the *Tiqla* suggests playfulness and rebirth. The Zoharic parable of the artisan teaches us that the creation of tools and their diverse qualities is dependent upon the will of the creator and his thoughts. By harmonizing the story of Lot's daughters with the verse from the Book of Job, the text illustrates that human beings are actually vessels rotating under God's hands: "He revolves wheels by His devices, according to their deeds, whatever He commands them on the face of the inhabited earth" (Job 37:12). God has the power to devise playful strategies, to change events and outcomes and to cause all that he commands to take place.

In the same manner, in the *Saba de-Mishpatim*, which is linked to our passage through the singular term *Tiqla*, King David is described as a royal artist, a "joker" and comedian of the king. There, the *Zohar* says that "Every artisan when he speaks, speaks by his craft."[50] The principle of eroticism and the playfulness of creation categorize the heroes and heroines of the Davidic dynasty, who know how to put in motion the *Tiqla*'s wheel.

B: From the feminine and gender perspective, the tactic of the *Tiqla* is linked to the idea of birth and motherhood, which is in keeping with the act of creation. From the root letters *ḥet*, *bet*, and *lamed* that appear in the above verse from Job quoted in the *Zohar*, it is possible to see links between God's supervision of the world and the act of giving birth. I suggest that the word "device" (*taḥbulah*) hints at labor pains, the manner in which the birthing mother is torn, and the depiction of the double millstone upon which women gave birth in the ancient world.[51]

---

50 *Zohar*, II: 107a. Matt, Pritzker, 8:124
51 The rabbinic expression "the birthpangs of the Messiah" implies the pain involved in the process of redemption along with its feminine and metaphorical symbolism.

In the story of Lot's daughters, we see an additional hardship in labor, meaning the preconditions which allow it to take place: the failure of the world and destruction of Sodom, seduction as an act of survival, and the messianic redemption inherent in that paradoxical deed. Rabbi Moses Cordovero emphasized the feminine face and motherliness of the *Ṭiqla* in his interpretation of our passage: "And that holy spirit [of the messiah] does not leave its place other than by a female, which is the soul, which was thrown down by the crime of the first man in the depth of those shells."[52]

C: From the eschatological perspective, the *Ṭiqla* is intended to represent the birth of the redeemer. The birth of the messiah symbolizes the other side of the circle and the tempestuous wheel, from the beginning of creation through to the redemption at the End of Days. Creation, like redemption, is characterized by breaking the taboo of incest.[53] By transgressing this obligation, or returning to its pre-existence, a new world can be realized.

The circumstances governed by the *Ṭiqla* and its circular movement echo ancient myths and archetypes. Gershom Scholem claims that the turning wheel represents *Fortuna*, the Roman goddess of Fortune and Luck.[54] It is also possible, as Yehuda Liebes suggests, that the word *Ṭiqla* reflects the influence of the name *Clotho*, one of the Three Fates (*Moirai*) in ancient Greek mythology. *Clotho*, the youngest of the three goddesses of destiny, spins the spindle, once to the right and once to the left, thus determining the fate of all human souls. Like the *Ṭiqla*, the principle of the circular and playful fate is recalled in the crafting of the Zoharic passages. The purpose of the movement of the female stories here is the birth of the Messiah; the *Zohar*'s passage in *Parashat va-Yera* begins with the daughters of Lot and concludes with the birth of Ruth and the messiah, the son of David. The *Ṭiqla* also represents the greatest possible amendment to the mystery of *yibbum* and transmigration in the section of *Saba de-Mishpatim*. It is no accident that in both cases, the *Zohar* chooses the mothers of the Davidic dynasty to be responsible for bringing about redemption.

---

52 Cordovero, *'Or Yaqar*, 21: 40–41.
53 For expansion on this notion, see Idel, "Secret of the 'Arayyot.'" For other approaches to the taboo of incest and its appearance in myths of creation and redemption, see Freud, "Totem and Taboo"; Rank, *Birth of the Hero*; Lévi-Strauss, *Elementary*; Fromm, *Psychoanalysis and Religion*.
54 Scholem, *Annotated Zohar*, 3: 1455.

D: From the perspective of ethics and norms, the *Ṭiqla* is described as an earthly court. When a human being sins, the wheels turn to the left, the side that symbolizes *Din*. This spinning continues according to the *Zohar* until the person repents and atones for his deeds. On the other hand, when human actions, powered by positive motivations, fit God's plan—then the spinning moves to the right, the side of *Ḥesed*.

Metaphorically and psychologically speaking, the movement to the right is almost unnoticeable, because human beings feel themselves "merging" into divinity; however, the movement to the left is agonizing, since it creates a dissonance with the "natural flow" of reality. The gap between God's devices and human deeds is the actual source of suffering and a deeper meaning of the idea of "Sin" (*ḥeiṭ*), which in Hebrew is connected to the word for "missing the mark" (*haḥti*):

> All this, *according* to human *deeds*: if they act well, that kick-wheel spins them to the right, so events in the world come about for them favorably, fittingly. The wheel spins constantly to the right, never dragging, and the world revolves accordingly. However, if humans begin to do wrong, the blessed Holy One spins *His* constantly spinning device—which had maintained a rightward spin—to the left, rotating wheels and previously fashioned vessels leftward. Then the potter's wheel spins and events in the world come about harmfully for humans. The wheel keeps spinning in that direction until people return to acting well.[55]

On the eschatological level, the *Ṭiqla* is the pillar which raises the righteous from earth to heaven and adjudicates justice for all humans. The *Ṭiqla* holds two faces and two directions of movement: divine and human. Although on the surface they appear to sin, the mothers of the Davidic dynasty personify the idea of righteousness that God intends to govern the world. The two *Ṭiqla* passages in the *Zohar*, *Parashat va-Yera* and *Saba de-Mishpatim*, emphasize the earthly source of the pillar and the theurgic power of women in utilizing judgment and tilting it toward the side of compassion. Lot's daughters set in motion the swaying of the *Ṭiqla* from the side of *Din* to the side of *Ḥesed*, a process continued by Ruth and Tamar, as the *Zohar* teaches in other passages.

---

55 *Zohar* I: 109b–110a; Matt, Pritzker, 2:158–59.

E: The sexual and seductive aspect of the *Tiqla* illuminates the antinomian aspect of the Mercy (*Ḥesed*) that allows for the birth of the redeemer. The definition of *Ḥesed* is generosity and largesse on the one hand, and ruin and shame on the other hand. As I showed above, *Ḥesed* is also a description of incest in the Leviticus 20:17.

In both Zoharic passages, sexual deviation propels the *Tiqla*'s movement. This deviation characterizes the acts of women who seduce men who do not understand what is being done. Lot is drunk when his daughters seduce him in the Zoar cave (Gen. 19), Judah did not recognize Tamar, because she is masked when she seduces him in *petaḥ einayim* (Gen. 38), and Ruth walks toward Boaz on the threshing night, leaving *"before one person could recognize another"* (Ruth 3:14). The women's initiatives are seen as a unique power in keeping with the divine plan that spins the cosmic wheels.

CONCLUSION

We have seen how the *Tiqla* is active in the realms of seduction and intention, playfulness and devices, the creation of life and birth, thereby generating the End of Days and the coming of the redeemer. The symbolism and the dialectic of the *Tiqla* represent the double structure in an oppositional motion: right versus left and upward versus downward. The upward forces are dependent on the downward forces: acts of compassion and law, of erotic creativity and the mystery of feminine seduction are all embedded in the model of the *Tiqla*. The mystery of the hidden is linked to the Davidic matriarchs through all of its schemes in accordance with the mystery of the multilayered *Tiqla*. The feminine leftward tilt and the overpowering strength of the demonic realm that rules it, eventually bring about redemption and the birth of the messiah through incest.[56] The *Tiqla* passage points to the paradoxical link between sin and redemption, in that both are revealed and resurge through bursts of compassion and creativity.

Ruth the Moabite walking to the threshing floor that night led to the Messianic restoration, and so echoed her forbearers, the daughters of Lot, who "used" their bodies as an act of Charity (*Ṣedaqah*) for the birth of the future

---

56 This matter was explored mainly in the Sabbatean literature and in the Lurianic kabbalah. Scholem, *Sabbatai*; Scholem, *Sabbateanism*; Tishby, *Paths*; Liebes, *On Sabbateanism*; Idel, *Ben*, 425–9; Wolfson, *Venturing Beyond*.

redeemer. Through its mythopoetical style, the *Zohar* summons these women from beyond the generational breach and grants their acts of sexual union the characteristics of essential human and divine repair. The justification of the daughters of Lot completes the literary and mythical circle, which grants feminine justification to all of the mothers of the messianic dynasty, from ancient times until Ruth, the grandmother of David.

In this context, form and content encounter one another, since the Zoharic passage joins together and "couples" paradoxes and contradictions. The capacity to combine ideas and to nurture a unique idiom such as *Tiqla* reveals the author's artistic ability to reflect new realities through language. The language of the *Tiqla* developed in the *Zohar* reaches beyond the concepts of good and evil, permitted and forbidden, and creates a poetic reflection of the dynamic connection between the upper and lower realms. Divine and human inspirations work in this passage side by side, and through "the middle pillar" reveals the sway of the *Tiqla*, whose devices influences the ways of the world.

In the Zoharic exegesis, Lot's daughter's seductiveness begins a theurgic process and propels the divine reality and transmigration of souls, from the aspect of *Din* to *Ḥesed*. Nevertheless, it is an act of concealment and hiddenness, objecting to the sacred edicts and the familial structure, precisely the very same that it seeks to establish, similar to the incestuous relations between a brother and sister written about in Leviticus 20:17 "it is kindness/incest (*ḥesed*)." The development of the exegesis is built around the terms "device" (*taḥbulah*) and "*Tiqla*" which are linked to one another, and stem from the verses in Job, as is written in the passage's beginning "Rabbi Yiṣḥaq opened, 'He revolves wheels by His devices, according to their deeds, whatever He commands them on the face of the inhabited earth'" (Job 37:12). In the passage's opening is a superstructure of the ways of the crooked and hidden providence of God in the world is described. Just as Sodom's overturning causes the finding of the Messiah within the destruction according to the sages, in the *Zohar* the entire reality is reversed from Judgment to Grace, and changes its intentions, and even the essence of the deed that humankind have done. The "*Tiqla*" reflects the divine jouissance and eros and the device allows the movement of the wheels and changing of actions. In the quasi-rabbinic argument, the *Zohar* offers two models of the divine reversal of man's deeds in light of the understanding of the cryptic word "*mesibot* (wheels)" in the verse from Job: the first is the reversal of human intentions; and the second is the reversal of the consequences and actions themselves. The *Qere* and *Ketiv* of the word "device (*taḥbulah*)" in the verse originating from Job reflect doubleness: as the one and only divine device controlled only by God on the one hand, and as many devices, and "feminine ruses," dependent on human deeds, on the other hand.[57] "[Read] (*Be-taḥbulotav*), *By His devices* spelled (*be-taḥbulato*), *by His device*," the distinction between the two is explained through the disclosure of the mysterious mechanism of "*Ṭiqla*", revealing the ways of divine providence.

Our discussion in connection to the Zoharic locution "*Ṭiqla*" to the ancient irrigation instrument, *Antiliya*, elucidates the centrality of the mystery of incest in the messianic idea. While there is only a slight phonetic similarity between the terms "*Antiliya*" and "*Ṭiqla*," however in both cases there is a connection between a wheel image and an image of a scale pumping water from the source, which in the Zoharic text alludes to the drawing forth of the Messiah's soul and his descent to the world. The messianic reparation of the Davidic foremothers is conceived as a balance between the forces of judgment and wine and those of water and grace, whose beginning is in the incestual act of Lot's daughters and its end in the birth of Obed and his elected progeny. In the *Zohar* eros, paradox, and the artistic act occupy the place of the dominant ethical questions of the sages regarding Lot's daughters' story. The mystical and theurgic meaning of the passage is reflected in the dialectical relation of the *Zohar* regarding illicit relations, from one perspective—as a negative and dangerous potency, and from another perspective—as the potency of disclosure and breaching that is necessary to bring the redemption. By emphasizing the feminine and messianic aspects of the mysterious "*Ṭiqla*," the complex facets of creation and revelation are revealed.

---

57 Scholem, *Sabbatai*, 1:49-50, 243-9; Liebes, *On Sabbateanism* 87-8; Beracha Sack, *The Kabbalah of Rabbi Moshe Cordovero* (Beer Sheva: Ben Gurion University Press, 1995), 94-102.

CHAPTER 6

The Burning Face of the *Shekhinah*—Tamar in *Zohar Aḥrei Mot*

As we viewed in the previous chapter, the mystery of incest plays a central role in the kabbalistic messianic myth, which ends with the birth of the chosen son. This chapter will explore the story of Tamar and discuss a more moderate sexual transgression in the ensemble of the Davidic stories. Through the figure of Tamar, it appears that the *Zohar* focuses on the assuaging process that the *Shekhinah* undergoes in order to enable the coupling and messianic birth. The first stage of this process includes an outbreak of the forces of Judgment (*Din*), emphasizing the symbolic role of feminine sin in the Zoharic messianic narrative. Additionally, we will examine the connection between the biblical story and the Zoharic authors' consciousness as reflected through their mythopoetical exegesis.

As Yehuda Liebes has illuminated, the uniqueness of the kabbalists in the *Zohar* stems from their ability to maintain a personal and intimate discourse with the evil potencies.[1] This intimacy is connected to their identification with the *Shekhinah* and its dangerous and destructive facets. Not only is the *sefirah* of *Malkhut* seized by evil, but at times the demonic realm is in a sense her "other side."[2] Hence the kabbalists' contact with divinity cannot attain its full experience without entering the *Shekhinah*'s dangerous zones, her transgressions and promiscuity. This issue is intensified in *Zohar Aḥrei Mot*, in the passage concerning the story of Tamar and Judah that explores feminine sexuality and the question of how to assuage the divine fury.

---

1 Liebes, "*Zohar* and Eros," 79-82.
2 Scholem, *Godhead*, 140-96; Tishby, *Wisdom*, 219-31, 285-307; Idel, *Kabbalah and Eros*; Elliot R. Wolfson, *Circle in the Square: Studies in the Use of Gender in Kabbalistic Symbolism* (Albany: SUNY, 1995); Wolfson, *Language*, 46-110; Hellner-Eshed, *A River Flows*; Abrams, *The Female Body of God*; Meroz, "The Weaving of a Myth."

In the remarkable scene at the center of our study is a description of a feminine figure whose revealed face is bound with flames. Should she not immediately cover her face, she stands on the verge of being burned and consuming the entire world in the ensuing conflagration. This figure is Tamar, sitting at the "entrance to Enaim" expecting Judah's arrival, but she is also the *Shekhinah*, consumed by the erotic and destructive potencies pulsating within her. *Eros*, the essence of the Zoharic work is, in addition to its platonic sense, identified with the forces of *Din* and sexuality, as well as Lilith, the anti-heroine of the *Zohar*.[3] The question that consequently arises is whether the Zoharic authors view the *Shekhinah* and Lilith as two contradictory figures or as different aspects of the same figure. In order to answer this question, it is necessary to consider the fact that the seductive and threatening description of Tamar's figure in the *Zohar* reveals the kabbalists' desire to unite with the evil potencies, which contain the potential for life but also for destruction and annihilation. In the *Introduction to the Zohar* the kabbalists are required, like Tamar, to gaze through the *Shekhinah*—termed *petaḥ einayim* (opening of the eyes)—and contemplate the supernal realms.[4] This unique idiom is mentioned in only two places in the *Zohar*: in the *Introduction* and in *Parashat Aḥrei Mot*. In both cases we will discuss its uniqueness while exploring the relation between the *Shekhinah* and Lilith.

The choice of the authors of the *Zohar* to place the expanded reading of Tamar's story in *Parashat Aḥrei Mot*, and not in *Zohar* Genesis (which features only short passages about her), thereby sets Tamar as an alternative to the death of Aaron's sons.[5] The mythic question, "how can one enter the sacred without dying?" engages the relation between the mundane and divine worlds, as well as the perception of copulation and its potential for holiness and profanation. This passage demonstrates that the encounter

---

3 Liebes, *God's Story*, 265-9; Liebes, "*Zohar* and Eros."
4 *Zohar* I:1b
5 An additional passage about Tamar can be found in *Zohar* I: 185a, and we shall discuss it in the following chapter. Tishby claimed that the editing of the sections in the *Zohar* is haphazard and I will argue against his position. Tishby, *Wisdom*, xvii, xxi-xxiv. On the integration of textual units, like the *Idra* literature, into the *Zohar*, see Liebes, *Studies*, 15-75; Shifra Asulin, "The Flaw and its Correction: Impurity, The Moon and the Shekhinah—A Broad Inquiry into Zohar 3:79 (Aharei Mot)," *Kabbalah* 22 (2010): 193-251, 214-21, 236-47. On the kabbalists' religious consciousness, see Liebes, "Myth vs. Symbol"; Melila Hellner-Eshed, "The Zealot of the Covenant and the Estatic Elijan and Habakkuk in the *Zohar*: On the Masculine and Feminine in the Human Psyche," *Kabbalah* 22 (2010): 178, 186.

with Lilith, representing the dark side of the *Shekhinah*, is intrinsic to the mystical experience and the kabbalist's spiritual journey.[6]

THE PASSAGE'S FRAMEWORK—AN OPENING TO SUPERNAL MYSTERIES

At both the beginning and end of the reading on Tamar in *Parashat Aḥrei Mot*, the *Zohar* states that her story demonstrates the mystery of faith and embodies the concealed and disclosed in God's name and the Torah:

> There we learned: The Holy Name is concealed and revealed; and Torah, which is the Supernal Holy Name, is concealed and revealed; and every verse in Torah and every portion in her is concealed and revealed. For it has been taught in the name of Rabbi Yehudah: **From the impudence of one righteous woman many benefits emerged to the world**. Who is that? Tamar, as is written: *She sat by the entrance to Enaim*. Rabbi Abba said: This portion demonstrates that Torah is concealed and revealed. I have looked through the entire Torah and have not found a place called *petaḥ einayim* (the entrance to Enaim). But really, all is concealed, mystery of mysteries. It has been taught: What prompted this righteous woman to engage in this act? Well in her father-in-law's house she learned the ways of the blessed Holy One: how he conducts this world with human beings. And because she knew, the blessed Holy One fulfilled this matter through her ... We have established as follows: **Tamar fulfilled the matter below, bring forth blossoms and sprouting branches in mystery of faith**.[7]

How do Tamar's actions attest to these mysteries? According to the *Zohar*, her singularity is due to her seduction in the mundane world, sprouting flowers and budding branches in the "mystery of faith," and it is precisely within her audacity that her righteousness is enrooted. It appears that this oxymoronic description of her actions, "From the impudence of one righteous woman," is further

---

6 This claim has been made by Liebes about Jacob's journey towards Haran to Lilith in the *Sitrei Torah*. I wish to demonstrate that it is also in regards to the body of the *Zohar*. Zohar I: 148a-b. Liebes, "Zohar and Eros," 100-1.
7 *Zohar* III: 71b-72a. Matt, *Pritzker*, 7: 478-80.

developed in Hasidic literature and transformed in the writings of Naḥman of Bratslav into the familiar idea of "holy audacity."[8]

The palm (*tamar*) tree, generally interpreted in the *Zohar* as the *Ṣaddiq*, here indicates a feminine figure with which the kabbalists identify. Seemingly, the text reverses the literal meaning of the verse, "The righteous (*Ṣaddiq*) flourish like the palm tree" (Psalm 92:13), and demonstrates that the divine male, *sefirah* of *Yesod*, will flourish like the palm tree that includes within it both male and female.[9] It is through these images that Tamar's masculine facet is highlighted, a heroine whose human acts of seduction, beginning with the fight against the human injustice she suffered—repair the supernal realm.[10] Tamar's very name alludes to her androgynous nature and the motif of exchanging (*ha-temura*) as well as the changeability of her actions.[11] The biblical story already draws the noticeable contrast between her being covered by a veil and her exposure, as it is written, "and [she] sat down at the entrance to Enaim" compared to "for she had covered her face" (Gen. 38:14-15). The Zoharic passage intensifies the tension between revealed and concealed and describes the feminine drama as a key to divine mysteries, as it emerges from its beginning: "The Holy Name is concealed and revealed ... This portion demonstrates that Torah is concealed and revealed." In this preface, the *Zohar* thereby conjoins kabbalistic traditions regarding the two levels of the Torah and God's

---

8 According to the translation of Yehuda Leib Ashlag, *Ba'al ha-Sulam*, "boldness of one righteous woman." While Cordovero says, "she set her face, as is written, 'through the physical action the spiritual allusion is concealed,'" Cordovero, *'Or Yaqar*, 13:66. Naḥman of Bratslav uses the term "holy audacity" in other contexts, for example *Liqquṭei MoHaRaN*, 22, 30, and Nathan of Nemirov, *Liqquṭei Halakhot* employs this expression regarding King David and the messianic dynasty.

9 On the androgynity of the palm tree, see b. *Pesaḥim* 56a; *Zohar* II: 126a; Daniel Abrams, *The Book Bahir: An Edition Based on the Earliest Manuscripts*, (Los Angeles: Cherub Press, 1994), 139; Wolfson, "Gender and Heresy," 255. Also as Philo wrote, "And when she [Tamar] has brought them to the birth, she wins the meed of conquest over her adversaries, and is enrolled as victor with the palm as the symbol of her victory. For Tamar is by interpretation a palm." (*On the Unchangableness of God*, 137) Colson and Whitaker, *Philo*, 79. Shinan and Zakovitch, *Story*, 44.

10 For an exploration of the theurgic role of the earthly woman, see Idel, *Kabbalah and Eros*, 67-74, 220, 364-8; Garb, *Power*. Charles Mopsik suggests that Tamar belongs to the "masculine woman" model, like Ruth, who is also in the passage as well as the other Davidic heroines. This model's roots are embedded in the Zoharic literature and the development of the mystery of "impregnation" and "transmigration." Mopsik, *Sex of the Soul*, 42-4.

11 Also emerging from the depiction of *Malkhut* as the "mystery of the possible," which we discussed in the previous chapter.

name enclosed therein, with Tamar's story representing a theurgic process.[12] Not only is the Torah perceived in the *Zohar* as "an archetype of man and the world," but the biblical stories and its heroes' actions also precipitate the relations of the *sefirot* and the divine saga.[13]

The link between the mystery of faith and Tamar's story is created through the term *petaḥ einayim*, which alludes to the *Shekhinah*. The *Shekhinah* is, in many ways, the opening to the supernal: she is the gateway to divine mysteries, she is the *pargod* (curtain) and mirror in which the *sefirot* are reflected, she symbolizes the "absence" and "feminine deficiency." It is in this capacity that she invites the kabbalists to heal her brokenness.[14] It can be said that the "opening" symbolizes the mystic's liminal position in traversing between *Din* and *Ḥesed*, and heaven and earth.[15]

The phrase *petaḥ einayim* is mentioned once more in the *Introduction to the Zohar*, in the revelatory passage interpreting Isaiah's words: "Lift your eyes on high and see: Who (*mi*) created these (*eleh*)," (40:26) which deals with mankind's ability to comprehend mysteries and through them, influence reality. The authors of the *Zohar* are well aware of the original meaning of the idiom *petaḥ einayim*. Its placement in the introduction is not random and enables the presentation of a central principal of the mystical experience: while illuminating the kabbalist's place facing the *Shekhinah*, Tamar's seductive figure is revealed to him. According to this passage, the feminine *sefirot* (*mah* [what]— *Malkhut*, and *mi* [who]—*Binah*), connect to the six masculine *sefirot* born from *Binah* (*eleh* [these]), and form the word "*Elohim*," which symbolizes the dual directional nature of the emanation process. Like Tamar's sitting veiled at "the entrance to Enaim," the kabbalist's uniqueness lies in his dual ability to gaze and comprehend the mystery of faith and its revelation, but also to recognize its limitations and the appropriate time for its concealment.[16]

---

12 For the perception of Torah as God's name, *Zohar* II: 87a, as well as, Gikatilla, *Sha'arei*, 1: 201, 249; Moshe Idel, "The Concept of the Torah in Hekhalot Literature and Its Metamorphoses in Kabbalah," *Jerusalem Studies in Jewish Thought* 1 (1981): 23-84; Liebes, "Zohar Lexicon," 174-6; Wolfson, *Language, Eros, Being*, 39; Halbertal, *By Way of Truth*, 60-1. On the disclosure and concealment in Torah, Scholem, *Symbolism*, 32-86; Liebes, *Studies*, 40-60; Moshe Halbertal, *Concealment and Revelation: Esotericism in Jewish Thought and its Philosophical Implications* (Princeton: Princeton University Press, 2007), 70-2; Hellner-Eshed, *A River Flows*, 187-221.

13 Idel, "Concept of the Torah," 58.

14 Gikatilla, *Sha'arei*, 1: 53-92. For a cultural criticism of the perception of the feminine as lacking, see Luce Irigaray, *This Sex Which Is Not One* (Ithaca: Cornell University Press, 1985).

15 Pedaya, *Vision and Speech*, 209-236; Turner, *Ritual Process*.

16 *Zohar* I: 1b. Liebes, "Zohar and Eros," 67-8; Hellner-Eshed, *A River Flows*, 225, 390; Wolfson,

The term *petaḥ einayim* that appears in the *Introduction to the Zohar* alludes to Tamar, whose life is endangered (as related in her story: "Bring her out, and let her be burned" Gen. 38:24), and hints at the dangerous experience embedded in each revelation.[17] On a reflective level it can be said that—already on the opening page—the *Zohar* "seduces its learner" as Tamar seduces Judah at the "entrance to Enaim." This interpretation's importance is emphasized by its repetition at the conclusion of the discussion about Tamar in *Zohar Aḥrei Mot*. Accordingly, a framework is constructed, at the core of which is an inspection of a human story and, at its edges, a description of the divine mysteries learned from Tamar's actions:

> Rabbi El'azar said, "This portion affirms supernal wisdom in various aspects. When words are contemplated, one perceives mysteries of the Blessed Holy One and His judgments everywhere ... Rabbi Abba said, "This portion is linked to mysteries of the wisdom of Torah, and all is concealed and revealed. The entire Torah follows this pattern. Every single word in Torah includes a holy name, concealed and revealed. (*Zohar* 3:72a; Matt, *Pritzker*, 7:484-5)

This passage teaches that reality oscillates upon the tension between concealment and disclosure which is expressed in relation to the body, *eros*, secrecy, God's name, and the Torah. According to the *Zohar*, the earthly relations between the masculine and feminine engender a supernal reality of the disclosure of the divine name which is given to Tamar at the end of the passage: "*Ṣedaqah*, (she is righteous), surely, and the name proves ... *Ṣedaqah* (She is righteous)—*Ṣedeq, he* (is Righteousness). *From me* She received this name; *from me* She inherited this; *from me* this came." This name is not only given to

---

Through a Speculum, 330-45; Chana Ripple-Kleiman, "*Petaḥ Einayim*: On Eyes and Vision in the *Zohar*" (master's thesis, Hebrew University, 2008), 86-93; Monique Biber, "Raza de-Eina: A Study in the Secrets of the Eye in the *Zohar*" (master's thesis, Bar Ilan University, 2006), 173-4. On the glance as an erotic-hermeneutic act, see Daniel Boyarin, "The Eye in the Torah: Ocular Desire in Midrashic Hermeneutic," *Critical Inquiry* 16, no. 3 (1990): 532-550.

17 On the threatening erotic core in the depictions of theophany in Hekhalot literature, see David J. Halperin, "A Sexual Image in *Hekhalot Rabbati* and Its Implications," in *Proceedings of the First International Conference on the History of Jewish Mysticism: Early Jewish Mysticism*, ed. Joseph Dan (Jerusalem: Hebrew University, 1987), 117-132. On the desire of God to reveal himself and the mystic's desire to view divinity in the Hekhalot literature, Halbertal, *Concealment and Revelation*, 21; Schäfer, *Synopse*, 159, 70.

her by Judah saying "she is more righteous than I," but by God as well. Thus the Ṣedeq (righteousness), which symbolizes *Malkhut* at her time of judgment, becomes Ṣedaqah (she is righteous), by uniting with *Tif'eret* (termed in the *Zohar* as Ṣaddiq).

The letter *he* added to Tamar's name transforms her anger at the injustice in the mundane realm into contemplation of grace (ḥesed). Tamar is thus the *Shekhinah* in both states—in her judgment and assuagement—and indeed, according to the *Zohar*, she is awaiting this coupling from time immemorial.[18] The longed for union does not, however, happen as easily and speedily as it does in the Bible. Tamar must undergo a complex journey, entailing an encounter with the demonic realm, the danger of exile, and even survive her own destructive forces.

THE BURNING IMAGE—THE SMOLDERING *SHEKHINAH*

According to *Zohar Aḥrei Mot*, the gist of the redemption drama occurs in the moments between Tamar's sitting at the "entrance to Enaim" and Judah's arrival and their copulation. This drama is played out simultaneously in heaven and earth. The divine mystery of faith is developed within the mystique of the biblical scene in which Judah comes to his daughter-in-law without knowing her identity. At the beginning of the account in Genesis 38, Tamar is described as a passive figure, taken and transferred from one man to another: going from Judah, to Er and Onan, and subsequently to her father's house in a state of "living widowhood," in which she is denied the promised union with Shelah. After sitting on the road to Timnah, she merits the mothering of Judah's progeny through ruse and seduction. However, at this stage her life is also endangered due to the rumor of "her playing the whore." The Bible indeed emphasizes Tamar's struggle and miraculous rescue, yet does not dwell on her feelings during the story. The *Zohar*, in contrast, focuses on the feminine experience and seeks to highlight the moment that Tamar—*Shekhinah*—covers her face.

By freezing the burning scene and amplifying it through parallel images that discuss the heroines in similar circumstances, the *Zohar* identifies with Tamar's unique voice and understands the dangerous experience in which she is trapped. Furthermore, the *Zohar* intentionally refrains from discussing the

---

18 *Zohar* III: 71b. Scholem also writes that this passage deals with "the aspect of judgment in *Shekhinah*... interpreting everything according to the mystery of *Malkhut* and *Tif'eret*." Scholem, *Annotated*, 5: 2456.

known results of the story, the birth of Perez and Zerah and the founding of the messianic dynasty; rather, it focuses on the meeting of *Malkhut* and *Tif'eret*. The fire grasping Tamar is understood from two perspectives: on the one hand, it represents the positive forces of *eros* and seduction that ultimately lead to the birth of a son to the Davidic line, while on the other hand it is the destructive flame of the feminine divine which seeks to completely destroy her surroundings. The attitude towards the flame (*eish*) and the woman (*isha*), and specifically, regarding their annihilative and invigorative potencies, teaches much about the mythopoetic process of the texts' formation, and the dialectic voices within their creators' souls. At the heart of Zoharic exegesis is a fabric of enigmatic images placed one upon the other, the aim of which is to stimulate the reader and transform him into a partner in the experiential and visual drama. Verses from Genesis, Proverbs, and the Song of Songs are interwoven in order to emphasize the *Shekhinah*'s demonic features:

> Judah saw her and he took her for a whore (Gen. 38:15)—as is said: Such is the way of an adulterous (Prov. 30:20) For she had covered her face (Gen., ibid.)—as we have established, for it is written: she eats and wipes her mouth (Prov., ibid.). She scorches the world with Her flames, and says, 'I have done no wrong' (ibid.). Why? For she had covered her face, and no one knows Her ways, to save Himself from Her. He turned aside to her by the road (*el ha-derekh*) (Gen. 38:1)—el ha-derekh (by the way), really, to join white with red. And said, 'Havah (Come on) let me come to you' (ibid.)—and we have established havah everywhere. For he did not know that she was his daughter-in-law (*khallato*)—that she was the destruction (*khallato*), of the world, and we translate this: 'that she was destruction.' Why did not He know? Because Her face shone to receive from Him, and She was ready to be sweetened and bestow compassion on the world. That she was his daughter-in-law (*khallato*)—alternatively, an actual bride (*kallah*) as is written: With me from Lebanon bride (*kallah*) (Song. 4:8).And she said, 'What will you give me for coming in to me?' (Gen. 38:16). Now the Bride seeks Her jewels. He said, 'I myself will send a kid from the flock' (ibid, 17). (*Zohar* 3:72a; Matt, Pritzker, 7:480-2).

This passage is charged with phonetic and linguistic play and loaded with multiple meanings. I seek to examine it through two readings: according to the first, in the *Shekhinah*'s blazing face it is possible to see a constant state, characterizing a permanent quality of feminine nature, whereas according to the second, this is but a temporary stage in the assuaging process of the female. Both options exist without negating the other and each is anchored in a reversed understanding of the verses while illuminating a different perspective of Tamar's story and the *Shekhinah*'s figure in the redemption myth. Either way, a powerful feminine archetype is formed, one that embodies the link between the sacred, sexuality, and death, and attests to the dangerous entrance to the holy, while drawing the kabbalist towards the threatening face of divinity. I will begin by discussing the image of the *Shekhinah*'s burning at the "opening of the eyes," comparing it to Lilith's descriptions in the *Zohar*. Subsequently, I will highlight the process of mitigation and reparation, unique to the description of the *Shekhinah*, as described in *Zohar Aḥrei Mot*.

A. "Scorches the World in Her Flames": The Fixed Quality in Feminine Nature—Tamar, *Shekhinah*, and Lilith

The *Zohar* draws parallels between Tamar and the foreign woman of Proverbs, ascribing to both of them the verse: "This is the way of an adulteress: she eats, and wipes her mouth, and says, 'I have done no wrong'" (Prov. 30:20). Similar to the foreign woman, Tamar is also portrayed as a harlot ("When Judah saw her, he thought her to be a prostitute, for she had covered her face"), the covering of her face necessary in order to conceal her threatening essence. The passage connects the word *paneha* (her face)—in Aramaic *anpaha*—and *mena'afet* (the adulterous woman).[19] The phonetic weaving of the verses also relies on the symbolic link between the mouth (*peh*), face (*panim*), and eyes (*einayim*) as erotic symbols. The adulterous woman in Proverbs suppresses the signs of her actions and claims her innocence, as does Tamar, sitting at the "entrance to Enaim" and hiding behind a veil. The *Zohar* highlights the impossibility of rescue from these two women and of comprehending their ways, both due to their concealed dangers. Tamar is configured here as a split-faced figure, a woman shining outwards, coming as it were, "to bestow compassion on the world." Behind the mask, however, she remains merely Lilith. This is an image complimenting two aspects of a single essence: the danger embedded in the erotic and vibrant potencies of the feminine figure. As emerges from the text's beginning and end, Tamar's personal danger pertains to the divine mysteries and driving forces of the universe. The act of copulation has the simultaneous potential of both pleasure and cosmic destruction, of danger and of reparation.

---

19 For the development of this idea and an exploration of Cordovero's commentary on the *Zohar*, see Hellner-Eshed, "On Love," 166-8.

The Zoharic account of Tamar reveals the archetype of "the devouring (*mekhalleh*) bride (*kallah*)," with the bridal canopy symbolizing the ecstatic union, but also destruction and death. The biblical description "**she eats, and wipes her mouth**" has a double and triple meaning, as an act of burning, satiation, and even as an image of lethal copulation: Tamar, widowed of two husbands, is portrayed in the *Zohar* as a positive *femme fatale*.[20] The *Zohar*, unlike rabbinic Midrash, makes no attempt to cleanse her name and motives, but rather, describes the burning and face covering without concealing the fire. The mythic image of the devouring female is transformed into part of the redemption journey, which begins by meeting the burning *Shekhinah*. The verse "she eats, and wipes her mouth" situated at the heart of the passage about Tamar, is interpreted a number of times in the *Zohar* in connection to demonic women. These descriptions, some of which I will examine below, illuminate the kabbalists' ambivalent attitude towards feminine seductiveness as, on the one hand, an irresistible ominous force and on the other, as a positive essential feature of the *Shekhinah*. Thus, for example, it is said about Lilith in *Parashat va-Yakhel*:

> *Her feet descend to death* (Prov. 5:5)—*Her feet descend* to whom? To the one called *death* ... Come and see what is written: *Such is the way of an adulteress* ... (ibid, 30:20), and we have established this. But, *Such is the way of an adulteress*—the Angle of Death, and so he is called. *She eats and wipes her mouth* (ibid.)—she scorches the world with her flames and kills people before their time. *And says, 'I have done no wrong'* (ibid.)—'for I demanded justice against them and they were found guilty and died justly.'[21]

In similar language that describes Tamar, Lilith is presented in the *Zohar* as one who "scorches the world in her flames." She slays men and kills their infants, while subsequently proclaiming her innocence.[22] In other places, Lilith is characterized by descriptions of seductive and perilous beauty. So, for example, in the *Sitrei Torah* on *Parashat va-Yeṣe*, Lilith wears a royal purple garment adorned with rare jewels, her mouth and lips rose-flushed, and is suddenly transformed into a man holding a sword who ascends to kill Jacob on his way to Haran. Lilith's

---

20 b. *Yevamot* 34b, Rashi on Genesis 38:11 "This is a woman whose husbands presumably die young," however in contrast to the Talmud, the *Zohar* doesn't condemn her deeds. Also Cordovero, *'Or Yaqar*, 13: 66, 68.
21 *Zohar* II: 196b. Matt, *Pritzker*, 6:117-8. Also *Zohar* I: 27b, III: 47a.
22 Tishby, *Zohar*, 1: 361-77; Idel, *Kabbalah and Eros*, 104-146; Yisraeli, *The Interpretation of Secrets*, 159-63.

depiction there, as "full of horrific eyes," echoes Tamar's "entrance to Enaim (*eyes*)."[23] Tamar's masculinity, which R. Moses Cordovero terms "tigerliness," is revealed in the beginning of the passage in which she makes flowers bloom in the mystery of faith, while Lilith's masculinity emerges when she takes revenge on the thoughtless who come to her.[24] The identification between Lilith and the Angel of Death seemingly attests to the Zoharic authors' concealed fears and their tendency to ascribe blame and responsibility for such threatening natural elements as birth, intercourse, and death, to women.[25] An additional treacherous feminine figure can be found at the end of the *Aḥrei Mot* section, following Tamar's account. There, the menstruant woman is portrayed as being controlled by the demonic realm, red and full of judgment like Lilith. Similarly, the menstruant, like Tamar, is presented as double-faced, and at the moment of her purification transforms the judgment (*Din*) and blood into whiteness and grace (*Ḥesed*). At the time of her judgment, the menstruant is perceived as a demonic figure, however one also possessing seductive aspects as reflected in the depiction of her hair, tongue, and fingernails.[26] These detailed descriptions allude to the kabbalists' recoiling from, but also attraction to her figure, as one who encapsulates the features of "the other woman" whom the midrashic literatures "loves to hate." This contrasts with the mystery of the red heifer that contains a portrayal of a hospitable feminine figure who suddenly becomes a snake and devours the world, like Tamar in our text: "*the statute of* (*Ḥuqqat*), *the Torah*—the verse should read (*ḥoq*), *the rule of, the Torah*; why *ḥuqqat*?... For now, Her face is beaming; yet She commits fraud against human beings—afterward striking like a snake, destroying and killing, and she says, 'I have done no wrong'* (Proverbs 30:20)."[27]

The similarity between Tamar's, the *Shekhinah*'s, and Lilith's descriptions in the Zoharic passages require interpretation.[28] All of these figures are recognized

---

23 *Zohar*, I: 147b (*Sitrei Torah*); Liebes, "*Zohar* and Eros," 101.
24 Cordovero, *'Or Yaqar*, 13:66; Mopsik, *Sex of the Soul*, 42-4; Wolfson, "Gender and Heresy."
25 Neumann, *Mystical*.
26 Asulin, "The Stature of the Shekhina," 103-81; Asulin, "The Flaw and its Correction." Boyarin claims that the demonization of the menstruant was prominent in the Middle Ages, thus "we must not, however, read the texts of classical rabbinic literature through the fear and hatred of women characteristic of the later period." On menstruation laws, as an atonement for Eve's sin, while simultaneously blaming her for bringing death into the world. Boyarin, *Carnal Israel*, 96; Fonrobert, *Menstrual Purity*, 32-8.
27 *Zohar* III: 180b, Matt, *Pritzker*, 9:195. The letter "*tau*" in the word *ḥuqqat* is composed of the letters "*dalet*" and "*nun*," both symbolizing the *Shekhinah* and Lilith (as a fish and a snake of destruction), while Scholem remarks that these passages deals only with the *Shekhinah*. Scholem, *Annotated Zohar*, 2:600-3; 6:3334).
28 As Liebes writes, "sometimes the 'adulterous woman' is interpreted as Lilith, situated as a

by their doubled and threatening faces. The eye and mouth feature with recurring depictions as liminal limbs, symbolizing the transition from the internal to external and the trepidation caused by the feminine body and its mysteries. The danger's intensity is viewed in the margins, cracks, and the outlines, as Mary Douglas suggests:

> All margins are dangerous. If they are pulled this way or that the shape of fundamental experience is altered. Any structure of ideas is vulnerable at its margins. We should expect the orifices of the body to symbolize its especially vulnerable points.[29]

Indeed, the eyes in Tamar's and Lilith's depictions are connected on the one hand to *petaḥ einayim* in its erotic and positive sense, and on the other, to the "evil eye" and the Angel of Death, who is "all eyes."[30] The *Zohar* warns against the foreign and seductive woman, the menstruant, Lilith, and advises to avoid these dangerous figures.[31] So what then is the difference between them and the *Shekhinah*? The answer likely lies in the narrow gap between potential destruction and its realization. Lilith actualizes her threat and burns, whereas the *Shekhinah*, in the figure of Tamar, suspends the perilous situation and "covers her face," thereby causing the fire to be calmed.

This topic is clarified in light of another scene of fire, which arises from R. Shim'on bar Yoḥai's (Rashbi) ecstatic statement at the end of the *Idra Zuṭa* when he ascends to heaven: "I testify that all my days I have been distressed for the world, that it not encounter the judgment of Righteousness (Ṣedeq) and be consumed by its flames—as is written: *She eats and wipes her mouth*."[32] As in the Zoharic text about Tamar, here too the *Shekhinah* is called Ṣedeq (Righteousness) in her state of burning, and Ṣedaqah (mercy/charity) when

---

polar opposite of *Shekhinah*... yet in other places in the *Zohar* this 'adulterous woman' is specifically the *Shekhinah* herself, in the *Zohar* opposites like these only contribute to the enrichment and diversification of myth." Yehuda Liebes, "A Bride as She is: On R. Moshe Cordovero: Ma'ayan Ein Ya'aqov," *Massekhet* 9 (2009): 197-8.
29 Douglas, *Purity and Danger*, 122.
30 In the *Idra* literature the "white eye of *Atiqa*" receives a closer look, alongside the destroying angels being depicted as a "master over his eyes." Liebes, *Studies*, 1-84; Wolfson, *Through a Speculum*, 383-92; Abrams, "Knowing the Maiden."
31 On the dialectical relation of Lilith and *Shekhinah* to motherhood, see Kara-Kaniel, "Eve, the Gazelle, and the Serpent." In the passage here, the seductive tone is prominent, while motherhood is only alluded to in the background of the portion.
32 *Zohar* III: 292a; Matt, *Pritzker*, 9:804.

she is coupling with a male who sweetens her judgments. Rashbi's crying out about the flames that may engulf the world upon his death, attests to his deep identification with the *Shekhinah*'s destructiveness. According to his own testimony, Rashbi dedicated his life to protecting the world from the *Shekhinah*'s flame, by absorbing her within him and through his identification with her.

According to Gershom Scholem, the dark side of the *sefirah* of *Malkhut* stems from two principles: on the one hand, the sins of man and human injustice that transform the *Shekhinah* into the executer of judgment, and on the other hand, the absence of abundance from the divine male which causes an empowering of the demonic realm and subsequently, the cleaving of the *qelippot* to her vulnerability and inner poverty.[33] The words of Rashbi in the *Idra Zuṭa* and Tamar's story in *Parashat Aḥrei Mot* elucidate how these two motifs connect the issues of righteousness and its absence. Generally, mankind's sins cause the appearance of the *Shekhinah*'s flame, however at times it is precisely her state as "*Ṣedeq*" (when she is alone without the balance of the male and *Ṣaddiq*), which causes the world's burning. The injustice done to Tamar by her husbands and the unfulfilled promise of her being wed to Shelah are the earthly causes of the ascent of evil forces, and alongside them, of the internal dynamics of judgment (*Din*) in the divine realm. In the absence of union with *Tif'eret*, the *Shekhinah*'s burning is intensified as the demonic realm cleaves to her.

Why did the authors of the *Zohar* choose to identify Tamar with the *Shekhinah* and place such a dramatic declaration regarding "the mystery of faith" at the beginning and conclusion of the passage? Obviously this identification is not accidental. In the kabbalists' description of the feminine divine, they did not choose a figure that is entirely white (pure) and kind (*ḥesed*), but rather preferred a stormy and scorching figure, the burning and perilous face. The choosing of Tamar's story in order to reflect the *Shekhinah*'s journey, demonstrates the understanding of a complicated process that divinity must undergo until the *Shekhinah*—like Tamar—can be transformed into a "messianic mother," symbolically and literally. The preference of a figure full of contradictions, "audaciously righteous," is meant to reflect the variegated appearances of *Malkhut*. On an innermost level, the image of the concealing and disclosing of the burning face allows an observation of the kabbalists' personal knowledge of the evil potencies and their attraction to the demonic aspects of the feminine divinity. This passage is also likely a type of prayer to cover and calm the mystic's burning face and arouse the source of mercy during the revelatory experience.

---

33 Scholem, *Godhead*, 189-90.

It is possible to say that the apocalyptic battles accompanying the Messiah occur within the *Shekhinah*'s being and are reflected in Tamar's face—that is, the kabbalist's soul.[34] Even the description of exile throughout the passage emphasizes their longing for redemption and their identification with the real perils in which Tamar finds herself at the moment of her being placed on the pyre: "What is written? *Take her out to be burned* (Gen. 38:24)—as is written: *Tif'eret Yisra'el (the beauty of Israel) has cast down earth from heaven* (Lam. 2:1). *To be burned*—by flames of noon in exile. What is written? *As she was being taken out* (Gen. 38:25)—to be drawn into exile."[35] Together with the metaphorical depiction of exile, the *Zohar* portrays a living image of a woman sent out to be burnt and who almost perishes by fire. Just as Tamar, who is meant to be punished on the pyre, the *Shekhinah* is also purged in exile, and like Tamar endangering her life, so too the *Shekhinah* is in the grips of the demonic realm:

> It happened about three months (*ke-mishlosh ḥodashim*) later (Gen. 38:24). What is *ke-mishlosh ḥodashim*?... that the fourth month had begun to arouse judgments in the world due to the sins of humanity, and She suckled from the Other Side (demonic realm). Then, *Judah was told, saying, 'Tamar your daughter-in-law has played the whore*—look, the Bride is located on the Other Side.[36]

In this description the daughter-in-law is found on the "other side," presented here as a terrifying and actual experience. The *Shekhinah*'s nourishment from the demonic realm is inevitable, for when the male fails to couple with her she is forced to seek sustenance elsewhere. Nevertheless, as we saw above, her cleaving to evil also happens justly (and as is well known, justice is blind), due to the overflowing of injustice in the mundane realm, both in Tamar's story and that of the *Shekhinah*'s situation in the supernal realm. The act of coupling indicates the depth of danger and the forces demanding to be struggled with, both from the male and female, as it is written in our text: "*He turned aside to her by the road (el ha-derekh)* (Gen. 38:1)—*el ha-derekh* (by the way), really, to join white with red." Judah too, as symbolizing *Tif'eret*, experiences a parallel voyage corresponding to the *Shekhinah*'s journey, and for this purpose leaves his place

---

34 *Zohar* II:7b-10a; Pedaya, *Vision and Speech*, 225-9; Pedaya, "The Sixth Millenium"; Liebes, *Studies*, 10-20..

35 *Zohar* III:72a, Matt, *Pritzker*, 7:483.

36 Ibid. According to the priestly tradition of Jubilees 41:25-26, Tamar was sentenced to the fire due to Judah being her father-in-law. Shemesh, *Halakha*, 80-95.

of security, deviating from his familiar path. The conjunction of red and white compels him to encounter the forces of judgment and temper them with good without forfeiting their intensity and danger.

B. Annihilation and Destruction as a Stage in the Reparative Process and as a Condition for the Arrival of the Redemption

Another reading of the *Shekhinah*'s voyage may emerge from a different understanding of the verses woven into the passage. The phrase "For she had covered her face" (Gen. 38:15) is referenced three times in the Zoharic passage interwoven with the verse from Proverbs 30:20. The recurring template "For he did not know that she was his daughter-in-law (*khallato*)" may thus be interpreted in contradictory ways: "he did not know" that she is a destructive and demonic woman—"that she was destruction"—and therefore he comes to her. "He did not know" that she is his daughter-in-law intended for his son, and was therefore unconcerned of possible illicit relations. "He did not know" that she is his intended bride, and thought that she was a mere *qedeshah* on the road. "He did not know" that she covered her face—that is to say she is not dangerous towards him and the world, for she calmed the forces of judgment. Finally, possibly Judah "did not know" anything of her destructive and perilous features, for she was kind towards him, willingly welcoming him and copulating with him.[37] The passage continues this ambiguity, suggesting a double reading of Proverbs 30:20 "she eats and wipes her mouth." On the one hand, as we saw previously in terms of burning and destruction, and on the other, as a soothing act, identified with Tamar's covered face. "For she had covered her face"—for she shielded herself and her surroundings from ruin and annihilation.

That being the case, there are then three stages of the process that the *Shekhinah* undergoes, and which are based on the mixture of verses in the text. First, "and he took her for a whore" / "Such is the way of an adulterous," a state of danger and threat. Second, "For she had covered her face" / "she eats and wipes her mouth," a moment of sweetening, covering, calming, and righteous justice. Finally, "For he did not know" / "that she was his daughter-in-law (*khallato*)," unraveling the plot by revealing the intended union of

---

37 Cordovero views in this depiction two contradictory images, which the *Zohar* is trying to unite. According to one, Tamar is externally attractive and Judah does not know that she is dangerous. Whereas according to the other reading, Judah is unaware that she is his destined bride through the "mystery of *du-Parṣufin*," and only sees the exterior harlot. Cordovero, *'Or Yaqar*, 13: 67.

Tif'eret and *Malkhut* and mitigating the red with white. The passage's main concern focuses on the covered face, thereby highlighting Tamar's and the *Shekhinah*'s experience. This is the place in which they encounter self-annihilation and the devouring fire within them. The reader of the text is similarly roused and, through the interwoven verses, experiences the potential fearsome annihilation. At this stage, following the danger's depiction, the *Zohar* presents the covered face—not as a disguise for the sake of pure seduction and concealment, rather as concealment for the sake of disclosure and salvation. Tamar covers her face to enable the encounter with Judah and the mending of the fracture in divinity. The exegetical delay regarding the image of the covered face allows an understanding vis-à-vis the quick sequence of the chain of events and the coupling leading to the world's deliverance: "And she said 'What will you give me for coming in to me?' (Gen. 38:16). Now, the Bride seeks Her jewels ... signs of *Matronita*, blessed by the King in Her union ... Immediately, 'He gave them to her and he came in to her and she conceived by him' (Gen. 38:18).[38]

Only after Tamar covers her face, thereby enabling the union, does Judah turn to the *Shekhinah* with conciliatory words, unacceptable in her former smoldering state. As in many Zoharic images, here too we witness *Malkhut*'s ability to switch between extreme states and transform the destructive forces of judgment within her into forces of grace, prepared to cordially welcome the male.[39] In the passage, Tamar transitions from the extreme state of the devourer of the world, the woman scorching without mercy, "that she was the destruction (*khallato*) of the world," to a relaxed and assuaged state: "Because Her face shone to receive from Him, and She was ready to be sweetened and bestow compassion on the world."[40] Here she becomes a "Bride" (*kallah*), and in the words of the *Zohar* the "actual bride" of the Song of Songs. Seemingly, Judah acts alongside Tamar, fulfilling his role opposite her: he is able to sweeten her only after she covers her face, while she covers her face only after he exposes his intention to copulate with her, thus rendering her judgments into forces of grace. These interactions apparently reflect a circular paradox within the *sefirotic* relations. Nonetheless, it appears that the *Zohar* alludes to the beginning of the sweetening process in the opening of

---

38 *Zohar* III: 72a, Matt, *Pritzker*, 7:482.
39 For example, see *Zohar* I: 221a; III: 191a; Hellner-Eshed, *A River Flows*, 262-4, 404-7; Liebes, *God's Story*, 71-90, 123-57.
40 According to Ashlag, "Bride is from the word 'destruction,'" *ha-Sulam*, *Aḥrei Mot*, 96; Sokoloff, *Dictionary*, 548.

Parashat Aḥrei Mot. The female's readiness to be sweetened by the male is bound to the *Ṣaddiq* coming to the *Shekhinah* at precisely the right "time":

> So, *All of them look in hope to You, to give them their food in its time* (Ps. 104:27) Who is *its time*? The *time* of Righteous One (*Ṣaddiq*)—*Matronita*, who is called so. Therefore all of them await this *time*, all those below are nourished from this place. We have established this mystery: *The eyes of all look in hope to You, and give them their food in its time* (ibid. 145:15), as we have established. Come and see: When this *all* sweetens *its time*, who is blessed by Him, all worlds are in joy, all worlds in blessing; then peace prevails above and below.[41]

Zohar Aḥrei Mot begins with an emphasis on the mystery embedded within the correct entrance to the sacred (*qodesh*), as reparation for the act of Aaron's sons, who failed to understand the importance of precise timing concerning the *Shekhinah*. This issue is derived from the words: "he is not to come just **at any time** into the sanctuary (*ha-qodesh*)" (Lev. 16:2-3). Judah, in our passage, embodies the manner in which *Ṣaddiq*, *sefirah* of *Yesod*—which is *all*, discovers its *time*, *Malkhut*, and joins her, responding to her state.[42] It appears that Judah's main reparation, besides that related to identifying the time, is his treatment of the *Shekhinah* and the way he observes her. The supernal *Ṣaddiq* is required to direct his gaze towards her, against her covered face. The text implies that in contrast to Aaron's sons, Judah did not feast his eyes and thereby "he merited to receive the *Shekhinah*."[43] The man, who began by looking for a *qedeshah* on the road—"he thought her to be a prostitute,"—is forced to see her differently after she covers her face and is introduced to her internality.

The face covering thereby has a sense of coupling, whether by conjoining the contradictory parts of the *Shekhinah*'s soul or through the union of opposites, which are, as it were, "concealed within each other." On a different level, the burning scene and face covering are linked to the intensity of revelation and mystical experience. It can be said that Tamar, who constitutes a model for the mystic, covered her face because of the magnitude of the sacredness and greatness of his position, and in order not to defile the revelatory experience. This meeting is bound with fear, as is written about Moses at the burning

---

41 *Zohar* III: 58a, Matt, *Pritzker*, 7:373.
42 On "all" and "time" as monikers for *Yesod* and *Malkhut*. Gikatilla, *Sha'arei*, 1:134-5.
43 *b. Eruvin* 63a; *Leviticus Rabbah* 20:10.

bush: "And Moses hid his face, for he was afraid to look at God" (Ex. 3:6).⁴⁴ This notion is reinforced in Tamar's depiction through the unique word "*va-tit'alaf*" (wrapped herself up), which literally means that she covered herself, but in our context may also be interpreted as a state of ecstatic fainting.⁴⁵ This experience is likely connected to an eye-rolling mystical technique, also entailing concealment and disclosure.⁴⁶ Ostensibly, in the journey that Tamar undergoes, it is the moment of fainting that allows her to show her face and receive the light of *Tif'eret* embodied in the figure of Judah. Indeed, only after the face covering does a conversation between them occur and it seems that it is due to the revelatory moments that the coupling takes place. Tamar's refined and precise speech in turning to Judah demonstrates the transformation she underwent when her face was covered, the short moment in which her soul swooned to its origin: "She said, 'What will you give me, that you may come in to me?'"... "And she said, 'Only if you give me a pledge, until you send it.'"... "She replied, 'Your signet and your cord, and the staff that is in your hand'"—these are supernal bounds, jewels of the bride, who is blessed from the three of them. *Neṣaḥ, Hod, Yesod*, and all are found in these three. 'The Bride is blessed by [*Neṣaḥ, Hod, Yesod*].' Immediately, 'He gave them to her and he came in to her and she conceived by him.'"⁴⁷ Like the Zoharic heroes, Tamar is situated here with "eyes wide open," and by virtue of her face being covered at the moment of burning, is granted the ability to see and process visions. Therefore, she finally merits the supernal jewels, *Neṣaḥ, Hod, Yesod*, which are the "limbs of the King," signs attesting to the seal of revelation in her flesh.

From an eschatological perspective, the passage from *Aḥrei Mot* discusses an encounter with evil, a necessary stage in the process of creation and

---

44 Similar imagery of the face being covered by the holy *ḥayyot* can be found in the Merkabah literature. Halperin, "Sexual Image," 123, fn. 33; Schäfer, *Synopse*, 82 (§ 189). Also compare *Hekhalot Rabbati*, ibid, 109-10 (§ 247). According to Halperin's psychoanalytic interpretation the viewer of the 'chariot' is similar to the child's exposure to the primal scene and his parents' threatening coupling. As well as Wolfson, *Through a Speculum*, 340-2.

45 Gen. 38:14; the connection between sorrow and fainting, in Tamar's story, arises from Psalm 102:1 and Isaiah 57:1. On states of fallenness, faintness, and convulsion in the mystical experience, see Pedaya, *Vision and Speech*, 95.

46 *Zohar* II: 247a; I: 18b; On mystical techniques of eye rolling, see Liebes, "Zohar Lexicon," 291-3, 316-7.

47 The mention of *Neṣaḥ, Hod, Yesod* appears in manuscript form at the end of the passage, without an acronym, this is in contrast to the Margolioth's edition. Also see Matt's 'reconstructed' edition: supernal bounds, jewels of the Bride, blessed by these three. For all is found in these three, all is blessed by these three—*Neṣaḥ, Hod, Yesod*. Matt, *Pritzker*, 7: 482.

redemption. According to this reading, Tamar's covering her face is interpreted as an apotropaic ritual and a bribing of the demonic realm to which the word "*va-tit'alaf*" (wrapped herself up) hints in its meaning of hiddenness and concealment. In this mystical text, Tamar's hiding symbolizes the first stage of the emanation process, paralleling impregnation and birth. The principle of "the shell precedes the fruit" teaches that the encounter with destruction and the forces of evil precedes the construction and concatenation of the beneficial, and that the sorting of dross and shells is an essential element in every beginning. The contact with evil is interpreted as a return to the source of emanation and to the forces of chaos and destruction entailed in creation. In our passage, Tamar and the *Shekhinah* represent the ultimate femininity and motherhood and symbolize archetypes of origin. Therefore, when the burning Tamar "covers her face," she is saved from the evil external to her and imbibes it internally. It is possible to say that she became a type of "nut in its shell" and fruit in its peal, in order to enable creation and birth and thus Perez is born, ancestor of King David.[48]

Tamar "wrapped in evil," faces and sweetens it, like Rashbi, who attests how all his days he contained the *Shekhinah*'s flame within himself, sheltering the world from her fire. It is likely that the source of destruction in *Malkhut* is embedded in the higher *sefirot*, and that precisely because of this it "demonstrates," in the Zoharic words, the mystery of Torah in which God's name is concealed. The very same divine force that Tamar arouses, demonstrates that in each important creation—such as the moments of the Messiah's birth or the formation of exegesis—the chaotic potencies burst forth with great power, and need to be enclosed and assuaged.

PETAH EINAYIM—FROM RABBINIC MIDRASH TO ZOHARIC EXEGESIS

To conclude our discussion on the kabbalists' attraction towards the flaming face of the divine feminine, we will examine the rabbinic Midrashim discussing Tamar's story and the manner in which they are adapted in the *Zohar*. The tension between concealment and discreetness on the one hand, and seduction

---

48 Asi Farber-Ginat, "'The Shell Precedes the Fruit'—On the Question of the Origin of Metaphysical Evil in Early Kabbalistic Thought," in *Myth and Judaism*, ed. Haviva Pedaya (Jerusalem: Bialik Institute, 1996), 118-142. On *sod ha-egoz* (secret of the nut) as a "feminine androgynous" in which the masculine is absorbed into the feminine, see Abrams, *The Female Body of God*, 68-79. Mopsik, *Sex of the Soul*, 139-49.

and exposure on the other, exists in the Bible, and is intensified by the sages discussing the term "*petaḥ einayim*" in Genesis Rabbah.[49] Tamar and Judah's meeting at the "entrance to Enaim" is likely a unique variation on the engagement type-scene. The eyes (*einayim*) hint at a source of water (*ma'ayan*), an encounter leading to marriage, like the meetings of Jacob and Rachel and Moses and Zipporah that occur by a well.[50] On the symbolic level, "*petaḥ einayim*" reflects the point of departure from the impasse in which Tamar finds herself, and attests to the liminal and oppressed position from which the Davidic messianism blooms. The phrase of symbols—*petaḥ* (opening) *einayim* (eyes)—provokes the imagination of the sages who interpret it in two ways:

> Rabbi said: We have searched through the whole of Scripture and found no place called *Petaḥ Einayim*. What then is the purport of *Petaḥ Einayim*? It teaches that she lifted up her eyes to the gate (*petaḥ*) to which all eyes (*einayim*) are directed and prayed: 'May it be Your will that I do not leave this house with naught.' Another interpretation: It teaches that she opened his eyes by declaring to him: 'I am clean, and I am unmarried.'[51]

This Midrash features two contrasting openings—the feminine womb and the gate of heaven—that demonstrate the twofold sphere in which the story occurs. The heavenly gate, to which the carnal eyes are directed, and to which Tamar turns in her plea for divine assistance, is located at the center of the first section. This Midrash indicates her passiveness and dependence and her anticipation for redemption, both by God and the man who faces her. The emphasis at the center of the second opening moves towards the eye as a sexual symbol, and is transformed into a verb describing the seductive act.[52] The first position focuses on the feminine lacking and Tamar's crisis and vulnerability facing God, while the second stresses erotic delight and the proactivity that she adopts towards Judah. Consequently, the Zoharic exegesis reveals the connection linking these two existences. The "other interpretation" is essentially the very same

---

49 Genesis Rabbah 85:7-8 (ed. Theodor-Albeck), 1037-8; Huddlestun, "Unveiling the Versions"; Frymer-Kensky, *Women*, 270.
50 On the ritualistic quality of the biblical betrothal type-scene, see Alter, *Biblical Narrative*, 61-77.
51 Genesis Rabbah 85:7 (ed. Theodor-Albeck), 1041; also *b. Sotah* 10a.
52 The eye and mouth are linked to water sources and symbolize the source of life and therefore are sexual metaphors in the Ancient Greek world and literature of the Middle Ages. The metaphorical link between the mouth of a spring and wellspring is also linked in this passage to the perception of Tamar as one who "*eats and wipes her mouth.*" Nacht, *Simlei 'Ishah*, 183-5.

topic: the divine plan is fulfilled through earthly seduction, while the feminine lack and dependence induce divine and messianic reparation. The Zoharic exegesis, based on the sages, illuminates that the womb, eye, heart, and heavenly gates are conjoined through Tamar's actions. Similar to rabbinic Midrash which grants Tamar a "voice" as well as the ability to depict her circumstances—from the prayer "May it be Your will that I do not leave this house with naught," to the practical words "I am clean, and I am unmarried"—the *Zohar* places the *Shekhinah*'s feminine experience in the center. The primal connection that the sages formed between the gate of heaven and the womb's opening, is transformed in the *Zohar* in light of the journey of the Shekhinah sitting at the "entrance to Enaim," into a discussion of the supernal realms and the "mystery of faith."

Similar to the Midrash, the *Zohar* also highlights the concealed covenant between God and the seductive and cunning messianic mother. However, in contrast to the rabbinic trend of justifying Tamar's actions which "were done for the sake of heaven," the Zoharic exegesis deals with an aspect which does not engage in ethical and personal questions but rather, discusses the source of wrath in divinity. An additional example of this process can be seen in the *Zohar*'s treatment of the story of Lot's daughters in *Parashat va-Yera*. In contrast to rabbinic Midrashim, in which the future motherhood provides validation and purpose to the seductive act, the Zoharic text intentionally skips the story's outcomes, briefly refers to the pregnancy and returns to discuss Tamar's internal embryo, called here "*Ṣedeq he*" (righteous, *he*). The fact that this passage does not refer to Perez and Zerah's birth—the climax of the biblical story—indicates that the *Zohar* seeks to focus on the birth occurring within the *Shekhinah* and not the story's aftermath.

The messianic and nationalistic motivations prominent in the rabbinic Midrashim on the signet, cord, and staff, are transformed in the *Zohar* and are refitted for the internal messianic process, which are intended to appease the divine from its judgments and mitigate the evil in the kabbalists' soul. Furthermore, the combat of the masculine desire, a central feature of rabbinic Midrashim, is converted in the *Zohar* into a struggle with the feminine flame—in reality and divinity.[53] The face covering in rabbinic Midrashim is directed towards the other man, Judah. In contrast, the focus of the Zoharic passage is the *Shekhinah*'s psychological experience, whereby the face covering is meant to first and foremost guard her. The *Zohar* consequently explores the capability of the two sexes to meet face to face in spite of the destructive forces within them.

---

53 The aspect of Judah being coerced against his will, as described in Genesis Rabbah 85:8 [17] (ed. Theodor-Albeck, 1041-2) is totally absent in the Zoharic text.

Generally, it is possible to see in the Midrash how the biblical heroes are set against God as human figures who, at times, merit to integrate into the divine plan. This is in contrast to the *Zohar*, in which the divine drama perpetually reflects the individual figures' experience. Judah and Tamar are people with wishes and desires, simultaneously also being *Tif'eret* coming to *Malkhut* when her destructive forces erupt. These matters are not stated in abstract symbolism, but rather in paralleled actuality occurring in the "mythic-real," "mythic-symbolic," and "psychological-existential" dimension.[54] This passage exemplifies how myth in the *Zohar* weaves the symbolic, real, and deep psychological descriptions within the mysteries of divine being.

From the midrashic foundation, the *Zohar* develops a model in which the gates of heaven and the womb converge and *eros* becomes an entrance for the experience of *devequt* (cleaving to God). Besides the identification of Tamar and the *Shekhinah*, the Zoharic innovation is embedded in the creation of the bond between the *Shekhinah* and Lilith and its complex fondness for these two figures. Retrospectively, it is clear that the *Zohar* does not only intensify the mystery of the dark judgments in divinity, but also allows for a deeper and bolder understanding of the earthly woman. An additional exegetical transformation can be seen in the *Zohar* following the sages in the interpretation of the word "timnatah" (to Timnah): "*She sat by the entrance to Enaim (einayim) … for all eyes of the world look to this opening. Which is on the road (timnatah) to Timnah … As is said and the image of (u-tmunat) YHVH he beholds.*"[55] Similar to the mythization of *petaḥ einayim* and its displacement from a geographical location to a theosophic state, *timnatah* here also represents a mystical state of consciousness connected to the ability to view images and comprehending divine mysteries. Thus the *Zohar* links Tamar's liminal state with the "opening" of the *Shekhinah* and *tmunat YHVH* (the image of God) revealed to the mystic. The combination of this passage and the kabbalists' invitation to gaze at "*petaḥ einayim*" (opening of the eyes) in the *Introduction to the Zohar* demonstrates that an echo of Tamar's action exists in every revelation and that there are visionary states that only occur when the heavenly opening is situated opposite the opening of the feminine womb. Both passages demonstrate that mystical

---

54 According to Yisraeli, this passage belongs to the "mythic-symbolic" and the "mythic-real" model. In this chapter I have sought to also add the "psychological-existential" dimension to it. Yisraeli, *Temple*, 19.
55 *Zohar* III: 71b–72a; Matt, *Pritzker*, 7:480.

vision is multifaceted and conditional on concealment and disclosure of the male and female.

The basic similarity between the rabbinic Midrash and the Zoharic passages emphasizes the difference between the corpuses. The main difference, in my opinion, is the *Zohar*'s unique treatment of the body. In the rabbinic Midrash there is a clear moderation of Tamar's burning scene.[56] In contrast, by configuring the *Shekhinah* burning, the *Zohar* returns to the realness of the biblical scene in which Tamar is taken to the pyre and transforms it into a physical and concrete image. The fire—symbolizing the beginning of the forces of judgment and danger, and afterwards, the union from which a son is born to the House of David—clutches at Tamar's face. This is not a metaphor, but rather a sharp embodiment of danger occurring on the corporeal stage.

The best example of the exegetes' substituting process and the *Zohar*'s treatment of the body is found in the interpretation of the three signs given to Tamar at the heart of the plot: "Your signet and your cord, and your staff (Gen. 38:18)." In the Bible's straightforward meaning the three are identity signifiers of Judah, whereas the sages describe them as national and political signs that God bestows upon Tamar as a gift: "Whence then are kings to arise, whence are redeemers to arise? *Your signet* alludes to royalty ... *and your cord* alludes to the Sanhedrin ... *and your staff* alludes to the royal Messiah."[57] The Midrash presents spiritual and ideological gifts which are also physical: royalty, greatness, honor, sacredness, and messianism. In light of the nationalistic and historical conceptions, the Zoharic myth's return to the body is noteworthy. The *Zohar* teaches that the cord, signet, and staff are *Neṣaḥ*, *Hod*, and *Yesod*, limbs of the divine male, and that their delivery is expressed in the actual act of copulation: "these are supernal bounds, jewels of the bride, who is blessed from the three of them. *Neṣaḥ*, *Hod*, *Yesod*, and all are found in these three."[58] The three signs are thereby a ritualistic and theurgic performance of earthly intercourse that drives the supernal union.

---

56 The sages wrote that God had provided Tamar new signifiers in place of the lost ones moments before her punishment, Genesis Rabbah 85:11 [25] (ed. Theodor-Albeck, 1044-5).

57 Genesis Rabbah 85:8-9 [17-8] (ed. Theodor-Albeck, 1041-3).

58 Zohar III: 72a; Matt, *Pritzker*, 7: 482. It is likely that this passage's audacious source is to be found in Philo's words: "And Tamar too; she bore within her womb the divine seed, but had not seen the sower... But she closely scanned the symbols and tokens, and judging in her heart that these were the gifts of no mortal she cried aloud, *To whomsoever these belong, he it is by whom I am with child*. Whose is the ring, the pledge of faith, the seal of the universe? Whose is the cord, that is, the world-order? Whose is the staff, that is the firmly planted, the unshaken? Whose are they? Are they not God's alone?" (*On the Change of Names* 134-6),

The Zoharic passage thus demonstrates that the erotic relations between people are an opening for understanding the relations between heaven and earth. By insisting on the human body, the *Zohar* again recounts that the *Shekhinah*'s face is not an abstract idea, rather a real occurrence. It also explains that it is only through contemplation of the biblical stories and the experiences of the figures participating in them that it is possible to comprehend the mystery of concealment and disclosure embedded in the Torah and in God's name. The text focuses therefore on the feminine motivations for seduction, the concealed forces of the corporeal body, the artful convergence of the masculine and feminine, the connection of *eros* and exegetical creativity, and finally, the internal reparation dependent on the conjoining of the facets of *Din* and *Ḥesed* in one personality. The techniques of concealment and disclosure are revealed here as a poetic instrument, maintaining infinite meanings in the text. The dynamism of revealing and concealing occurs within each figure, each verse, each word, and in their conjoining.

By emphasizing the link between Lilith and the *Shekhinah*, the *Zohar* presents desire as an extraordinary experience allowing one to encounter his and the Other's mysteriousness. To "the otherness of sexuality," which has been discussed by Foucault, Bataille, Laplanche, Stein, and others, the *Zohar* adds multi-faceted aspects of the erotic experience, hiddenness and self-concealment, essential powers which defend against the devouring *eros*.[59] Alongside the humanly, erotic, and psychological reading, the biblical story receives a mystical understanding in the *Zohar*. The familiar items, such as the signet and staff, undergo a symbolic transformation and then return to their literal and corporeal sense, like the limbs of a living body. They are intentionally chosen to reveal the supernal secrets and to attest to the mystery of faith. Like the signet, cord, and staff, Tamar's veil also signifies the changes of the figures and the dynamism in the divine tales.

TAMAR'S STORY AND THE MOTIF OF FIRE IN *ZOHAR AḤREI MOT*—A MIRROR TO THE WORLD OF THE KABBALISTS

As has been seen, Tamar's story does not only come to teach us about Tamar herself, but also about the mysteries of Torah and divinity learned through her actions. Examples of such are the seductive process, the union of male and female, the sweetening of *Malkhut*'s judgments, and the dialectic of danger and

---

Colson and Whitaker, *Philo*, 5:210-3.
59 Bataille, *Death and Sensuality*; Laplanche, *Otherness*; Stein, "Sexuality."

desire. The choice of Tamar as a reflection of the *Shekhinah*'s figure allows a glimpse into the souls of the passages' authors and the editors of the Zoharic compilation. The question arises as to why Tamar's story is situated at the heart of the *Zohar* on *Parashat Aḥrei Mot*, following the passages of the Yom Kippur services and the death of Aaron's sons? Seemingly, the *Zohar* forms a connection between Tamar and Aaron's sons by focusing on the fire motif. According to the sages, Nadab and Abihu "feasted their eyes upon the *Shekhinah*."[60] In contrast, Tamar is depicted here as withdrawing her gaze when the *time* is unbefitting.

In the Zoharic text, Tamar's sitting at the "entrance to Enaim" with her face covered repairs and assuages the acts of Aaron's sons by mitigating the destructive burning forces. This passage, like other Zoharic images, actualizes the fire's outburst on the threshold of revelation and its miraculous calming. Moreover, the kabbalists apparently describe themselves in the figures of Tamar and the *Shekhinah*, viewing themselves as restitutions for the tragic deaths of Nadab and Abihu. They are familiar with the destruction entailed in the mystical experience and identify with the desire for *unio mystica* within the fire, and therefore as a mythic and poetic resolution. In the moment before Tamar goes up in flames, like Aaron's sons, the kabbalists portray the reparation within the covered face figure. This resolution suggests a beneficial reproduction of the sons' traumatic death and a possibility of delaying the burning scene of the *Shekhinah*. Tamar's covering of her face saves her life and all of existence. Thus, the sequence of passages in the section beginning with "after the death of the two sons of Aaron, when they drew near before the Lord and died" (Lev. 16:1) is clarified. Interweaving Tamar's story into this section in the *Zohar* intends to teach the kabbalists how to enter the sacred without being burned.[61] Fire is a central raw material through which the passages of *Parashat Aḥrei Mot* are joined. Like Tamar, who transforms her face from *Din* to *Ḥesed*, so Aaron the High Priest, and the kabbalist, are forced to find the precise and appropriate time to come into the sacred.[62] The many coverings appearing in the sacred areas, such as the veil, *kapporet* (mercy-seat), screen, and *pargod*, embody a quality of con-

---

60 *b. Eruvin* 63a; Leviticus Rabbah 20:10.
61 On the perception of Aaron's sons in the *Zohar*, see Yehuda Liebes, "Clothed Nudity: The Esoteric Cult of Philo," *Jerusalem Studies in Jewish Thought* 24 (2015): 9-28. Yisraeli, *Temple Portals*, 220-38; Hellner-Eshed, "The Zealot"; Asulin, "The Flaw and its Correction," 214-21; Ruth Kara-Kaniel, "Consumed by Love: The Death of Nadav and Avihu as a Ritual of Erotic Mystical Union," *Teuda* 26 (2014): 585-653.
62 *Zohar* III: 58b.

cealing and withholding, and yet their nature allows for a partial reflection of reality and existence that is significantly richer.[63] If so, Tamar's face, like the *Shekhinah*'s essence, reflects the *pargod*, the "veil of being"—that divides and conceals, but also materializes a platform for revelation in the ecstatic crossing point between danger and salvation.

It appears that the covering of Tamar's burning face is a mythic development of an earlier image: that of the High Priest entering the Holy of Holies with a censer full of fire in hand, sheltered within the vessel called a *maḥtah* (censer), when he is at first protected by the veil and smoke of incense. I believe that this is what the *Zohar* is alluding to by situating Tamar's account in contrast to Aaron's sons' death and depicting the *Shekhinah* as "**eating and wiping her mouth.**" Consequently, the veil that covers Tamar's face is likely a parallel to the High Priest's garments, constituting divine presence and apotheosis in the sacred.[64] As emerges from the academic literature, the barrier and mystical veil have an essential connection to the divine garment, and it is through them that an additional meaning is revealed—in Tamar's story they "show" the mystery of divinity. Two parallel processes of "concealing the fire," the quintessence of the kabbalists' service, are in operation here: preserving the potency of the *Shekhinah*'s fire while protecting reality from her flames. This duty is similar to the High Priest's role on the Day of Atonement: his entrance into the Holy of Holies entails endangerment of life, but also results in reparation for the people of Israel.

Zohar Aḥrei Mot describes the redemption as a maturing process that allows a controlling of *eros* and even unharmed entrance to the sacred. The conclusion that arises from this passage is that the reparation is impossible without coupling and the erotic forces, and that the mitigating of *Malkhut* is a pre-condition for revelation and messianic birth. Mankind's role then is double. On the one hand, there is the desire to rectify the fragmented conditions existing between *Tif'eret* and *Malkhut*, determined by their dual capability and derived from Tamar's story, sitting at the "entrance to Enaim" and seducing, and on the other hand, to gaze on high and pray for salvation. The passage about Tamar in *Zohar Aḥrei Mot* sharpens a few fundamental kabbalistic questions: what is the source of wrath and smolder in divinity, and specifically in the feminine divine? Why are passion, destructiveness, and annihilation so powerful in the supernal realms? Why is devastation summoned regularly? And lastly, whether—and how—is it possible to influence occurrences in the supernal realms in

---

63 Pedaya, *Vision and Speech*, 237-55; Liebes, *God's Story*, 272-9.
64 Schneider, *Priest*, 49-96; Scholem, *Major Trends*, 72-4.

order to assuage the titanic struggles whose ramifications are seen in this world? In the course of this chapter, I have sought to show that in this passage the kabbalists retelling of Tamar's story is but a testimony about themselves, their identification with the *Shekhinah's* internal burning, the quest for reparation and their search to assuage and relieve her burning. The kabbalists, who already in the *Introduction to the Zohar* identify with Tamar and her sitting at the "entrance to Enaim," are even referred to in many passages as "Face of *Shekhinah*," for as Yehuda Liebes writes: "they are the external aspect of the *Shekhinah*, and she is revealed through them in our world."[65] Tamar's story initiates the divine drama and enables the imagination of events behind the covered face and beyond the *pargod*, to the very depths of concealment of the supernal realms. Through this illustration the kabbalists attempt to (re)construct a concealed realm that reflects the divine mysteries by describing it in human shape and language. The passage clarifies the understanding that the symbolic processes of reparation and "messianic birth" are unable to occur without a face-to-face encounter with the forces of evil and their transformation into forces of redemption.

---

65 *Zohar* II: 163b; Liebes, "*Zohar* and Eros," 104, fn. 240.

CHAPTER 7

The *Shekhinah's* Exile and Redemption in Ruth and Naomi's Journey

Having examined the incestuous relations of Lot's daughters and Tamar's seductiveness in "the entrance to Enaim," this chapter will concentrate on the figure of Ruth and her portrayal as the feminine divinity in the Zoharic literature. We will follow the motif linked to the stages of editing and formation of the different strata of the Zoharic corpus in their relation to the figure of the *Shekhinah*, and we will discuss conflicting readings of the threshing night in the body of the *Zohar* (the sections of the *Zohar* on the Pentateuch, henceforth: the *Zohar*), *Midrash ha-Ne'elam Ruth*, and *Tiqqunei Zohar*.

As it is known, the Zoharic literature is made up of many layers. In contrast to the clear lateness of the *Ra'ya Mehemna* and *Tiqqunei Zohar* strands, earlier and later views have been presented regarding the compilation of the *Midrash ha-Ne'elam* (*MhN*).[1] Portions included in this stratum are differentiated by their anonymous voices, the integration of Hebrew and Aramaic, their allegorical and philosophical aspects, and different theosophic hermeneutics. Nonetheless, there are differences between the passages attributed to the *MhN*; for instance the *MhN* on Genesis and Exodus, which are set in the main body of the *Zohar* in printed editions, are not similar to those passages printed in the *Zohar Ḥadash*, like *MhN* on the Song of Songs, *MhN* on Lamentations, *MhN* on Ruth, and others.

---

1 Tishby, *Zohar*, xxi; Goldreich, *Self-Image*, 459-96; Liebes, "The *Zohar* and the Tiqqunim." Scholem, *Major Trends*, 181-6; Tishby, *Zohar*, xviii, cvi-cvii; 2-31, 38-9; Liebes, *Studies*, 85-138; Oron, "Artistic Elements."

There are many passages exploring the mystical significance of the Book of Ruth in the sections of the *Zohar* and later pseudo-Zoharic works. The main composition dedicated to the mystical interpretation of the Book of Ruth is the *Midrash ha-Ne'elam* Ruth (henceforth: *Zohar Ruth*). The first printers of the *Zohar*, the Mantua and Cremona editions, knew this work and affirmed its inclusion in their printing, but only later and separately, under different names—first as *Yesod Shirim* and *Tapuḥei Zahav* and afterwards as *MhN* Ruth—finally included in *Zohar Ḥadash*.[2] Daniel Abrams emphasizes the work's importance as a transition point from the allegorical kabbalah (based on the conception of the uniqueness of the Hebrew letters), to the theosophic-theurgic kabbalah. According to him, *Zohar Ruth*, mostly written in Aramaic and including theosophic-sefirotic foundations alongside allegorical readings, was written by Castilian kabbalists and is "an early testimony to a developing gradual change of thought in their circle in the second half of the 13th century."[3] Opposing him, Efraim Gottlieb suggests that *Zohar Ruth* and *Sitrei Torah* present a different perception of the soul than the *Zohar*, which resembles ideas presented in later Zoharic strata.[4] Through an analysis of the thematic connections between the messianic mother figure and the *Shekhinah* in *Zohar Ruth* and in *Tiqqunei Zohar*, we may advocate Gottlieb's position and demonstrate the lateness of *Zohar Ruth* and its proximity to the layer of *Tiqqunei Zohar*.

I suggest that an analysis of the recurring expression "and she uncovered his feet" reflects a range of perceptions of the *Shekhinah*'s exile and redemption in Castile in the 13th and 14th centuries, showing the development of the messianic idea in the *Zohar*. Here is evidence of the transition from a "personal-active" description of the *Shekhinah* appearing in the *Zohar* to an "allegoric-passive" description characterizing *Zohar Ruth* and the *Tiqqunim*.

---

2   On the relation of *Zohar Ruth* to *Midrash ha-Ne'elam*, see Scholem, *Trends*, 162, 387, fn. 3; Tishby, *Zohar*, xviii. Daniel Abrams, *Midrash Ha-Ne'elam Ruth*, (Jerusalem: Personal Publisher, 1992), 3-8, notes that the first printers of the *Zohar* considered it as a separate composition. In the first printing (1559) the composition was entitled *Yesod Shirim* as well as *Tapuḥei Zahav*. In the Venice edition (1565) it was entitled *Midrash ha-Ne'elam* to the Book of Ruth. Kabbalists like Recanati, Ibn Gabbai, Judah Ḥayyat, and others did not consider it as part of the *Zohar* (Huss, *Radiance of the Sky*, 89, 99, fn. 62, 110-2; 84-139). Another work entitled *Zohar Ruth*, was printed in 1711 and renamed "*Har Adonai*." In 1791 it was printed together with *Ṣaddiq Yesod Olam*, a work attributed to R. Isaac Luria, but as Liebes has shown the composition was written by Judah Leib Prossnitz. Liebes, *Sabbateanism*, 53-69.

3   Abrams, *Midrash Ha-Ne'elam Ruth*, 3.

4   Ephraim Gottlieb, *Studies in Kabbalistic Literature*, ed. Joseph Hacker (Tel Aviv: Rosenberg, 1976), 540-4; Tishby, *Zohar*, 2:38-40.

This transition attests to the substituting of the active-theurgic stance—which is designed to hasten the coming of the redemption in the *Zohar*—in favor of a passive stance linked to the identification with the *Shekhinah*'s forsakenness in exile. Biti Roi and Haviva Pedaya have extensively discussed the models of identification with the exilic *Shekhinah* in *Tiqqunei Zohar*.[5] To these studies I seek to add the hypothesis that the change in the perception of redemption impacts the attitude towards femininity and sexuality: from an active and redeeming heroine in the *Zohar*, the *Shekhinah* becomes a submissive and suffering figure in the later strata, a topic which I will discuss from a gender perspective. Overall, an examination of the myth of the messianic mother in connection to the *Shekhinah* highlights the differences between the *Zohar* and other works included in the Zoharic corpus. In addition, the change in the *Shekhinah*'s conception may demonstrate the influence of *Zohar Ruth* on later Zoharic layers and the transition point between the *Zohar* and the prominent conceptions in the *Ra'ya Mehemna* and *Tiqqunei Zohar*.[6] This reading joins the views of Yehuda Liebes and Ronit Meroz regarding circles of authors who expand on their predecessors' work, as well as challenging the claims regarding the antiquity of *Midrash ha-Ne'elam*, while showing later developments of exile and redemption in Zoharic literature.

THE BOOK OF RUTH AND THE THRESHING FLOOR SCENE— FROM THE BIBLE TO SECOND TEMPLE LITERATURE

As we saw in the first chapter, the genealogical list at the end of the Book of Ruth echoes the array of the Davidic tales. The book creates an intertextual restoration of Ruth's foremothers, who are not necessarily embedded in the overt actions of the figures, but in the gaps and obscurity of the text.[7] It is observable

---

5   For a discussion of the modes of identification with the *Shekhinah* in the *Tiqqunim*, like her lameness, see Biti Roi, "The Legs of the Shekhina as a Founding Image of an Ethos in Tiqqunei ha-*Zohar*," *Kabbalah* 23 (2010): 181-217. On the centrality of the exilic experience in the *Tiqqunei Zohar*, see Haviva Pedaya, *Walking through Trauma: Rituals of Movement in Jewish Myth Mysticism and History* (Tel Aviv: Resling, 2011), 46-9, 80-7. Also Roi, "Shekhina," 89-232.
6   *Zohar Ruth* has several layers of editing, which effect the *Shekhinah*'s different portrayals, see also Meroz, "The Weaving of a Myth." Benarroch suggests that *Zohar Ruth* represents the "middle stratum" between the body of the *Zohar* and the *Tiqqunim* and *Ra'ya Mehemna*. Benarroch, "'Yanuqa' and 'Sabba,'" 263-9.
7   This obscurity allows the subversive voices of the Book of Ruth to be heard. Bal, *Lethal Love*, 83-5; Pardes, *Countertraditions*, 98-117. In rabbinic Midrashim, see Boyarin, *Intertextuality*.

that, in contrast to the harshness in the description of the incestuous episode in Genesis 19 ("Thus both the daughters of Lot became pregnant by their father," 19:36) and the description of Tamar's harlotry in Genesis 38:15-24 ("When Judah saw her, he thought her to be a prostitute ... Judah was told, 'Your daughter-in-law Tamar has played the whore; moreover she is pregnant as a result of whoredom.'"), the Book of Ruth does not elucidate what occurred between Boaz and Ruth that night. Previous scenes of seduction and deception are indeed implied in the setting of the book, but this is a sublimated scene, assuaging and softening the previous tales.

The force of the threshing floor scene stems from its multifacetedness and significations. This scene begins with the secret arrival of Ruth, "Then she came quietly and uncovered his feet, and lay down" (Ruth 3:7), and concludes with her leaving "before one person could recognize another" (3:14)—two descriptions maintaining the privacy and mystery of the action, alongside its implied boldness. It is likely that only Boaz and Ruth know what happened between them that night, and even that they are in a state of unsureness—"she got up before one person could recognize another," whose prior parallel is "he did not know when she lay down or when she rose" in the cave of Zoar.[8] Noticeable in this scene are Ruth's hasty actions—the washing and preparation, changing of garments, coming to the threshing floor, uncovering his feet, lodging on the threshing floor, taking the barley and its concealment, her leaving before dawn, returning to Naomi—in contrast to Boaz's vague response, which conceals his pragmatic intentions (Ruth 3:10-13). Ruth says but a single statement that night "I am Ruth, your servant; spread your cloak over your servant, for you are a redeemer," (3:9) but it speaks volumes, for in contrast to Naomi's proposal "go and uncover his feet and lie down; **and he will tell you what to do**," (3:4) Ruth decides how her redemption will be achieved.

Despite Ruth's dominance in that moment, joining her predecessors' stories, it is possible to state that the book is wrapped in an atmosphere of fertility, nature, and harmony, used as camouflage for the human tensions hidden within it. The poetic speech of the figures stands in tension with the narrative's background: the poverty and hunger of the two women, Ruth's gender, ethnicity, and social vulnerability, the fact that Ruth possibly goes not of her own volition, but as an instrument for Naomi and her needs, the tension between

---

8   Ruth 3:14; Gen. 19:33. For a comparison of these two scenes see above chapter 1 and 2, as well as Fuchs, *Sexual Politics*, 78-9; Brenner, *Ruth and Naomi*, 101-3; Zakovitch, *Ruth*, 98-97; Doniger, *Bedtrick*, 253-63.

the romantic encounter and the determined licentiousness and seductiveness of the House of David. The seduction in the threshing floor scene may be read as the heroine's choice or as an act motivated by crisis, poverty, and feminine vulnerability. The playful tones and narrative methods—like the letter *lamed* rolling around in *"lini ha-lailah"* (remain this night) and the exhilarating and mysterious phrase *"va-tegal margelotav"* (and she uncovered his feet)—transforms the threshing floor scene into a poetic moment providing cover for the implied radicalness of what has occurred.

Rabbinic literature develops and intensifies the tension between the pastoral atmosphere of the book and the enigmatic events that occur on the threshing night. Prominent in these Midrashim is their ambiguity regarding the meeting between the heroes and the question of whether intercourse happened that night. There are voices that stress Boaz's overcoming his desire.[9] Others, meanwhile, create an expectation for a familiar narrative development: the seductive act and its realization for the sake of the Davidic progeny.[10] Apparently, the sages are aware of the possibility that there was intercourse between the two and therefore reject this tradition.[11] This tension arises from Naomi's question about what occurred between Ruth and Boaz in her return from the threshing floor: "She came to her mother-in-law, who said, 'Who are you my daughter?' Did she then not recognize her? Yes, but she meant, '**Are you still a virgin or a married woman**?' She answered, 'A virgin.'"[12]

Josephus adopts an even more innocent reading in his description of the threshing floor scene, which concludes like this: "He woke her up and

---

9 b. *Sanhedrin* 20a; Ruth Rabbah 6:4; Ruth Zuṭa 3:13 (ed. Buber, 52-3); Numbers Rabbah 15:16; Tanḥuma Be-haʻalotekha 10. On Boaz's glorification in the misradh, Maren R. Niehoff, "Constructing Ruth's image in the Midrash," *Jerusalem Studies in Jewish Thought* 11 (1993): 49-78. On the battle against sexual desire in the Davidic dynasty, Rosen-Zvi, *Demonic Desires*, 103, 199, fn. 4, 6. David himself (*y. Sanhedrin* 2:5, 20a) as well as Boaz swear not to fulfill their desire (*Sifre* Numbers 85), a Midrash that mentions also the story of Tamar and Judah; Leviticus Rabbah 23:11 (ed. M. Margulies, 543-5).

10 The depiction of Boaz's *yeṣer* strengthens the polemical stance, Ruth Rabbah (ed. Lerner) 6:8: "R. Judan said: All that night his *yeṣer* accused him, saying, 'You are unmarried and seek a wife, and she is unmarried and seeks a husband. Arise and have intercourse with her, and make her your wife. And he took an oath to his *yeṣer*, saying, 'As the Lord lives, I will not touch her.'" (Lerner, "The Book of Ruth," 176-7). An even more noticeable depiction is found in the *Midrash ha-Gadol* on Genesis 38:9 "'Lie down until the morning' (Ruth 3:13)—teaches that he took his 'middle finger' (a euphemism for his penis) and placed it by the graveside and swore to his *yeṣer* that he would not sin." Whereas Zakovitch insists that Ruth "only does a symbolic act," in contrast to Lot's daughters and Tamar, Zakovitch, *Ruth*, 26.

11 Ginzberg, *Legends*, 2:866, fn. 60.

12 Ruth Rabbah (ed. Lerner) 7:4; Lerner, "The Book of Ruth," 182-3.

directed her to take what she could of the barley and go to her mother-in-law before anyone should see that she had slept there. For in these matters it was prudent to guard against slander—**all the more so since nothing had happened.**"[13] The sages' and Josephus's opposition to the idea that the two copulated on the threshing floor is due to the act's implications. By Boaz, the judge and city elder, taking a Moabite woman that night, one who even a relative refuses to redeem lest he forfeit his inheritance, he instantly reverses her marginal position of being a poor and foreign widow into a royal family member.

In contrast to these sublimative descriptions, from other Midrashim a clear trend of sexual fulfillment emerges:

> "*And turned over* (Ruth 3:9)—She clung to him like ivy, and he began to finger her hair. 'Spirits have no hair,' he thought, so he said, '*Who are you? A woman or a spirit?*' She answered, 'A woman.' [He said to her] 'A single or a married woman?' She answered, 'Single.' [He said to her] 'Are you pure or impure?' She answered, 'Pure.' *A woman*, purest of women, *lying at his feet* (ib. 8), He said, '*Who are you?*' And she answered, '*I am Ruth, your servant.*' (ib. 9)[14]

This Midrash recounts the intentional seduction and the unequivocal feminine initiative. "She clung to him like ivy"—Ruth is described like a plant wrapped around and clutching the tree trunk. Initially, Boaz views her as a type of phantom belonging to the imaginary realm, but expressed in his series of questions—if she is a woman, single, pure, and lastly her name—is a clear intention of copulation. Seemingly, the sages wish to configure both of them as active partners preparing for intercourse. Even if nothing actually happened the exegetes insist on a covenant made between them that night: "*And she answered, I am Ruth, your servant and he said... Remain this night* (Ruth 3:8-13) ... She said to him: You wish to send me away with mere promises! Said he to her: As the Lord lives, I will not send you away with mere promises."[15]

---

13 [Flavius, *Antiquities*, 5:330] Begg, *Judean*, 83.
14 Ruth Rabbah (ed. Lerner) 6:3; *Ruth Zuṭa* (ed. Buber) 3:8. Niehoff, "Ruth," 75-8. In contrast to the claim that this Midrash condemns Ruth, I find an explicit validation of her actions. According to Fonrobert, the biblical Boaz is presented as a passive figure lacking all sexual desire, while in my opinion these Midrashim intensify the tension present in his figure. Fonrobert, "Birth of the Messiah," 261.
15 *Tanḥuma* (ed. Buber) *Bo* 16. Also see *Ruth Zuṭa* (ed. Buber) 3:9.

The interpretation that intercourse occurred that night is supported by the paralleling verses at the end of Boaz's series of questions: "Cursed be the wicked! Elsewhere it is said, "She caught hold of his garment, saying, 'Lie with me!'" (Gen. 39:12), but here, she said, "spread your cloak over your servant" (Ruth 3:9)."[16] According to the sages, Ruth, like Potiphar's wife, intends the very same action, but she hints at it modestly. The idiom "spread your cloak (*kanfekha*)," located in the story's foundation, may be interpreted as a type of request for shelter and marriage or as an act of intercourse (for a wing—*kanaf,* has sexual characteristics), and in light of the connection to Potiphar's wife this possibility appears to be the midrashist's intention.[17]

RUTH IN THE *ZOHAR*—"AND SHE UNCOVERED HIS FEET"

As we have seen, the threshing floor scene, in biblical and rabbinic literature, is at the heart of the tension between the virginal and erotic language that emerges from idioms like "and she uncovered his feet" and "she lay," which can be understood as blatant seduction and temptation, but also as an innocent act and a request for shelter.[18] The *Zohar* follows the same path. The diversity of interpretations, which the *Zohar* gives for the mysterious encounter between Ruth and Boaz on the threshing floor, explore the multiple meanings of the phrase "and she uncovered his feet," in the verse "When Boaz had eaten and drunk, and he was in a contented mood, he went to lie down at the end of the heap of grain. Then she came quietly and uncovered his feet, and lay down" (Ruth 3:7). We shall discuss the two trends that explain this verse in contrasting manners: The first finds in it evidence for the *Shekhinah*'s resurgence and salvation, whereas the second trend views it as evidence of her fall and exile. The roots of these two trends are in rabbinic literature, which describe the copulation and active seduction, alongside abstention and anticipation of the future redemption.

The *Zohar* chooses to establish the phrase "and she uncovered his feet," a *hapax legomenon*, as a key-term in the passages exploring the individual and feminine redemption, as well as the national and cosmic. Embedded within this term are complex and contradictory imagery and diverse literary allusions: the

---

16 Ruth Rabbah (ed. Lerner) 6:3; Genesis Rabbah 87:4 (ed. Theodor-Albeck, 1065).
17 Rosen-Zvi, *Sotah Ritual*, 187; Ruth Rabbah 6:4; *y. Ḥagigah* 2:1, 77c.
18 The idiom "and she uncovered his feet" is repeated and is reminiscent of the description of adulterous Israel in Ezekiel 23:10; 18; Hosea 2:11. On the euphemistic understanding of the feet being exposed, see Biale, *Eros and the Jews*, 234, fn. 7; Niditch, "Genesis 38."

motif of exile and revelation (*galut* and *hitgalut*), the myth of transmigration of souls (*gilgul*), the metamorphosis (*gilgul*) of figures in the biblical tales, the removal of the well-stone (*ha-golel*), the exposing of Noah's feet (*gilui margelotov*) when he is rolling drunkenly in his tent, the seductive act and illicit relations (*gilui arayot*) of the Davidic dynastic mothers, the foot of the mountain and the entrance to the cave of Lot's daughters, the joy (*gil*) embedded in the redemption (*ge'ula*) in contrast to the rolling around (*hitgolelut*) inherent in exile, and more. In our context, we will focus on the two contradictory directions derived from the term itself.

The symbolism of "the feet" is connected in the *Zohar* to Ruth's courage and daring, and also her weakness and vulnerability. From one perspective, the feet represent the acts of copulation, resurgence, and redemption, but from a different perspective they represent the *Shekhinah*'s difficult circumstance for she is described as lying in the dust "crushed by his feet" in *Tiqqunei Zohar* and *Zohar Ruth*. The feet are bound to dust, in their lowly, negative, and serpentine sense, "And dust you shall eat all the days of your life" (Gen. 3:14), alongside a description of dust's positive sense as the source of life. In the *Zohar*, the feet and shoes are distinctive marks of the *Shekhinah*'s multifaceted identity, called "the dust of the earth."[19] Also the word "**va-tegal**" (and she uncovered) carries a double meaning and is connected to exile (*galut*) and the mystery of disclosure (*gilui*) and redemption (*ge'ulah*), two motifs that the *Zohar* connects to the Davidic dynastic stories.

Ruth's name reflects the two contradictory conditions of the *Shekhinah*: from one perspective, Ruth is compared to the Assembly of Israel (*kenesset yisra'el*) and *Shekhinah* when she is "brimming with sorrow, overflowing with pain" and enveloped by the darkness of the night of exile.[20] From another perspective, in the Zoharic passages, Ruth is portrayed as an individual who merits resurgence and reparation. Likewise, her name (*r.v.t*) hints to Torah (*t.v.r.h*, by adding the letter *he*) and to a turtledove (*tor, t.v.r*) that "saturates the Holy One blessed be He with songs and praise."[21] This reading does not only constitute

---

19 Isaiah 26: 19; *Zohar* I: 124a, 139b; *Tiqqunei Zohar* 17b. Roi, "Legs." On the *Shekhinah* as the "shoe," see *Zohar* III: 180a.
20 *Zohar Ḥadash* 88a. Hecker, *Pritzker*, 11:237.
21 For the image of Ruth as a turtledove, see *Zohar Ruth* 75a, 78a. Also as it says in *Zohar Ruth* 85b: "Ruth—in the image of the lower world, saturating the blessed Holy One with songs and praises perpetually. Ruth, (*rut*) like the name, turtledove (*tur*). As the turtledove has a unique song among all others, so Assembly of Israel has a song of praise unique among all other calls—praise of awakening (*tur*). "The turtledove emits two calls as one: one high and one low—all as one. Assembly of Israel, too, arouses above and arouses below—all at once and with a single voice." Hecker, *Pritzker*, 11:281.

an optimistic alternative to the version of exile and downfall, but also a creative and feminist rendering of the interpretation of King David's name in rabbinic literature.[22] While in the allegoric passages Ruth symbolizes the lower letter *he* in the Tetragrammaton (*yud, he, vav, he*), Naomi, by contrast, is identified with the *sefirah* of *Binah* and the upper letter *he*.[23]

The Zoharic passages treating Ruth and the threshing night exist in the tension between redemption and exile, exposure and hiddenness, and their interpretations fluctuate between the extremities. From one perspective, prominent in the *Zohar*, is the perception of feminine resurgence and actual copulation that happened that night and led to the construction of the messianic dynasty: "That day, she really rose—for Boaz united with her."[24] From a different perspective, in *Zohar Ruth* and *Tiqqunei Zohar* a pessimistic picture is configured, according to which reparation is impossible: "What is the meaning of the verse *Then she came stealthily and uncovered his feet and lay down* (Ruth 3:7)? Lying down by his feet—not opposite him, or next to him."[25] Here the exegesis emphasizes the exilic state of the *Shekhinah* displaced at the feet, without any possibility of being rescued from her location.[26] It is likely that the basis for this reading is based on the sages stressing that she is laying *at his feet* (and not coupling with him), but the *Zohar* intensifies the description here of the calamity and vulnerability of the Assembly of Israel as a symbolic figure.[27]

These two contradictory trends interpret verses from the Book of Ruth. The first reading identifies Ruth with the *Shekhinah* and interprets the threshing floor episode as a tragedy occurring also in the supernal realm, while simultaneously

---

22 As is written: "Ruth. What is the meaning of Ruth? R. Johanan said: Because she was privileged to be the ancestress of David, who saturated the Holy One, blessed be He, with songs and hymns. How do we know that the name [of a person] has an effect [upon his life]? R. Eleazar said: Scripture says: Come, behold the works of the Lord, who hath made desolations in the earth. Read not *shammot*, [desolations], but *shemot*, [names]." b. Berakhot 7b, b. Bava Batra 14b, *Ruth Zuṭa* 1:4. The Zohar feminizes this Midrash, while simultaneously transferring the emphasis from Ruth's descendants to her. For more on rabbinic interpretation of her name, see Neihoff, *Ruth*, 61.
23 At times, this identification is linked to the Written Torah and Oral Torah. *Zohar Ruth* 83b, 85b; *Tiqqunei Zohar, Tiqqun* 31.
24 *Zohar* I: 111a, Matt, *Pritzker*, 161.
25 *Zohar Ruth* 87b-88a; Hecker, *Pritzker*, 11:234-5.
26 *Zohar* I: 93b, I: 214, there the phrase "remain this night" as a pessimistic state of the *Shekhinah* in exile.
27 Ruth Rabbah (ed. Lerner) 7:1. For variant formulations, Lerner, "The Book of Ruth," 176-7. This Midrash is missing from many manuscripts, seemingly with these words the sages are disputing an opposing tradition, which Flavius confronts as well.

emphasizing the difficult setting in which the Book of Ruth begins, with both women abandoned in a world where death, famine, and crisis reign. The second reading, conversely, presents a personal and optimistic trend that relies on the book's conclusion, with the women's blessing at the city's gates and the birth of Obed, while relying on Ruth's figure's description in rabbinic exegesis. Alongside the focusing on the passages on the juxtaposition *"va-tegal margelotav"* (and she uncovered his feet), we will refer now to additional phrases through which these two trends are constructed in different layers of the *Zohar*. For example, the phrase *"lini ha-lailah"* (remain this night), is interpreted as an anticipation for the redemptive morning from the long exilic night and also as a depiction of the night of coupling bringing the personal and messianic reparation.

THE PERSONAL STANCE—RUTH AS AN ACTIVE MESSIANIC MOTHER IN THE *ZOHAR*

The *Zohar*'s exegesis of *Parashat va-Yeshev* develops the feminine model of the biblical type-scene and the dynastic heroines' vindication in rabbinic Midrash, while comparing Ruth to Tamar, who are both motivated, according to the *Zohar*, for the sake of heaven, and therefore receive divine assistance. The multiple actions and efforts in the passage bring to light a coupling scene which ends with the birth of the messianic son:

> "She took off her widow's garments … (Genesis 38:14). Come and see: Tamar was the daughter of a priest. Now, would you ever imagine that she set out to whore with her father-in-law, given that she was inherently modest? Rather, she was righteous and did this out of wisdom. She offered herself to him only because she possessed knowledge and contemplated wisdom. So she approached him to act kindly and faithfully; that is why she came to him and engaged in this affair. Come and see: Because she possessed knowledge and exerted (*hishtadlah*) herself in this affair, the blessed Holy One offered assistance in that very act and she immediately conceived. All issued from Him. Now you might ask: 'Why did not the blessed Holy One bring those sons through some other woman? Why through this one?' But precisely she, and no other woman, was need for this act (*Zohar* I: 188a; Matt, *Pritzker*, 3:148).

These heroines are chosen to establish the Davidic dynasty due to their foreignness and worthy intentions. In the passage's continuation, the *Zohar* presents a shared model of the Davidic mother's justification in light of Ruth and Tamar's similar actions:

> There were two women through whom the seed of Judah was established, from whom issued King David, King Solomon, and King Messiah. These two women correspond to one another: Tamar and Ruth, whose husbands died first, who exerted themselves in this action. Tamar enticed (*hishtadlah*) her father-in-law, who was next of kin to his sons who had died. Why did she entice him? As is written: *for she saw that Shelah had grown up and she had not been given to him as wife.* That is why she engaged in this act with her father-in-law. As for Ruth, her husband died and then she engaged in this act with Boaz, as is written: *She uncovered his feet and lay down.* Engaging with him, she later gave birth to Obed. Now you might ask 'Why did not Obed issue from another woman?' But precisely she was needed, no one else. From these two, the seed of Judah was established and consummated. Both of them acted properly, acting kindly toward the dead so that the world would later be enhanced ... Both of them exerted themselves to act kindly and faithfully toward the dead, and the Holy One assisted in that act. All was fitting! Happy is one who engages (*she-mishtadel*) in Torah day and night (*Zohar* I: 188b; Matt, *Pritzker*, 3:149-50).

The significant innovation in this passage lies in the comparison of the two stories of seduction: Tamar's daring actions parallel, according to the *Zohar*, Ruth's more ambiguous actions, and in both cases it is a seduction which leads to actual copulation between a man and woman. Based on the Midrashim that vindicate the dynastic mothers, the *Zohar* depicts them as righteous women benefiting the dead and living, without any criticism or polemic against their deeds.[28]

The root *sh.d.l* (exert/engage/entice) is repeated again and again in the passage: "who exerted (*hishtadlu*) themselves in this action ... Tamar enticed (*hishtadlah*) her father-in-law ... she engaged (*hishtadlah*) in this act with Boaz ... *She uncovered his feet and lay down.* Engaging (*hishtadlah*) with him ... Both of them exerted (*hishtadlu*) themselves to act kindly and faithfully toward the dead." Surprisingly the *Zohar* links the feminine enticement and the engagement

---

28 Genesis Rabbah 51:7-11 (ed. Theodor-Albeck, 537-41); Genesis Rabbah 85:7-8 (ed. Theodor-Albeck, 1038-42); Ruth Rabbah (ed. Lerner) §3, 6-7. There is no doubt that the *Zohar*'s statement: "There were two women through whom the seed of Judah was established," is based on the opening of the Midrash in *Ruth Zuṭa* (ed. Buber) 1:12 "Two women gave themselves for the tribe of Judah."

in Torah study, and teaches that thanks to their labors God assists in the execution of "the act," according to the principle of *midah ke-neged midah* (proportional reciprocation).

Despite the commandment of levirate marriage (*yibbum*) being placed on the man—the levir—in both of these stories, Tamar and Ruth actively initiate a levirate marriage and seek to perpetuate their deceased husband's name. Both demonstrate the *mise-en-scène* of the seduction and coupling and in the end both give birth to a son for the Judean dynasty. According to the Zoharic exegesis on *Parashat va-Yera*—which we examined in the chapter about "*Tiqla*"—Ruth going to the threshing floor that very night causes a messianic resurgence, alluding to her foremother's actions. This rising and resurgence, according to their erotic and mystical meanings, to use the Zoharic terminology, occurred "precisely" as a result of the feminine initiative and divine providence of the action.[29] We may summarize and say that Ruth's coupling with Boaz is described in a few passages in the *Zohar* as an exertion meriting divine justification and earthly bounty. The phrase "*Then she came uncovered his feet and lay down*" is interpreted as an actual act of seduction during the threshing night, leading to Obed's birth. The use of the term "this act" in both cases shows that the *Zohar* seeks to emphasize the reparation embedded in Ruth's and Tamar's efforts, which are repeated in each other's acts.

RUTH AND TAMAR—THE SHARED MODEL

In the Zoharic exegesis of *Parashat va-Yeshev*, a four-stage model is repeated in Ruth's and Tamar's stories: seeing, understanding, the seductive act, and lastly divine support and the birth of a son for the messianic dynasty. Indeed, there are many parallels in the two biblical stories: beginning with the husbands' deaths, afterwards the need for *yibbum*, alongside a woman in need of redemption, and the act of *yibbum*, not done by the closest redeemer, but by the further redeemer. The similarities are also prominent in the description of the seductive act, the feminine initiative and varieties of deceit: the walking at night, the threshing floor and cloak, next to the disguise and face cover, sitting at the crossroads, the six measures of barley as parallel to the signet, cord and the staff, the men's elderliness, Tamar's mention in the blessing at the gate for Ruth, and the birth of a son woven into the royal messianic dynasty.

---

29 *Zohar* I: 111a. Also see chapter five.

Tamar and Ruth are portrayed in the *Zohar* as archetypical figures recurring over many generations, returning and doing the very same action of reparation, which entails perception and opening the eyes, understanding and awareness, until the redemption arrives through it. Similar to the Davidic heroines, all the men of these stories also symbolize Judah, the primary father of the dynasty. This emerges from the *Zohar*'s text on *Saba de-Mishpatim*, which interprets Judah's persistence to perform the act of *yibbum* with Tamar from the words: "And he did not continue, to know her any longer" (Gen. 38:26), which is translated as—"and he did not cease."[30] This picture completes the feminine effort described in the Zoharic exegesis of *Parashat va-Yeshev*: just as Judah's character recurs throughout the generations, likewise it is possible to understand that these heroines have been designated for "that act" since time immemorial. As is written about Tamar and Ruth: "She knew, and acted zealously in this matter, to fulfill the ways of the blessed Holy One, so that royal rulers would issue from her, destined to reign over the world. And Ruth acted similarly."[31] We will briefly discuss the model's stages that reoccur in the stories.

A. The Motif of Seeing and the "Eyes" by Tamar and Ruth

The motif of the eyes in these stories is highlighted by the *Zohar*, associating "your eyes on the field" from the Book of Ruth with the idiom "entrance of *Enaim* (eyes)" in Genesis 38. The *Zohar* develops the rabbinic Midrashim, according to which Tamar and Ruth both gazed, cried, and prayed in order to merit progeny from Judah's family and not leave them "empty."[32] Tamar covered her face and therefore Judah did not recognize her and from afar she fixed her gaze to "the gate to which all eyes are directed"; while Ruth casts "her eyes on the field" and understood that in the future, a son and grandson would be born to her from Boaz who will "saturate the Holy One blessed be He with songs and praise."[33] Both stories are built upon the principle of concealment and disclosure: the active feminine seduction,

---

30 *Zohar* II: 104b; Matt, *Pritzker*, 5:71; *b. Sotah* 10b.
31 *Zohar* III: 72a; Matt, *Pritzker*, 7:484.
32 Genesis Rabbah 85:7 [14] (ed. Theodor-Albeck, 1041), and as is written in *Ruth Zuṭa* (ed. Buber) 1:12, "Two women gave themselves for the tribe of Judah: Tamar and Ruth. Tamar would cry out saying that she would not leave the house empty handed, and Ruth, every time her mother-in-law would say to her to return home, would sob, as it is written, 'Then they wept aloud *again*.'" In contrast to their passivity in this Midrash, the *Zohar* emphasizes their dominance through the 'eye' motif. An additional link between them emerges from *Midrash Tehillim*, 116.
33 Genesis Rabbah 85: 7-8 [14-15] (ed. Theodor-Albeck, 1038-42); Ruth Rabbah (ed. Lerner) 3, 6-7.

sitting at "the entrance of Enaim," and going to the threshing floor, while drawing the eyes to the place's opening, symbolizing the source of mercy (*raḥamim*) and the feminine womb (*reḥem*). Boaz says to Ruth to set "your eyes on the field," and the *Zohar* stresses that he saw "that supernal holy eyes (kings and ministers) were destined to issue from her" for she set good eyes on the field "and she did not move her eyes to look anywhere but in front of her ... and had no impudence in her."[34] The heroines' singularity is emphasized here. Concerning everyone else there is a rule "not to follow the lust of your own eyes," whereas they cast their good eyes on "that very act," and their perception changes the face of reality.

B. Understanding and Awareness

Similar to God vindicating Lot's daughters' act, with the birth of Ruth from the same "other seed" (hinted at in Gen. Rabbah 51), it is possible to say that the Davidic dynastic mothers desire one, specific son, and for his sake insist on establishing their house. According to *Zohar va-Yeshev*, each detail of their actions are directed towards this end, linking the sexual seduction to the labor of Torah study and the mystery of *yibbum* and transmigration. In this way, the *Zohar* indicates the circle of life and death in the Davidic dynasty, wherein the transmigration of souls is a reflection of the cosmic wheel.

In this way, both of these heroines draw down a "thread of grace (*ḥesed*)" from the realm of death to the world of the living, and thereby merit long lives. On the mystical level, Tamar and Ruth enact the mystery of *yibbum* and transmigration, establishing a name for Er, Onan, and Mahlon through the figures of Perez and Obed.[35] Each birth, especially when it is a messianic birth, is an objection to the universal order, an opening to the unknown. It is possible to say that the dimension of unknowing, stemming here from the future, occurring in the "world of truth" and future generations. Only in the fourth stage's completion—the birth of a son and divine vindication—is a circular observation of their acts of kindness made possible.

C. The Seductive Act

As stated, Tamar's and Ruth's seductive actions termed in *Zohar va-Yeshev* as **"hishtadlut"** (exertion), are not only directed at their individual deeds, but also at

---

34 *Zohar* II: 217b-8; Matt, *Pritzker*, 6: 241-2.
35 On the "mysteries of *yibbum* and transmigration," see Scholem, *Godhead*, 197-250; Mopsik, *Sex of the Soul*, 42-4; Yisraeli, *The Interpretation of Secrets*, 113-29.

the generations preceding and following them. The perception of sexuality here is not situated unto itself; rather it appears in the context of dynastic and national fertility, beginning by Ruth going to the threshing floor and Tamar sitting at the "entrance of Enaim." The *Zohar* stresses that the Judean tribe is built thanks to bold women who fought death by giving birth. The connection between the stories of Tamar and Ruth intensifies the suffering and crisis surrounding both heroines: the deaths of Elimelech, Mahlon, and Chilion, the famine and difficult return to Bethlehem, the deaths of Er and Onan, Tamar's abandonment at her father's house, Judah's callous attitude, and her almost being burned. The death appearing in these passages clarifies that in both stories it is not merely a passing seduction due to momentary lust, but rather an intentional process designed to overcome past ruptures and grow within them new life. The erotic potencies are enlisted in the Zoharic exegesis for a theurgic action that drives the divine through the seduction, and arouses it to collaborate in the birth of the messianic son. In this way, these heroines' choice to continue the chain of being forms a myth of birth occurring in both the supernal and mundane realms.

D. The Divine Assistance and Birth of the Son to the Messianic Dynasty

The entangled seductive acts of both women are successful thanks to the heavenly assistance hidden in each Davidic story. As already highlighted in the Midrash regarding Tamar losing Judah's identifiers: "*As she was being brought out* (Gen. 38:25). R. Judan said: They [the signet, cord, and staff] had been lost, and the Holy One, blessed be He, provided others in their place." For Ruth the Midrash creates an even more dramatic assistance, the creation of a womb, as it is stated: "She lacked the main portion of the womb, but the Holy One, blessed be He, shaped a womb for her."[36] The shaping of the womb in Ruth's case and providing of identifiers for Tamar, are designed to hasten the messianic births of Perez and Zerah, and Obed and David. Furthermore, the sages purposefully disrupt the natural way of things, in order to highlight the divine efforts on behalf of these heroines and their actions' realizations. Similar to the Midrash that we discussed in the third chapter, describing the manner in which God "creates the messianic light," this Midrash adds that God contributes his part to the mission's success: "R. Eliezer said: Boaz played his part, and Ruth

---

36 Genesis Rabbah 85:11 [25] (ed. Theodor-Albeck, 1044). Ruth Rabbah 7:14 (ed. Vilna), as well as Ruth Rabbah 6:4 (ed. Lerner): "Ruth was forty years old and was not remembered, and once this righteous man prayed for her, she was immediately remembered."

played hers, [and Naomi played hers]. Whereupon the Holy One, blessed be He, said, 'I too must play mine.'"[37]

If in the rabbinic Midrashim God assists the women, in the *Zohar* the picture is reversed, and it is the women who are helping divinity and creating a theurgic rectification in the supernal realms.[38] This assistance is described in the *Zohar* as a circle of grace (*ḥesed*), conjoining upper to lower. After examining the descriptions of Ruth and Tamar as archetypical figures laboring "in the same action," we will study the passive and tragic readings of the threshing night. As opposed to the foremothers who are "revivers of the dead" through the *yibbum* that they initiate, in the passages of *Tiqqunei Zohar* and *Zohar Ruth*, a different perspective of the *Shekhinah*'s exile emerges.

THE ALLEGORICAL STANCE—*ZOHAR RUTH* AND *TIQQUNEI ZOHAR*

In contradiction to the passages of the *Zohar*, which view Ruth as an actual figure whose initiative and struggle bring her redemption, we shall present two passages that view Ruth's action as an allegory of a vulnerable feminine figure, pleading to merit an external redemption. According to the symbolic-allegorical position—arising from *Tiqqunei Zohar* and *Zohar Ruth*—Ruth symbolizes the Assembly of Israel in exile, while Boaz signifies God who is meant to rescue her in the coming future.[39]

Zohar Ruth: At Midnight

The passage in *Zohar Ruth* begins with a description of Boaz viewing the celestial precious stones and magnificent jewels surrounding the holy throne, and while he delighted in "consuming heavenly life," suddenly he became frightened:

> "*He went to lie down at the end of the heap of grain* (Ruth 3:7). Rabbi Nehorai and Rabbi Yehudai came to Tiberias, where they heard Rabbi Shim'on expound upon this verse: *Boaz ate and drank* ... (ibid.). *His heart was glad* (ibid.)—consuming heavenly life—this life gladdened his heart. After rejoicing, at once he went to lie down at the end of the heap of grain. These are the celestial precious stones and magnificent jewels surrounding

---

37 Ruth Rabbah 7:7.
38 Idel, *Kabbalah and Eros*, 247–50.
39 Although the symbol and the allegory differ from one another, it is possible to identify both orientations in *Zohar Ruth* and *Tiqqunei Zohar*.

the holy throne, as is said: *Your belly is a heap of wheat edged with lilies* (Song of Songs 7:3). What is the meaning of the verse: *Then she came stealthily and uncovered his feet and lay down* (Ruth 3:7)? Lying down by his feet—not opposite him, or next to him. From here we learn that until midnight he did not know. And the blessed Holy One does not enter the Garden of Eden with the righteous until after midnight ... When night is split, a voice arouses, calling out, aroused from the north side ... And he cries out: Then upper and lower abide under the aegis of Judgment (*Din*) of the left" (*Zohar Ḥadash Ruth* 87b-88a, Hecker, *Pritzker* 11:234-235).[40]

The passage connects the Song of Songs (7:3) "Your belly is a heap of wheat," to the verse "When Boaz had eaten and drunk, and he was in a contented mood, **he went to lie down at the end of the heap of grain**. Then she came quietly and uncovered his feet, and lay down." (Ruth 3:7). In this manner, a dissonance is created between Boaz's state of spiritual elevation and expectation of uniting with the *Shekhinah*, and his astonishment entailed in his encounter with Ruth rolling at his feet. Midnight in the kabbalists' view is a time of awakening and stormy happenings in the supernal realm; it is a time of God's jouissance playing with the righteous souls in the Garden of Eden on the one hand, and a frightful time in which the proclamations of Judgment go out from the heavens, on the other hand.[41] In this passage it is the moment in which Boaz discovers Ruth at his feet, together with the forceful rooster's crowing, and the forces of the left coming from the north. The divine roar over the destruction known to us from rabbinic literature here joins Ruth's cry to Boaz:[42]

> "*At midnight*. We have learned: There are three watches of the night; and during each watch, the blessed Holy One sits and roars like a lion ... At the moment that the rooster crows—when the flame from the northern side is aroused ... He crows loudly, proclaiming, 'Arise to wail for the Temple, all masters of peace!' ... all gather to weep over the Temple ... And the

---

40 *Zohar Ḥadash* 87b-88a. This is from The *Zohar*: Pritzker Edition, volume 11, translation and commentary by Joel Hecker. My deep gratitude to Dani Matt and Joel Hecker and the *Zohar* Education Project, Inc, for allowing me to make use of this material before publication.
41 Hellner-Eshed, *A River Flows*, 149-63.
42 As it is written in *b. Berakhot* 3a: "The night has three watches, and at each watch the Holy One, blessed be He, sits and roars like a lion." Michael Fishbane, "The Holy One Sits and Roars," 61-75; Hellner-Eshed, *A River Flows*, 150-1. Also compare, de León, *Sheqel*, 88-90; Scholem, *Symbolism*, 146-9.

> Holy One blessed be He wailing, crying, and kicking in the 390 firmaments. Then, at that precise moment, *At midnight, the man trembled and twisted away* (Ruth 3:8). *The man*—the blessed Holy One bellowing a mournful wail for the Temple, as is written: *YHVH roars from on high, and from His holy habitation He utters His voice* ... (Jeremiah 25:30), Roaring he does roar over his abode—this is the *Shekhinah*" (Ibid, 88a, Hecker, *Pritzker*, 11:235-6).

Boaz symbolizes God, "the man," and the one with the power (*bo ha-oz*, Boaz) to redeem the *Shekhinah*. Fashioned here is the transformation from the personal drama to its allegorical significance. God's roaring and kicking of the 390 firmaments parallels the scene of Boaz awaking frightened at midnight, in the transition between the second and third watches, in which he cries over the Temple's destruction. It is significant that the juxtaposition of "and she uncovered his feet" is not interpreted regarding the copulation, rather the divine wail over the *Shekhinah* and the destroyed sanctuary. The identification of the night with the suffering of exile is sourced in the rabbinic exegesis of the Book of Ruth: "Remain this night—in this world which is all night, and in the morning—refers to the world which is all good," an idea which is repeated many times in the *Zohar*.[43] The difficult wait "until morning" is intensified through God's identification with the Assembly of Israel in exile, as it arises from the passage's continuation:

> "*And twisted away*. Why? Because *Behold! There was a woman lying at his feet!*—lying in the dust crushed by His feet—this is Assembly of Israel. Then, at that moment, she was aroused toward him and he asked her, saying, 'My daughter, *who are you* (Ruth 3:9) in exile? Who are you at this moment?' And she replied, 'I am *Ruth (Rut)*, your handmaid (ibid.)'— brimming (*meravvat*), with sorrow, overflowing with pain over my children in exile, and over the holy palaces, for I have been exiled from My sanctuary. And it is not enough that I have been banished, but they abuse and curse Me every day on account of them, and I have no voice in exile to respond!" (Ibid, 88a, Hecker, *Pritzker*, 11:237).

The ambiguous description of Ruth and Boaz's conversation at the threshing floor in the Bible is transformed in the *Zohar* into an intimate and direct discussion between two disassociated lovers. In this dialogue God asks the

---

43 Ruth Rabbah 6:7 (ed. Lerner); Lerner, "The Book of Ruth," 170; for example *Zohar* II: 17a.

Shekhinah: "My daughter, *who are you* in exile? *Who are you* at this moment? And she replied, 'I am Ruth (Rut), your handmaid (ibid.)'—brimming (*mer-avvat*) with sorrow, overflowing with pain over my children in exile."[44] The *Shekhinah* associates her condition with that of her children—the nation of Israel suffering in exile. The drama presented here occurs first and foremost in the divine *familia*.[45] Ruth, the *Shekhinah*, and the Assembly of Israel, tell the Holy One blessed be He about her excessive degradation, inherent in her inability to answer those who abuse and curse her. On the symbolic and psychological level this description portrays the feminine weakness of a figure "lacking a voice."[46] This is not the only place in the *Zohar*, in which the exile is represented as a state of feminine dumbness, while redemption is identified with speech and masculine success.[47]

This passage recognizes the pain of the feminine heroine, and even marks a struggle with the *Shekhinah*'s internal muteness. Through the allegorical reading the emotional world of the figures is stressed, while the *Zohar* deepens the connections between the human and divine drama. Already in the Talmud the sages present the third watch of the night as an intimate time in which the feminine figure "recounts with her husband," but also as a dangerous time of God's painful roaring. Therefore, the *Zohar* chooses to describe this conversation at the heart of the third watch, in which the *Shekhinah* is left lying at his feet, crushed into the dust, lamenting the cursed exile, and her speechlessness in facing her abusers. The mythopoetic design of the passage reaches its peak here—for the very response to the question, "who are you my daughter" is an act of exposing the feminine voice and its disclosure, paralleling in many aspects the "revealing" of Boaz's feet. The beginning of this motion is the feminine arousal, "at that moment, she was aroused towards him," for even if there is not a personalistic redemption and copulation, there is yearning and longing meriting a reparation through speech. Exile is described in the passage through the mute state of the *Shekhinah*, while God's responsiveness to her pain implies a beginning of *tiqqun* and redemption.

The ability of the exegetes to cause the *Shekhinah*'s pain to speak stems from their identification with her exilic state. However, it is possible to say that

---

44 As aforesaid, this interpretation of her name, is an exact opposite to the rabbinic Midrash. b. *Berakhot* 7b.
45 Idel, *Ben*, 377-506; Hellner-Eshed, *A River Flows*, 143-4.
46 Carol Gilligan, *In a Different Voice* (Cambridge: Harvard University Press, 1982), 5-23; Cixous and Clément, *The Newly Born Woman*, 138-46; Kristeva, *Black Sun*. See also ch. 4 fn. 15.
47 *Zohar* I: 36a, 116b. Pedaya, "The Sixth Millenium," 67.

the descriptions of the *Shekhinah*'s pain and degradation in exile reproduce her passive condition, stifle her agency, and attribute her salvation to an external redeemer. The *Shekhinah* is entirely dependent on the masculine reparation of the husband or sons. In contrast to Ruth's image in rabbinic Midrashim, grasping Boaz "like ivy," or her description in the *Zohar* as a resourceful woman who gets what she wants, the Assembly of Israel in the passage of *Zohar Ruth* is a passive figure pleading for salvation, "with no voice" or phallicness in her exilic state.[48] Her identity is condensed into "your handmaiden," the one "brimming with sorrow, overflowing with pain," and therefore she stays in that position until the end of the night:

> "*Stay for the night*—stay now in exile and guide Your children there with Torah and good deeds. If their good deeds aid Your redemption, You will be redeemed. If not, [*then in the morning ...*] *I will redeem you myself, by YHVH's life! Lie down until morning* (Ruth 3:13). For morning and the light of redemption will come" (Ibid, 88b, Hecker, *Pritzker*, 11:239).

Indeed, God's promise to eventually redeem the *Shekhinah* from the dust himself, "in its time I will accomplish it quickly," offers an alternative model of personal and active redemption. The suggestion that she waits until dawn if the good deeds of her children will not help her, is presented as an act of divine reconciliation. In contrast to the interpretation in the *Zohar* exploring "that act," the seduction, and *yibbum*, this passage suggests that the kindness of Ruth and the Assembly of Israel does not stem from their labors and deeds, but precisely from their inactivity. The *Shekhinah*'s redemption will arrive as a result of her not doing anything. She will neither be worried about the nations' abuse, nor frightened that her sons are not saving her; rather she will wait until the night's end. In God's words at the end of the passage of *Zohar Ruth*: "stay now in exile," until the morning comes.

Tiqqunei Zohar: Tiqqun 21—"And She Uncovered His Feet"

Tiqqunei Zohar interprets a number of times the threshing floor image as a symbolic scene and divine drama, in a similar manner to *Zohar Ruth*. However, here is a different literary genre constructing a remarkable world of significations and relying on a unique expressive virtuosity.[49] We will discuss the meaning of

---

48 Freud, "Female Sexuality"; Freud, "Essays"; Irigaray, *Sex Which Is Not One*.
49 See an example below, and fn. 53.

the term "and she uncovered his feet" in *Tiqqun* 21, and the means in which the compiler of the *Tiqqunim* interprets the tension between the first redeemer, the "closer" one, and the second redeemer. This tension is reflected in Boaz's words in the Book of Ruth: "But now, though it is true that I am a near kinsman, there is another kinsman more closely related than I. Remain this night, and in the morning, if he will act as a redeemer for you, good; let him do so. If he is not willing to act as a redeemer for you, then, as the Lord lives, I will act as a redeemer for you. Lie down until the morning" (Ruth 3:12-13).

Who is the closer redeemer that Boaz refers to, on the symbolic plane, and who is the second redeemer, seemingly the further one? In the passage in *Zohar Ruth* we saw that God asks the *Shekhinah* to wait until night's end in order for him to redeem her himself. This approach is reinforced in the *Tiqqunei Zohar*, and is presented in an even harsher form. Here the divine Boaz does not request, rather he announces to the *Shekhinah*, after he confronts her with his disappointment from the acts of the earthly *Ṣaddiq* (righteous one). This exegesis stresses man's dependence in general, and specifically that of the feminine divinity, on the supernal divine salvation. Simultaneously, the masculine phallic aspect is intensified, binding *Yesod* and the figure of the Supernal *Ṣaddiq*. In these readings the oath terminology "as the Lord lives" attests to the identity of the divine redeemer, while the statement "I will redeem you" transforms Boaz into a divine apotheosis, who will raise the *Shekhinah* in the future from the dust, with the assistance of the supernal *sefirot*.

In a paradoxical manner, the first redeemer is called "good," identified here with Boaz as a human figure who disappoints and is unable to redeem Ruth, whereas God, who has the power (*bo ha-oz*), is described as the second chosen redeemer.[50] In this lengthy *Tiqqun* the phrase "and she uncovered his feet" is interpreted six times in different tragic contexts, while intensifying the disappointment from reality and the anticipation for the divine redemption from above:

> And when she falls, **she falls at his feet, as it is written "and she uncovered his feet and lay down,"** and she falls in front of him, falling on her face (*nefilat apaiyyim*) in front of the *Ṣaddiq* (righteous one) who sustains the world, is poor in exile, and the *Ṣaddiq* when he is displaced ... is called *Bar*

---

50 On the identity of "good" and its connection to Boaz in rabbinic literature, see Ginzberg, *Legends*, 2:866-7, fn. 61-4.

(son/outcast) and she is called *Baraita* (daughter/external) of Sabbath, who adds to the poor *Ṣaddiq*, who is certainly The Day of Sabbath ... bile (*marah*), spleen (*teḥol*), and liver (*kaveid*) symbolize the exile of *neshamah*, *ruaḥ*, and *nefesh* (three parts of the soul), which is the *Shekhinah*, who is exiled in the liver as it is written about the limbs, that the holy people are her hosts, "Let heavier (*tikhbad*) work be laid on them" (Ex. 5:9) ... "and made their lives bitter (*va-yemareru*)" (Ex 1:14) ... "but they would not listen to Moses, because of their broken spirit and their cruel slavery" (Ex. 6:9) and they cried out to the Holy One blessed be He because of it ... **and the soul (*neshamah*) in the last exile, it is written "and she uncovered his feet" is lying in the dust. Woe to the man whose soul descends to his feet**, which at the same time it is said "Fallen, no more to rise" (Amos 5:2) and he cannot ascend or rise except when the Holy One and the Holy Name go to the right, and raises her, The mystery of the matter, "remain this night," if he will redeem you good, which is *berit* (covenant), he will redeem "if he is not willing to be a redeemer for you, then I (*anokhi*) will be a redeemer for you" (Ruth 3:13) I (*anokhi*) – who is the Supernal Mother, I (*anokhi*) of exodus from Egypt ... "Lie down until the morning" – which is the right, the strength of the Written Torah, the central column. The Written Torah was given from the right and from the left the Oral Torah, the feminine. And thus it is good that the *Ṣaddiq*, who is "mighty one (*gibor*) conquers his desires" and sustains the world, comes from the left ... Simultaneously **the soul is crushed beneath the feet, which is written "and she uncovered his feet and lay down" and thus is returned to the heart, which is Jerusalem**, and then the heart sees ... the heart hears ... while Israel is sullied in the filth of the nations, the soul, which is the *Shekhinah*, says "Do not gaze at me because I am dark" (Song of Songs 1:6) and the prayer falls, which is written "Fallen, no more to rise, is maiden Israel" (Amos 5:2) **and when she falls she lays in the dust beneath his feet, and when she is raised "and she uncovered his feet and lay down" and she prays to the Holy One blessed be He that he will raise her from the dust**, which is written, "spread your cloak over your servant, for you are a redeemer," while simultaneously "the man was startled and turned over" as it is written "The Lord is a warrior" ... he will come and say to her "Remain the night" which is the left, "and in the morning" which is mercy, the right, which from there light comes forth, as it is written "the morning was light" (Genesis 44:3), "if he will act as a redeemer for you, good," if Israel will do for you good deeds to raise you from beneath the feet, good. If you will be redeemed by your husband, Supernal Israel, certainly good, and if they will not do good deeds for you, I will redeem you. Simultaneously, "Jonah (*yonah*), meanwhile, had gone down into the hold of the ship" (Jonah 1:5), this is the lower *Shekhinah*, **which is written about her, "and she uncovered his feet and lay down" – lying in the dirt,** and this is "and had lain down, and was fast asleep" (Ibid.), and why did she fall? Because the *ruaḥ* (soul) departed from her, which is the central pillar that supports her, and she fell, at the same time, it is written about her, "How lonely [she] sits" (Lam. 1:1). And who caused her fall? It is because Israel violated the commandments. **And while she is fallen beneath the feet, Israel her sons are crushed beneath the feet, and they are ill and wounded.** Simultaneously, the body is in the house of the sick, which is Israel, and the *Shekhinah* is with them, for she is a turtledove (*yonah*).[51]

From all the complex allusions in *Tiqqun* 21, I will explicate those relevant for the interpretation of the threshing floor scene, specifically the phrase "and she uncovered his feet." The text's style creates an ecstatic effect, in which image is joined to image, in order to intensify the description of the *Shekhinah*'s hard fall—she is the soul, the nation of Israel in exile, the fallen prayer, the Ṣaddiq in distress, the lamenting Jerusalem, Jonah seeking his death, Noah's dove looking for a place to rest, and a limb of the divine figure.[52] All of these are gathered in the body of Ruth the Moabite, who goes to the threshing floor and falls at Boaz's feet.

The choice of Ruth as a heroine, someone who represents the layered experience of fallenness, is due to the author's identification with the totality of foreign states in the human condition. The figure of an isolated, poor, and alien widow, reveals an autobiographic tone in the figure of the author of the *Tiqqunim*, who expresses through Ruth, the human longing to be wrapped in God's redeeming protection: "and she prays to the Holy One blessed be He that he will raise her from the dust, that which is written,

---

51 *Tiqqunei Zohar, Tiqqun* 21, 45b-53a. It should be stated that this is an exceptionally long *Tiqqun*, and that the passage I explore is spread over nine folios, of which a large section doesn't engage in exegesis on the Book of Ruth.
52 On the style of the *Tiqqunim*, Liebes, "The *Zohar* and the Tiqqunim," 269; Goldreich, *Self-Image*, 459-96; On the *Shekhinah*'s centrality in this work, see Roi, "Shekhina"; Pedaya, *Walking through Trauma*, 104-7 and in Safedian kabbalah, ibid, 124-46.

spread your cloak over your servant, for you are a redeemer."⁵³ The passage stresses that the belief that redemption is possible is conditioned on man's identification with the depth of the *Shekhinah*'s fall, and thus it configures a spiritual conception of appealing to divinity from a feminine stance of lacking and absence.

The passage's literary formulation shakes the foundations of rationality and the sequential logical structure to which the reader is accustomed. Thus, all the metaphoric, symbolic, and mystic worlds are directed towards the *Shekhinah*, and her multiple falls. The phrase "and she uncovered his feet" receives in *Tiqqun* 21 a sensory demonstration as a performance of the "theatre of the disintegrating body": she is at his feet, oppressed, fallen, imprisoned, exiled, lying in the dust, displaced, descended to the liver, blackened and filthy, poor, crushed beneath his feet, and then she blossoms and rises to the heart and returns, and her soul leaves, and is enslaved in Egypt, facing Amalek, ill and wounded. Each of the readings exemplify different aspects of the feminine figure's exile. Following Haviva Pedaya's study on the ritual of going and wandering in the *Tiqqunei Zohar* as an expression of the exilic trauma, and that of Biti Roi, who illustrates the empathetic and emulative practices of the suffering *Shekhinah*, it is possible to say that in the *Tiqqun* here the author rolls in the dust together with the *Shekhinah*, and completely identifies with her distress.⁵⁴

The cosmic fall of the *Shekhinah* is comparable to the way that the psychoanalyst Donald Winnicott links the fear of breaking down, falling, and death with the pathological states of "disintegration," an experience of the self falling into pieces, without an anchor to gather the personality from within.⁵⁵ These states are due to the absence of a strong maternal foundation and they are reminiscent of the perception of the biblical Ruth in the eyes of the author of the *Tiqqunim*. The figure wandering from land to land, in poverty and hunger, with no secure protection, and pushed onto the threshing floor for the sake of saving

---

53 This depiction alludes to the custom of *nefilat apayyim*, which originates in kabbalistic literature, Hallamish, *Kabbalah*, 474-79; Roi, "Dying While Living" [forthcoming]

54 As Pedaya states "My starting point in discussing this section is that the text's author indeed experiences states of wandering in actual reality." Pedaya, *Walking through Trauma*, 79-87, 104-7; and Roi "The kabbalist identifies with the *Shekhinah* and her difficult exilic circumstance. He imitates the 'legless' *Shekhinah*, he is destitute, wandering, and crippled." Roi, "Shekhina," 156-232, 301-4.

55 Winnicott, "Fear of Breakdown"; Thomas H. Ogden, *The Primitive Edge of Experience* (Northvale: Jason Aronson, 1989), 146-7. Melanie Klein, in contrast, interprets frequent falls as symptoms connected to the Oedipus complex and feelings of guilt. Klein, *Writings*, 44-5.

her life and Naomi's, is transformed into an "eternal faller," in the continuous present.

Despite the rich imagery and allegories of the falling scenes, the passage has a strong feminine and corporeal base, reflected in the description of the internal bodily organs and the author's treatment of the liver's, bile's, and spleen's roles as symbols of exile. While the *Zohar* describes the feminine active seduction that has already happened, here the author of the *Tiqqunim* emphasizes the *Shekhinah*'s passive, arrested, and desperate state, in order to arouse the kabbalist to act and accelerate her redemption.[56]

Elliot Wolfson states that "according to the kabbalistic ontology there is only one gender, for the feminine has no significance or value except in terms of the masculine."[57] Indeed, we may ask whether the sequence of images in this passage deal with the loss of a limb or part of the male body (which in the future will be restored to him at the time of the redemption), or perhaps here is a description of a separate and independent feminine body? In a few places in *Tiqqun* 21 it is possible to identify a conception of the integration of *Malkhut* in *Tif'eret* and *Yesod*, and her being a part of the masculine body, in accordance with Wolfson's view. So for example, arising from the description "and it is said about the soul (*neshamah*) in the last exile "and she uncovered his feet" lying in the dust, woe to the man whose soul goes below his feet." Despite this, in the passage's continuation it says:

> While Israel is sullied in the filth of the nations, the soul, which is the *Shekhinah*, says "Do not gaze at me because I am dark" (Song of Songs 1:6) and the prayer falls ... and when she falls she lays in the dust beneath his feet, and when she is propped up "and she uncovered his feet and lay down" and she prays to the Holy One blessed be He that he will raise her from the dust.

It is clear that here is a description of a drama involving partners, in which the *Shekhinah* represents an independent entity, having her own divine dimension (*shi'ur qomah*) and separate body, similar to other passages in the Zoharic literature.[58] If so, what is the feminine divine dimension that the author of the

---

56 Roi, "Legs"; Pedaya, *Walking through Trauma*, 127.
57 Wolfson, "Gender and Heresy." In his view in kabbalistic literature, only the male androgyne or androgynous phallus exist and the *Shekhinah* is reabsorbed into his body as the phallic corona (*ateret ha-berit*). Wolfson, *Circle in the Square*, 49-78.
58 On the conception of the *Shekhinah* as an independent figure, see Roi, "Shekhina"; Asulin, "The Stature of the Shekhina," 103-82; Hellner-Eshed, "On Love"; Felix, "R. Joseph of Shushan"; Abrams, "The Condensation of the Symbol 'Shekhinah.'"

Tiqqunei Zohar offers in this passage? The description of the *Shekhinah* in terms of absence and loss—as a fallen, injured, and broken figure—makes one wonder if the author truly sees an actual feminine entity. Perhaps he wishes to present a bounty of "negative descriptions," or fragmentations of an imagined feminine character, which is defined in terms of lacking and portrays the "basic fault" of the human condition.[59] At the same time, it seems that the author of the *Tiqqunim* sees in front of him a complete androgynous body, feminine and masculine, and one shared heart. According to this suggestion, the *Shekhinah* is sometimes located in the heart, and that is the organ which is exiled to the feet and is fallen during the hour of crisis. Support for this can be found in the interpretation of the locution "and she uncovered his feet" in *Tiqqun* 70:

> R. El'azar said to him: Father, is the soul situated in a known place in the heart or is it circulated throughout all of the heart's organs? He said to him: My son, behold it is written, "and she uncovered his feet and lay down," according to the deeds of man she exits her place, and descends from outside of her place, like the *Shekhinah*, which it is written "and for your transgressions was your mother put away" (Is. 50:1) and complete repentance—is one who returns her to her original place, for when the soul is in the heart she is called, Queen (*Malka*), and when she exits the heart, she is not called Queen, according to the transgressions of man does she descend level by level, and organ by organ, until she falls to his feet, and according to his merits does she ascend until she reaches her place. Because of this in each place that she descends, she does an extra movement with that organ more than the other ones (*Tiqqun* 70, 132b).

We see in this passage that man's deeds establish the *Shekhinah*'s location in the body. In a repaired state she is in the heart, *Matrona* and *Malka*, whereas in a mournful state she is the expelled mother, exiled at his feet.[60] Perhaps this image provides a solution to the tension between the conceptions presented: those who view the *Shekhinah* as an independent divine essence and those who see her as the "phallic corona" of the male body. One may suggest that when the *Shekhinah* is in her place, she has a divine dimension of her own, whereas when she is weary at his feet in exile, her essence is transformed and becomes part of

---

59 Michael Balint, *The Basic Fault: Therapeutic Aspects of Regression*, (London: Tavistock Publications, 1968).
60 Hellner-Eshed, *A River Flows*, 143-4; Roi, "Shekhina," 98-150.

the masculine body. In the future, the redemption is marked by the *Shekhinah*'s independent stature; this is in contrast to her being restored to the masculine body, which symbolizes the undeveloped pre-embryotic state and therefore is identified with exile.[61]

As we saw, the emotional and symbolic world stands at the center of the passages of *Zohar Ruth* regarding the *Shekhinah* lacking a voice in exile, as an expression of the experience of destruction in the divine. In contrast, within the *Tiqqunei Zohar*, the trigger is not personal or psychological, but rather theurgic, stylistic, and poetic. The interchanging metaphors of subjects and objects and the increasing tempo of substituting figures and analogies create a cataclysmic experience, which happens in the present, as it were—the *Shekhinah* is falling now—and we must hurry to raise her from the dust. In this manner the crisis experience, which Gershom Scholem stresses in the description of the messianic idea, is intensified.

In his view, beginning in the biblical literature and the apocalyptic trends in rabbinic literature, the messianic idea signifies a sharp transition between the historical reality and the moment of redemption: "Redemption as a new state of the world wholly unrelated to anything that had gone before, not the product of a purifying development of the preceding state ... Hence for them the world unredeemed and the world in process of redemption, were separated by an abyss ... [redemption is a] colossal uprooting, destruction, [and] revolution."[62] In the threshing floor scene's formation in the *Tiqqunei Zohar* we view how the fractured image is constructed and intensified until its brink, in order that after the apocalypse a new world will be created. Ruth's coming to the threshing floor wanders between images, thereby increasing her desperate dependence on the one who will place her upright. Seemingly, her figure's passivity empowers the activeness of the author of the *Tiqqunei Zohar*, and his desperate desire to redeem her, voiced in his unique literary style.

THE DISTANT REDEEMER, THE CLOSE REDEEMER— *TIQQUNEI ZOHAR* IN CONTRAST TO *ZOHAR RUTH*

At this point, we shall return to the redemptive act and the figure of the redeemer identified with the *sefirah* of *Yesod* in the *Tiqqunei Zohar*.[63] The Ṣaddiq represents

---

61   Idel, *Kabbalah and Eros*, 104-25. For a reversed reading of the eschatological unification, see Wolfson, *Language, Eros, Being*, 333-71.
62   Scholem, *Messianic Idea*, 38.
63   Idel, *Messianic Mystics*, 104-18; Liebes, *Studies*, 1-84.

the fulfillment of the commandments and good deeds, which are meant to save Israel from exile. Particularly, the Ṣaddiq is responsible for "guarding the covenant" (*shemirat ha-berit*), as it emerges from multiple passages in the *Zohar* and the *Tiqqunim*: "And it is said, 'and she uncovered his feet'—to whom does this refer? The Ṣaddiq, and this is circumcision (*berit milah*) who is Boaz, who has the power (*bo oz*), overcoming his evil inclination ... and this is the middle column, of which it is said 'Israel is my firstborn son' (Ex. 4:22)."[64]

In the passage of *Zohar Ruth*, we saw that God is prepared to save the *Shekhinah* himself, since there is no other redeemer. The *Shekhinah*'s wait during the long exilic night following God's request and exertion, suggests that possibly the Ṣaddiq is unable to redeem her. In the passages of the *Tiqqunei Zohar*, the disappointment in the Jewish people and Ṣaddiq's functioning hints at a failure in the area of *shemirat ha-berit*. The exilic state is constant and permanent, not only because of the *Shekhinah*'s heightened fall, but because of the continuous transgressions of Israel.

Tiqqun 21 emphasizes that God wants to be the *Shekhinah*'s only redeemer, a conception that creates a deterministic attitude towards Israel's sins. Instead of wrestling with their situation, the author configures an inbuilt and compulsory failure of the human realm—portrayed through Boaz and the lower Ṣaddiq—in order that the supernal Ṣaddiq, who has the power (*bo ha-oz*), shall redeem her. The verses discussing the Ṣaddiq in this passage hint at Jacob's struggle with the angel "until daybreak." Since Jacob failed and "did not prevail against him," God arrives at daybreak to lift the Assembly of Israel, who is also the fallen prayer.[65] This prayer is in need of *Yesod*—the lifeblood of the worlds, and of *Tif'eret*—the middle column who raises her, in order that she may reach the supernal place to which she is directed. The conjunction of these images intensifies the *Shekhinah*'s dire state and her dependence on the two redeemers, neither whom can liberate her. The man, the mortal Ṣaddiq, is unable to redeem, since he is weak and his vitality is disappointing; while God is busy throughout the exilic night in a struggle with the forces of judgment (*Din*) of Samael, Amalek, and Egypt.

The future morning represents grace (*Ḥesed*), which will come only when God's right hand is free to raise the *Shekhinah*. Since the morning has not yet come, God is unable to place her upright. The threatening atmosphere is

---

64 Tiqqun 31. Also, *Zohar* Ruth 85b; *Zohar* II: 91b (*Ra'ya Mehemna*).
65 In contrast to the emphasis on the future redemption in this image, the raising of *tefilah* (prayer) by de León is conceived as a theurgical performance in the present. Idel, *Messianic Mystics*, 104-5; Roi, "Legs."

reinforced through the verses of harsh revenge woven into the passage and creates a sense of futility and human vulnerability. In contradiction to the imagery of fertility and idyllic nature in the Book of Ruth, an image of powerlessness emerges here, and instead of a seductive scene, there is exilic impotence. The author of the *Tiqqunei Zohar* chooses to focus on the *Shekhinah*'s suffering and he is in no hurry to continue the plot towards its optimistic resolution. Removing the phrase "and she uncovered his feet" from its biblical context demands that the author configure a new literary context for the *Shekhinah*. Indeed, alongside the two heroine characters who are incapable of being delivered that night, he adds to the threshing floor story another feminine figure.

SORORAL LOVE—NAOMI AND RUTH AS *BINAH* AND *MALKHUT*

Tiqqun 21 portrays Naomi, who is absent from our Zoharic readings thus far, as a figure who redeems Ruth in the end. This choice highlights the comradery between the two heroines in the Book of Ruth, thereby demonstrating the link between the feminine *sefirot* of *Malkhut* and *Binah* in the sefirotic tree. The unique relationship between the two is implied in the description of the mother who is meant to redeem her daughter and raise her from the dust, as it is written later in *Tiqqun* 21: "and the mystery of 'remain this night,' if he redeems you good—that is the covenant (*berit*), let him redeem, 'If he is not willing to—then I (*anokhi*) will redeem you,' I (*anokhi*)—is the Supernal Mother, the I (*anokhi*) of the exodus from Egypt."

The supernal name "*anokhi*" (I) symbolizes *Binah*, who took Israel out of Egypt, the one who will raise Ruth after the masculine *sefirah* of *Yesod* and the earthly *Ṣaddiq* disappoint.[66] This Supernal Mother alludes to Naomi, who sends Ruth to the threshing floor, safeguards her from afar, and even receives her at the end of the night. In opposition to the critical claim, according to which women become "agents of oppression" against each other in stressful situations, the possibility of feminine support and the participation of the divine *familia* in rescuing the fallen *Shekhinah* arises from this passage.[67] In an additional passage from *Zohar Ruth*, Naomi is described as

---

66 Compare with Gikatilla, *Sha'arei*, 2:19. For a doubled feminine model, in which Naomi and Ruth represent "two Torahs," "two tablets," and the relation between the body and soul, *Tiqqun* 31, 75b. The interpretation of exile in the continuation of this *Tiqqun* resembles the allegorical interpretation of *Zohar Ruth*.

67 In the passage's continuation the father *Hokhmah* and *Tif'eret* join as forces of balance and "central columns," in order to redeem the *Shekhinah* together.

saving the *Shekhinah* from above, through the collaboration between both feminine *sefirot*:

> It is written: *Now Naomi had a kinsman on her husband's side* (Ruth 2:1). This is where this scroll should have begun! Rabbi Nehorai said to him, "Open your mouth, for these are new-ancient words, from the day that the world was created!" ... Naomi, as it is written: *Let the favor (no'am) of the Lord our God be upon us*. And through this name, the very same name was planted in the world. Who is *no'am*, kindness? *Teshuvah*. *To gaze on (no'am), kindness of YHVH* (Psalms 27:4)—*Teshuvah* and the World That Is Coming. *And to contemplate His palace* (ibid.)—another world, below (*Zohar Ruth* 85a).

It emerges from this passage that the connection between the *sefirah* of *Malkhut* (Ruth) to the *Ṣaddiq*, the *sefirah* of *Yesod* (Boaz), occurs through the mediation of the *sefirah* of *Binah*—*Teshuvah* and the Supernal Mother (Naomi). This description is comparable to that which is written in the Introduction to the *Zohar*, where the mother affixes her daughter's adornments and garments for the sake of observing the masculine ritual of pilgrimage, in which "all your males shall appear."[68] Naomi's name alludes to the divine pleasantness abounding from above, and she is situated at the head of the seven *sefirot* and directs the system from a consciousness of "the world to come," which as R. Joseph Gikallita says, is the maternal world that "is always coming," birthing and constantly summoned by her children.[69]

Apparently, the author of the *Tiqqunim* adds an additional layer to the image of the active mother, adorning and fashioning her daughter. Alongside the dependence on the Supernal Mother for redemption and the lower redeemer's inability to do so, the passage adds the myth of the exodus from Egypt to the threshing floor scene of the Book of Ruth. What do these two scenes have to do with one another? By linking the divine maternal figure to the exodus

---

68 *Zohar* I: 2a. According to this passage, the *Shekhinah* reveals her masculine facets like *Binah*, who is called in other Zoharic passages "world of the masculine." This term stresses the alterity found within the Great Mother—the otherness of the son who born of her, as well as the otherness of the father, with whom she occasionally clothes herself, as demonstrated in *Sefer Ma'arekhet ha-'Elohut* (Ch. 4, 58-62) in the description of *Hokhmah* as a *ṭallit* (prayer shawl), spirit, cover, in which *Binah* is enclothed. For more on this term, fn. 95.

69 Gikatilla, *Sha'arei*, 2:57-61. On the concept of "new-old" ideas in the *Zohar*, Matt, "Matnita Dilan."

from Egypt, it echoes the motif of the national delivery in the Book of Exodus and the difficult birth pangs that preceded the nation's creation.[70] According to the passage of the *Tiqqunim*, the nation is born in the moments of the splitting of the sea, thanks to the intervention and help of the Supernal Mother. Similarly, Ruth is finally redeemed precisely because of Naomi's assistance, as a supreme archetypical heroine who saves the messianic dynasty. She is the one who transverses from the personal and feminine space—of nature and agricultural harmony—to the areas of, the "law of the father," rules and culture, and creates within them a new reality.[71]

AN EXISTENTIALIST READING—THE *SHEKHINAH* IS THE SOUL

After examining a variety of interpretations of the locution "and she uncovered his feet," I wish to linger on the choice of the author of *Tiqqunei Zohar* to identify Ruth and the *Shekhinah* with the soul. The soul, according to this passage, at times drops within the body and collapses at his feet, due to the discontent of the liver, bile, and spleen, as it is later written in *Tiqqun* 21: "Bile (*marah*), spleen (*teḥol*), and liver (*kaveid*) are the exile for *neshamah, ruaḥ,* and *nefesh* (the lower three parts of the soul), which is the *Shekhinah* who is exiled in the liver." Additionally, this text raises the image of the heart that is unable to elevate its pleas and prayers, at the time that the clouds blocks its path, and also the image of the city, which is like a body ruled by foreign forces: "simultaneously what was the soul, crushed beneath the feet, that which is written 'and she uncovered his feet and lay down (Ruth 3:7)' she is returned to the heart, which is Jerusalem."[72] The ensemble of these images are joined to the depiction of the *Shekhinah* as Jonah (*yonah*) the prophet, descending to the hold of the ship and from there to the belly of the whale, as well as her comparison to Jonah:

> Simultaneously, "Jonah (*yonah*), meanwhile, had gone down into the hold of the ship" (Jonah 1:5), this is the lower *Shekhinah*, which is written about her, "and she uncovered his feet and lay down" lying in the dirt, and this is "and had lain down, and was fast asleep" (Ibid), and why did she fall? Because the *ruaḥ* (soul) departed from her, which is the central pillar

---

70 Ilana Pardes, *The Biography of Ancient Israel: National Narratives in the Bible* (Berkeley: University of California Press, 2000), ch. 1.
71 Deem, *Zot ha-Pa'am*, 268-71, suggests that Naomi binds redemption of land with the act of *yibbum*.
72 *Tiqqunei Zohar* 21; Idel, "Fragments"; Pedaya, *Walking through Trauma*, 105.

that supports her, and she fell at the same time, as it is written about her, "How lonely [she] sits" (Lam. 1:1) ... While the body is in the house of the sick, which is Israel, and the *Shekhinah* is with them, for she is a turtledove (*yonah*). (*Tiqqun* 21)

The chain of images embodies the variegated expressions of the downfallen *Shekhinah*'s pain. The supporting pillar, no longer able to stand, elucidates the collapse of the sefirotic system, beginning in the physical dimension and culminating in the allegoric spiritual dimensions of the soul. The passage's end reveals a powerful existential scene. The scenes of the *Shekhinah* as a bird that cannot fly, a turtledove whose voice is unheard, and the soul falling to the body's feet, intensify the existentialist tragedy in the Book of Ruth.

According to this passage, Ruth collapses at the feet of Boaz, not only as a character in need of union and feminine redemption, but also as a soul seeking to return to her place and (re)construct her complete individual stature. Thus the questions of gender, which we raised earlier pertaining to the independence of the feminine figure, are converted, from the differentiation between passivity and activity, to a question of the individual soul's resurgence. By describing the *Shekhinah*'s dependence on an external redemption, *Tiqqun* 21 reveals the hope for redemption hidden within fractured images. The longing for repair is developed from within an existence of deficiency and the *Shekhinah*'s multiple agonies. As is written in Lamentations, expounded upon in the Introduction to the *Zohar* about the *sefirot* of *Binah* and *Malkhut*: "What can I say for you, to what compare you, O daughter Jerusalem? To what can I liken you, that I may comfort you, O virgin daughter Zion? For vast as the sea is your ruin; who can heal you?"[73]

THE *ZOHAR* IN CONTRAST TO THE *TIQQUNIM* AND *ZOHAR RUTH*— THE PERSONALISTIC MODEL AND THE ALLEGORICAL MODEL

As noted, in opposition to the active language in the descriptions of Tamar and Ruth in the *Zohar*, prominent in the passages from *Zohar Ruth* and *Tiqqunei Zohar* is the dependent, passive, and tragic feminine position, stimulating the apocalyptic feeling of crisis in the human and divine realms. The threshing night is transformed from an agricultural, bountiful, and dionysiac scene into a metaphor of exile and suffering.

---

73   Lam. 2:13. Also see the passage on the daughter and mother, *Zohar* I: 2a.

In accordance with the well-known gender division, these scenes specifically describe the feminine figure as suffering, fallen, and speechless. This identification is meant to arouse the kabbalists to rescue the *Shekhinah*, while highlighting the theurgic power of the kabbalists. However, an opposite outcome may occur: the emphasis on the *Shekhinah*'s deficiency forms a destitute worldview in which the person—man or woman, is destined to a hopeless and passive state.[74] Until God Himself redeems the *Shekhinah*, the mortal Ṣaddiq or people do not have the possibility of meriting redemption. In the words of *Zohar Ruth*, which encourage passivity and restraint, all that remains for him is to wait, as it is written, "remain this night."

Minimizing the role of the personalistic feminine figure in the *Tiqqunei Zohar* and *Zohar Ruth* speaks volumes and raises a question about the relation between the biblical corpus, rabbinic exegesis, and Zoharic passages. In the *Zohar*, we can identify a sequential development and reliance on rabbinic readings that vindicate Ruth, together with the rest of the dynastic heroines who cause the redeemer's birth. In contrast, Ruth's portrayal in the *Tiqqunim* and *Zohar Ruth* is bereft of erotic aspects, and refrains from describing feminine and maternal myths. This reading diverges from the biblical narrative and the rabbinic midrashic continuum that discusses the threshing night. The known narrative is placed onto the mystical and allegorical map, which explores the drama that occurs within the divine instead of individual mortal characters. Not only is there no coupling or resurgence in these passages, they do not even echo Boaz's restraint and his struggle with his inclination. The oath in the *Tiqqunei Zohar* refers to God who fights against the forces of evil, while directing the sexual theme towards the nationalistic field and ethnic struggle.

The cosmic enlargement of the scene and the dynamism of the sefirotic realm allow the understanding of the Davidic dynastic story as a mythic multidimensional plot, as emerges from another passage in *Zohar Ruth*: "Ruth, Naomi, and Boaz—three of them in the image of sashed, exalted, enduring rungs. And the progeny of David, from the image of a tree, was planted in the world."[75] The human tale, according to this reading, reflects supernal actions and the states of the *sefirot*. The three heroes of the Book of Ruth, Naomi, Boaz, and Ruth, are not recounting about themselves, rather about the sefirotic system and the theory of emanation. As Melila Hellner-Eshed writes, this is an example of a "hyper-extensive" interpretation discussing the concatenation of the

---

74 Abrams, *The Female Body of God*; Mopsik, *Sex of the Soul*, 5-52.
75 *Zohar Ḥadash Ruth*, 85a. For a variant text, see Hecker, *Pritzker*, 11:195.

divine worlds "from their subtle source (unable to be materialized in differentiated reality and symbolized by the name Elimelech) to the *sefirah* of *Malkhut* and the reality of the everyday world (symbolized by the birth of David.)"[76]

Here as well, as noted in the aforementioned allegorical passages, Naomi symbolizes *Binah*—connected with pleasantness and the origin of Supernal Motherhood, Ruth symbolizes *Malkhut*—the Oral Torah, voice of the turtledove, the wife and daughter, while Boaz represents *Yesod*—the Ṣaddiq accumulating the abundance and transmitting it to *Malkhut* for the sake of raising her. The relations between the three and the additional interconnected *sefirot*, are designed to tell how the Davidic dynasty was structured in the likeness of the supernal divine tree. In this manner, Gershom Scholem's claim is supported: in many Zoharic texts, the theory of redemption is actually the theory of creation. In other words, the human and messianic genealogy is set aside in favor of a description of the order of concatenation and creation of the world.

Our study has revealed that the phrase "and she uncovered his feet" in Zoharic passages indicates, on the one hand, a feminine action of seduction that leads to a reparation, while on the other hand it describes the harsh fall of *Malkhut*, which is not liberated until the future redemption. Is this evidence for editorial stages of the Zoharic passages and the evolution of its relation towards the *Shekhinah*? It appears that the more we focus on the later strata of the Zoharic literature, from the *Zohar* to the *Tiqqunim* passages, Ruth is transformed from a particular character into an allegorical construction of the *Shekhinah* and a symbol carrying meanings of fracturedness and dependence. Additionally, the general structure of the Book of Ruth is changed and is transformed from a description of a national and personal story into a description of the unfolding of the divine and supernal drama.[77] Concurrently, here is a transition from an "optimistic" perception linked to the personal figure of Ruth, as a woman who is successful in her mission, to a "pessimistic" perception embedded in the recesses of the story in the book. The biblical Ruth, the epic figure, is imagined as a woman whose central purpose is to be received in Boaz's household and to beget Obed. This appears

---

76 Hellner-Eshed, *A River Flows*, 192.
77 Generally, in the later Zoharic strata, the personal wishes of Boaz and Ruth are replaced by more symbolic questions.

very clearly in the establishment of the dynasty, and in the emergence of David and Solomon's offspring. The heroes of the messianic family receive a noticeable presence in the *Zohar* and are positioned as archetypical models.

A description of Ruth's figure in the later strata of the *Zohar* does not deal with the particular redemptive act, rather the dire state of the Assembly of Israel and the *Shekhinah* in the unceasing exile, who only God himself can save. In light of this understanding, the Book of Ruth describes a journey of a feminine figure seeking shelter and pursuing redemption and a home, a process that continues existentially and universally.[78] These passages highlight the aspect of *Malkhut*'s "having nothing of her own," and because of it she cries out and marks the fracture and the expectation for the redemption from above.

Here are two different readings of the Book of Ruth, sketching different consciousnesses of the time of redemption: the first observes a personal and actual tale which occurred in the past and is projected as a living myth on the present, whereas the second sees a future desire and aspiration which is unfulfilled. Obviously, from these two readings, it is possible to derive two conceptions of messianism and redemption: the first is catastrophic and based on crisis and hope for salvation from above, while the second is more optimistic and harmonious, dependent on man's deeds. Regarding our opening question, concerning the riddle of the threshing night, the sources answer contradictorily. According to the *Zohar*, copulation occurs that night, and the actual redemption process has begun and it materializes in Ruth's story as an individual figure. In contrast, according to the reading of the *Tiqqunim* and *Zohar Ruth*, the coupling designated for *Tif'eret* and *Malkhut* has not yet occurred, and everything described in the Book of Ruth deals with the future eschatological tale, unto which the Assembly of Israel awaits. Hence the *Shekhinah*, crushed in the dust and crying out for salvation, does not merit an earthly redemption or human salvation, be it from the *Ṣaddiq*, Boaz, or the people of Israel. On the contrary, she is still lying and waiting, still crushed beneath his feet, overflowing with pain, and waiting for the arrival of morning.

Both perspectives of messianism in the *Zohar* are thereby in a complex relationship with each other. The personalistic-active view and the symbolic-passive view are intended to arouse the kabbalist to identify with the

---

78 In gender and psychoanalytic context, see Cixous and Clément, *The Newly Born Woman*; Anzaldúa, *Borderlands La Frontera*.

Shekhinah and the messianic mother. One way is identification, stemming from the pessimistic description in which the fracturing reaches its limits—and thereby a fantasy of a future repaired world is formed—according to the biblical and prophetic model which Scholem identifies, in which the exile and redemption do not sprout organically one form the other.[79] The other way is of reparation, developing within reality and creating a narrativic continuum between exile and redemption. This position accords with the optimistic perspective in which Ruth's actions are described corporeally and bring about her reparation.

Besides illuminating different facets of the messianic myth in the Zoharic literature, both of the models have gender ramifications. In the layers of the *Zohar* discussing Ruth's actual figure, there emerges, as mentioned, an optimistic conception of the redemption contingent upon the success of the feminine seduction. In contrast, in the later sources, the destruction and exile are represented by the feminine figures' unembodied and voiceless portrayal, in need of a spiritual and physical redemption, and lacking an opportunity to actualize their eroticism.[80] This reading leaves the redemption—identified with the act of coupling—as an unrealized yearning, which is intensified by virtue of the feminine figure's vulnerability and weakness. The savior's role in these passages is attributed to a man, whether Boaz, the *Ṣaddiq*, or God who has the power (*bo ha-oz*) and not Ruth the Moabite or the rest of the messianic mothers, on which the earlier Zoharic texts rely.

Tamar and Ruth, Lot's daughters and Bathsheba, and Rachel and Leah, are described from the biblical story and through their development in the rabbinic midrash and different Zoharic strata, as heroines forced to fight for their own redemption. As personal characters, they are configured as women who are forced to do something, to strive, to seduce. In this sense, here is the well-known identification between woman, temptation (*yeṣer*), and corporeality, consistently appearing already in ancient literature. Contrary to this identification, the abstention of the *Shekhinah* in *Zohar Ruth* or her fall in the *Tiqqunei Zohar*, raises the possibility that the symbolic or allegorical tradition liberates the woman from the burden of "seducing the other," and allows her internal voice to be heard. The Zoharic anxiety of speechlessness, in the

---

79 Scholem, *Explications*, 196-201. On apocalyptic time-consciousness, see Pedaya, "The Sixth Millenium."

80 On desire as belonging to men and the cost of the split between femininity and sexuality, see Benjamin, *The Bonds of Love*, 114-29; also in the context of rabbinic literature, see Rosen-Zvi, *Demonic*.

identification of Ruth with Jonah and a turtledove as well as the description of the fallen soul, presents an alternative model of feminine freedom. A freedom not situated in respect to an other or for the purpose of realizing an external, familial, national, or divine goal. These passages create a language structured on the tension between the passivity of the figures and the activeness of the interpreters, thus creating a new construction of feminine divinity which rises from the downtrodden and dependent state, beginning with "and she uncovered his feet."

CONCLUSION

Gender Reversal and the Poetics of Redemption

In the transitions of the type-scene of the Davidic Messiah's birth through the biblical, rabbinical, and Zoharic literature, there are consistent themes that are sequentially developed, but also prominent are the changes that occur in the different corpuses. The biblical literature forms the epic narrative and myth, whereas the rabbinic Midrashim emphasize the ethical and normative vindication of the Judean dynastic mothers. The Zoharic literature, in contrast, explores the implications of the feminine drama in the supernal realm. Sometimes the Zoharic passages begin with a description of the human figure and her emotional and psychological world, but quickly we find ourselves documenting the *Shekhinah*'s journey of exile and redemption. In several texts, the difference between the mundane and divine world is minimal and the images almost converge, while other texts are structured on the tension between the human and divine acts of redemption.

The Davidic mothers and their antinomian interpretations in the *Zohar* filled a central role in the development of the messianic idea for future generations, specifically in the 16th century Kabbalah, Sabbateanism, and Hasidism. This development widens the dialectical tensions between transgression and redemption, challenging the kabbalistic understanding of the demonic forces in divine and earthly realms, as well as emphasizing the feminine role in the myth of redemption. Generally, the mortal figures in the world of the *Zohar*—like the divine *sefirot*—bear a double identity, both feminine and masculine. Unlike in the biblical narrative and rabbinic literature, where it is clear that it is feminine figures fulfilling "feminine functions," like seduction, pregnancy, and birth, in the Zoharic literature the Davidic heroines represent an androgynous function, feminine and masculine together. On the one hand, as we have seen throughout this book, the *Zohar* identifies them with the *Shekhinah* and feminine characteristics. On the other hand, in the body of the *Zohar*, the messianic mothers express a masculine aspect in their identification with the active *sefirah* of *Yesod*. Thus, the Messiah is transformed into a feminine figure in the *Zohar*, arising from the widespread identification of King David with the *Shekhinah* and the *sefirah* of *Malkhut*.[1]

This model hints at the array of passages we have examined, also emerging from the messianic passage exploring the mystery of *gilgul* (transmigration) and *yibbum* in *Saba de-Mishpatim*. In this text, Judah represents all of the dynastic men, while Tamar represents all the women. However, surprisingly the masculine figures, known there as "you (masculine)," symbolizes *Malkhut*, while the dynastic mothers represent active "masculine" figures rectifying the mystery of *yibbum*.[2] It is possible to say that David inherits the messianic quality of *Malkhut* thanks to his foremothers, who fulfill the role of the *Ṣaddiq* in their going to the cave, threshing floor, and sitting at the "entrance of Enaim," as well as their strength of abstention and anticipation for the redemption. Thus, the hierarchal order is reversed, and the women are placed "above" *Malkhut*, which represents the Messiah, while strengthening the link between the Lower Mother who rises to *Yesod*, to the Supernal Mother, *Binah*.

Following Elliot Wolfson, it is possible to claim that the feminine seduction and sexual activeness are identified in the *Zohar* as masculine activities, for any act of overflowing is male, and only consequently are the messianic mothers' subversive initiatives justified and perceived in a positive light. This view corresponds to Thomas Laqueur's claim that in the scientific discourse of the Middle Ages there are not "two sexes, rather only "one sex" is conceived, in which the female reflects an imperfect male physiology, and she is reversed from "external to internal."[3]

However, any binary model can be reversed, and what was an imperfection may become supernal and preferred, similar to the mystical idea of "raising of the diadem" at the time of redemption.[4] It appears therefore, that the theory

---

1 See fn. 38. For the development of the "masculine woman" in the *Zohar*, see Mopsik, *Sex of the Soul*, 5-52.
2 *Zohar* II: 103b-104b. As well as ibid, I: 188b; 155a. Also a parallel in Gikatilla, *Sha'arei*, 1:148-9. Liebes, "*Zohar* and Eros"; Yisraeli, *The Interpretation of Secrets*, 113-29.
3 For a discussion of Wolfson's view, see Part 3 fn. 3; Thomas Laqueur, *Making Sex: Body and Gender from the Greeks to Freud* (Cambridge: Harvard University Press, 1990); Caroline W. Bynum, *Fragmentation and Redemption: Essays on Gender and the Human Body in Medieval Religion* (New York: Zone Books, 1992), 108-17, 151-79.
4 On the ascension of the *Shekhinah*, see Scholem, *Godhead*, 283; Idel, *Kabbalah and Eros*, 38-42, 210-2; Idel, *Kabbalah*, 205-11; Arthur Green, *Keter: The Crown of God in Early Jewish Mysticism*, (Princeton: Princeton University Press, 1997); Hellner-Eshed, "On Love,"

of one sex does not necessarily express the assimilation of the feminine in the masculine or the integration of the mother in the father; rather, it can represent a reversed model—in which the masculine is assimilated into the feminine, expressed by Gershom Scholem's as the "dialectics of femininity."[5] Thereby, the independence of the feminine divinity and her sefirotic placement above the "son" reflects, as it did in the messianic mothers' stories, her elevation, not only in the future redemption, but also in the present.

In addition to these models, it may be suggested that the *Zohar*'s perception is not of "one sex" or even "two sexes," but rather "multiple identities" and a conception of unique sexuality and gender fluidity. The "divine biology" is not bound by human rules, thus allowing for downward and upward movements, traversing from left (*Din*) to right (*Ḥesed*), enabling gender and sex reversals, expressed through different roles like father, mother, son, daughter, groom, bride, etc.[6] The *sefirot* and the figures identified with them, carry these personas—simultaneously and perpetually—while freely moving between them. For example, the *Zohar* depicts feminine and masculine figures that identify with divine *sefirot* as representing the opposite sex, like Rebecca who, in order to balance the aspect of *Din*, becomes the aspect of *Ḥesed* in her marriage to Isaac (despite the tendency to see in *Ḥesed* a masculine aspect). In the same manner, the letter *yod* in Sarai's (*sh.r.y.*) name alludes to her masculine being and is therefore uprooted. Through her agreement to descend from the "masculine world" to *Malkhut* in order to give birth, she becomes Sarah (*sh.r.h.*)

170-6; Shifra Asulin, "The Mystical Commentary of the Song of Songs in the *Zohar* and its Background" (PhD diss., Hebrew University, 2006), 206-15; Roi, "Shekhina," 61-78. Elliot Wolfson sees in the teachings of Ḥabad a reverse model in which the *Shekhinah* ascends atop the male and is not reabsorbed, in contrast to the assimilatory model which he claims characterizes the *Zohar* and most kabbalistic works. Elliot Wolfson, *Open Secret* (New York: Columbia University Press, 2009), 200-23.

5 Liebes (*Messiah*, 27) connects *Malkhut* to the revealed aspect of reality and *Yesod* to the concealed aspect. Seemingly the Davidic stories demonstrate the masculine and covert potencies of the *Shekhinah*. Regarding the "dialectics of femininity," see also Scholem, *Godhead*, 187.

6 For a discussion of the divine *familia* in the *Zohar*, see Idel, *Ben*, 380-5, 403-25. In addition, I suggest that the figures of *Hokhmah* and *Binah* (who are portrayed in the *Zohar* as "two lovers who are inseparable from one another") function as the absent parents of Adam and Eve. The divine father and mother "contain" and "strengthen" the entire sefirotic system. As an internalized figures, they are linked to the fantasy of the "primal scene", and are reconstructed in the childish imagination as a "unified figure." On this concept, see Klein, *Writings*, 246, an idea which Meltzer (*Aesthetic*, Ch. 4; 9) developed. Also, Aron, "The Internalized Primal Scene"; Halperin, "Sexual Image."

and relinquishes the letter *yod*.⁷ In this passage, Abraham in turn ascends to the *sefirah* of *Binah* which is feminine, while King David is identified with *Shekhinah* in numerous Zoharic passages, who at times is portrayed also by Rashbi, the main hero of the *Zohar*.⁸ Ruth and Tamar's primal masculinity is also hinted at in the Zoharic literature and transformed later to miraculous pregnancies.⁹

These substitutions are prominent in the *Zohar*'s description of the human figures as well as the dynamism of the *sefirot*. In addition to the *Shekhinah*'s identification with the figures of David and Rashbi, the *Shekhinah* is referred to with explicit masculine terminology, like "you (*ata*- masculine)," "lad (*na'ar*)," "deer (*ayil*)," "in you (*be-kha*-masculine)," and "covenant (*berit*) of the rainbow," which generally symbolize, in Castilian contemporaneous works, masculine *sefirot* like *Tif'eret* and *Yesod*.¹⁰ Also, *Binah* is specifically termed in the *Zohar* as "world-of-the-masculine," precisely when she is fulfilling the feminine and motherly function of giving birth.¹¹ These examples demonstrate

---

7 For the passage on Rebecca, see *Zohar* II: 257b; the transition of Abraham and Sarah, *Zohar* I: 96a. The source of the Zoharic conception of Sarah's masculinity is likely in Philo's exegesis, Niehoff (*Sarah*, 439-44) suggests that the masculine figure of Athena serves as inspiration for Philo's allegoric readings.

8 Liebes, *Studies*, 1-84; Liebes, *King*.

9 This follows the rabbinic conception that Ruth did not have a womb, and the similarity between the two figures, which we discussed in Ch. 7. These gender reversals are developed by R. Joseph Karo in connection to his personal biography (*Maggid Meisharim, Parashat va-Yeshev*).

10 For the connection between Rashbi and the *Shekhinah*, see Liebes, *Studies*, 1-84. The epithet "*atah*" (you) symbolizes in *Sefer ha-Shem* (17b, 19b) and in Gikatilla (*Sha'arei*, 1:267-9), *Tif'eret*; also the term "*berit ha-qeshet*" (covenant of the rainbow) which in the *Zohar* symbolizes *Malkhut* (for example *Zohar* I:71b), whereas in *Sefer ha-Shem* (23-24b) and in *Sha'arei Orah* (1:114-7) it symbolizes *Yesod*; the terms "*bekha*" (in you (male)) and "*na'ar*" (lad) commonly refer to *Malkhut* in the *Zohar* and are absent from most contemporaneous works. On similarities between the *sefirot*'s epithets in the *Zohar* and the Hebrew works of de León, Elihayu Peretz, *Ma'alot ha-Zohar—Mafte'aḥ Shemot ha-Sefirot* (Jerusalem: Academon, 1987), 1-10, his examination demonstrates that some terms denote *Malkhut* in the *Zohar*, while in *Tiqqunei Zohar* refer to *Yesod*.

11 As Scholem noted, this is a rare Zoharic term. Scholem, *Qabbalot*, 65-7. This term appears a total of six times in the *Zohar* and barely in de León Hebrew writings. (For example, in *The Book of the Pomegranate* [ed. Wolfson] 191-4). Wolfson obviously views this as evidence for the assimilation of the maternal into the paternal, however in my opinion the term "world of the masculine" is different than the term "male" and attests to the mutual exchange of identities (*Zohar* I: 246-7) and the *sefirot*'s transitions, like the human figures—Abraham and Sarah, David and Solomon (*Zohar* II: 127)—through the "second sex." It is interesting to compare the body of the *Zohar*'s attitude and the locution "world of the masculine," to the choice of the *Ra'ya Mehemna* to denote *Binah* as female and not male, *Zohar* III: 264b. For the link between the term "world of the masculine" and the perception of the "womb" of *Binah* as a "closed *mem*" (the letter "*mem*" at the end of a word) Liebes, *On Sabbateanism*, 63-4, 320; Liebes, *Studies in the Zohar*, 148, fn.44. Idel, *Kabbalah and Eros*, 205, fn. 10.

the intentional choice of the Zoharic authors to use multi-directional gender reversals that unite the realms and create a "transformational poetics" meant to hasten redemption. Therefore, it is hardly surprising that the messianic mothers' journey expresses the multifacetedness of the *Shekhinah*, and her leaping over familiar and static identity templates, as an expression of their labors in giving birth to the Messiah. Their actions accelerate the private redemption, and consequently create a theurgic reparation in divinity and complete the deficient figure of the *Shekhinah*.

The view that the messianic mother represents an active and actuated figure, masculine and feminine, stresses Victor Turner's claim that states of "*communitas*" are characterized by a reversal of identities and hierarchies.[12] Yet, it should be mentioned that Caroline Bynum, in her critique of Turner's concept of "liminality," states that only in men's imaginations are women conceived as the liminal "other." By contrast, actual women and female Christian mystics in the Middle Ages did not consider themselves as undergoing gender reversals or identifying with "the second sex." As she has shown, many men in the late Middle Ages viewed Jesus as a feminine and motherly figure, and even described themselves with feminine imagery (even while in roles of authority—which surprisingly were identified with motherly functions). The religious experience of women, according to Bynum, reflects "traditional" feminine roles and classic identities that continue in their present condition: in their being the wife, sister, or mother of Jesus. Moreover, during mystical experiences and Eucharistic rituals, women continue to express non-liminal states, compared to the crisicality that characterizes men's model of reversal.[13] Haviva Pedaya, following Bracha Ettinger, adds a clarification to this critique that the maternal matrix presents a matrilineal structure contesting the patrilineal model of Turner. In this structure, the feminine does not necessarily function as a chaotic and semiotic force undermining the surface. Rather, it often represents the symbolic order of *communitas*, which covertly acts in the relations of fathers and sons and exposes the longing for "maternal love."[14]

---

12 For an examination of his claim that women represent perpetual liminal states and that "matrilaterality represents, in the kinship dimension, the concept of *communitas*," see Bynum, *Fragmentation and Redemption*, 33; Pedaya, *Expanses*, 130.

13 Bynum, *Fragmentation and Redemption*, 27-51. According to Chodorow, sons must go through an identity transformation due to the psychological disconnect from the mother as "other," while daughters mostly have to take a part in the continuous model in which there isn't any dramatic identity reversal. Chodorow, "Gender, Relation, and Difference."

14 Pedaya, *Expanses*, 126-37.

Following Bynum and Pedaya, it can be said that the Zoharic corpus is indeed based on perceptions of female liminality, reflecting the experiences of its male authors. Those writers chronicle their "ritual process" and then project them on the "other," whether it be feminine figures or divine *sefirot*.[15] Additionally, we may note that while Turner believes liminality is temporary and serves the acclimatization to a new state, the suggested model of fluid identities attempts to not only mediate a human (masculine) experience and an imagined (and competing) feminine structure, but also initiate a continuous religious and "androgynistic" mystical experience.[16] The conception of eros and redemption in the book of the *Zohar* thus combines transgression, liminality, and the changing of gender roles.

Whereas in the supernal realm these changes are entirely "fluid," there are questions concerning their implications for the actual lives of women. As Ada Rapoport-Albert emphasizes, in Judaism the sexual abstinence of women was perceived as a perversion and a threat to the religious order, in contrast to Christianity (and Islam) in which women held sacred and spiritual positions by living a life of abstinence, allowing them to deviate from their gender roles. Although in the Sabbatean movement we can find examples of women holding mystical positions, those were rare in the normative Jewish system—even including the kabbalistic realm.[17] Thus, I would claim that the only way for "real women" to diverge from the male order—without completely violating the rules—was through sexually licentious behavior, as we have seen in the stories of the messianic mothers. However, promiscuity and licentiousness only deepen the identification of the woman with her corporeality and sexuality, in contrast to the image of virginity which intensifies female freedom and thereby greatly threatens the Jewish patriarchal order.

The Oxymoronic Poetics of Redemption in Zoharic Literature

The *Tiqla* of Lot's daughters, Tamar's story at *petaḥ einayim*, and the uncovering of feet in Ruth's story, apart from their ideological and mystical content, suggest

---

15 In this context, Pedaya suggests that in contrast to the cosmic cyclicity linked to the Great Mother in Naḥmanidean kabbalah, in the *Zohar* a masculine binary model is presented, which focuses on the "Small" Mother, the *Shekhinah*. Pedaya, *Mother*; Pedaya, *Expanses*, 139-41.
16 For a discussion of androgyny (that does not strive for integration, but rather separateness, which brings about fertility and birth) as a formative principle of divinity and of the perception of *eros* in kabbalah, Idel, *Kabbalah and Eros*, 104-25; Idel, "Androgynes"; Liebes, "*Zohar* and Eros."
17 Rapoport-Albert, *Women*, 143-8.

a unique language that reflects the singularity of the messianic mothers. Here is a "poetics of redemption," which the interpreters create while reconstructing the messianic myth in their own image. Oxymoronic idioms prominently characterize these stories: for example, Tamar's appellation in the *Zohar* as "the impudence of a righteous woman" or the justification of the actions of Lot's daughters, Tamar, and Ruth in the Talmud, through the term "transgression committed for the sake of God." So too, the eschatological depictions bringing divine and human worlds together for the sake of the redeemer's birth through "the seed that comes from another place," and the portrayal of God who "creates the light of the Messiah." These phrases are typified by their double meanings and inspired by the Messiah's depiction in the Bible. Like the description of Tamar's concealment and disclosure at the "entrance of Enaim," the idiom "that we may preserve seed of our father" in the story of Lot's daughters, attests to the violation of incestual taboos, but also the saving of the world, and the locution "and she uncovered his feet" on the threshing night, is embedded with contradictory meanings of exile and redemption. The pinnacle of this complexity is reflected in the unique word "*Tiqla*," which appears only twice in the *Zohar* in connection to the Davidic mothers. These linguistic terms dialectically and purposefully arouse the reader, reflecting the exegetical interplay which engenders the Davidic stories by uniting the mythic and gender, feminine and messianic, aesthetic and poetic, ethic and ritualistic, halakhic and antinomianistic.

The connections between transgression and redemption in the Davidic dynasty merit paradoxical resolutions in the Zoharic literature. At its foundation is the premise that the threatening facets of reality complement the forces of good. According to this approach, the redeemer is the one capable of uniting contradictory aspects within himself, for the personal integration allows a general reparation and the sweetening of evil within good to occur. Redemption, in this conception, expresses an "incorporation" of potencies, whereas the demonic realm constitutes a catalyst, like the yeast leavening the dough. According to one approach, "only good" exists, and evil is an illusion, or not yet purified and distilled. If there is no evil in the entire world, then the Davidic stories are neither transgressive nor subversive. In contrast, an opposite position emphasizes the antinomianism of the dynastic heroines' stories. Similarly, the redeemer is conceived in the Sabbatean world as one who is meant to transmutate the evil forces into forces of good, through his plunging to the depths of the demonic realm. This approach stresses the feminine transgression and its important repetition, as part of the historical redemptive process. Furthermore, feminine practices were derived from the actions of Ruth, Tamar, and Lot's daughters, not only by Frankists and Sabbateans, but also in the redemption doctrine of R. Moses Ḥayyim Luzzatto, as we saw in chapter four. In Hasidic doctrines, models of "descent for the purpose of ascent" or "transgression for the sake of repentance" seek to make room for sin as part of the messianic reparation in the soul of the individual and subsequently the nation.

The *Zohar* proposes an additional solution to this question by describing the complex "*Ṭiqla*" model, which expresses an instrument of intentional providence, but also is evidence of instability and the playfulness of human nature in its connection to the divine realm. The "*Ṭiqla*" reflects the mystery the transmigration of souls and cosmic wheels, in which only God understands their paths, although his plan is dialogically woven with the deeds of man. Zoharic passages on the House of David emphasize the dynastic heroines' unique personalities and the idea that this is not a general perception of "sin," instead a specific case, permitted at its time, for these figures only. The *Zohar*'s innovation is the claim that divine reparation is dependent on their actions.

The perception of David in the Palestinian and Babylonian Talmuds, as the immortal or the future resurrected Messiah, is joined to the idea that David symbolizes the convergence of his foremothers, in a multifaceted figure.[18] The vindication of David, identified with *Malkhut*, is derived from the model of "transgression for the sake of God," and in the *Zohar* it is a vital key for bringing about redemption. Therefore, in the *Zohar*, David represents paucity and absence as well as fullness and androgyny. In his figure, the unbridled sexuality of the dynastic mothers is reflected, as well as the concentration, exertion, and intention for heaven's sake that characterizes their personalities. As a result of the potency of his archetypical foremothers, David is able to draw down the abundance onto the lower world and influence the upper world. Just as Obed had two mothers in the Book of Ruth, similarly David—beginning in *Yalkut ha-Makhiri*—has at least two mothers partnering in his birth. The messianic mothers' recurrence in each other's actions demonstrates that these figures contend with annihilation, death, and exile by giving birth and increasing life. In contrast, the men in these stories are incapable of struggling with this harsh reality, let alone repairing it. Beginning in the Bible, the messianic fathers are portrayed as sleeping or "unaware" when the women initiate and labor, in order that the sons will become elected. Afterwards, the gendered division is mended, and according to the Zoharic narrative, the men take part in the

---

18 See Introduction fn. 2-3. On the figure of David in the *Zohar*, I am dedicating a separate study (in preparation).

reparation that the women are arranging. We saw that the seduction does not stand alone in the Judean model, rather it is a part of a genealogical sequence of breaching and innovation. On these two foundations, continuity and novelty, the world subsists, and through them the House of David is built. In this sense, the Davidic heroines play the role of the Creator, redeeming the world through the essence of seduction and birth.

The returning feminine myth attests to a wound that seeks healing and assuaging. I suggest, in summary, that the messianic mothers' stories form a reparation not only for the injustices of reality and divinity in general, but also for the figure of the *Shekhinah* crushed in the dust. The Davidic mothers show that the *Shekhinah* has many facets, active and passive. The dominance of the dynastic heroines, prominent in the Bible, continuing through the rabbinic literature and culminating in the Zoharic corpus, demonstrates the potency of the feminine figure to redeem reality and heal it.

EPILOGUE

The Messianic Mother in Judaism and Christianity

The messianic mother in Jewish myth represents a feminine *topos* and genealogical tree, whose roots are planted in the Bible and developed in rabbinic sources and Zoharic literature. In spite of these figures, Mary is characterized in stark contrast to her predecessors: she is one, they are many. She is a virgin, they are harlots. She is impregnated effortlessly and without choice, whereas they fight for the sake of giving birth to their sons and realizing their motherhood. The following epilogue is devoted to the question of what nevertheless connects Mary, the virgin messianic mother, to these figures.

In this section I compare and contrast the Jewish developments regarding the "mother of the Messiah" with the Gospel narratives and the Church Fathers' developing Mariology. While tracing the continual development of the figure of the messianic mother from antiquity to the Middle Ages, I discuss, from both gender and psychoanalytic perspectives, the similarities and differences between Mary and the Davidic mothers. This analysis revolves around issues concerning sexuality and virginity in Jewish and Christian sources, and the way both cultures imposed their interpretations on earlier biblical materials.[1] My aim is to challenge the current scholarly assumption that traditions about the mother of the Messiah were not important or prominent in Judaism until after the development of the Christological image of Mary: for example, Raphael Patai's claim that "In contrast to Christianity, in Judaism the Mother of the Messiah remained a shadowy and enigmatic human figure to whom

---

1   Due to the enormous scope of the theoretical material pertaining to Mary, I focus here only on a comparison to the Davidic dynasty figures, concerning perceptions of motherhood and sexuality in the two religions. For a general introduction and bibliographical references on Mary see the works of Warner, Pelikan, Rubin, Flusser, Lang, and others. For an overview on concepts of gender, body, and sexuality in Christianity and Judaism from historical and psychoanalytical perspectives, see Kristeva, *In the Beginning*; Boyarin, *Dying for God*.

little attention was paid" or David Biale's statement, "In any event, the mother of the Messiah plays a very important role in the *Sefer Zerubavel*, one that is unprecedented for a woman in the Jewish eschatological traditions, at least until Sabbatai Ṣevi."[2] I counter their assertions that the very existence of such a figure is a defining distinction between Christianity and early Judaism by showing how Christianity responded to a notion of the messianic mother that has existed in Judaism since antiquity, and thus I argue to reverse the direction of influence.

Judaism and Christianity have both given a central place to the messianic idea in which the mother of the Messiah has played a crucial role.[3] My thesis of the uninterrupted development of this figure also accounts for the rise of the *Shekhinah* in kabbalistic thought in the Middle Ages, countering claims that the *Shekhinah*'s image is rooted in the Virgin Cult. In fact, a parallel process of gradual growth of the "messianic mother" can be shown to have occurred simultaneously in both religions.[4] I introduce examples of mutual influences regarding Christian and Jewish texts from antiquity through the Middle Ages, and discuss their implications from the perspectives of gender and psychoanalytic thought.

THE MOTHER OF THE MESSIAH IN THE BIBLE AND IN EARLY CHRISTIANITY

It has already been suggested that the story of the birth of the Messiah serves as a bridge between the Hebrew Bible and the New Testament.[5] Both Matthew and Luke use Old Testament characters and type-scenes to ground Jesus in the biblical history of Israel. However, in contrast to Luke, who uses the template of the "barren heroines" such as Hannah's story and the birth of Samuel as a background for the infancy narratives of Jesus, Matthew highlights the Davidic lineage as Jesus' main characterization. The descriptions of the Davidic genealogy as an introduction to the Virgin Birth of Jesus in Matthew bear witness to

---

2 As was shown by Himmelfarb, Dan, Knohl, Schäfer and others, the messianic mother in *Sefer Zerubavel* was dialectically influenced by Christianity. See also *Midrashei Geulah*, 55-142; Raphael Patai, *The Messiah Texts* (Detroit: Wayne State University Press, 1979), 122; Biale, "Counter-History and Jewish Polemics Against Christianity," 139.

3 Nevertheless, scholars usually discuss messianic ideas in early Judaism and Christianity while ignoring the Davidic mother of the Messiah. Scholem, *Messianic Idea*; David Flusser, *Jesus* (Jerusalem: Magnes Press, 2001).

4 For further discussion and critique see below paragraph F.

5 Levine, "Ruth," 252–5; Brown, *The Birth of the Messiah*; Campbell, *Ruth*, 173; Doniger, *Bedtrick*, 253–69.

the influence the "messianic mothers" of the house of David have had on the image of Mary.

While focusing on the narrative in Matthew 1, and by applying psychoanalytic concepts, I suggest that Mary represents the "return of the repressed" in the Bible, as she embodies the sexual sins of her foremothers in an attempt to transform them back to a model of virginity. According to Sigmund Freud, the myth of "the Egyptian Moses" symbolizes the return of the repressed and serves as a memory of the "male sin" of the murder of the primordial father. Similarly, Mary can be said to represent the maternal and the "female sin" of Davidic genealogy.[6] In fact, Mary embodies acts of incest, seduction, and adultery committed by the female progenitors of the House of David, who are mentioned at the end of the Book of Ruth (4:11-18). The descriptions of the birth of Jesus in the Gospels shows striking similarities between the genealogies found in Matthew 1 and Ruth 4. It appears that the hand of an editor is directing us to read the two texts side by side. The opening of the Gospel of Matthew continues a known biblical model. Here we find again a list of men seemingly giving birth to men, while a few heroines are intertwined:

> An account of the genealogy of Jesus the Messiah ... Judah the father of Perez and Zerah by *Tamar*, and Perez the father of Hezron ... and Salmon the father of Boaz by *Rahab*, and Boaz the father of Obed by *Ruth*, and Obed the father of Jesse, and Jesse the father of King David. And David was the father of Solomon by *the wife of Uriah*, and Solomon the father of Rehoboam ... and Jacob the father of Joseph the husband of Mary, of whom Jesus was born, who is called the Messiah (Matt. 1:1–17).

Four extraordinary women appear in this list. Here again are mentioned Tamar, Ruth, Bathsheba (who is called "Uriah's wife," thus emphasizing the sin of her adultery with David), and another figure—Rahab, who seems not to belong to the House of David. Why is Rahab mentioned here? Most likely because she was a prostitute "by profession," as we learn from the opening of the Book of Joshua.[7] From her addition to the Davidic lineage, we can conclude, as

---

6   Freud, "Totem and Taboo"; Freud, "Moses and Monotheism." Yosef Hayim Yerushalmi (*Freud's Moses*, 39–57, 89) expands on the idea of "the return of the repressed," while Art Green suggests that the *Shekhinah* signifies the "return of the repressed" of Mary in kabbalistic literature.
7   Joshua 2:1; according to Talmudic tradition (*b. Megillah* 14b), Joshua married Rahab after she converted to Judaism. Longstaff, Niditch and Doniger discuss the parallels between the

St. Jerome suggested, that the character of Mary is in complete opposition to her deviant predecessors.[8] Henceforth, an alternative image of a holy and pure heroine will replace her sinning ancestors.[9] By introducing the problematic background of the House of David and the identity of its female lineage, the author of Matthew achieved a dual purpose: Mary's holiness is intensified in light of her predecessors, and the Christian redeemer is perceived as coming out of the abyss of sin. Jesus is qualified to bear the sins of mankind by the virtue of Mary's ability to absolve the sins of her foremothers.

On the other hand, St. Ephrem the Syrian emphasized in his hymns the bold and sinful acts of Mary, who continued in the same path of sexual promiscuity of her foremothers listed in Matthew 1. "On your account women have hurried after men ... even Rahab, who caught men, was caught by you ... for it was a holy thing, the adultery of Tamar for your sake ... she ran and became even a whore for your sake. ... Ruth with a man on the threshing floor she lay down, for your sake. Her love was bold for your sake, you who teach boldness to all the repentant."[10] It is apparent from his reading that by adding Mary to the Davidic dynasty, the author is following a subversive biblical model of sinful women who transgress "for the sake" of bearing the Messiah. According to St. Ephrem, Matthew calls attention to the centrality of the female figures since they are the mothers who enable their sons to become chosen ones. This is despite the fact that Jesus' father, Joseph, and not Mary, is the one who is officially attributed to the tribe of Judah in this genealogy. Here, as David Flusser notes, the feminine mythology is stronger than biology and "Mary is the certain link between Jesus and the Jewish people."[11]

---

stories of Tamar and Rahab, the motifs of "the crimson thread of hope" and the foreign woman who uses methods of harlotry and deception for the sake of deliverance.

8 Levine, *Matthew*; Brown, *The Birth of the Messiah*; Doniger, *Bedtrick*. St. Jerome stressed the acute tension between Mary and her predecessors as portrayed in the Old Testament and the New Testament. This is contrary to my claim that the tension indicates an integration of these heroines, through the "return of the repressed."

9 Matthew 1:18. It should be noted that Mary's passivity in Matthew is replaced by her active behavior in Luke 1:26–38 and 2:5. Janice C. Anderson, "Mary's Difference: Gender and Patriarchy in the Birth Narratives," *Journal of Religion* 67, no. 2 (1987): 183-202.

10 De Nativitate 9; Phil Botha, "Tamar, Rahab, Ruth, and Mary, the Bold Women in Ephrem the Syrian's Hymn De Nativitate 9," *Acta Patristica et Byzantina* 17 (2006): 1–21; Miri Rubin, *Mother of God: A History of the Virgin Mary* (New Haven: Yale University Press, 2009), 34–40.

11 David Flusser, et al., eds. *Mary: Images of the Mother of Jesus in Jewish and Christian Perspective* (Minneapolis: Fortress Press, 2005), 12.

Based on the Annunciation in Luke 1:2-38 and Matthew 1:18-21, the Protoevangelium of James claims that Mary herself is born to her mother, Anne, through an exceptional impregnation. This is reminiscent of Jesus' birth; similar to Mary's virginity, her mother Anne merited an immaculate conception.[12] Mary's parents' union is designed to institute a genealogy without sexual sin or the serpent's filth. Therefore, Mary and Jesus are untouched by Original Sin, in which the rest of humanity is entrenched. In contrast to the "Original Eve," who represents the source of sexual transgression in the Garden of Eden story, Mary is referred to as *Nova Eva* or a "Second Eve," who symbolizes an unblemished figure who has not tasted sin.[13]

This dichotomy emphasizes that in contrast to Eve who unites her maternal and sexual identity, thereby symbolizing the "source of sin" in the traditions of early Christianity, the depictions of Mary and Anne giving birth challenge the link between sexuality and motherhood and represent a division between the mother figure and woman figure.

Through her miraculous pregnancy, Mary continues the biblical maternal model and is portrayed as suspected of harlotry (as in Math. 1:19-20; and hinted at in Luke 2:5), and only then is introduced as having conceived without any masculine intervention. Similar to the biblical genealogies, which often appear as an opening and closing of a text, the Gospels of Matthew and Luke start with the infancy narratives of Jesus that Mark, John, and Paul chose to ignore.[14] Matthew and Luke emphasized the role of the "mythical pair," the mother and the redeeming son, in the opening of their Gospels, while Matthew clearly echoes back to the Davidic genealogies in the Old Testament. It is possible to say that both of them mark the Virgin Birth as a continuation to the biblical narrative, without censoring its stories. *Their readings are not oppositional nor polemical, but rather are a continuation of the Jewish view*, which connects the transgressive feminine genealogy to the hero's birth scene.[15]

Additionally, Jesus and his mother are later incontestably placed into the core of the earthly Holy Family that corresponds to the Divine Trinity.

---

12 Cross and Livingstone, *Dictionary*, 821-2; Warner, *Mary*, 50-67, 236-54; Rubin, *Mary*, 173-6, 303-312.
13 Jaroslav Pelikan, *Mary through the Ages: Her Place in the History of Culture* (New Haven: Yale University Press, 1996), 46–52, 236.
14 On the identities of Matthew and Luke, see Anthony J. Saldarini, *Matthew's Christian-Jewish Community* (Chicago: University of Chicago Press, 1994); Serge Ruzer, *Mapping the New Testament* (Leiden: Brill, 2007); Rubin, *Mother of God*.
15 Alan Dundes, Lord Raglan, and Otto Rank, *In The Quest of the Hero*, ed. Robert Segal (Princeton: Princeton University Press, 1990); Cohen, "Traditions."

Occasionally, in some Gnostic trends, the image of Mary is displayed in the trinity of the Father, Son, and Holy Spirit. At such times, the entities of the mother and son are united into one symbolic figure that has not been infected by the primordial sin and rises to heaven as the result of their purity.[16] The two share not only the resurrection, but other unique motifs that have been absorbed in Christian doctrines and Mariology.

I claim that the Bible echoes the resemblances between Mary, the holy virgin, and her innocent son and the seductive mothers of the dynasty of David and their son, David, the "adulterer." Through his sexual sins, David reflects the heroic and seductive characters of his maternal roots, as well as the justification his behavior receives in rabbinic literature. David is described by the sages as an archetype of the "repentant," who came "to establish the Yoke of Repentance" (*b. Shabbat* 56b), similar to the role of Jesus who, from the womb, was destined to atone for the sins of all humanity (Matt. 1:21). Moreover, the Sages ascribed to David the drama of a miraculous birth, which might have been influenced by the virgin birth of Jesus in Matthew and Luke.[17]

The Gospels' attitude toward the biblical description puts an emphasis on the common psychoanalytic principle in the two religions, according to which the Messiah is not the chosen one as a result of his deeds (or the "potential" he bears by being anointed), but first and foremost due to his past and primordial origins.[18] The mothers are those who have caused the son to be chosen—and therefore, it is by virtue of his mothers that he is a Messiah. With this background, we can understand the surprisingly positive attitude of the Sages toward the sexual transgressions of the heroines of the Davidic dynasty, as opposed to the sexual abstinence imposed on Mary and the implications arising in Christianity from the model of her virginity.

---

16 Elaine Pagels, "What Became of God the Mother? Conflicting Images of God in Early Christianity," *Signs* 2 (1976): 293-303. Mollenkott, Sheingorn and King discuss Jesus' identification with female figures, such as the image of Sofia (*wisdom*), while Bynum explored images of Jesus as a maternal and nursing figure, a theme that was reflected in medieval visual art. Bynum, *Fragmentation and Redemption*, 104–11, 207–13.

17 As Alter and Cohen have shown, the birth of Jesus in the Gospels is parallel to biblical stories about heroes who were born with divine intervention. On David's miraculous birth, see *b. Sukkah* 52a. According to this Midrash, David was born lifeless and was saved due to the years lent to him by Adam, a notion which reflects motifs in the "family romance." The myth of the birth of the hero was studied by Freud, Rank Campbell, Dundes and others. Alter, "Convention"; Cohen, "Traditions."

18 In the words of Lord Raglan: "The attribution of divine birth to a hero is not the result of his heroism, but is derived from the ritual union of a princess to her own husband, disguised as a god." *The Quest of the Hero*, 149.

It could be said that Jesus is a messiah because of the tension between his sinful mothers of the Old Testament and his impeccable mother of the New Testament. This tension is also expressed in the duality of Mary, who on the one hand represents motherhood and fertility, while on the other hand is a disembodied ideal.[19]

In popular tradition, Mary was named Theotokos, "the mother of God." This title was afterwards enshrined as doctrine during the heated discussions at the Councils of Ephesus (431 CE) and Chalcedon (451 CE), but the Nestorians insisted on the independent human nature of Jesus, and thus called her Christotokos, "the mother of the Messiah." According to some interpretations, even after the birth of Jesus, Mary remains a virgin. In the words of St. Augustine: "*Concipiens virgo, pariens virgo, virgo gravida, virgo feta, virgo perpetua.*"[20] We can now understand why Mary's maternity has been viewed in some streams as a "virginal maternity" and solely as a symbolic idea. Not only was she denied sexuality, but also motherhood.[21] Moreover, the notion that Jesus was conceived not like other men, but rather came through his mother "like water through a pipe," is prevalent in some gnostic trends.[22]

From the very beginning of both western and eastern churches, the corporeality and concreteness of Jesus' birth has been theologically contentious. While Mary's undoubted virginity—an identification of her innocence and perfection—poses a serious challenge to women wanting to realize their sexuality and motherhood. Attempts to strengthen the image of Joseph, the father of Jesus, mostly failed and demonstrated the weakness of the "male model" of

---

19 As Julia Kristeva claims: "In the rare instances when the mother of Jesus appears in the Gospels, she is informed that filial relationship rests not with the flesh but with the name or, in other words, that any possible matrilinealism is to be repudiated and the symbolic link alone is to be last." Kristeva, *Tales*, 237.

20 "Mary conceived as virgin, gave birth as a virgin, carried him as a virgin, pregnant as a virgin, a perpetual virgin." Saint Augustine, Sermon 186, 1 in PL edition (J. P. Migne, *Patrologiae Cursus Completus, Series Latina*, Paris 1844–64), Vol. 38, p. 999.

21 When comparing Mary's role to the mothers of the Davidic line, we may conclude that Mary possessed only partial freedom of choice in regard to her sexuality and motherhood. Yet, as Fulton and Anderson stress, tradition based on the *Magnificent* in Luke (1:46–55) emphasize Mary's choice to become the mother of Jesus.

22 Irenaeus, "Against Heresies," 1:7:2. According to St. Proclus, Jesus entered Mary's womb through her ear and exited the same way, Burton L. Visotzky, *Fathers of the World: Essays in Rabbinic and Patristic Literature* (Tübingen: Mohr Siebeck, 1995), 103. Mary's pregnancy is unusual as well. According to the *Proto Gospel of James*, she gave birth after the sixth month, and in *Ascension of Isaiah*, her pregnancy lasts only two months and "takes Mary by surprise." Jonathan Knight, "The Portrait of Mary in the Ascension of Isaiah," in *Which Mary—The Marys of Early Christian Traditions*, ed. S. Jones (Leiden: Brill, 2003), 101.

identification in Christianity. Mary was perceived as the dominant parent, as well as his symbolic sister, daughter, and wife – manifested in the character of the Christian church—the *ecclesia*.[23] According to some traditions, Mary is even the bride of her son, a perception that testifies from another direction the "return of the repressed" in the Bible, wherein incest and adultery are central motives in the biography of the Messiah.

CHRISTIAN TRADITIONS AND JEWISH RABBINIC LITERATURE

In an old polemic tradition, it is said that Mary conceived Jesus not by divine impregnation, but by a Roman soldier named Pandira. This legend was first found in the lost treatise of the second-century pagan philosopher Celsus and cited in the writings of Origen and Tertullian in the second and third centuries. The same narrative is also mentioned with slight changes in the Babylonian Talmud and found throughout the Middle Ages in a few versions of *Sefer Toledot Yeshu*, a Jewish polemic composition on the life of Jesus. In addition to the perception that the book is a counter-narrative of Jesus' birth in the Gospels and a parody of Mary's conception, I claim that it is an attempt to associate Mary with the sequence of her ancient mothers.

In the latest version of the book, Jesus is denounced as a despicable bastard, conceived during the menstrual period of his mother. However, closer examination of the descriptions of Mary reveals continuous references to the sexual transgressions of the mothers of the Davidic dynasty, both in the Hebrew Bible and in early Christianity.[24] The possibility of Jesus being born

---

23 Clarissa W. Atkinson, *The Oldest Vocation: Christian Motherhood in the Middle Ages* (Ithaca: Cornell University Press, 1991); Patrick J. Geary, *Women at the Beginning: Origin Myths from the Amazons to the Virgin Mary*, (Princeton: Princeton University Press, 2006), 60–75. This is probably the reason why apocryphal sources from the second century relate Mary to the lineage of the House of David [*Protoevangelium of James* (ed. Elliot), 61]. Hollywood, Warner, and Ruether expand upon gender roles in Christianity while Wolfson discussed in depth the theme of sexual-fluidity in Christian and Jewish mystical literature. Bynum has shown that the tendency of priests to identify Jesus with motherly figure posed another challenge to the male identity in the church, while female mystics usually experienced stable identity with continuous gender roles. Bynum, *Fragmentation and Redemption*, 27–51, 200-65.

24 Biale, "Counter-History and Jewish Polemics Against Christianity"; Rubin, *Mother of God*, 57–9. Peter Schäfer (*Mirror*, 211; *Jesus in the Talmud*, 10) claims that in opposition to *Sefer Toledot Yeshu* which presents Mary as a victim of rape (Krupp edition, 33), the tradition in the Babylonian Talmud illustrates a strong Jewish polemic on Mary as prostitute who deviated from her husband. Accordingly, Jesus was called in the Talmud *Ben Stada* (son of the harlot), and Mary was viewed as an adulterous woman who symbolically uncombed her hair (*Migdalit*).

from a woman who had committed harlotry lies already in the literal layer of the Gospels: in the recounted suspicion that arises in Joseph when he reveals that his virgin bride has suddenly become pregnant (Matt. 1:19; Luke 2:5). One way or another, whether in references to her sexual sin or in her portrayal as a virgin, Mary belongs to the heroines of the House of David. Although the two possibilities seem to contradict one another, both are actually an expression of the very same idea.

The connection between sexual transgression and the messianic idea is shared by both religions from their outset. As previously mentioned, King David, the "Messiah," had sinned by committing adultery with a married woman, just as his foremothers had violated sexual prohibitions. A similar narrative had developed about Jesus himself, in the story of his marriage to Mary Magdalene, who is presented in later traditions as a prostitute—an example for the effect that the biblical model had on certain trends on the margins of early Christianity.[25]

Of course, the influences were not one-sided. Just as the Davidic myth informed the formation of Mary as a complement or contrast to her predecessors, so Christian images influenced rabbinic literature. In the Midrash we find prominent evidence of discourses, polemics, and apologetics over the image of the messiah's mother, as we can learn from the following examples that deal with sexuality, virginity, and the idea of miraculous conception.[26]

A) Miraculous Conception: "A Seed That Comes from Another Place"

The act of incest between Lot and his daughters, described in Genesis 19, is the first link in the chain of the Davidic Dynasty. Actually, this story brings together both the beginning and the end through its description of the birth of Moab, the first ancestor of Ruth the Moabite, from whom the Messiah, representing

---

25 See King, *The Gospel of Mary of Magdala: Jesus and the First Woman Apostle*, (California: Polebridge Press, 2003); Jansen, *The Making of the Magdalen*; Warner, *The Myth and the Cult of the Virgin Mary*; Ruether, *Mary, the Feminine Face of the Church*; and others.

26 Daniel Boyarin emphasized the Judeo-Christian ideas regarding virginity and prostitution as well as the connection between gender and ethnic identity. Boyarin, *Dying for God*, 67–92. Developing these concepts, Charlotte Fonrobert suggested that the Jewish rituals and laws of *Niddah* served as an equivalent to the Christian practices of virginity, stating: "In spite of and against the textual evidence we have to at least try to conceive of how Jewish women might have argued about their 'Jewishness' as an ethnic identity." Fonrobert, *Menstrual Purity*, 38. Recently, Avital Davidovich stressed the role of virginity in rabbinic literature and medieval culture. Davidovich, *Virginity*, Ch. 2, 4.

future redemption, is born. The story reinforces the idea that every creation involves incest: just as myths of incest appear in descriptions of world-creation in many cultures, incest is also involved in the birth of the messianic scion.

The taboo on incest symbolizes the beginning of civilization and the transition of humanity from the primitive phase to the dominance of the "law of the father." The renunciation of the semiotic (matriarchal) mode, in favor of the symbolic (patriarchal) mode, releases anarchical sexual forces. These forces sink and bubble beneath the surface to erupt in extreme liminal transitional situations. The story of Lot's daughters, who fulfill a threatening and prohibited fantasy, is a manifestation of this process. In the Freudian sense, this story involves sexual transgression, guilt, and voyeurism, a glimpse into a place of danger—an embodiment of the "primal scene" of the messianic lineage.[27]

The sages were fully aware of the antinomy of the trends found in the story of Sodom, and thus tried to soften it by adding a third hero to the messianic drama: from then on, God is the father who impregnates the daughters of Lot, rather than their flesh and blood father. As it is presented in the following Midrash:

> "*Come, let us make our father drink wine, and we will lie with him, that we may preserve seed through our father*" (Genesis 19:32). R. Tanhuma said in Samuel's name: It is not written that we may preserve a child of our father, but "that we may preserve seed (*zera*), through our father": viz. the seed that comes from another place [from heaven]—and this is the Messiah (Genesis Rabbah 51:8).

According to this Midrash, the messiah is a "seed that comes from another place." Thus, the name "Moab"—though implying incest ("from my father")—is also evidence of the exoneration of Lot's daughters. The divine Father is God himself who impregnated Lot's daughters, and consequently the Jewish Messiah is "*Divi Filius*" (the son of God).[28] This daring Midrash—written in Palestine during the Byzantine era, parallel to the emergence of Christianity as the religion of the Roman Empire—reflects most clearly how the virginal myth

---

27 Levi-Strauss, *Elementary*; Lacan, *Écrits*; Kristeva, *Powers of Horror*. For example, Freud, *Dreams*; Freud, *Totem*. For other developments of this notion, see Klein, *Love, Guilt and Reparation*; Aron, "The Internalized Primal Scene."

28 This is similar to the ancient Near East and Egypt, where God "gives birth" to the king or adopts him and crowns him as his son, as Hangel, Knohl, Idel, Schneider and Lorberbaum have shown (ch. 1 fn. 36).

influenced the Sages.[29] I assume that in order to neutralize the severe sin of incest underlying the birth of the messiah, the Sages are ready to *adopt* the idea of Virgin Birth as a commentary on the preexisting biblical story. Here we find an example of an innovative genre of exegesis that transforms the ancient plot and imbues it with new meaning.

Ideas about the mother of the Messiah continue to develop in a reciprocal way in both religions. Consequently, we can suggest that the tradition of *hieros gamos* (holy marriage) of Mary and her son, and the illustration of the bridal mysticism which is prominent in medieval writings, leans on the old biblical core in which incest and messianic birth are intertwined. The union of the mother and her son, in light of the coupling of Jesus and Mary in later traditions, or the union between Lot and his daughters, reflects the depth of the desire to bring salvation—a situation in which the differences between right and wrong, male and female, and even parents and children disappear.[30]

B) Sexuality and Virginity: "All Those Women of the House of Rabbi Who Crushed with Their Finger"

A Midrash describing the ceremony and a ritual of the women in the House of R. Judah the Prince emphasizes the differences between the image of the messianic mother in Judaism and Christianity:

> Surely Tamar conceived from a first contact! The other answered him: Tamar crushed with her finger; for R. Isaac said: All women of the house of Rabbi who crushed [the hymen] with their finger [to destroy their virginity] are designated Tamar. And why are they designated Tamar?— Because Tamar crushed with her finger (*b.Yevamot* 34b).

This is one of the most revolutionary sources in rabbinic literature, documenting a practice exercised for generations by women of the leading families in late antiquity. According to ancient medical and gynecological concepts, a virgin could not conceive from her first intercourse. To resolve this dilemma, the

---

29 Fonrobert, "Birth of the Messiah," 262.
30 At the same time, the symbiosis between the mother and her son highlights the exclusion of the father and prevents a sexual relationship between the parents. As Alan Dundes suggests, the inseparable connection between Jesus and Mary represents an Oedipal struggle of the son with the father: "A son who is born to a virgin can deny that his father ever had sexual access to his mother." Dundes, *Hero*, 195.

Sages recount that Tamar "crushed [her hymen] with her finger" so she could conceive immediately.

This surprising sermon teaches that Tamar, who disguised herself as a prostitute and conceived from her father-in-law, became a model of inspiration for the women of the house of Rabbi (second century CE), who attributed to themselves Davidic lineage.[31] The women in the ruling family even named themselves "Tamar," thus showing their empathy with the behavior of their symbolic ancestor. I believe that by means of this technique, the young women of the House of Rabbi freed themselves from the "demand of virginity." As brides, they liberated themselves by rejecting the examination of their sheets after the wedding night, which would formerly have verified their virginity.

If all the women of the chosen tribe "deflowered" themselves, none of them could be checked and the men could not have control over their sexuality. In a parallel Midrash, the Sages say that the daughters of Lot also deflowered themselves and conceived Ammon and Moab on their first intercourse.[32] Here we learn not only about an ancient tradition that had been attributed to the biblical heroines, but about a practice that was assumed to be exercised by women in late antiquity. The image of Tamar, like other figures of the Davidic dynasty, was relevant to the world of real women in the rabbinic era. It seems that these heroines had become archetypal models for the resistance of patriarchal oppression and for exercising an independent, active choice of motherhood.

One can indeed read this sermon in a converse way: as a male fantasy on the licentiousness of the women from the House of Rabbi, or as a testimony of an oppressive custom of dismembering the hymen for the purpose of immediate conception. However, it is hard to ignore the way in which this rabbinic commentary connects between the audacity of the biblical Tamar and the noble women related to the dynasty of House of David in the first centuries CE. In many abundant Midrashim, the Sages express a remarkable degree of sympathy for the mothers of the House of David and sweeping justification of their deeds, such as Tamar sitting in the place called "the opening of the eyes" (*petaḥ einayim*), which is presented as an ally of God. This Midrash and other sources underline the secret covenant between God and the mothers of the messiah. Moreover, in the Babylonian Talmud, there is a concluding, bold,

---

31 Urbach, *Sages*, although Goodblatt and Schwartz challenged the claim of the historical connections between the house of Rabbi and the Davidic dynasty.

32 *Genesis Rabbah* 45, 4; 51, 9; *Pesiqta Rabbati* 42; Malkiel, "Virginity," presents another understanding of this technique in late antiquity and medieval Jewish culture.

and morally affirmative statement relating to all the heroines of the dynasty: "*Gedolah averah lishmah me-mitzva she-lo lishma.*"[33] From these testimonies, I conclude that the phrase "crushed with their finger" used by the Sages is not defamation, but a positive outlook on the bold women who built the messianic lineage by means of transgression.

In fact, there is great similarity between the descriptions of the practices of the women of the House of Rabbi and the proposed action of Tamar. Just as they first destroy their virginity—physically and symbolically—by tearing off the illusion of purity and freeing themselves from the patriarchal pillory through the irruption of their bodies, so does Tamar assert control over her body, and by its irruption undermines the religious order and breaks social boundaries to attain female freedom and motherhood. As it says in Genesis 38:15–16: "When Judah saw her, he thought her to be a harlot, for she had covered her face. ... She said, 'What will you give me, that you may come in to me?' ... She replied, 'Your signet and your cord, and your staff that is in your hand.' So he gave them to her, and went in to her, and she conceived by him."[34] Only after dressing like a harlot and conveying her abandonment does she receive symbols of identity from Judah and can bravely confront him as a way to save her own, Perez's, and Zerah's lives.

Rabbinic commentaries add details to emphasize the role of virginity in Tamar's story, in order to create a polemical dialogue with the Christian messianic idea of sexuality and motherhood. Their Midrashim deny the validity of the "virginal mother" and her chastity, while the mothers of the Davidic dynasty are presented here, as well as in other commentaries, as heroines who "have control over their own bodies" (Gen. Rabbah 51: 9), making an active choice to embrace motherhood. This is in contradiction to Mary, who does not choose to become pregnant and is compelled to conceive a child via divine impregnation. Following this, we can say that through the mothers of the Davidic dynasty, the rabbis introduce a feministic model, in which are joined into one figure the images of the "virgin," the "mother," and the "harlot."

C) "Qedeshot" and "Qedushot"—The Holy Harlots

Simone de Beauvoir called upon women to avoid giving birth in order to free themselves from the oppressive identification between femininity and

---

33   Ch. 4.
34   Douglas, *Purtiy*. In the beginning, Tamar's passivity is conspicuous, as evidenced in the story of her abandonment by Judah and his sons and her confinement to her father's house (Gen. 38). However, after verse 14, her bold activism becomes prominent. Alter, *Biblical Narrative*.

motherhood. She and other feminist theorists pointed to the primal split between the figure of a virgin/mother and the figure of the harlot, while offering various explanations as to its origins.[35] To examine the myths of the mother of the Messiah in Christianity and Judaism demonstrates that each religion represented complex aspects of this primal split. The heroines of the House of David actively chose to become mothers and thus left a mark on world history, even though their motherhood includes posttraumatic and oppressive aspects. In contrast to them, Mary's choice was not active, since she was chosen to conceive Jesus in a miraculous way, through the annunciation scene. She symbolizes the problematic and paradoxical identification between motherhood and virginity, in which a woman's sexuality is controlled by forcing her to retain her virginal innocence. It turns out that she—who avoided giving birth in the simple sense of the word—has become the archetype of the impeccable mother.

The mothers of the Davidic dynasty win appreciation in Jewish rabbinic commentary due to their daring sexual deeds that lead to motherhood, while Mary is glorified for her virginal motherhood in Christianity. Each of the religions treats with contempt the opposing sexual model—unsurprisingly, given that both idealization and contempt stem from the same source of dominance over women and their bodies. Like Mary, the heroines of the House of David also constitute an example of the transition from motherhood as a personal experience to motherhood that is controlled by the patriarchal institution. Likewise, both examples reflect the high value attributed to fertility in each culture. And yet, in the rabbinic literature, along with the glorification or contempt, we encounter another attitude. As we have learned from the Midrash regarding the House of Rabbi, the biblical mothers of the dynasty have become an example of a ritualistic identification and of everyday life practices.

The mention of the defloration of Tamar and the daughters of Lot in these commentaries suggests a creative way of unifying the virgin and mother figures with that of the prostitute. The heroines of the House of David (both the

---

35 According to one interpretation, man's fears of "the big mother" and her destructive powers purify her from any sexual component and transfer passion to a subordinate feminine figure. However, the glorification of the mother and the irreverent attitude toward the sexual woman actually stem from the same source, as they reflect man's inability to regard a woman as an independent subject. See de Beauvoir, *The Second Sex*; Gilbert and Gubar, *Madwomen*; Rich, *Of Woman Born*. On the other hand, according to Freud's, "Totem and Taboo," the taboo on incest and the son's forbidden desire for his mother force him to turn his erotic feelings from her to an "alien," "other" woman.

ancient and the new) win their liberty by the destruction of their virginity, while in the background echoes the saintly figure of Mary. These women, through provocative sexual behavior, choose to conceive in an active way. In their accession to and establishment of the royal lineage, they win God's sympathy and theological glorification. While being in dialogue and partial consent with the Christian myth, the sages undermine it through their creation of a new feminine model—a woman who is both a virgin and a harlot, a mother and a prostitute.

By associating the technique of defloration with the mothers of the Davidic dynasty, the Sages benefit twice: on the one hand, they refute the words of the Gospels in favor of actual sexual conception, while simultaneously reflecting their deep and repressed fear of virginity.[36] On the other hand, they preserve the *aura of virginity* in the background, implying the fundamental innocence of the Davidic mothers, because their intentions were "for the sake of Heaven." As the description of these women contains varying and contradictory qualities of "a woman"—her motherhood and sexuality—these feminine models and deeds have become objects for identification.

In contrast, Mary is portrayed as an ideal and unattainable figure. Indeed, can one identify with her? Surely, the model of virginity has offered women an intellectual freedom and liberation in social and family life. Christian culture had developed models of liberated women, as in convents, where educated nuns engaged in a life of study (as opposed to Jewish women, who all had the obligation to marry and have children), or women who escaped reality by martyrdom while uniting with Jesus at their death. Yet one cannot ignore the ascetic demand from Mary to renounce her body and her sexuality, and the consequent difficulty women and mothers have had in identifying with her. Indeed, virgins, nuns, and martyrs who followed Mary's lead were often regarded as "masculine" women.[37] In fact, there exists a profound incongruity

---

36 Freud argued that the danger primitive man saw in female virginity derived from the crucial and liminal moment tied to the loss of virginity as a dangerous stage in the development of female sexuality, during which arose contradictory feelings of "thraldom and enmity" (*Virginity*, 235). In order to protect them, along with the women's anxiety around the first sexual relations, there was a custom in primitive tribes to separate the defloration of girls from the act of marriage. Interestingly, this task was given to male authority figures, as though to confirm that the passion of a girl was really to her father and not to her husband. As Freud says, "The duty of defloration is given to an elder, a priest, or a holy man—that is, to a father substitute" (ibid, 229). In our context, it is fascinating to see that the pairing of Davidic mothers also occurs with "father figures." And yet, in this case, it is the women themselves who make the choice to remove their virginity and deflower themselves.

37 Boyarin, *Dying for God*. As Coon, Warner, Fulton, Artman and others claim, during the first

between the women who joined the cult of Mary and Mary herself, who had a son and fulfilled her motherhood.

From a psychoanalytic perspective, the myth of the Holy Virgin deepens the split between femininity and motherhood and between the mother and the harlot. While idealizing the actual qualities associated with motherhood, such as nurturing, nourishing, and holding, the myth of virginity neutralizes the relationship with the mother without relating to a real living entity. She is not a "subject" but a concept of an "ideal mother" or "idol." This way, man can control his fears of the "big mother" and her consuming and destructive powers, as they were described by Erich Neumann, Julia Kristeva, and others. Indeed, the image of incorporeal, asexual motherhood intensifies the existing hierarchy in gender relations.

D) Seduction, Trauma, and Relationships

Do the sexual transgressions of the Davidic mothers liberate these heroines, unlike Mary's virginity which preserves the existing gender power relations, or are these stories yet another act of oppression disguised as acts of freedom?

In the stories of prostitution, incest, and seduction of the mothers of the Davidic lineage, we bear witness to a deep trauma that these heroines are trying to process and repair. "Trauma" is defined as an exceptionally threatening event that interrupts the continuous flow of time and the feeling of existence in a subject. A person who has been overpowered by trauma is compelled to restore her memory constantly and cannot "move on." Trauma has a disruptive impact on the experience of temporality; in other words, it erases "historical time," transferring it into "mythical time." On the one hand, trauma blurs the differences between good and bad, past and present, self and the other. In the context of sexual trauma, it erases the borders between the private body and others, thus causing transgressive behavior, while at the same time it gives rise to binary structures in human experience.[38]

---

centuries, some of these women were not concerned with following Mary; rather their goal was to follow Jesus and the apostles (as we learn from the example of Perpetua and Thecla), but for the medieval period, we find that they follow Mary herself. On the model of "chastity marriage" as a paradoxical combination of marriage and celibacy: see Dyan H. Elliott, *Spiritual Marriage: Sexual Abstinence in Medieval Wedlock*, (Princeton: Princeton University Press, 1993).

38 Laplanche and Pontalis, *Psychoanalysis*, 465–70; see also LaCapra, *Writing History, Writing Trauma*, MacKinnon, Herman, Dworkin and Stolorow.

Based on Freud's "trauma theory," Jacques Laplanche explores the meaning of a mother's communication with her child, positing that it is a process of seduction that imprints her subconscious in the mind of the little boy or girl, causing trauma, which is later aroused and re-expressed in mature sexuality.[39] Laplanche stresses that seduction is the foundational process of the human being, although sometimes, and in a normal process, it can lead to a "humanizing trauma," enabling formative aspects of the development of the self. In the stories of the mothers of the Davidic dynasty, we can identify a traumatic sequence in which women use their bodies as the only resource of power that they have.

Ostensibly, these stories liberate women, but the oscillation between promiscuity and virginity shows a self-destructive and continuous pattern, repeated generation after generation. This phenomenon was defined by Freud as "repetition compulsion," introduced in the Bible through narratives that reflect a wound in need of healing. However, here the stories represent not a simple repetition, but a process of sublimation, as each story refines the one previous to it, turning the initial trauma into a tool of healing and amendment. It is as though perpetuating the same patterns differently can repair their inner mythical damages.

The daughters of Lot carry within themselves a terrible wound, since they are being offered by their own father to the Sodomites to be raped (Gen. 19:4–8), which, later on, led to their incestuous relations with him. This is the most grievous wound of the dynasty, and it appears as the core story that is inherited by daughters of the Davidic lineage. Later on, the primordial sin between Lot and his daughters follows a lesser perversion, in Tamar's copulation with her father-in-law; Tamar disguises herself as a harlot, and is abandoned both by her husbands and by Judah, who prevents her from marrying his third son. These narratives are repeated in the most moderate way in the seduction scene of Ruth and Boaz on the threshing floor. Here, with each passing generation, we witness not only a sublimation and decline in the severity of the sexual sins depicted, but also a transformation in the heroine's choice, which might be a result of conscious attempts of later authors to cope with the paradoxical heritage of the Davidic narratives.

Tamar and the daughters of Lot are lonely women in a dangerous male world. They have no other alternative but to seduce and give birth. Ruth, by

---

39 In fact, Freud referred to trauma as part of his seduction theory and the development of the "trauma theory" attributed to the Object-Relations theory. Also, Stein, "Enigmatic"; Tsoffar, "Trauma."

contrast, freely chooses to go to Bethlehem and to Boaz's place. As a result of her relationship with Naomi and of their commitment to each other, there emerges a new model of relations, in which sisterhood substitutes for the lack of biological female support. It is not only the least sinful act of seduction, between a single woman and unmarried old man, but also a story that summarizes the entire narrative of the dynasty. Retelling these stories as a blessing at the gate in the end of the book of Ruth signifies a persuasive attempt to heal their wounds and liberate themselves from inner and outer oppression.

The agency of these women and their "excessive behavior" is a response to the complete failure of the respective men in the stories: Lot, who abused his daughters and yet, we are told twice, still "*did not know* when she lay down or when she rose" (Gen. 19:33–35); Judah, who after sending Tamar away to her father's house, "*did not know* that she was his daughter-in-law" (Gen. 38:16) but coupled with her; Elimelech, the "Judge," who escaped from the famine in Bethlehem to Moab, abandoning his city and family to the hunger; and even Boaz, who did not recognize Ruth since she "got up before one person could recognize another" (Ruth 3:14). The stories of these heroines always begin with distress: widowhood, abandonment, abuse, neglect, hunger, and poverty. Nevertheless, their choice to survive, live, and give birth prevails. While processing these changes, the Davidic mothers transform conventional perceptions toward kinship, sexuality, and redemption, each in her own way. Facing oppression and violence, these women try to heal the "basic fault" that underlies the infrastructure of their dynasty and to extricate themselves and their descendants. Though the details of the stories differ, each woman does so by turning the frozen "mythical" time that resulted from the particular trauma that she experienced to actual "historical" time, and by changing the "acting out" to "working through" her history.

Compared to this development, Mary's virginity signifies a static mode that might stem from a different kind of trauma, which cannot progress or transform metaphorically.[40] Her unstained ("immaculate") body—from

---

[40] Clues can be found in Freud's discussion on hysteria, implying that "virginity" represents trauma and latent sexual anxiety as women who were exposed to dangerous or prohibited sexuality tended to develop hysteria, frigidity, and fear from the sexual act; Freud, "Three Essays on the Theory of Sexuality." I assume that this motif is used in the description of the antichrist in the polemic apocalypse titled *Sefer Zerubavel*. In this "counter-history" composition, the mother of Armilus symbolizes Mary (Biale, "Counter-History and Jewish Polemics Against Christianity") and is situated as a beautiful "stone idol." This image reflects her both seductive and static (rigid and frigid) position in the eyes of Jewish narrators. According to Biale, the author of *Sefer Zerubavel* "sexualizes the idolatry he identifies with Christianity.

both the perspective of her own birth and the birth of her son—represents a perfect and eternal being, which has no real presence in the context of "object relations." By reconstructing Mary's biography from the Gospels and later sources, I want to suggest that due to the circumstances of *her birth*, Mary is unable to be a carnal, sexual, and maternal woman. The Immaculate Conception prevents her from having a physical connection with Joseph, the father of her son.[41] Her body has been taken from her and has become a symbol of "absence," a "void," "a lacuna": motherhood and womanhood with no substance, no flesh. A world without relationships is created here through pure conception, suspicious fatherhood and motherhood, a resurrected messiah, and the presence of the Holy Spirit. Virginity, along with the illusion of wholeness, represents a nontransformative state.[42] Comparing the sexual characterizations of the messianic mothers in these religions, we can discern three different models: (1) the "static model" of the Virginal Birth, (2) its opposite, the "relationship model," which dates back to the Hebrew Bible, and (3) the Immaculate Conception of Mary. The third model can be viewed as an "intermediary model," since it includes, on the one hand, intercourse and real sexual relations, but on the other hand presents them as "neutral," "unstained," and without the "otherness" of sexuality.

In the biblical model seen in the stories of Lot, Judah, Jacob, Boaz, and David, an affinity of flesh and familial ties heightens the sense of adultery that exists in the relations between the mother and the father of the chosen son. I suggest that it is precisely the prohibited sexual relations between *the father* and *the daughter* that create the sacred relations between *the mother* and *the messianic son*. In all these cases, the real affinity is between the "other" and the "self," as a projection of the "self in relations." The Jewish messiah is born from

---

In so doing, he inverts the image of Mary from virgin to harlot" (Biale, "Counter-History and Jewish Polemics Against Christianity," 140). At the same time, Martha Himmelfarb convincingly shows that the image of Mary is split between the stone idol and Hefzibah herself, reflecting contradictory emotions toward Mary's cult, Himmelfarb, "The Mother of Messiah in the Talmud Yerushalmi and Sefer Zerubbabel," in *The Talmud Yerushalmi and Graeco-Roman Culture*, ed. Peter Schäfer (Tübingen: Mohr Siebeck, 2002), 369-389.

41 Matthew claims that there has been no sexual contact between the spouses before Jesus' birth, unlike later readings of the myth of Mary that support the idea of total sexual abstinence of the Messiah's parents.

42 Kathleen C. Kelly, *Performing Virginity and Testing Chastity in the Middle Ages* (New York: Routledge, 2000); Davidovich, *Virginity*. The motif of the resurrection of Jesus could have been developed in Christianity as a way to compensate the mother and her son with continuous birth, due to the absence of a first actual birth.

the "relationship model" in which the forbidden seduction is transformed into an act of redemption. The trauma is perceived here to be a basis for repair and transformation, while in the model in which no trauma exists, there is also no movement: redemption, whether personal or feminine, is merely a possibility.[43]

E) Late Subversion in a Medieval Midrash

All the stories of the Davidic dynasty in the Hebrew Bible reveal the "relationship model" and the affinity between the Messianic mother and the chosen son, while at the same time emphasizing the absence of a birth story for King David himself. The medieval Midrash in *Yalkut ha-Makhiri* tries to complement this absence and strengthen the "relationship model" by bringing three partners to the conception of David. While arguing against the Christian model, on the one hand, they simultaneously develop it by emphasizing female subjectivity and the choice of motherhood.[44]

According to this Midrash, King David was born following a secret alliance between the handmaid of David's father, Jesse, and his rejected wife. Jesse, who intended to be with his handmaid, unknowingly impregnated his legal wife. We can see how the rabbinic commentators process the tension between fertility, sexuality, and motherhood, while elevating the forbidden lust to a level of fantasy without allowing it to be actually realized. Jesse did not have intercourse with his desired handmaid, but rather with his abandoned and neglected wife.[45] And yet, the child was born a redhead because of his father's "sinful thought"—just a thought, and not an actual forbidden deed. The subversion of this Midrash stems from the reverberations of the known ancient motifs, while processing and developing them to new directions. Between the lines, we can hear criticism against the earlier rabbinic institution, as Jesse is presented as the "Head of the Sanhedrin" (the high court of assembled Sages), yet an immoral figure whose non-Jewish maid rescued him from severe sin.

What stands out here is the criticism of the law and the patriarchal order. The Midrash emphasizes the blindness of men, who do not understand the situation, while women manipulate events behind the scenes. Above all, this commentary is unique because it favors the model of "sisterhood" over the male

---

43 Chodorow, "Gender, Relation, and Difference." However, in Christianity, there is still social and religious salvation, and a real relationship between the "one" mother and the "one" son.
44 Ch. 3.
45 Zakovitch, *David*; Fonrobert, "Birth of the Messiah."

"urges." The alliance between the wife and the concubine, who together cope with the crisis, is an amendment to the old biblical struggle between Rachel and Leah over the love of Jacob and motherhood. *Yalkut ha-Makhiri* indicates that the wife and the handmaid share roles that were split in the past, continuing the blessing of the elders at the city gate: "May the LORD make the woman who is coming into your house, like Rachel and Leah, *who together built up the house of Israel*" (Ruth 4:11).

I claim that in this legend, David is the son of two mothers: one redheaded, foreign, and desired, and the other his permissible and actual mother.[46] Written as a well-known biblical narrative, this late version of the Midrash demonstrates how "mythological" stories are reprocessed in a feminist mode. This is achieved by portraying the birth of the savior as originating in triangular relations and solidarity between women. The Midrash matches the model of the Mother of the Messiah that was developed in the Judeo-Christian discourse throughout the generations: the women here are not prostitutes, though this motif is implied in the image of the handmaid, and the women's bed trick echoes the biblical plots of the Davidic dynasty.[47] It could be that the triangular relations in the tale are an alternative to the Christian Trinity, while the two mothers that turn the son into a "messiah" are an opposition to the absence of relations between Mary and the biological father of Jesus, Joseph.[48]

However, it seems that this late Midrash, which appears in medieval Christendom, not only challenges the myth of Mary's virginity but is also profoundly influenced by it. Along with the actual relations between Jesse and his wife, the Midrash includes the possibility of a symbolic and "virginal" conception. David was born a red-head due to Jesse's thoughts about his forbidden red-headed concubine. Jesse's desire emphasizes the power of the mental imprinting and the "sinful thought" (*maḥshavah zarah*; *hirhur averah*) hinting at the development and violation of the "virginal birth" of the chosen son of the

---

46 Doniger (*Bedtrick*) reveals a parallel pattern in the Davidic lineage, according to which it is always two men who shares the fatherhood in the messianic plot. Tamar, Ruth, Bathsheba, and Mary have children not with the legal fathers, but from "other," surprising sources. According to my reading, double fatherhood changed in the legend of *Yalkut ha-Makhiri* through "double" and ironical motherhood.

47 As we learn also from Leviticus Rabbah (14: 5). This Midrash already reflects the idea of *hirhur averah* (mental sinful imprinting) in David's birth and implies that he is son of a menstruant.

48 By quoting the verse "The Lord said unto me, you are my son" (Ps. 2:7), this Midrash implies that the Messiah is the "Son of God," just like David who declares in Psalms: "If my father and mother forsake me, the Lord will take me up" (27:10).

messianic dynasty. At the same time, this Midrash also alludes to the idea of the "Immaculate Conception" of Mary, since it includes both a sinful thought and the act of sexual intercourse, not with the same woman.

Through the dialogues between Jesse's wife and his concubine, the Midrash focuses on feminine subjectivity and the personal experience of the Messiah's mother. It begins with the wife's confession of her desolation, continues with the maid's plan to help her mistress trick Jesse, and ends poignantly with the mixed feelings of David's mother, who is "inwardly happy and outwardly sad" at the anointment ceremony of her son. Moreover, the Midrash emphasizes that Jesse's wife makes an active choice of motherhood and fights for it: she uses all possible means, including artifice, just like the foremothers of the Davidic dynasty.[49]

F) The Messianic Mother as a Virgin and Harlot—Influences on the Perception of the *Shekhinah* in the *Zohar*

Martha Himmelfarb claims that "unlike so many aspects of Christianity, veneration of the mother of the messiah does not have roots in Judaism. Indeed the importance of the mother of the messiah is a feature that sets Christianity apart from Judaism."[50] A similar view is expressed by David Biale, Peter Schäfer, and others who view the Jewish messianic mother as a reaction to the traditions of Jesus's birth, and identify Mary's birth scene as an independent myth that begins in the Synoptic Gospels.[51] In contrast to these positions, the narrative that I have presented highlights the centrality of the messianic mother in the ancient Jewish traditions and indicates the links that exist in the biblical literature, Midrash, and early Christian traditions. It is even possible to strengthen this claim and say that the Bible forms a messianic mother model, which Christianity adopts or reacts to. According to this model, Mary is not just a negative image of her predecessors, but a figure who symbolizes the "return of the repressed" of the biblical heroines.

---

49 Fonrobert, "Birth of the Messiah"; Doniger, *Bedtrick*.
50 Himmelfarb, "The Mother of Messiah," 369.
51 Peter Schäfer, *Mirrors of His Beauty: Feminine Images of God from the Bible to the Early Kabbalah* (Princeton: Princeton University Press, 2002), 214; Biale, "Counter-History." For a discussion of the messianic narrative as a dialogic literature: Hasan-Rokem, *Web of Life*, 163-72. This analysis focuses on the birth legends of Menahem in Lamentations Rabbah 1:1; *y. Berakhot* 2:4 (17b) a story discussed also by Frenkel and Knohl. On Christian influence on Jewish-Ashkenazic ritual in the Middle Ages, see Marcus, *Rituals*, Ch. 6.

An analysis of these traditions intensifies the centrality of the mother figure in both religions, and illuminates the connection between Mary's virginity and the Davidic heroines' promiscuity. To conclude our study and its evolution from the Bible through the literature of the Middle Ages, I shall suggest that the figure of the *Shekhinah* in Zoharic literature is developed in two parallel channels: she flourished due to the influence of internal Jewish traditions regarding the mother of the Messiah, and in dialog with mariological trends in Christianity. Thus the *Shekhinah* is portrayed in the Zoharic literature as a figure who is simultaneously a harlot and a virgin, a *qedeshah* and a *qedoshah*.

If we accept this claim, we may make peace between two positions currently argued in kabbalah scholarship. One position sees the origin for the figure of the *Shekhinah* in kabbalah, in the rise of the cult of Mary beginning in the 12th century (paralleling the appearance of the *Bahir*).[52] The oppositional attitude points to the ancient sources of the *Shekhinah*'s figure and its development within internal Jewish traditions.[53] According to this approach, biblical, rabbinic, gnostic, philosophic, and mythic motifs were integrated in the figure of the *Shekhinah* in kabbalah, and characteristics of *Sofia*, Helen of Troy, Daughter of Zion, Ishtar and Asherah, Miriam the sister of Moses, Mary the mother of Jesus, Mary Magdalene, Davidic matriarchs, Esther, Bathsheba, and others were combined and formed the *Shekhinah*'s multifaceted figure, which is certainly not a virgin.[54]

---

52 Schäfer, *Mirrors*, 147-72. Arthur Green, "Shekhinah, the Virgin Mary, and the Song of Songs: Reflections on a Kabbalistic Symbol in Its Historical Context," *AJS Review* 26, no. 1 (2002): 1-52. Although Green notes that both religions share "close" symbols, he concludes with the statement that "Recognizing Jewish indebtedness to Christianity, especially on the level of popular piety, is often much more difficult." Ibid, 52, 56.

53 According to Idel, (*Kabbalah and Eros*, 46-7, 80-2, fn. 116) this hypothesis needs further exploration. In contrast to the *Shekhinah* in the *Zohar*, in *Sefer ha-Meshiv* Idel identifies clear Christian influences (Idel, *Ben*, 437-40), while Liebes' critique of Green's view emphasizes the centrality of copulation in the *Zohar*, standing in total contradiction to the virginity myth: Liebes, "Indeed the Shekhinah a Virgin? On the Book of Arthur Green," *Pe'amim* 101–2 (2005): 303–313. Nevertheless, in "Christian Influences in the *Zohar*," Liebes shows how Christological concepts were integrated into the *Zohar*, as he writes, "the author of the *Zohar* did not close his eyes nor refrain from drawing upon handfuls of Christian material and infuse it into his magnificent structure." Liebes, *Studies*, 139-62; Liebes, *On Sabbateanism*, 319-21. For the development of the conception of the *Shekhinah* in the *Bahir* and a criticism of her feminine presentation in earlier versions of the composition, Abrams, "The Condensation of the Symbol Shekhinah."

54 On the gnostic influence on the *Shekhinah*'s appearance in kabbalah, Scholem, *Origins*, 13-22, 23-65; Scholem, *Godhead*, 274-94. Liebes, Shekhinah," 83-119; Liebes, *Studies in Jewish Myth*, 1-64. Abrams, "The Virgin Mary," as well as Shoham, *Miriam*, dealt with

However, I would suggest that the admixture of virginity and licentiousness is seen in many central passages in the *Zohar*. For example, in *Zohar Emor*, the *Shekhinah* is forced to undergo the "*Sotah*" (errant woman) trial and is found to be "pure" each year anew. The *Zohar* parallels the "seven complete weeks" counted between Passover and Pentecost and the seven clean days of a woman, as well as the *sotah*'s barley offering and the wave offering. The *sotah*'s trial and the suspicion and fault cast on the *Shekhinah*, prepare her for annual copulation with the divine partner that occurs on Pentecost.[55] The *Zohar* echoes here the transitions from suspicion and transgressive sexuality to purity, virginity, and immaculateness. In the same manner, also the menstruant at the time of her impurity is perceived as a harlot, whereas when pure, she is in the *Zohar*'s words "a new bride," meaning a "virgin." These descriptions of the *Shekhinah* stress the desire to renew her virginity and purity, precisely after she is accused and cleansed of guilt. In this ritualistic ceremony the *Shekhinah* each year presents a "new grain offering," which symbolizes her becoming a "new bride." This figure is also identified with Torah, disclosed in its entire splendor and virginity on Pentecost.

In a parallel passage within the "*Pequdin*" stratum in the *Zohar*, the duality and proximity of virginity and harlotry are exacerbated, up to the author's portrayal of Lilith as the other side of *Shekhinah*, similar to the conception of Tamar's double face in *Zohar Aḥrei Mot*. By bringing the "wave offering" the licentious woman departs from the *Matronita*, and leaves Israel "unadulterated in regards to the mystery of faith."[56] The *Zohar* on the "wave offering" references the midrashic story of the two sisters, in which one "erred," and the second attempts to save her by undergoing her *sotah* trial instead—still it causes death to the first sister when they embraced—highlights the binary opposition between purity and impurity, life and death. While the rabbinic Midrash portrays the tragic and deterministic aspect in the *sotah*'s punishment, the Zoharic exegete presents the psychological perception of choice: "And this is the advice that the Holy One blessed be He gives to his sons, to bring this offering in order that the licentious woman will be

---

the Ashkenazic traditions and Sephardic kabbalah, which turn to the figure of Miriam as a polemic or alternative to the Virgin Cult. For further discussion of the Judeo-Christian discourse see Wolfson, *Language, Eros, Being*.

55 Zohar III: 96a-97a. According to one version after the trial the *Shekhinah* is revealed as a virgin, "for here is the renewal of the bride." Sharon Koren, *Forsaken: The Menstruant in Medieval Jewish Mysticism* (Waltham: Brandeis University Press, 2011), 77-9.

56 Zohar III: 97, the statement is published in the *Ra'ya Mehemna*, but belongs to the *Pequdin* stratum. Gottlieb, *Studies*, 226.

expelled [from] the woman of valor." The emancipation from the "false self" and from the "shadow" figure, which reflects the "other side" of the purified woman, emerges from this Zoharic statement. Thus, the risk of death in licentiousness transformed into a force of life and renewed fecundity.[57]

In cases where it is clear that the *Shekhinah* is identified with heroines who were not virgins, the *Zohar* also underlines the motif of the "bride" emphasizing the aura of virginity entailed in this image. For example, the *Shekhinah*'s journey of redemption and her moving from the side of Judgment (Red) to Grace (White), correlates, as we saw in *Zohar Aḥrei Mot*, Tamar's story, which in the beginning she is a "destroyer of the world" and at the end she is "an actual bride, of the Song of Songs." As I have shown, the fire and judgments, which characterize Tamar in the beginning ("For she had covered her face," "she eats and wipes her mouth"), have a great similarity to the promiscuous figure of Lilith, while in the end the revelation of her face illuminated and whitened, corresponding to the purification and redemption that parallel the Christian virginity myth. In the *Zohar* there are multiple passages on the adornment of the bride's jewelry, which are the ornaments of Torah, whose virginity is constantly renewed.

The high value of virginity in Christianity is rendered in rabbinic and Zoharic exegesis into corresponding values and primal experiences such as Torah study: "R. Samuel b. Nahmani expounded: 'Loving hind and a graceful roe,' why were the words of the Torah compared to a 'hind'? To tell you that as the hind has a narrow womb and is loved by its mate at all times as at the first hour of their copulation, so it is with the words of the Torah—They are loved by those who study them at all times as at the hour when they first made their acquaintance."[58] According to the sages, Torah study is an erotic activity, compared with copulating with a virgin. Similarly, the *Zohar* stresses the veneration of the *"peshat"* (simple explanation) paralleling the original and virginal state, as the final stage in the encounter with the beloved Torah, in the allegory of the maiden in the palace, in the section of *Saba de-Mishpatim*.[59]

In another passage the *Zohar* states that the *Shekhinah* is like Esther, who moves from lap to lap, whether she belongs to the Holy One blessed be He or the human Ṣaddiq, yet in the eyes of each of them she is his sole and exclusive woman. This conception is grounded in rabbinic Midrashim, which

---

57 Tanḥuma, Parashat Naso 10; Numbers Rabbah, 9:9.
58 b. Eruvin 54b. For the ornamenting ritual of the bride—Torah, for example, Zohar I: 8a.
59 Zohar II: 99a-b. Liebes, "Zohar and Eros," 94-5; Wolfson, "Beautiful Maiden"; Yisraeli, *The Interpretation of Secrets*, 219-26; Ruth Kara-Kaniel, "From *Petaḥ Einayim* to 'The Beautiful Maiden Without Eyes'—Fear and Vision in the *Zohar*," *Massekhet* 11 (2013): 61-97.

question how Esther, Mordecai's wife, could commit adultery by marrying Ahasuerus.[60] On this basis the *Zohar* develops an antinomian position portraying the *Shekhinah* as a bride and harlot, through its statement: "*In the evening she comes* to Her husband; *and in the morning she returns* to the righteous on earth—all with the permission of Her husband."[61] Through this reading a quasi-patriarchal template is preserved, since each man is granted the sense of exclusivity. Still, the passage receives a subversive mystical meaning: God sends the *Shekhinah* to the righteous ones (*Ṣaddiqim*), while each one sees her as his unique partner. This "polyandrous" arrangement, in which the *Shekhinah* has multiple husbands, is designed to remove the suspicion of adultery, which is originally ascribed to her only in order to cleanse her of all guilt and prove her innocence. Although there is not a clear expression here attesting to Esther's virginity, it may be said that the practice of immersion and purification in the Midrash upon which the *Zohar* is based ("that she used to rise from the lap of Ahasuerus and immerse and sit in the lap of Mordecai"), serves as a parallel to the idea of deliverance from the *sotah* trial.

As Charlotte Fonrobert has demonstrated, already in rabbinic literature the laws regarding menstruation may be seen as a Jewish parallel to "virginity practices" in Christianity.[62] The menstruation laws signify a borderland, which may be explained on the one hand as a masculine control of feminine sexuality and an instrument of reproduction and regulation of fecundity, and on the other hand as a space that provides Jewish women a spiritual and liberating way to be freed from masculine sovereignty. Esther is described in the *Zohar* as an exclusive "bride" for each husband, but at the price of promiscuity, which is gently alluded to in this passage.

---

60 b. *Sanhedrin* 74b and Ch. 4. As well as, b. *Megillah* 13a-14b: "Read not 'for a daughter' [*le-bat*], but 'for a house' [*le-bayit*] ... R. Jeremiah said: [This means] that she used to show the blood of her impurity to the Sages. Like as when she was brought up with him. Rabbah b. Lema said in the name of Rab: [This means] that she used to rise from the lap of Ahasuerus and bathe and sit in the lap of Mordecai."

61 *Zohar* III: 220b, Matt, *Pritzker*, 9:542. On Esther as a virgin bride paralleling Mary by Alkabetz and Hugh of St. Victor, see Green, "Shekhinah," 45. In contrast to this position, *Tiqqunei Zohar*, *Tiqun* 21 (58a), this passage suggests that Esther was not with Ahasuerus at all, and in her place was a demon in her likeness. This position is reminiscent of the view of Christian Docetism, according to which Jesus was not actually hung on the cross, but only "appeared to be," and is also echoed in the views of Euripides, Stesichorus, and others, for Helen did not actually arrive to Tory, but rather her eidolon. Yehuda Liebes, "Helen's Porphyry and Kiddush Ha-Shem," *Da'at*, 57-59 (2006): 83-120.

62 Fonrobert, *Menstrual Purity*, 38, 165; Boyarin, *Dying for God*, 67-92.

Similarly, in the passage about the biblical Miriam, the *Zohar* quotes a unique verse which does not exist in the Bible: *"raise a lament for the Virgin of Israel."* The fabrication of such a verse constitutes, in my opinion, evidence for the impact of the Christian myth on the *Zohar*.[63] In this context, it is important to emphasize that in spite of Miriam being conceived as a symbol of a "national mother" as Ilana Pardes has explicated, nowhere in the Bible is there evidence of her being a mother or wife. Seemingly, because of the concern that Miriam—an archetypical redeemer in Egypt who is called "maiden" (Exodus 2:8)—would be perceived as a virgin similar to Mary, the sages painstakingly portrayed her as a mother and married woman.[64] In contrast to the rabbinic Midrashim, the *Zohar* does not hesitate to present Miriam as *Shekhinah* and the *sefirah* of *Malkhut* corresponding to "Virgin Israel," whereas Moses her brother is portrayed in the same passage as the masculine divine and *sefirah* of *Tif'eret*. This model implies erotic relations between siblings, who both represent on the one hand, earthly celibacy and on the other hand complete *devequt* (cleaving) to the divine.[65]

Moses is already presented in the Bible as a quasi-naziritic figure cleaving to divinity, and subsequently the *Zohar* highlights his identity as the "master of the house and Torah," married to the *Shekhinah*.[66] This description of Miriam

---

63 *Zohar* III: 181b, Matt, *Pritzker*, 9.207. It appears as interweaving of verses from Amos 5:2 and Ezekiel 19:1, (see valso *Zohar* III: 6a). *Niṣuṣei Zohar* on *Zohar* I: 151a hints that sometimes the *Zohar* quotes verses "that have been lost to us," an explanation that is difficult to accept in this case. Abrams, "The Virgin Mary," 46, views this quotation as a slip of the pen in regards to the verse in Ezekiel 19:1. I stress that the change from "the princes of Israel" to "Virgin of Israel" is far too critical to be dismissed as merely a polemic or scribal error.

64 For a depiction of Miriam as a national mother, see Pardes, *Countertraditions*, 6-13. In *b. Sotah* 11b and *Exodus Rabbah* 48:4, she is presented as Caleb's wife and Hur's mother. Also Bithya, Pharaoh's daughter merits a child without any male intervention, thus implying, together with her name ("the daughter of God") that redemption depends on independent women and "virgins" in Judaism and Early Christianity. See *Pesiqta Zutarta* (*Leqaḥ Ṭov*) on Exodus 2. Deem, *Zot ha-Pa'am*, 253-61. Whereas Sachs-Shmueli, "The Image of the Prophetess Miriam," *Kabbalah* 33 (2015): 183-210 suggests that Miriam should be seen as a symbol of physical and mystical marriage and copulation.

65 *Zohar* III: 181b; Matt, *Prtizker*, 9:207-8. Between the three siblings prevailed a closeness similar to the body's limbs conjoined as one. Abrams, "The Virgin Mary," 17-24, 45-56, claims that this is a polemic against Mary's virginity and Jesus's singlehood, however this reading ignores the similarities between Mary and her son, and Miriam and her brother in the Bible.
Despite the tradition of the three siblings dying with the "kiss of God" (*b. Bava Batra* 17a), it appears that the *Zohar* is highlighting the unique relation between Moses and Miriam, and is portraying them as divine figures.

66 For example, see *Zohar* I: 236b; 239a; II: 235b; 244b, ect. Liebes, "Zohar and Eros," 98, fn. 189-91.

as the *Shekhinah* and Moses as her spouse radicalizes the tension between the marital ethos and earthly copulation in the *Zohar*, and the exaltation of special individuals like Miriam and Moses, who atone for the sins of the world with their deaths. This conception may easily be interpreted as demonstrating or at least alluding to Miriam and Moses as being free of sin, like Mary and her son. Daniel Abrams claims that this passage indicates an anti-Christian polemic regarding the issues of Mary's sexuality and the atoning death of the redeemer, whereas Ephraim Shoham demonstrated that in Ashkenaz in the 12th and 13th centuries Jews turned towards internal traditions about Miriam the Prophetess, in order to respond to the challenge presented to them by Christianity's Cult of the Virgin.[67] It appears that the *Zohar* reflects a multi-directional discourse, and a unification of traditions and reciprocal influences, which are not necessarily polemical. Just as Miriam's figure in the Bible—the independent leader who adopts her brother like a "son"—is able to influence the depictions of Mary and her miraculous impregnation in the beginning of Christianity, so too the Marian devotees and the reinforcement of the views that depict her marriage to Jesus in the Middle Ages, were able to influence the passages alluding to the "divine marriage" of Miriam and her brother in the *Zohar*.[68]

Implicit references to Mary's virginity also appear in the *Zohar* polemically. For example, in *Zohar Pinḥas* there is a passage concerning the rose, about which is written that when "closed" she does not emit a fragrance, paralleling the people of Israel: "As long as they are hard-hearted, not opening with *teshuvah*, they do not emit fragrance ... When they open with *teshuvah*, they immediately emit fragrance." In the frame-story a great eagle arrives and plucks the rose, and the text ends with a statement emphasizing the significance of the act as a transition from virginity to intercourse: "When it opens, it emits fragrance, and then it is brought forth from among the thorns, and Assembly of Israel delights in them. As is written: *Open to me, my sister, my love* (Song of Songs 5:2)."[69] In the background of this passage an additional allusion to the anti-virginal stance can be found, for the verse from Psalms that R. Pinḥas interprets

---

67 Abrams claims that the polemic against the Virgin Cult was prominent in Castile as much as Provence or Ashkenaz, despite the inclination of scholars to ignore this fact. Abrams, "The Virgin Mary," 23-4. According to Shoham-Steiner Jews in Ashkenaz responded to the external challenge by developing intra-Jewish traditions and rituals that sought to create "inner self-empowerment." Shoham-Steiner, "The Virgin Mary, Miriam, and Jewish Reactions to Marian Devotion in the High Middle Ages," *AJS Review* 37 (2013): 75-91.
68 On additional links between Mary and Miriam, Hosen-Rokem, *Web*, 135, 169, 246; Green, "Shekhinah."
69 *Zohar* III: 233a-b.

"*For the leader, on shushan edut* (rose of testimony) *A mikhtam of David*" (Psalm 60:1), sets the menstruant against the virgin.

The *Zohar* interprets the words "*Mikhtam* of David" (literally meaning epigram, but alluding to the word stain) as the stains that David saw on the moon—which symbolizes the *Shekhinah*. Here, the *Zohar* creates links in an exegetic-associative manner between the *Mikhtam* and the "*ketem*" (stain) of the bride, the Assembly of Israel, and King David himself in the *Zohar*. Further along in this homily, the Zoharic exegete discovers a sign of her wholeness and completeness within her defectiveness and ostracism, due to the possibility of her being purified before copulation.[70]

Just as the rose is plucked and deflowered—and does not preserve her "virginity"—so to Israel emits its fragrance at the moment that they repent from their sins and their love is accepted before God. Israel is identified in this passage with the moon and *Shekhinah*, which have signs of deficiency and seclusion, and therefore symbolize rectification and cyclical fulfillment. A similar text appears in *Zohar Ḥadash Song of Songs*, as an interpretation of the Talmudic ruling according to which a virgin is married on the fourth day of the week. In contrast to the perception of virginity as "immaculate," the *Zohar* connects the virgin with the waning moon and the figure of Lilith, as implied in the verse "Let there be lights in the firmament" (Gen. 1:(14(the word lights [*me'orot*] appearing in a defective form [without a *vav*] so it may be read as *me'arat* [curse] and the diphtheria disease).[71] Subsequently, the *Zohar* states that the marriages of virgins on the fourth day are evidence of disgrace and blemish, whose very virginity corresponds to darkness and hell, from which the virgin releases herself through her marriage.

Elliot Wolfson has discussed the connections between Lilith and Mary, suggesting that Lilith with her partner Samael express in the Zoharic exegesis a polemical treatment of Jesus and his mother.[72] However, as we saw in the sixth chapter, Lilith also merits a certain sympathy in the *Zohar*, as emerges from the attempt to depict her desires and motivations as well as emphasizing the dynamics of seduction and sexual potency that drive her. Biti Roi demonstrated

---

70 The connection to menstruation is alluded to in this passage not only through the word "stain" (already identified with David in *Midrash Tanḥuma* on Deut. 3), but also in the description of the Sanhedrin and Torah. See also *Pesiqta Rabbati* 10; *Canticles Rabbah* 7:7; *Tanḥuma Ki Tissa* 2; *Midrash Tehillim* 2.
71 *Zohar Ḥadash* 99b; following Gen. Rabbah 8:12.
72 Wolfson, *Venturing Beyond*, 93; Koren, *Forsaken*, 89-96; Shoham-Steiner, "The Virgin Mary." On the multiple negative images of Mary in kabbalistic literature, see Garb, "Gender and Power," 106.

from a different angle that the *Shekhinah* is perceived in *Ra'aya Meheimna* as a virginal and pure figure whom Moses slanders. Therefore, Moses must redeem her and marry her, following the biblical law: "*they shall fine him one hundred shekels of silver which they shall give to the young woman's father because he has slandered a virgin of Israel* (Deut. 22:19)."[73] While this trend seeks to highlight the conception of virginity as a stage towards the *Shekhinah*'s marriage, nonetheless, the harsh criticism of Moses emphasizes the use of virginity for the purpose of vindicating the feminine figure while condemning the male. Thus, the kabbalists' seemingly ambivalent attitude toward the common Christian ethos of the Middle Ages is exposed.

These views allude to different aspects of the virginity myth and are founded on creative Zoharic interpretations of biblical law and narrative—such as the laws regarding the *sotah* and menstruant, Esther's actions in Ahasuerus's house, and the stories of the Davidic heroines, Miriam, and Bathsheba.[74] It can be seen that the *Zohar* carefully chose these images in order to sympathetically present different facets of the *Shekhinah*'s personality and her capricious character. This choice indicates that the authors of the *Zohar* are reacting to the centrality of the virginity motif, while integrating it into the model of sexual promiscuity emerging form the development of an "internal-Jewish" messianic idea. Therefore, the disclosure of the *Shekhinah*'s whitened and purified face, as well as her being established as a pure bride following her being suspected of licentiousness, bears messianic significance and parallels the coming of the redemption. The sources of these conceptions are likely in the Ashkenazic areas in which Jews were exposed to the public and ritualistic character of the Cult of the Virgin, and they attest, as scholarship has suggested, to the migration of these ideas to the *Zohar* and Castile.[75]

For instance, Yehuda Liebes has shown that the figure of Mary and her son Jesus are alluded to in the Zoharic passages regarding the open *mem* and closed *mem*; Moshe Idel has presented motifs that have been transferred from the

---

73 *Zohar* III: 275b; Roi, "Shekhina," 274-5. On the emphasis on virginity in Philo's thought see Niehoff, *Sarah*, 436-9.
74 Bathsheba symbolizes the *Shekhinah* as a virgin in *Zohar* III: 6a-b. Through interpretation of the verse "Fallen, no more to rise, is maiden Israel; forsaken on her land, with no one to raise her up" (Amos 5:2) the *Zohar* stresses the *Shekhinah*'s dependence in the future redemption. This description is based on the perception of the Bathsheba as taken by David—unlike the other active dynastic mothers, but also as an initiating seducer, following the late Midrash (Ginzberg, *Ginze Schechter*, 1:166). An additional passage hints at Bathsheba's virginity when she was married to Uriah, *Zohar* I: 8b.
75 See Ta-Shma, *Revealed in the Hidden*; and the beginning of Ch. 5.

ancient Christian world to the Zoharic literature, such as conceiving Jerusalem as a bride descending from the heavens, and different perspectives of the "son" myth; Elliot Wolfson has discussed links between Christianity and the *Zohar* in a variety of gender and theological contexts, and more.[76] As mentioned before, Arthur Green and Peter Schäfer have contributed to this comparative discussion as well, by highlighting the parallels between Mary and the *Shekhinah* as sustaining and nourishing figures, who mediate between the divine and mundane worlds. Recently, Tzahi Weiss and Haviva Pedaya have suggested that the well-known parable in *Saba de-Mishpatim* about the beautiful maiden without eyes, is connected to the Christian imagery of *Ecclesia* and *Synagoga*, an image prominently displayed in the front of buildings and churches in the Ashkenazic public domain, and from there apparently it arrived to Spain and the *Zohar*.[77]

Indeed, the image of the beautiful maiden integrates an intentional mixture of the virgin and harlot figures within her. The maiden's bound eyes in the riddle of the old man hints at virginity, in light of the prevalent connection in the *Zohar* between intercourse and vision, in addition to the maiden's seductiveness, intermittently revealing herself to and disappearing from her beholders. As Pedaya has suggested, the riddle constitutes an example of the adoption of the motif of blindness associated with *Synagoga* and transforming it into a positive characterization. In addition, the tower and the palace in the continuation of the section, symbolize a chastity belt, acting as an oppositional symbol to the maiden's seductiveness. In the parable of the Torah the lover quotes just one verse: "You that are simple, turn in here," a verse loaded with dual erotic significance, and is attributed in Proverbs both to the harlot and wise woman (Proverbs 9:4, 16). The resemblance of *Ecclesia* and *Synagoga*'s femininity and beauty implies that the *Shekhinah* is capable of being a harlot and virgin concomitantly. In my understanding, the kabbalists feel free to adopt the imagery of virginity, which possesses a solid biblical and rabbinic tradition.[78] Alongside the presentation of

---

76 Liebes, *Studies*, 139-62; Idel, *Ben*; Idel, *Jerusalem*; Wolfson, *Language, Eros, Being*; Wolfson, "Eckhart." For a review of the studies, which began with Jellinek and Graetz until contemporary research, Abrams, "The Virgin Mary," 9-10.
77 Weiss, "Beautiful Maiden," 73, fn. 39; Pedaya, *Expanses*, 237-9. Yoav Elstein, "The Theme of The King Daughter Locked-Up in a Tower" in *Encyclopedia of the Jewish Story*, eds. Yoav Elstein, Avidov Lipsker, and Rella Kushelevsky (Ramat Gan: Bar Ilan University, 2004), 79-104, discusses the legend's transition from the motif of the "locked garden" which is identified with Mary's virginity, to the castle erotic symbolism in kabbalistic literature. See also Chapter five, fn. 38-9; Rachel Elior, "A Pretty Maiden Who Has No Eyes"; Kara-Kaniel, "Fear and Vision."
78 In contrast, Arthur Green claims that "Christianity developed a rich and variegated world of symbols, which are mainly maternal and virginal," in contrast to Judaism, which doesn't have

the *Shekhinah*'s transgressive side, the *Zohar* also stresses her virginity. In this way it is similar to the Christian myth, which itself does not lack for paradoxes, particularly the conception of Mary as a virgin but also as a mother, as well as her being presented as the bride, daughter, and even lover of her son.

***

The request to redeem and to be redeemed represents, on a psychoanalytic level, a universal wish, exposing the first primary fractures in individuals. This desire reveals humans' deepest perception of deficiencies (in the sense of "Tell me who your redeemer is, and I will know who you are"). The wish to bring redemption motivates the analytic process and is based on the belief that healing and repairing (*tiqqun*) is possible, even when a miraculous transformation is required to bridge the gap between reality and "the desired."[79] Furthermore, according to Freud, every woman wishes for a son, who represents her redemption and reconciliation of her phallic lack. Continuing in this line of thought, the wish to "give birth to a Messiah" symbolizes an attempt to break the existing order to establish a new and better world. Creativity, while linked to a basic "successful narcissism" and "healthy exhibitionism" according to Kohut and Mitchel, is also connected to the messianic wish to unite poles. It therefore resists divisions, whether of gender differences or other limits on the infinity of the soul. Overcoming gender differences is an ideal rooted in the messianic myths of the Hebrew Bible as well as in the OT, given expression through verses like Genesis 1:27 or Galatians 3:28.[80]

From the sources we have examined above, we find that in Judaism and Christianity, the mother of the Messiah represents a "liminal stage," within which two extremes of virginity and promiscuity complement each other. Both cultures share a mutual structure of linkage between antinomianism and

---

"a tradition glorifying virginity or celibacy," rather only emphasizes the sexual union. Green, "Shekhinah," 60.

79 According to Wilfred Bion, the birth of a messianic son is one of the major wishes of any dynamic group. However, this son must never be born, or all the erotic energy of the group will be lost. Wilfred Bion, *Experiences in Groups and Other Papers* (London: Tavistock, 1961). For more on the paradoxical relations between the messianic ideal and the necessity of not bringing it to full realization, see Scholem, *Messianic Idea*.

80 "There is no longer Jew or Greek, there is no longer slave or free, *there is no longer male and female*; for all of you are one in the Messiah Jesus" (Galatians 3:28). While it suggests equality between male and female, this verse was interpreted by the Church patriarchy as the necessary subordination and inferiority of the female to the male, thus losing its redemptive power and messianic ideal. Wolfson, *Venturing Beyond*.

redemption as an eschatological principle in which the profane is united with the sacred. The choice of such aberrant characteristics and sexual anomaly has implications not only for theological and philosophical fields, but also for questions of gender and ethics. The messianic mothers in both religions present complex models which are difficult to emulate. Displaying the female body in its abnormal context—in its absolute avoidance of sexuality, or in its radical externalization and promiscuity—enables a wide range of possible behaviors between these two extremes. However, in practice, as this model gains support from both God and the Sages, it seems that female sexual "perversion" is encouraged, and the destruction the borders of the self is promoted.

There is scholarly debate regarding the influence of myths and their role in the oppression or liberation of women. A range of scholarship examines the mythic model of "ideal motherhood" as one of the means of domination over women in reality. In the case of the mother of the Messiah, however, I believe that it is reality that has influenced the myth, rather than the opposite. In fact, mythical thinking by itself is not the source of oppression, but the way we read ourselves into it. As Robert Segal states: "Myths *solve* problems rather than *perpetuate* them, are progressive rather than regressive, and abet adjustment to the world rather than flight from it. Myths serve not, or not just, to vent bottled-up drives but also to sublimate them."[81]

Thus, it seems that in both religions, the messianic myth deepens the split between reality and fantasy, and neglecting the real mother in favor of phantasmic, idealized forms of motherhood. The contrasting perceptions of the mother of the Messiah in Judaism and Christianity derive from the split between the virgin and the harlot, as one model leans on the image of Mary, while the other leans on the biblical heroines of the Davidic dynasty. At the same time, in both religions, the myth of the messiah's mother challenges the existing order by encouraging transgression and antinomian behavior, as well as ideological, ethical, and theological rethinking. Furthermore, as we learn from Freud, virginity actually signifies the opposite fantasy of promiscuity, and vice versa. Thus, the attempt to unite the radicalized parts of the mother of the Messiah in the development of the discourse about her, allows us to see these opposite facets as a unified structure.[82]

---

81 Segal, *Hero*, ix; Ashur, "To Read and Write"; Gilbert & Gubar, *Madwomen*.
82 Since trauma splits reality into binaries and disrupts the experience of temporality, the configuration of the virgin image with the harlot may reflect an attempt to unite "mature consciousness" (such as sexualized parts of the self) with infantile unconscious levels (symbolized by the "virginal" aspects of the self). This combination accepts contradictions and

The myth of the messiah's mother may serve as a key to the greater appreciation of women, even to their liberation. This can be based on the return to a vibrant, positive, multi-faceted model of a messianic mother which includes aspects of the harlot and the virgin, paralleling the development of the male messianic hero in Jewish traditions.[83] As I have suggested, Mary's purity actually embodies the "repressed" in the biblical narratives and enables the reconstruction of the female genealogy of the house of David. As paradoxical as it may seem, Mary's virginity makes us aware of the biblical heroines' licentious sexuality and active choice of motherhood, thus forging a union from radical cultural poles.

Focusing on the image of the mother of the Messiah in Jewish myth emphasizes the concept of woman as a free subject who engages in real relationships. The Sages examine her independence and choices in the precarious situations in which she acts. Simultaneously, in these narratives, they offer creative solutions to the tension between motherhood and seduction. In the psychoanalytic context, the messianic myth proves that, indeed, as Winnicott states, "There is no such thing as a baby," and that "a baby cannot exist alone." The chosen son is an essential part of a relationship, a woven fabric built of mutual relations between mother and child who meet on the hinges of establishing an identity, procreation, separation and individuation, perversion and sexuality, which are all part of a repetitive process. Throughout history, the messianic couple (the Redeemer and his mothers), create one other time and again. Thus, King David is not "the chosen" as a result of his deeds, but thanks to his mothers, who processes their traumas and sexual transgressions into the transformative power of life. David reflects his maternal dynasty through the narrative of his life, as an "heir" of their seductive characters. His life patterns demonstrate an attempt of repairing their "sins" and traumatic spots. Therefore, it is by virtue of his mothers that he is a Messiah. Both the symbolic impregnation of Mary, as well as the "deviations" of the mothers of the Davidic dynasty, bear witness to the way in which the desecrated creates the holy. Moreover, they testify to the controversial relationship between the formation of a norm, transgression, and the establishment of Jewish sovereignty, as the foundation of the messianic idea.

---

allows the "Multiple Selves" to appear, as Bromberg, Mitchel and Loewald suggest; or, in Aron's terms, attributed to the metaphor of the primal scene that "illuminate the capacity to hold two contrasting ideas in mind at once without either fusing them or splitting them apart" ("The Internalized Primal Scene," 197). Therefore, giving birth to a messiah and bringing about redemption means achieving a playful stage where we can ""celebrate multiplicity" (ibid, 201), and bridge the gap between the image of the mother as an idol, and her real subjectivity.

83 On the feminine aspects of King David I will expand in the future.

Bibliography

Abramovitch, Dorit. *The King is Naked: Incest in a Feminist Perspective*. Tel Aviv: Babel Publishing House, 2004. [Hebrew]

Abrams, Daniel. *The Book Bahir: An Edition Based on the Earliest Manuscripts*, with an introduction by Moshe Idel. Los Angeles: Cherub Press, 1994. [Hebrew]

———. *Kabbalistic Manuscripts and Textual Theory: Methodologies of Textual Scholarship and Editorial Practice in the Study of Jewish Mysticism*. Jerusalem: Magnes Press, 2010.

———. "The Virgin Mary as the Moon that Lacks the Sun: A Zoharic Polemic Against the Veneration of Mary." *Kabbalah* 21 (2010): 7-56.

———. "The Condensation of the Symbol 'Shekhinah' in the Manuscripts of the 'Book Bahir.'" *Kabbalah* 16 (2007): 7-82.

———. *The Female Body of God in Kabbalistic Literature: Embodied Forms of Love and Sexuality in the Divine Feminine*. Jerusalem: Magnes Press, 2004. [Hebrew]

———. "Knowing the Maiden without Eyes: Reading the Sexual Reconstruction of the Jewish Mystic in a Zoharic Parable." *Da'at* 50-52 (2003): 487-511.

———. *Midrash Ha-Ne'elam Ruth*, Facsimile edition of Venice 1566 edition, with a critical introduction. Jerusalem: Personal Publisher, 1992. [Hebrew]

Adelman, Rachel. "Seduction and Recognition in the Story of Judah and Tamar and the Book of Ruth." *Nashim* 23 (2012): 87-109.

Alter, Robert. "How Convention Helps Us Read." *Prooftexts* 3 (1983): 115-130.

———. *The Art of Biblical Narrative*. New York: Basic Books, 1981.

Amit, Yaira. *Hidden Polemics in Biblical Narrative*. Translated by Jonathan Chipman. Leiden: Brill, 2000.

Anderson, Janice C. "Mary's Difference: Gender and Patriarchy in the Birth Narratives." *Journal of Religion* 67, no. 2 (1987): 183-202.

Anzaldúa, Gloria. *Borderlands La Frontera: The New Mestiza*. San Francisco: Spinsters/Aunt Lute, 1987.

Aron, Lewis. "The Internalized Primal Scene." *Psychoanalytic Dialogues* 5 (2005): 195-237.

Ashur, Dorit. "To Read and Write as If Your Life Depended on It: Personal Voices in American Feminist Writing on Literature in the 1970's and 1980's." PhD diss., Hebrew University, 2005. [Hebrew]

Asulin, Shifra. "The Flaw and its Correction: Impurity, The Moon and the Shekhinah—A Broad Inquiry into *Zohar* 3:79 (Aharei Mot)." *Kabbalah* 22 (2010): 193-251.

———. "The Stature of the Shekhina: The Place of the Feminine Divine Countenance (*Parzuf*) in Idra Rabba and Idra Zuta." In *Spiritual Authority: Struggles over Cultural Power in Jewish Thought*, edited by H. Kriesel, B. Huss, U. Ehrlich, 103-83. Beer Sheva: Ben-Gurion University Press, 2009. [Hebrew]

Atkinson, Clarissa W. *The Oldest Vocation: Christian Motherhood in the Middle Ages*. Ithaca: Cornell University Press, 1991.

Bal, Mieke. *Lethal Love: Feminist Literary Readings of Biblical Love Stories*. Bloomington: Indiana University Press, 1987.

Balint, Michael. *The Basic Fault: Therapeutic Aspects of Regression*. London: Tavistock Publications, 1968.

Barkai, Ron. *Science, Magic and Mythology in the Middle Ages*. Jerusalem: Van Leer Institute, 1987. [Hebrew]

Bataille, Georges. *Death and Sensuality: A Study of Eroticism and Taboo*. New York: Walker and Company, 1962.

Beauvoir, Simone de. *The Second Sex*. Translated by Howard M. Parshley. New York: Vintage Books, 1989.

Begg, Christopher T. *Judean Antiquities Books 5-7*. Flavius Josephus: Translation and Commentary 4. Leiden: Brill, 2005.

Benarroch, Jonatan. "'Yanuqa' and 'Sabba'—Two that are One: Allegory, Symbol and Myth in Zoharic Literature." PhD diss., Hebrew University, 2011. [Hebrew]

Benjamin, Jessica. *The Bonds of Love: Psychoanalysis, Feminism, and the Problem of Domination*. New York: Pantheon, 1988.

Ben-Naftali, Michal. *Childhood, a Book—A Novella*. Tel Aviv: Resling, 2006. [Hebrew]

———. *Chronicle of Separation: On Deconstruction's Disillusioned Love*. Translated by Mirjam Hadar. New York: Fordham University Press, 2015.

Biale, David. "Counter-History and Jewish Polemics Against Christianity: The *Sefer Toldot Yeshu* and the *Sefer Zerubavel*." *Jewish Social Studies* 6 (1999): 130-145.

———. *Eros and the Jews: From Biblical Israel to Contemporary America*. New York: Basic Books, 1992.

Biber, Monique. "Raza de-Eina: A Study in the Secrets of the Eye in the *Zohar*." Master's thesis, Bar Ilan University, 2006. [Hebrew]

Bion, Wilfred R. *Experiences in Groups and Other Papers*. London: Tavistock, 1961.

Bloom, Harold. *The Anxiety of Influence: A Theory of Poetry*. Oxford: Oxford University Press, 1997.

Bloom, Harold, and David Rosenberg. *The Book of J*. New York: Grove Weidenfeld, 1990.

Huss, Boaz. "A Dictionary of Foreign Words in the *Zohar*—A Critical Edition." *Kabbalah* 1 (1996): 167-204. [Hebrew]

———. *The Question about the Existence of Jewish Mysticism: The Genealogy of Jewish Mysticism and the Theologies of Kabbalah Research*. Jerusalem and Tel Aviv: Van Leer Institute Press and Ha-kibbutz Hameuchad, 2016. [Hebrew]

———. *Like the Radiance of the Sky: Chapters in the Reception History of the Zohar and the Construction of Its Symbolic Value*. Jerusalem: Bialik Institute, 2008. [Hebrew]

———. "A Sage is Preferable than a Prophet: Rabbi Shim'on Bar Yohai and Moses in the *Zohar*." *Kabbalah* 4 (1999): 103-139. [Hebrew]

Bollas, Christopher. *The Shadow of the Object: Psychoanalysis of the Unthought Known*. London: Free Association Books, 1987.

Botha, Phil. "Tamar, Rahab, Ruth, and Mary, the Bold Women in Ephrem the Syrian's Hymn De Nativitate 9." *Acta Patristica et Byzantina* 17 (2006): 1–21.

Botterweck, G. Johannes, Helmer Ringgren, and Heinz-Josef Fabry, eds. *Theological Dictionary of the Old Testament*. Cambridge: Eerdmans, 2003.

Boyarin, Daniel. *Carnal Israel: Reading Sex in Talmudic Culture*. Berkeley: University of California Press, 1993.

———. *Dying for God: Martyrdom and the Making of Christianity and Judaism*. Stanford: Stanford University Press, 1999.

———. "The Eye in the Torah: Ocular Desire in Midrashic Hermeneutic." *Critical Inquiry* 16, no. 3 (1990): 532-550.

———. *Intertextuality and the Reading of Midrash*. Bloomington: Indiana University Press, 1990.

Braun, Roddy. *1 Chronicles. Word Biblical Commentary*. Waco: Word Books, 1986.

Brenner, Arthur B. "Onan, the Levirate Marriage and the Genealogy of the Messiah." *Journal of the American Psychoanalytic Association* 10 (1962): 701-721.

Brenner, Athalya. "Biblical Attitudes toward Foreign Women and Exogamic Marriages." *Beth Miqra* 100 (1984): 179-185. [Hebrew]

———. *The Israelite Woman: Social Role and Literary Type in Biblical Narrative*. Sheffield: JSOT Press, 1985.

———. *Ruth and Naomi: Literary, Stylistic and Linguistic Studies in the Book of Ruth*. Tel Aviv: Sifriat Poalim, 1988. [Hebrew]

Bromberg, Philip M. *Standing in the Spaces*. New York: Routledge, 2001.

Brown, Raymond E. *The Birth of the Messiah: A Commentary on the Infancy Narratives in Matthew and Luke*. New Haven: Yale University Press, 1977.

Brown, Raymond E., et al., eds. *Mary in the New Testament*. Philadelphia: Fortress Press, 1978.

Buber, S., ed. *Lamentation Rabba*. Vilna 1899.

———. ed. *Midrash on Psalms (Midrash Tehillim or Shoḥer Tov)*. Vilna 1891. Repr. Jerusalem 1965.

———. ed. *Ruth Zuṭa*. Vilna: Rom, 1925.

———. ed. *Yalkut ha-Makhiri on Psalms*. Jerusalem, 1967.

Bush, Frederic W. *Ruth. Word Biblical Commentary*. Dallas: Word Books, 1996.

Bynum, Caroline W. *Fragmentation and Redemption: Essays on Gender and the Human Body in Medieval Religion*. New York: Zone Books, 1992.

———. *Jesus As Mother: Studies in the Spirituality of the High Middle Ages*. Berkeley: University of California Press, 1982.

Calderon, Ruth. *The Market, The Home, The Heart.* Jerusalem: Keter, 2001. [Hebrew]

Camp, Claudia V. *Wise, Strange, and Holy: The Strange Woman and the Making of the Bible.* Sheffield: Sheffield Academic Press, 2000.

Campbell, Edward F. *Ruth.* Anchor Bible 7. Garden City: Doubleday, 1975.

Campbell, Joseph. *The Hero with a Thousand Faces.* Cleveland: World Publishing Company, 1956.

Caspi, Mishael M., and Rachel S. Havrelock. *Women on the Biblical Road: Ruth, Naomi and the Female Journey.* Lanham: University Press of America, 1996.

Chodorow, Nancy. "Gender, Relation, and Difference in Psychoanalytic Perspective." In *Essential Papers on the Psychology of Women*, edited by C. Zanardi, 420-436. New York: New York University, 1980.

Cixous, Hélène. "The Laugh of the Medusa." Translated by Keith Cohen and Paula Cohen. *Signs*, 1, no. 4 (Summer 1976): 875-93.

Cixous, Hélène and Catherine Clément. *The Newly Born Woman.* Translated by Betsy Wing. Minneapolis: University of Minnesota Press, 1986.

Cohen, Jonathan. "The Traditions of Jesus' Birth against the Background of the Birth Stories in the Bible and Jewish Tradition." PhD diss., Hebrew University, 1989. [Hebrew]

Colson, F.H. and G.H. Whitaker, trans. *Philo.* 10 vols. Loeb Classical Library. Cambridge: Harvard University Press, 1929-1962.

Coon, Lynda. *Sacred Fictions: Holy Women and Hagiography in Late Antiquity.* Philadelphia: University of Pennsylvania Press, 1997.

R. Moses Cordovero. *'Or Yaqar.* 21 vols. Jerusalem: Ahuzat Israel, 1962-75.

Cover, Robert M. "The Supreme Court, 1982 Term—Foreword: Nomos and Narrative." *Harvard Law Review* 97, no. 4 (1983): 4-68.

Cross, Frank Leslie, and Elizabeth Anne Livingstone, eds. *The Oxford Dictionary of the Christian Church.* Oxford: Oxford University Press, 1997.

Davidovich-Eshed, Avital. "How Then Could I Gaze at a Virgin?" PhD diss., Tel Aviv University, 2014. [Hebrew]

Davies, Eryl W. "Ruth 4:5 and the Duties of the Goel." *Vetus Testamentum* 33, no. 2 (1983): 231-234.

Deem, Ariela. *Zot ha-Pa`am.* Tel Aviv: Reuven Mas, 1986. [Hebrew]

Doniger, Wendy. *The Bedtrick: Tales of Sex and Masquerade.* Chicago: University of Chicago Press, 2000.

Douglas, Mary. *Purity and Danger: An Analysis of Concepts of Pollution and Taboo.* London: Routledge, 1966.

Driver, S. R. *The Book of Genesis, with Introduction and Notes.* London: Methuen, 1904.

Dundes, Alan, and Lord Raglan, and Otto Rank. *In The Quest of the Hero.* Edited with an introduction by Robert Segal. Princeton: Princeton University Press, 1990.

Dworkin, Andrea. *Intercourse.* New York: Free Press, 1987.

Eben Shmuel, Yehuda, ed. *Midrashei Geula.* Jerusalem: Mesada Press, 1953.

Eliade, Mircea. *A History of Religious Ideas*, Volume 1: *From the Stone Age to the Eleusinian Mysteries.* Translated by Willard R. Trask. Chicago: University of Chicago Press, 1978.

———. *The Myth of the Eternal Return*. Translated by Willard R. Trask. Princeton: Princeton University Press, 1954.

Eliade, Mircea. *Rites and Symbols of Initiation: The Mysteries of Birth and Rebirth*. New York: Harvill Press, 1958.

Elior, Rachel. "A Pretty Maiden Who Has No Eyes". In *Blessed Who Made Me a Woman'* eds. David Joel Ariel, Maya Leibovich, Yoram Mazor, 37–56. Tel Aviv: Yedioth Ahronoth, 1999.

Elliott, Dyan H. *Spiritual Marriage: Sexual Abstinence in Medieval Wedlock*. Princeton: Princeton University Press, 1993.

Elliott, James K., ed. *The Apocryphal New Testament: A Collection of Apocryphal Christian Literature in an English Translation*. Edited by James K. Elliott. Oxford: Clarendon, 2005.

Elqayam, Avraham. "To Know the Messiah: The Dialectic of Sexual Discourse in the Messianic Thought of Nathan of Gaza." *Tarbiz* 65/4 (1996): 637-670. [Hebrew]

Elstein, Yoav. "The Theme of 'The King Daughter Locked-Up in a Tower." *Encyclopedia of the Jewish Story*, edited by Yoav Elstein, Avidov Lipsker, and Rella Kushelevsky, 79-104. Ramat Gan: Bar Ilan University, 2004. [Hebrew]

Epstein, Jacob N. *Introduction to Amoraic Literature*. Jerusalem: Magnes Press, 1962. [Hebrew]

Ettinger, Bracha L. *The Matrixial Borderspace*. Minnesota: University of Minnesota Press, 2006.

Farber-Ginat, Asi. "'The Shell Precedes the Fruit'—On the Question of the Origin of Metaphysical Evil in Early Kabbalistic Thought." In *Myth and Judaism*, edited by Haviva Pedaya, 118-142. Jerusalem: Bialik Institute, 1996. [Hebrew]

Feldman, Louis H. *Judean Antiquities Books 1-4*. Flavius Josephus: Translation and Commentary 3. Leiden: Brill, 2000.

Felix, Iris and Ruth Kara-Kaniel. "Fire that Bears Fire: The Literary Development of the *Zohar* and the Flourish of Zoharic Exegesis at the Beginning of the 14th Century: Menahem Recanati and Joseph Angelet." *Jerusalem Studies in Jewish Thought* 24 (2015): 157-200.

Felix, Iris. "Theurgy, Magic and Mysticism in the Kabbalah of R. Joseph of Shushan." PhD diss., Hebrew University, 2005. [Hebrew]

Fisch, Harold. "Ruth and the Structure of the Covenant History." *Vetus Testament* 32 (1982): 425-437.

Fishbane, Michael. "The Holy One Sits and Roars—Mythopoesis and the Midrashic Imagination." In *The Midrashic Imagination, Jewish Exegesis, Thought, and History*, 1-21. Albany: SUNY Press, 1993.

Flusser, David. *Jesus*. Jerusalem: Magnes Press, 2001. [Hebrew]

Flusser, David. "The Reflection of Jewish Messianic Beliefs in Early Christianity." In *Messianism and Eschatology*, edited by Zvi Baras, 103-134. Jerusalem: Zalman Shazar Center, 1983. [Hebrew]

Fonrobert, Charlotte E. "The Handmaid, the Trickster and the Birth of the Messiah.'" In *Current Trends in the Study of Midrash*, edited by Carol Bakhos, 245-275. Leiden: Brill, 2006.

———. *Menstrual Purity: Rabbinic and Christian Reconstruction of Biblical Gender*. Stanford: Stanford University Press, 2000.

Foucault, Michel. *Discipline and Punishment: The Birth of the Prison.* New York: Vintage Books, 1979.

———. *The History of Sexuality: Volume 1: The Will to Knowledge.* Translated by Robert Hurley. Harmondsworth: Penguin Books, l998.

———. *Language, Counter-Memory, Practice: Selected Essays and Interviews.* Ithaca: Cornell University Press, 1977.

Freud, Sigmund, and Josef Breuer. "On the Psychical Mechanism of Hysterical Phenomena." *International Journal of Psycho-Analysis* 37 (1983): 8-13.

Freud, Sigmund. *The Standard Edition of the Complete Psychological Works of Sigmund Freud*, 24 Vols. Edited and Translated by J. Strachey. London: Hogarth Press and Institute of Psychoanalysis, 1953-1974.

Fromm, Erich. *Psychoanalysis and Religion.* New Haven: Yale University Press, 1972.

Frymer-Kensky, Tikva. *Reading the Women of the Bible.* New York: Schocken Books, 2002.

Fuchs, Esther. *Sexual Politics in the Biblical Narrative: Reading the Hebrew Bible as a Woman.* Sheffield: Sheffield Academic Press, 2000.

Fulton, Rachel. *From Judgment to Passion: Devotion to Christ and the Virgin Mary, 800-1200.* New York: Columbia University Press, 2002.

Galpaz-Feller, Pnina. *The Sound of Garments: Garments in the Bible: Do the Clothes Make the Man?* Jerusalem: Carmel Publishing, 2008. [Hebrew]

Gamilieli, Devorah Bat David. *Psychoanalysis and Kabbalah: The Masculine and Feminine in Lurianic Kabbalah.* Los Angeles: Cherub Press, 2006. [Hebrew]

Gane, Roy. "Holiness Book." In *Leviticus. Olam ha-Tanakh*, edited by Moshe Weinfeld, 9. Tel Aviv: Revivim, 2002. [Hebrew]

Garb, Jonathan. "Gender and Power in Kabbalah: A Theoretical Investigation." *Kabbalah* 13 (2005): 79-107.

———. *Manifestations of Power in Jewish Mysticism: From Rabbinic Literature to Safedian Kabbalah.* Jerusalem: Magnes Press, 2005. [Hebrew]

Geary, Patrick J. *Women at the Beginning: Origin Myths from the Amazons to the Virgin Mary.* Princeton: Princeton University Press, 2006.

Gikatilla, Joseph. *Sha'arei Orah.* 2 vols. Edited by Joseph Ben-Shlmo. Jerusalem: Bialik Institute, 1981. [Hebrew]

Gilbert, Sandra M., and Susan Gubar. *The Madwomen in the Attic: The Woman Writer and the Nineteenth-Century Literary Imagination.* New Haven: Yale University Press, 1979.

Giller, Pinchas. *Reading the Zohar: The Sacred Text of the Kabbalah.* Oxford: Oxford University Press, 2001.

Gilligan, Carol. *In a Different Voice: Psychological Theory and Women's Development.* Cambridge: Harvard University Press, 1982.

Ginzberg, Louis. *Ginze Schechter: Genizah Studies in Memory of Doctor Solomon Schechter*, Volume 1: Midrash and Haggadah. New York: Jewish Theological Seminary of America, 1928.

———. *The Legends of the Jews.* Philadelphia: Jewish Publication Society, 2003.

Goldreich, Amos. *Automatic Writing in Zoharic Literature and Modernism.* Los Angeles: Cherub Press, 2010. [Hebrew]

———. "The Flaw and its Correction: Impurity, The Moon and the Shekhinah—A Broad Inquiry into *Zohar* 3:79 (Aharei Mot)." *Kabbalah* 22 (2010): 193-251.

———. "The Mystical Self-Image of the Author of Tiqqune ha-*Zohar*" in *Massu'ot*, edited by Michal Oron and Amos Goldreich, 459-496. Jerusalem: Bialik Institute, 1994. [Hebrew]

Gottlieb, Ephraim. *Studies in Kabbalistic Literature*. Edited by Joseph Hacker, Tel Aviv: Rosenberg, 1976. [Hebrew]

Graves, Robert. *The White Goddess: A Historical Grammar of Poetic Myth*. New York: Noonday, 1948.

Green, Arthur. *Keter: The Crown of God in Early Jewish Mysticism*. Princeton: Princeton University Press, 1997.

———. "Shekhinah, the Virgin Mary, and the Song of Songs: Reflections on a Kabbalistic Symbol in Its Historical Context." *AJS Review* 26, no. 1 (2002): 1-52.

Grossman, Abraham. "David—The Loathsome and the Repulsive: A Controversial Midrash of the Middle Ages." In *Studies in Bible and Exegesis*, Volume 5, edited by M. Garsiel, S. Vargon, A. Frisch, and J. Kugel, 341–349. Ramat Gan: Bar Ilan University Press, 2000.

Gruenwald, Ithamar. "Myths and Historical Truth." In *Myths in Judaism—History, Thought, Literature*, edited by Moshe Idel and Ithamar Gruenwald, 15-52. Jerusalem: The Zalman Shazar Center, 2004. [Hebrew]

Halbertal, Moshe, and Avishai Margalit, *Idolatry*. Translated by Naomi Goldblum. Cambridge: Harvard University Press, 1992.

Halbertal, Moshe. *Concealment and Revelation: Esotericism in Jewish Thought and its Philosophical Implications*. Translated by Jackie Feldman. Princeton: Princeton University Press, 2007.

———. *By Way of Truth: Nahmanides and the Creation of Tradition*. Jerusalem: Shalom Hartman Institute, 2006. [Hebrew]

———. *Interpretative Revolutions in the Making*. Jerusalem: Magnes, 1997. [Hebrew]

Hallamish, Moshe. *The Kabbalah in Liturgy, Halakhah, and Custom*. Ramat Gan: Bar-Ilan University Press, 2000. [Hebrew]

———. "Nefilat Apayyim as an Example of Kabbalistic Influence on the Order of Prayer." *Mahanayim* 6 (1994): 124–133. [Hebrew]

Halperin, David J. "A Sexual Image in *Hekhalot Rabbati* and Its Implications." In *Proceedings of the First International Conference on the History of Jewish Mysticism: Early Jewish Mysticism*, edited by Joseph Dan, 117-132. Jerusalem: Hebrew University, 1987.

Hangel, Martin. *Whose Child, The Son of God: The Origin of Christology and the History of Jewish-Hellenistic Religion*. Translated by John Bowden. Philadelphia: Fortress Press, 1976.

Hasan-Rokem, Galit. *Web of Life: Folklore and Midrash in Rabbinic Literature*. Translated by Batya Stein. Stanford: Stanford University Press, 2000.

Hellner-Eshed, Melila. "On Love and Creativity: Drops from Sea of Myths of Cordovero on the Shekhinah." In *Ma'ayan Ein Ya'aqov: The Fourth Ma'ayan from Sefer Elemah*, edited and annotated by Beracha Sack, 161-188. Beer Sheva: Ben-Gurion University Press, 2009. [Hebrew]

———. *A River Flows from Eden: The Language of Mystical Experience in the Zohar*. Translated by Nathan Wolowski. Stanford: Stanford University, 2009.

———. "The Zealot of the Covenant and the Estatic Elijan and Habakkuk in the *Zohar*: On the Masculine and Feminine in the Human Psyche." *Kabbalah* 22 (2010): 149-192. [Hebrew]

Herman, Judith L. *Trauma and Recovery: The Aftermath of Violence-From Domestic Abuse to Political Terror*. New York: Basic Books, 1992.

Higger, M., ed. Brooklyn: Moinester Publishing Company, 1936.

Himmelfarb, Martha. "The Mother of Messiah in the Talmud Yerushalmi and Sefer Zerubbabel." In *The Talmud Yerushalmi and Graeco-Roman Culture*, Volume 3, edited by Peter Schäfer, 369-389. Tübingen: Mohr Siebeck, 2002.

———. "Sefer Zerubbabel." In *Rabbinic Fantasies: Imaginative Narratives from Classical Hebrew Literature*, edited by D. Stern and M. J. Mirsky, 67-90. Philadelphia: Jewish Publication Society, 1990.

Hirshman, Marc. *A Rivalry of Genius: Jewish and Christian Biblical Interpretation in Late Antiquity*. Albany: SUNY Press, 1996.

———. "Changing Foci of Holiness: Honi and His Grandsons." *Tura* 1 (1989): 109–118. [Hebrew]

———. *Torah for the Entire World: A Universalist School of Rabbinic Thought*. Tel Aviv: Hakibbutz Hameuchad, 1999. [Hebrew]

Hollywood, Amy. "Sexual Desire, Divine Desire." In *Toward A Theology of Eros: Transfiguring Passion at the Limits of Discipline*, edited by V. Burrus and C. Keller, 119-133. New York: Fordham University Press, 2006.

Horowitz, Menachem. *Encyclopaedia Hebraica*, s.v. "Zenut." Jerusalem: Encyclopedia Publishing Company, 1965.

Horowitz, ed. *Sifre Ba-Midbar*. Leipzig 1917, 2nd ed. Jerusalem, 1966.

Huddlestun, John R. "Unveiling the Versions: The Tactics of Tamar in Genesis 38:15." *Journal of the Hebrew Scriptures* 3 (2001): 325-343.

Huizinga, Johan. *Homo Ludens: A Study of the Play Element in Culture*. London: Routledge & Kegan Paul, 1949.

Huss, Boaz. "A Dictionary of Foreign Words in the *Zohar*—A Critical Edition." *Kabbalah* 1 (1996): 167-204. [Hebrew]

———. *The Question about the Existence of Jewish Mysticism: The Genealogy of Jewish Mysticism and the Theologies of Kabbalah Research*. Jerusalem and Tel Aviv: Van Leer Institute Press and Ha-kibbutz Hameuchad, 2016. [Hebrew]

———. "A Sage is Preferable than a Prophet: Rabbi Shim'on Bar Yohai and Moses in the *Zohar*." *Kabbalah* 4 (1999): 103-139. [Hebrew]

———. *Like the Radiance of the Sky: Chapters in the Reception History of the Zohar and the Construction of Its Symbolic Value*. Jerusalem: Bialik Institute, 2008. [Hebrew]

Idel, Moshe. "Additional Fragments from the Writings of R. Joseph of Hamadan." *Da'at* 21 (1988): 47-55. [Hebrew]

———. *Ascensions on High in Jewish Mysticism: Pillars, Lines, Ladders*. Budapest: Central European University Press, 2005.

———. *Ben: Sonship and Jewish Mysticism.* New Haven and London: Continuum, 2007.
———. "The Concept of the Torah in Hekhalot Literature and Its Metamorphoses in Kabbalah." *Jerusalem Studies in Jewish Thought* 1 (1981): 23-84. [Hebrew]
———. "The Interpretations of the Secret of the 'Arayyot in Early Kabbalah." *Kabbalah* 12 (2004): 93-103. [Hebrew]
———. "Kabbalah and Elites in Thirteenth-Century Spain." *Mediterranean Historical Review* 9, no. 1 (1994): 5-19.
———. *Kabbalah and Eros.* New Haven: Yale University Press, 2005.
———. *Kabbalah: New Perspectives.* New Haven: Yale University, 1988.
———. "The Kabbalah's 'Window of Opportunities,' 1270- 1290." In *Me'ah She'arim: Studies in Medieval Jewish Spiritual Life in Memory of Isadore Twersky*, edited by Gerald J. Blidstein, Ezra Fleischer, Carmi Horowitz, and Bernard Septimus, 5-32. Jerusalem: Magnes Press, 2001.
———. *Messianic Mystics.* New Haven: Yale University Press, 1998.
———. *Messianism and Mysticism.* Tel Aviv: Broadcast University, 1992. [Hebrew]
———. "Patterns of Redemptive Activity in the Middle Ages." in *Messianism and Eschatology*, edited by Zvi Baras, 253-280. Jerusalem: Zalman Shazar Center, 1983. [Hebrew]
———. "Torah Ḥadashah: Messiah and the New Torah in Jewish Mysticism and Modern Scholarship." *Kabbalah* 21 (2010): 57-109.
Irigaray, Luce. *Je, Tu, Nous: Towards a Culture of Difference.* Translated by Alison Martin. New York and London: Routledge, 1993.
———. *This Sex Which Is Not One.* Translated by Catherine Porter. Ithaca: Cornell University Press, 1985.
———. *Sexes and Genealogies.* Translated by Gillian Gill. New York: Columbia University Press, 1993.
Iser, Wolfgang. *The Act of Reading: A Theory of Aesthetic Response.* London: Routledge and Kegan Paul, 1978.
Ish Shalom, M., ed. *Pesiqta Rabbati.* Tel Aviv, 1951.
Jansen, Katherine Ludwig. *The Making of the Magdalen: Preaching and Popular Devotion in the Later Middle Ages.* Princeton: Princeton University Press, 2001.
Jung, Carl G. *Memories, Dreams, Reflections.* Edited by Aniela Jaffé and translated by Richard Winston and Clara Winston. New York: Vintage, 1965.
———. *Psychology and Religion.* New Haven: Yale University Press, 1938.
———. *The Psychology of the Transference.* New York: Routledge, 1983.
Kafka, Franz. *Parables and Paradoxes.* New York: Schocken, 1971.
Kalimi, Isaac. *The Book of Chronicles—Historical Writing and Literary Devices.* Jerusalem: Bialik Institute, 2000. [Hebrew]
Kalmanofsky, Jeremy. "Sins for the Sake of God." *Conservative Judaism* 54, no. 2 (2002): 3-24.
Kara-Kaniel, Ruth. "Consumed by Love: The Death of Nadav and Avihu as a Ritual of Erotic Mystical Union." *Teuda* 26 (2014): 585-653
———. "From *Petaḥ Einayim* to 'The Beautiful Maiden Without Eyes'—Fear and Vision in the Zohar." *Massekhet* 11 (2013): 61-97. [Hebrew]

———. "To Write or Not to Write." In *The Zoharic Story*, edited by Jonatan Benarroch, Melila Hellner-Eshed, and Yehuda Liebes. Jerusalem: Yad Yitzhak Ben Zvi, 2017. [Hebrew] (forthcoming)

Katz, Jacob. *Halakhah and Kabbalah: Studies in the History of Judaism*. Jerusalem: Magnes Press, 1984. [Hebrew]

Kauffman, Tsippi. *In all Your Ways Know Him: The Concept of God and Avodah Be-Gashmiyut in the Early Stages of Hasidism*. Ramat Gan: Bar Ilan University Press, 2009. [Hebrew]

Kelly, Kathleen C. *Performing Virginity and Testing Chastity in the Middle Ages*. London and New York: Routledge, 2000.

Kessler, Gwynn. *Conceiving Israel: The Fetus in Rabbinic Narrative*. Philadelphia: University of Pennsylvania Press, 2009.

King, Karen L. *The Gospel of Mary of Magdala: Jesus and the First Woman Apostle*. California: Polebridge Press, 2003.

Klein, Melanie. *Love, Guilt and Reparation and Other Works 1921-1945* London: Hogarth Press, 1975.

Knight, Jonathan. "The Portrait of Mary in the Ascension of Isaiah." In *Which Mary—The Marys of Early Christian Traditions*, edited by S. Jones, 91–105. Leiden: Brill, 2003.

Knohl, Israel. *Biblical Beliefs*. Jerusalem: Magnes Press, 2007. [Hebrew]

———. *The Many Faces of Monotheistic Religion*. Tel Aviv: The Broadcasted University, 1995. [Hebrew]

———. *The Messiah Before Jesus: The Suffering Servant of the Dead Sea Scrolls*. Berkeley: University of California Press, 2000.

Knoppers, Gary N. *1 Chronicles 1-9: A New Translation with Introduction and Commentary*. Anchor Bible 12. New York: Doubleday, 2003.

Kohut, Heinz. "Forms and Transformations of Narcissism." *Journal of the American Psychoanalytic Association* 14 (1966): 243–272.

Koren, Sharon. *Forsaken: The Menstruant in Medieval Jewish Mysticism*. Waltham: Brandeis University Press, 2011.

Kosman, Admiel. *Femininity in the Spiritual World of the Talmudic Story*. Tel Aviv: Hakibbutz Hameuchad, 2008. [Hebrew]

Kramer, Phyllis Silverman. "Biblical Women that Come in Pairs: The Use of Female Pairs as a Literary Device in the Hebrew Bible." In *Genesis: The Feminist Companion to the Bible*, edited by Athalya Brenner, 218-232. Sheffield: Sheffield Academic Press, 1998.

Kristeva, Julia. *In the Beginning Was Love: Psychoanalysis and Faith*. Translated by Arthur Goldhammer. New York: Columbia University Press, 1987.

———. *Black Sun: Depression and Melancholia*. Translated by Leon S. Roudiez. New York: Columbia University Press, 1989.

———. *Powers of Horror: An Essay on Abjection*. Translated by Leon S. Roudiez. New York: Columbia University Press, 1982.

———. *Strangers to Ourselves*. Translated by Leon S. Roudiez. New York: Columbia University Press, 1991.

———. *Tales of Love*. Translated by Leon S. Roudiez. New York: Columbia University Press, 1987.
Kron, Tamar. *Us, Adam and Eve: Myths and Psychology of Couple Relationship*. Tel Aviv: Hakibbutz Hameuchad, 2004. [Hebrew]
Krupp, Michael. *Sefer Toldos Jeschu: A Jewish Life of Jesus*. Facsimile of the First Edition., Altdorf 1681. Jerusalem: Hebrew University, 2001.
Kugel, James L. *Traditions of the Bible: A Guide to the Bible as It was at the Start of the Common Era*. Cambridge: Harvard University Press, 1998.
Lacan, Jacques. "The Function and Field of Speech and Language in Psychoanalysis (1953)." In Écrits (A Selection). Translated by Alan Sheridan, 30–113. London and New York: Routledge, 1977.
LaCapra, Dominick. *Writing History, Writing Trauma*. Baltimore: Johns Hopkins University Press, 2001.
Laplanche, Jean and Bertrand Pontalis. *The Language of Psychoanalysis*. Translated by D. N. Smith. New York: W.W. Norton & Company, 1973.
Laqueur, Thomas. *Making Sex: Body and Gender from the Greeks to Freud*. Cambridge: Harvard University Press, 1990.
Leiner, ed. *Seder Olam Rabbah*. Warsaw, 1905.
R. Moses de León. *Sefer Sheqel ha-Qodesh*. Edited by Charles Mopsik. Los Angeles: Cherub Press, 1996. [Hebrew]
Lerner, Myron B. "A New Fragment of *Midrash Eshet Hayil* and the Opening Section of a Work Dealing with Twelve Women." In *Studies in Talmudic and Midrashic Literature: In Memory of Tirzah Lifshitz*, edited by M. Bar-Asher, A Edrei, J. Levinson, and B. Lifshitz, 265-292. Jerusalem: Bialik Institute, 2005. [Hebrew]
Lerner, Myron B. "The Book of Ruth in Aggadic Literature and Midrash Ruth Rabba." 2 vols. Ph.D. diss., Hebrew University, 1971. [Hebrew]
Levine, Amy Jill. "Matthew." In *The Women's Bible Commentary*, edited by Carol A. Newsom and Sharon H. Ringe, 252-262. London: SPCK, 1992.
———. "Ruth." In *The Women's Bible Commentary*, edited by Carol A. Newsom and Sharon H. Ringe, 78-84. London: SPCK, 1992.
Levinson, Joshua. *The Untold Story: Art of the Expanded Biblical Narrative in Rabbinic Midrash*. Jerusalem: Magnes Press, 2005. [Hebrew]
Lévi-Strauss, Claude. *The Elementary Structures of Kinship*. Translated by James Bell and John von Sturmer. Boston: Beacon Press, 1969.
Lichtenstein, Aaron. "Aveirah Lishmah in Halakha and Thought." In *The Other: Between Man and Himself and His Fellow*, edited by Haim Deutsch and Menachem Ben-Sasson, 99–125. Tel Aviv: Yedioth Aharonoth, 2001. [Hebrew]
———. "Does Jewish Tradition Recognize an Ethic Independent of Halakha?" In *Modern Jewish Ethics*, edited by Marvin Fox, 62-88. Columbus: Ohio State University Press, 1975.
Lieberman, Saul. *Sheki'in: Some Thoughts on Jewish Legends, Customs and Literary Sources Found in Karaite and Christian Works*. Jerusalem: Wahrmann Books, 1970. [Hebrew]

———. *Tosefta ki-Feshutah: A Comprehensive Commentary on the Tosefta*, 10 vols. New York: Jewish Theological Seminary, 1955-1988. [Hebrew]

Liebes, Yehuda. "A Bride as She is: On R. Moshe Cordovero: Ma'ayan Ein Ya'aqov." *Massekhet* 9 (2009): 191-198. [Hebrew]

———. "Clothed Nudity: The Esoteric Cult of Philo." *Jerusalem Studies in Jewish Thought* 24 (2015): 9-28. [Hebrew]

———. *God's Story: Collected Essays on the Jewish Myth*. Jerusalem: Carmel Publishing, 2009. [Hebrew]

———. "Helen's Porphyry and Kiddush Ha-Shem." *Da'at*, 57-59 (2006): 83-120. [Hebrew]

———. "Indeed the Shekhinah a Virgin?: On the Book of Arthur Green." *Pe'amim* 101-2 (2005): 303–313. [Hebrew]

———. "Mazmiah Qeren Yeshu'ah." *Jerusalem Studies in Jewish Thought* 3 (1984): 313-349. [Hebrew]

———. "Myth vs. Symbol in the *Zohar* and Lurianic Kabbalah." In *Essential Papers on Kabbalah*, edited by Lawrence Fine, 212-242. New York: New York University, 1995.

———. *On Sabbateanism and Its Kabbalah: Collected Essays*. Jerusalem: Bialik Institute, 1995. [Hebrew]

———. "Sections of the *Zohar* Lexicon." PhD. diss., Hebrew University, 1976. [Hebrew]

———. *Studies in Jewish Myth and Jewish Messianism*, translated by Batya Stein. Albany: SUNY Press, 1993.

———. *Studies in the Zohar*, translated by Stephanie Nakache, Penina Peli, and Arnold Schwartz. Albany: SUNY Press, 1993.

———. "'Two Young Roes of a Doe'": The Secret Sermon of Isaac Luria Before his Death." *Jerusalem Studies in Jewish Thought* 10 (1992): 113-169. [Hebrew]

———. "*Zohar* and Eros." *Alpayyim* 9 (1994): 67-119. [Hebrew]

———. "The *Zohar* and the Tiqqunim: From Renaissance to Revolution." In *New Developments in Zohar Studies*, edited by Ronit Meroz, *Te'uda* 21/22 (2007): 251-302. [Hebrew]

———. "The *Zohar* as a Halakhic Book." *Tarbiz* 64 (1995): 581-605. [Hebrew]

———. "The *Zohar* as Renaissance." *Da'at* 46 (2001): 5–11. [Hebrew]

Loewald, Hans W. *The Essential Loewald: Collected Papers and Monographs*. Hagerstown: University Publishing Group, 2000.

Loewenstamm, Samuel E. *Encyclopedia Miqra'it*, s.v. "Arayot," "Zenut u-Zenunim," Jerusalem: Bialik Institute, 1954-1971. [Hebrew]

Longstaff, Thomas R. W. "From the Birth of Jesus to the Resurrection: Women in the Gospel of Matthew." In *When Judaism and Christianity Began: Essays in Memory of Anthony J. Saldarini*, Volume 1, edited by Alan Jeffery Avery-Peck, Daniel J. Harrington and Jacob Neusner, 147-178. Leiden: Brill, 2004.

Lorberbaum, Yair. *Disempowered King: Monarchy in Classical Jewish Literature*. London: Continuum, 2011.

———. *In God's Image: Myth, Theology, and Law in Classical Judaism*. Cambridge: Cambridge University Press, 2015.

R. Moses Ḥayyim Luzzatto. "*Sefer Qine'at H' Ṣeva'ot.*" In *Ginzei Ramḥal*. Edited by Haim Friedlander. Benei Berak, Friedlander 1990. [Hebrew]

MacKinnon, Catharine A. "Prostitution and Civil Rights." *Michigan Journal of Gender and Law* 1 (1993): 13–31.

Maggid Meisharim. Edited by Y.A. Bar Lev. Petah Tiqwah, 1990.

Malinowski, Bronislaw. *Sex and Repression in Savage Society*. London: Routledge & Kegan Paul, 1927.

Malkiel, David. "Manipulating Virginity: Digital Defloration in Midrash and History." *JSQ* 13 (2006): 105-127.

Mandelbaum, B., ed. *Pesiqta de-Rab Kahana*. 2 vols. New York, 1962.

Marcus, Ivan G. *Rituals of Childhood, Jewish Acculturation in Medieval Europe*. New Haven: Yale University Press, 1996.

Margulies, M., ed. *Midrash Ha-Gadol*. Jerusalem: Mosad HaRav Kook, 1967.

———. ed. *Va yikra Rabbah*. 5 vols., 3rd ed., Jerusalem, 1993.

Matt, Daniel C. "*Matnita Dilan*: A Technique of Innovation in the *Zohar*." *Jerusalem Studies in Jewish Thought* 8 (1989): 123–145. [Hebrew]

Matt, Daniel C., and Joel Hecker, and Nathan Wolski. *The Zohar: Pritzker Edition*. 12 Vols. 11-12. Stanford: Stanford University Press, 2003-2016.

Matt, Daniel C., ed. David ben Yehudah he-Ḥasid. *The Book of Mirrors: Sefer Mar'ot ha-Ẓove'ot*. Chico: Scholars Press, 1982. [Hebrew]

———. "New-Ancient Words: the Aura of Secrecy in the *Zohar*." In *Gershom Scholem's Major Trends in Jewish Mysticism 50 Years After*, edited by Peter Schäfer and Joseph Dan, 181-207. Tübingen: J. C. B. Mohr, 1993.

Meltzer, Donald, and Meg Harris Williams. *The Apprehension of Beauty: The Role of Aesthetic Conflict in Development, Art and Violence*. Perthshire: Clunie Press, 1988.

Menn, Esther. *Judah and Tamar (Genesis 38) in Ancient Jewish Exegesis: Studies in Literary Form and Hermeneutics*. Leiden: Brill, 1997.

Meroz, Ronit. "The Middle Eastern Origins of Kabbalah." *Journal for the Study of Sephardic and Mizrahi Jewry* 1 (2007): 39-56.

———. "The Teachings of Redemption in Lurianic Kabbalah." Ph.D. diss., Hebrew University, 1988. [Hebrew]

———. "The Weaving of a Myth: An Analysis of Two Stories in the *Zohar*." In *Study and Knowledge in Jewish Thought*, Volume 2, edited by Howard Kreisel, 167-205. Beer-Sheva: Ben Gurion University Press, 2006. [Hebrew]

———. "Zoharic Narratives and Their Adaptations." *Hispania Judaica Bulletin* 3 (2000): 3-63.

Migne, Jacques P., ed. *Patrologiae Cursus Completus, Series Latina*. 221 vols. Paris: Garnier and Migne, 1844-1864.Milgrom, Jacob. *Leviticus 17-22: A New Translation with Introduction and Commentary*. Anchor Bible 3B. New York: Doubleday, 2000.

Mollenkott, Virginia R. *The Divine Feminine: The Biblical Imagery of God as Female*, New York: Crossroad Publishers, 1983.

Mopsik, Charles. *Sex of the Soul: The Vicissitudes of Sexual Difference in Kabbalah*, edited and with a forward by Daniel Abrams. Los Angeles: Cherub Press, 2005.

Mowinckel, Sigmund. *He That Cometh: The Messianic Concept in the Old Testament and Later Judaism.* Translated by G.W. Anderson. Oxford: Basil Blackwell, 1956.

Nacht, Jacob. *Simlei 'Ishah.* Tel Aviv: Private Production, 1959. [Hebrew]

Naeh, Shlomo. "Ḥeruta: A Talmudic Reflection on Freedom and Celibacy." In *Issues in Talmudic Research: Conference Commemorating the Fifth Anniversary of the Passing of Ephraim E. Urbach*, 10–27. Jerusalem: Israel Academy of Sciences and Humanities, 2001. [Hebrew]

Nachmanides (Ramban). *Commentary on the Torah: Genesis.* Translated and annotated by Charles B. Chavel. New York: Shilo Publishing House, 1978.

Nahman of Bratslav. *Liqqutei MoHaRaN.* Benei Beraq, 1972.

Nathan of Nemirov. *Liqqutei Halakhot.* Jerusalem, 1974.

Naveh, Hannah. "Heart of Home, Heart of Light: Representation of the Family in Hebrew Literature." In *The Love of Mothers and the Fear of Fathers*, edited by Aviad Kleinberg, 105-176. Tel Aviv: Keter and Tel Aviv University, 2004. [Hebrew]

Netzer, Ruth. *Journey to the Self: The Alchemy of the Mind – Symbols and Myths.* Ben Shemen: Modan, 2004. [Hebrew]

Neumann, Erich. *The Great Mother: An Analysis of the Archetype.* Princeton: Princeton University Press, 1963.

Neusner, Jacob. *Sifré to Numbers: An American Translation and Explanation, Volume Two: Sifré to Numbers 59-115.* Edited by J. Neusner. Atlanta: Scholars Press, 1986.

Newsom, Carol A., and Sharon H. Ringe, eds. *The Women's Bible Commentary.* London: SPCK, 1992.

Niditch, Susan. "'The Wrong Women Righted, Genesis 38." *Harvard Theological Review* 72, no. 1-2 (1979): 143-149.

Niehoff, Maren. "Constructing Ruth's image in the Midrash." *Jerusalem Studies in Jewish Thought* 11 (1993): 49-78. [Hebrew]

———. "Mother and Maiden, Sister and Spouse: Sarah in Philonic Midrash." *Harvard Theological Review* 97, no. 4 (2004): 413–444.

Nolan-Fewell, Danna, and David Gunn. "'A Son is Born to Naomi!'—Literary Allusions and Interpretation in the Book of Ruth." *Journal for the Study of the Old Testament* 40 (1988): 99-108.

Ogden, Thomas H. *The Primitive Edge of Experience.* Northvale: Jason Aronson, 1989.

Ogden Bellis, Alice. *Helpmates, Harlots, Heroines—Women's Stories in the Hebrew Bible.* Louisville: Westminster/John Knox, 1994.

Origen. *Homilies on Genesis and Exodus.* Translated by Ronald E. Heine. Fathers of the Church, Volume 71. Washington, D.C.: Catholic University of America Press, 1982.

Oron, Michal. "Artistic Elements in the Homiletics of the *Zohar.*" *Jerusalem Studies in Jewish Thought* 8 (1989): 299-310. [Hebrew]

Ortner, Sherry B. "Is Female to Male as Nature to Culture?" In *Woman, Culture, and Society*, edited by Michelle Zimbalist Rosaldo and Louise Lamphere, 67-87. Stanford University Press, 1974.

Pagels, Elaine. ""What Became of God the Mother? Conflicting Images of God in Early Christianity." *Signs* 2 (1976): 293-303.

Palgi-Hecker, Anat. *The Mother in Psychoanalysis: A Feminist View.* Tel Aviv: Am Oved, 2005. [Hebrew]

Pardes, Ilana. *The Biography of Ancient Israel: National Narratives in the Bible.* Berkeley: University of California Press, 2000.

———. *Countertraditions in the Bible—A Feminist Approach.* Cambridge: Harvard University Press, 1992.

Patai, Raphael. *The Hebrew Goddess.* New York: Ktav Publishing House, 1967.

———. *The Messiah Texts.* Detroit: Wayne State University Press, 1979.

Pedaya, Haviva. "Defect and Restoration of the Deity in the Works of Isaac the Blind." *Jerusalem Studies in Jewish Thought* 6 (1987): 157-285. [Hebrew]

———. *Expanses: An Essay on the Theological and Political Unconscious.* Tel Aviv: Hakibbutz Hameuchad, 2011. [Hebrew]

———. "The Great Mother: The Struggle Between Nahmanides and the *Zohar* Circle." In *Temps i Espais de la Girona Jueva*, 311-328. Girona: Patronat Call de Girona, 2011.

———. *Nahmanides: Cyclical Time and Holy Text.* Tel Aviv: Am Oved, 2003. [Hebrew]

———. "Sabbath, Sabbatai, and the Diminution of Moon—The Holy Conjunction: Sign and Image." *Eshel Beer-Sheva* 4 (1996):143- 191. [Hebrew]

———. "The Sixth Millenium: Millenarism and Messianism in the *Zohar*." *Da'at* 72 (2012): 51-98. [Hebrew]

———. *Vision and Speech· Models of Prophecy in Jewish Mysticism.* Los Angeles: Cherub Press, 2002. [Hebrew]

———. *Walking through Trauma: Rituals of Movement in Jewish Myth Mysticism and History.* Tel Aviv: Resling, 2011. [Hebrew]

Pelikan, Jaroslav, David Flusser, and Justin Lang, eds. *Mary: Images of the Mother of Jesus in Jewish and Christian Perspective.* Minneapolis: Fortress Press, 2005.

———. *Mary through the Ages: Her Place in the History of Culture.* New Haven: Yale University Press, 1996.

Peretz, Elihayu. *Ma'alot ha-Zohar—Mafte'ah Shemot ha-Sefirot.* Jerusalem: Academon, 1987. [Hebrew]

Perry, Menahem, and Meir Sternberg. "The King through Ironic Eyes: Biblical Narrative and the Literary Reading Process." *Poetics Today* 7 (1986): 275–322.

Philo. *Questions and Answers on Genesis.* Translated by Ralph Marcus. Loeb Classical Library. Cambridge: Harvard University Press, 1969.

Pomeroy, Sarah, ed. *Women's History and Ancient History.* Chapel Hill: University of North Carolina Press, 1991.

Rakover, Nahum. *Ends that Justify the Means.* Jerusalem: Library of Jewish Law, 2000. [Hebrew]

Rank, Otto. *The Myth of the Birth of the Hero, and Other Writings.* New York: Vintage Books, 1959.

Rapoport-Albert, Ada. *Women and the Messianic Heresy of Sabbatai Zevi, 1666–1816.* Oxford and Portland: Littman Library of Jewish Civilization, 2011.

Renan, Yael. *Goddess and Heroes: On the Limits of Power.* Tel Aviv: Am Oved, 2001. [Hebrew]

Rich, Adrienne. *Of Woman Born: Motherhood as Experience and Institution.* New York: Norton, 1976.

Rimerman, Yehuda. *Forbidden Relations in the Family: Sociology and Psychology of Incest.* Tel Aviv: Shercover, 1985. [Hebrew]

Ripple-Kleiman, Chana. "*Petaḥ Einayim*: On Eyes and Vision in the *Zohar*." Master's thesis, Hebrew University, 2008. [Hebrew]

Rofé, Alexander. *Introduction to the Literature of the Hebrew Bible.* Jerusalem: Simor, 2009.

Roi, Biti. "The Legs of the Shekhina as a Founding Image of an Ethos: An Inquiry into the Story of the Man on Crutches in Tiqqunei ha-*Zohar*." *Kabbalah* 23 (2010): 181-217. [Hebrew]

———. "The Myth of the *Shekhina* in *Tiqqunei ha-Zohar*: Poetic, Hermeneutic and Mystical Aspects." PhD diss., Bar-Ilan University, 1993. [Hebrew]

Rojtman, Betty. *The Forgiveness of the Moon: Essays on Biblical Tragedy.* Jerusalem: Carmel Publishing, 2008. [Hebrew]

Rosen-Zvi, Ishay. *Demonic Desires: "Yetzer Hara" and the Problem of Evil in Late Antiquity.* Philadelphia: University of Pennsylvania Press, 2011.

———. "The Evil Impulse, Sexuality and Yichud: A Chapter of Talmudic Anthropology." *Theory and Criticism* 14 (1999): 55-84. [Hebrew]

———. *The Mishnaic Sotah Ritual: Temple, Gender, and Midrash.* Leiden: Brill, 2012.

Rubin, Miri. *Mother of God: A History of the Virgin Mary.* New Haven: Yale University Press, 2009.

Rubin, Nissan. *The Beginning of Life: Rites of Birth, Circumcision and Redemption of the First-Born in the Talmud and Midrash.* Tel-Aviv: Hakibbutz Hameuchad, 1995. [Hebrew]

Ruether, Rosemary R. *Mary, the Feminine Face of the Church.* Philadelphia: Westminster, 1977.

Ruzer, Serge. *Mapping the New Testament.* Leiden: Brill, 2007.

Sachs-Shmueli, Leore. "The Image of the Prophetess Miriam as a Feminine Model in Zoharic Literature." *Kabbalah* 33 (2015): 183-210. [Hebrew]

Sack, Beracha. *The Kabbalah of Rabbi Moshe Cordovero.* Beer Sheva: Ben Gurion University Press, 1995. [Hebrew]

Sack, Beracha, ed. R. Moshe Cordovero, *Ma'ayan Ein Ya'aqov: Ha-Ma'ayan ha-Revi'i me-Sefer Elemah.* Beer Sheva: Ben Gurion University Press, 2009. [Hebrew]

Sagi, Avi, and Zvi Zohar. *Conversion and Jewish Identity: An Inquiry into the Foundations of the Halakhah.* Jerusalem: Shalom Hartman Institute and Bialik Institute, 1995. [Hebrew]

Saldarini, Anthony J. *Matthew's Christian-Jewish Community.* Chicago: University of Chicago Press, 1994.

Scarry, Elaine. *The Body in Pain.* Oxford: Oxford University Press, 2006.

Schaberg, Jane. *The Resurrection of Mary Magdalen: Legends, Apocrypha, and the Christian Testament.* New York: Continuum International Publishing Group, 2002.

Schäfer, Peter. *Jesus in the Talmud.* Princeton: Princeton University Press, 2007.

———. *The Jewish Jesus: How Judaism and Christianity Shaped Each Other.* Princeton: Princeton University Press, 2012.

———. *Mirrors of His Beauty: Feminine Images of God from the Bible to the Early Kabbalah.* Princeton: Princeton University Press, 2002.

Schneider, Michael. "The Angelomorphic Son of God, Yahoel and the Prince of Peace." *Kabbalah* 21 (2010):143–254. [Hebrew]

———. *The Appearance of the High Priest*, Los Angeles: Cherub Press, 1992. [Hebrew]

Scholem, Gershom. *Explications and Implications: Writings on Jewish Heritage and Renaissance.* 2 Vol. Tel Aviv: Am Oved, 1986. [Hebrew].

———. *Gershom Scholem's Annotated Zohar (Jozefoui 1873)*, with an introduction by Yehuda Liebes. Jerusalem: Magnes Press, 1992. [Hebrew]

———. *On the Kabbalah and Its Symbolism.* Translated by R. Manheim. New York: Schocken 1965.

———. *Major Trends in Jewish Mysticism.* New York: Schocken Books, 1941.

———. *The Messianic Idea in Judaism and Other Essays on Jewish Spirituality.* New York: Schocken Books, 1971.

———. *On the Mystical Shape of the Godhead: Basic Concepts in the Kabbalah.* Translated by Joachim Neugroschel, edited and revised by Jonathan Chipman. New York: Schocken Books, 1991.

———. "Qabbalot R. Yiṣḥaq ve-R. Ya'aqov, Benei R. Ya'aqov ha-Qohen." *Maddaei ha-Yahadut* 2 (1927): 227-230. [Hebrew]

———. *Sabbatai Ṣevi: The Mystical Messiah, 1626–1676.* Translated by R. J. Zwi Werblowsky. Princeton: Princeton University Press, 1973.

Scott, James. *Domination and the Arts of Resistance: Hidden Transcripts.* New Haven: Yale University Press, 1990.

Eleazar ben Judah of Worms. *Sefer ha-Shem.* Jerusalem, 2004.

Segal, Robert S. *Theorizing About Myth.* Amherst: University of Massachusetts Press, 1999.

Sheingorn, Pamela. "Appropriating the Holy Kinship: Gender and Family History." In *Medieval Families,* edited by Carol Neel, 273–301. Toronto: University of Toronto Press, 2004.

Shemesh, Aharon. *Halakhah in the Making: The Development of Jewish Law from Qumran to the Rabbis.* Berkeley: University of California Press, 2009.

Shinan, Avigdor and Yair Zakovitch. *The Story of Judah and Tamar: Genesis 38 in the Bible, The Old Versions and the Ancient Jewish Literature.* Research Projects of the Institute of Jewish Studies, Monograph Series 15. Jerusalem: The Hebrew University Press, 1992. [Hebrew]

Shochetman, Eliav. "Ma'aseh haba'ah be'aveirah." *Israel Law Review* 17, no. 3 (1982): 383–387. [Hebrew]

Shoham-Steiner, Ephraim. "The Virgin Mary, Miriam, and Jewish Reactions to Marian Devotion in the High Middle Ages." *AJS Review* 37 (2013): 75-91.

Sokoloff, Michael. *A Dictionary of Jewish Palestinian Aramaic of the Byzantine Period.* Jerusalem: Bar Ilan University Press, 1992.

Sokoloff, Michael. *A Dictionary of Judean Aramaic.* Ramat-Gan: Bar Ilan University Press, 2003.

Speiser, Ephraim Avigdor. *Genesis: A New Translation with Introduction and Commentary.* Anchor Bible 1. New York: Doubleday, 1979.

Stein, Ruth. "The Enigmatic Dimension of Sexual Experience: The 'Otherness' of Sexuality and Primal Seduction." *Psychoanalytical Quarterly* 67 (1998): 594–625.

———. "The Otherness of Sexuality: Excess." *The Journal of the American Psychoanalytic Association* 56 (2008): 43–71.

Steinsaltz, Adin. *Women in the Bible*. Tel Aviv: The Ministry of Defense, 1983. [Hebrew]

Stolorow, Robert D. *Trauma and Human Existence: Autobiographical, Psychoanalytic and Philosophical Reflections*. New York: Routledge, 2007.

Ta-Shma, Israel M. *The Revealed in the Hidden*. Tel Aviv: Hakibbutz Hameuhad, 1995. [Hebrew]

Theodor, J. and Ch. Albeck, eds. 3 vols. Jerusalem: Wahrmann Books, 1965.

Tishby, Isaiah. *Paths of Faith and Heresy*. Ramat Gan: Masada Publishing, 1964. [Hebrew]

———. *Studies in Kabbalah and Its Branches*. Jerusalem: Magnes Press, 1993. [Hebrew]

———. *The Wisdom of the Zohar: An Anthology of Texts*. 3 vols. Oxford: Littman Library of Jewish Civilization, 1989.

Trible, Phyllis. *God and the Rhetoric of Sexuality*. Philadelphia: Fortress Press, 1978.

Tsoffar, Ruth. "The Trauma of Otherness and Hunger: Ruth and Lot's Daughters." *Women in Judaism* 5, no. 1 (2007): 1-13.

Turner, Victor. *The Ritual Process: Structure and Anti-Structure*. Chicago: Aldine, 1969.

Urbach, Ephraim E. *The Halakhah: Its Sources and Development*. Translated by Raphael Posner. Jerusalem: Yad la-Talmud, 1986.

———. *The Sages: Their Concepts and Beliefs*. Translated by Israel Abrahams. Cambridge: Harvard University Press, 1975.

———. *The World of the Sages: Collected Studies*. Jerusalem: Magnes Press, 1988. [Hebrew]

Van Wijk-Bos, Johanna. "Out of the Shadows: Genesis 38; Judges 4:17-22; Ruth 3." *Semeia* 42 (1988): 37-67.

Visotzky, Burton L. *Fathers of the World: Essays in Rabbinic and Patristic Literature*. Tübingen: Mohr Siebeck, 1995.

Warner, Marina. *Alone of All Her Sex: The Myth and the Cult of the Virgin Mary*. New York: Alfred A. Knopf Press, 1976.

Weiss, Tzahi. ""Who is a Beautiful Maiden without Eyes? The Metamorphosis of a *Zohar* Midrashic Image from a Christian Allegory to a Kabbalistic Metaphor." *The Journal of Religion* 93, no. 1 (2013): 60-76.

Welldon, Astela. *Mother, Madonna, Whore: The Idealization and Denigration of Motherhood*. London: Karnac, 1988.

Winnicott, Donald W. *The Child, the Family and the Outside World*. Harmondsworth: Penguin Books, 1964.

———. "Fear of Breakdown." *International Journal of Psychoanalysis* 37 (1974): 386-388.

Wolfson, Elliot R. "Beautiful Maiden without Eyes: 'Peshat' and 'Sod' in Zoharic Hermeneutics." In *The Midrashic Imagination, Jewish Exegesis, Thought, and History*, edited by M. Fishbane, 155-203. Albany: SUNY Press, 1993.

———. *The Book of the Pomegranate: Moses de Leon's Sefer ha-Rimmon*. Atlanta: Scholars Press, 1988.

———. *Circle in the Square: Studies in the Use of Gender in Kabbalistic Symbolism*. Albany: SUNY, 1995.

———. "Gender and Heresy in Kabbalah Scholarship." *Kabbalah* 6 (2002): 231-262. [Hebrew]

———. *Language, Eros, Being: Kabbalistic Hermeneutics and Poetic Imagination*. New York: Fordham University Press, 2005.

———. *Open Secret Postmessianic Messianism and the Mystical Revision of Menahem Mendel Schneerson*. New York: Columbia University Press, 2009.

———. *Through a Speculum That Shines—Vision and Imagination in Medieval Jewish Mysticism*. Princeton: Princeton University Press, 1994.

———. "*Tiqqun ha-Shekhinah*: Redemption and the Overcoming of Gender Dimorphism in the Messianic Kabbalah of Moses Hayyim Luzzatto." *History of Religions* 36 (1997): 289–332.

———. *Venturing Beyond: Law and Morality in Kabbalistic Mysticism*. New York: Oxford University Press, 2006.

Yerushalmi, Yosef Hayim. *Freud's Moses: Judaism Terminable and Interminable*. New Haven: Yale University Press, 1993.

Yisraeli, Oded. *The Interpretation of Secrets and the Secret of Interpretation: Midrashic and Hermeneutic Strategies in Sabba de-Mishpatim of the Zohar*. Los Angeles: Cherub Press, 2005. [Hebrew]

———. *Temple Portals: Studies in Aggadah and Midrash in the Zohar*. Magnes Press, Jerusalem, 2013. [Hebrew]

Zakovitch, Yair. *David: From Shepherd to Messiah*. Jerusalem: Ben-Zvi Institute, 1995. [Hebrew]

———. *Ruth: Introduction and Commentary*. Miqra' le-Yisra'el. Tel Aviv and Jerusalem: Am Oved and Magnes Press, 1990. [Hebrew]

———. "The Threshing Floor Scene in Ruth." *Shnaton* 3 (1978–1979): 29–33. [Hebrew]

Index

A
Abigail, 19
Abrams, Daniel, 103n42, 106n47, 114, 115, 116n12, 123n41, 149n9, 174n2, 246
Alter, Robert, xiii, 5n15, 6n19, 26, 28n11, 55, 224n17
Androgynous/Hermaphrodite, 68, 149, 149n9, 164n48, 197n57, 198, 210, 215, 217
Antilia - see: *Ṭiqla*
Antinomian Deeds/Antinomianism, x, xvii, 18, 22-25, 69, 76, 84, 87, 105, 110, 117, 136, 140, 143, 210, 216, 244, 250-251
Aesthetic Conflict, 50n76, 81n16, 105, 216
Asulin, Shifra, 114, 147n5, 212n4
Augustine of Hippo, 225, 225n20

B
Bal, Mieke, xv, 3, 33, 59
Bataille, Georges, xin1, 21n38, 69n111, 97n26, 124n1, 169n59
Bathsheba, xi, 1-3, 8, 19, 23, 29, 34, 38, 40-41, 63, 68, 82, 94, 129, 208, 221, 239n46, 241, 248
"Beit-David", The House of David
    Davidic Dynasty, x-xi, xiii, xvi, 1, 3, 6, 10, 14, 17-19, 23, 30, 35, 39, 41, 48-50, 55-56, 62, 72-73, 80n13, 84, 88, 90, 93, 96, 99, 101, 118n18, 125, 128, 134, 136, 140-142, 177n9, 182, 186, 206, 216, 219n1, 222, 224, 226-227, 230n31, 232-233, 235, 238-240, 251-252
    Monarchic dynasty, 5, 16-17, 23-24, 27, 30, 52, 71, 88, 107, 124, 131
    Davidic Genealogy, 92, 220-221
"Beit- Shaul", The House of Saul 17, 83,
Benjamin, Jessica, xv, 17, 48n68
Biale, David, xiv, 3, 38, 220, 240

Birth
    Mythical Birth, x-xii, 1—2, 8—10, 13—15, 17, 19, 64, 84, 206
    Second Birth, 19, 64
    Theology and Birth
    Gender and Reproduction, 8, 11
Boaz, xi-xii, 1, 5, 7, 9, 12-16, 18, 29-30, 33, 36, 38, 40, 43, 45-47, 51-54, 56, 60, 66-68, 70, 75, 116-117, 118n20, 122n36, 131n28, 133n31, 134, 137-139, 143, 176-177, 177n9-10, 178-179, 178n14, 181, 183-193, 195, 200, 202, 204-208, 221, 235-237
Book of Judges, 8
Book of Ruth, xv, 5, 16, 25, 27, 29, 33-35, 38-39, 41, 43, 45, 78, 80, 134, 137, 174, 182, 185, 190, 193, 201, 205-207, 217, 221, 236
    assumption of judicial responsibility and identity of mutual recognition, 51
    characteristics of David's personality, 8, 22-23 genealogical lists, 6-7, 9-13, 18-19
    foreign women, 8
    intertexuality in, 3-4
    location of the blessing, 16-17
    motherhood and seduction, 61, 66-67, 70, 77
    "obscene" women, 94
    stories of Lot's daughters, Tamar, and Ruth, 2, 43, 46, 54, 56, 60
    threshing floor scene, 175-179, 181, 202
    use of the term "redemption" in, 36n37
Book of Samuel, 4, 8, 24-25, 81
Boyarin, Daniel, xiv, 107, 156n26, 227n26
Bush, Frederick, 9, 10n7

C
Campbell, Joseph, xiii, 10n7, 66n107
Carnival, 46

Chava, Eve
  Primordial Sin, 224, 235
  Chava and Lilith, xiv
  Heruta 95–99
Cixous, Hélène, xv, 109
Conversion, 75
Cordovero, Rabbi Moses, 114n5, 118n20, 141, 149n8, 154n19, 156, 160n37

D

David, x-xii, xiv, xvi, 1–2, 4, 8–14, 17–18, 22–25, 29, 31–32, 34, 38–39, 46, 56, 63, 66–68, 70–82, 94, 129–130, 138, 140–141, 144, 164, 181, 183, 205–207, 211, 213, 217, 224, 227, 237–240, 247, 252
Doniger, Wendy, xiv, 47, 77, 98n27, 221n7, 239n46
Dundes, Alan, xiii, 224n17, 229n30

E

Eschatological/ Eschatology, x, xvi, 102, 113, 133, 138–139, 141–142, 207, 216, 220, 251
Esther, 88, 88n4, 103–104, 241, 243–244, 244n61, 248
Evil Inclination, 97, 106n52, 111, 200
Excess, 52, 68, 81–82, 132n39, 191, 236

F

Fisch, Harold, 2n2, 3
Freud, Sigmund, 31n23, 32n27, 50n76, 70, 70n112, 114, 125, 125n5-6, 128n18, 132n29, 141n53, 192n48, 221, 221n6, 224n17, 228n27, 232n35, 233n36, 235, 235n39, 236n40, 250–251
Fonrobert, Charlotte, xiv, 12n13, 74n3, 75, 79–80, 80n13, 178n14, 227n26, 244
Fuchs, Esther, xv, 4, 11, 30, 56, 60, 126

G

Green Art (Arthur), 211n4, 221n6, 241n52, 244n61, 246n68, 249n78, 20n78

H

Hellner-Eshed, Melila, 114n5, 117, 147n5, 205

I

Idel, Moshe, xiii, 113, 117, 119n22, 121–122, 133, 241n53, 248
Incest, x, xiii, 1, 31–32, 35, 39–40, 48–49, 53–54, 59, 64, 67, 70, 88, 90–91, 90n7, 94, 100n35, 124–128, 125n2, 126n12, 127n13, 132n29, 134–135, 135n41, 137, 141, 141n53, 143–146, 173, 176, 216, 221, 226–229, 232n35, 234
Intertextuality, 3–4, 43
Infertility, 16–17, 26, 31, 77
Introduction to the Zohar, 120, 147, 150–151, 167, 172, 202, 204
Irigaray, Luce, xv, 7, 12n13, 12n15, 109, 114, 150n14
Irigaray, Luce, xv, 13, 109, 114

J

Jacob, 1–2, 16, 23, 35, 39–40, 44n59, 46–47, 68, 77–78, 84, 127, 148n6, 155, 165, 200, 221, 237, 239
Jerome, 129n20, 222
Jesus, xiv, xvi-xvii, 4, 123, 214, 220–224, 224n16-17, 225n19, 226, 226n23, 227, 229, 229n30, 232–233, 237n41-42, 239–241, 244n61, 245n65, 246–248
Jesse, 1, 7, 9, 11–13, 18, 39, 75–76, 79, 80n13, 221, 238–240
Jesse's Handmaiden, 73–78
Josephus, 128, 177, 178
Joseph, Son of Jacob and Rachel, 17, 83
Joseph, Mary's Husband, 221–222, 225, 237, 239
  Rabbi Joseph Karo, 213n9
Judah, xii, 1–2, 5, 9, 12–13, 15–16, 23, 28, 33–44, 46–47, 51–53, 55, 60, 65, 68, 70, 77–79, 84, 92, 116, 129, 143, 146–147, 151–154, 159–163, 160n37, 165–168, 176, 183, 185, 187, 211, 222, 231, 231n34, 235–236
Judah's Wife [*Shua's Daughter*], 18–19, 55
Jung, Carl Gustav, xi, 27n4, 40, 40n49, 50n75, 125–126

K

Kafka, Franz, xvi
Kristeva, Julia, xv, 31, 80, 82n17, 126, 225n19, 234
King David, xi, xiv, xvi, 1, 4, 8, 10, 22, 24, 46, 73, 83, 92, 94, 129, 132, 138, 140, 164, 181, 183, 211, 213, 221, 227, 238, 247, 252

L

Laplanche, Jacques, 235
de-León, Rabbi Moses, 116, 118, 200n65, 213n10-11
Levirate Marriage, yibbum, 2n2, 23, 34, 36, 184
  ḥaliṣa 53–54
Liebes, Yehuda, xiii, 63, 113, 116–117, 119, 120n25, 121, 121n30, 133, 136, 141,

146, 148n6, 172, 174n2, 175, 212n5, 241n53, 248
Lilith, xiv, 113, 147–148, 154–157, 157n31, 167, 169, 242–243, 247
Lot's Daughters, x, xii–xiii, 1–6, 3n9, 8, 13–15, 17, 19n30, 20, 22, 25, 27–28, 30, 31n24, 32–36, 38–40, 42–44, 46–47, 52–54, 56, 58–60, 62–68, 70, 76, 83, 88–95, 98–100, 110, 115n8, 123–125, 127–129, 128n19, 130n23, 131, 134–136, 138–141, 145, 166, 173, 177n10, 180, 186, 208, 215–216, 228
Lot's Wife, 34
Luke, xvii, 9n5, 58, 77, 220, 222–225, 227
Luzzatto, R. Moses Ḥayyim Luzzatto (Ramchal), 86–87, 101–106, 217

M

Mahlon and Chilion, 15, 34, 68, 186–187
Mamzer (Bastard), 53, 76, 226
Mary, xiv, xvii, 4, 58, 77, 115n8, 219, 219n1, 221–225, 222n8, 225n21–22, 226–227, 226n23–24, 229, 229n30, 231–234, 236, 236n40, 237, 239, 239n46, 240–241, 245, 245n65, 246–252
Masquerading, x, 44n59, 46, 48, 76
  Veil, Cloth 38, 42–49, 92, 149–50, 154, 169–171, 202n68
Matthew, 58, 220, 221, 222, 223, 224, 237
Menstruating Woman, *Nidda*, 11, 35, 156, 156n26, 157, 226, 239n47, 242, 244, 247, 247n70, 248
Meroz, Ronit, 116n9, 175
Messianic Idea, Messianism, x, 1, 5–6, 9, 20–22, 27, 31, 48, 58, 63, 69, 72, 76, 82, 112–113, 115, 118n18, 119–123, 139, 145, 165, 168, 174, 199, 207, 210, 220, 220n3, 227, 231, 248, 250n79–80, 252
Messiah, x–xi, xiii–xiv, xvi, 6, 8–9, 17, 20–22, 32, 41–42, 56, 58, 61, 63–64, 69, 77, 82–85, 88, 89n6, 90, 95n21, 99, 104n45, 105n48, 111, 120n26, 122–124, 130, 132–133, 135–136, 138–139, 140n51, 141, 143–145, 159, 164, 168, 183, 210–211, 214, 216–217, 219–222, 224–230, 232, 237, 237n41, 239, 239n48, 240–241, 250–252, 251n82
  Messiah son of David: *see* Davidic Dynasty
  Messiah son of Joseph, 17
Miriam, the Sister of Moses, 241, 241n54, 245, 245n64–65, 246, 248
Moab and Ammon, xii, 1–2, 28–30, 32, 34, 36, 46, 53, 57–59, 64, 67, 70, 75, 90–92, 95, 108, 129–132, 134, 230
Motherhood, xi–xii, xiv–xv, 5–6, 11, 16–18, 20–22, 27, 30, 41, 52, 76–77, 79, 99, 114n6, 118, 139–140, 157n31, 164, 166, 206, 219, 219n1, 223
  Motherhood and Fertility, 57–59, 61, 66–67, 225, 225n21, 230–234, 237–240, 251–252
Mothers and Daughters, 11, 13, 70
Mystical Union, 170n61
Myth, x–xvii, 1, 5–6, 13, 21, 24, 27, 38, 40–42, 48–51, 54, 57–58, 63, 67–73, 80, 82, 84, 86, 88, 94, 103, 105–107, 111–112, 114–116, 119–120, 122–123, 125, 128–129, 129n21, 131, 133, 135, 141, 141n53, 144, 146–147, 153–155, 167–168, 170–171, 175, 180, 187, 191, 202, 205, 207–208, 210, 216, 218–219, 221–223, 224n17, 227–228, 232–236, 237n41, 239–241, 243, 245, 248–249–252

N

Nahshon, 7, 9, 12, 18
Naveh, Hannah, 10
Nomos and Narrative, 4, 23n43, 35n36

O

Obed, 1, 7, 9, 12–13, 15, 17–18, 41, 57, 66–67, 77, 145, 182–184, 186–187, 206, 217, 221
Origen, 128, 226
Other, Otherness, 24, 31, 48, 79, 107, 109, 132, 169, 202n68, 232n34, 237

P

Pardes, Ilana, xv, 3, 16, 27, 45n62, 56, 245
Pedaya, Haviva, 112n1, 114n4, 117n14, 121n32, 122n37, 133, 164n48, 175n5, 196, 214, 249
Peretz *Ma'alot ha-Zohar—Mafteaḥ Shemot ha-Sefirot*, 213n10
Perez and Zerach, 1, 10n9, 18–19, 37, 42, 55–57, 65, 68, 153, 166, 187, 221, 231
Philo, 78n10, 128n19, 149n9, 168n58, 213n7, 248n73
Prostitution/Promiscuity, 1, 2n3, 8, 11, 22, 29, 35–36, 58, 88, 98, 98n27, 146, 215, 222, 227n26, 234–235, 241, 244, 248, 250–251

R

Rachel and Leah, xi, 1–3, 7–8, 12–17, 24, 33–34, 45n62, 47, 67–68, 77–79, 81, 82n17, 93, 208, 239
Rahab, 83, 221–222
Rank, Otto, xiii
Rape, 14, 28, 32, 34, 36, 38, 47–48, 52–53, 103–105, 104n45, 128, 226n24, 235
Rich, Adrienne, xv
Roi, Biti, 114n5, 175n5, 196, 247
Rosen-Zvi, Ishay, xiv, 98n28, 106n52

Rubin, Nissan, 11
Ruth, see Book of Ruth,

S

Salvation, xii–xiii, 17, 63, 74, 76, 86, 88, 89n6, 92, 96–97, 100, 104, 104n45, 105, 105n48, 119, 136, 138, 161, 171, 179, 192-193, 207, 229, 238n43
Scholem, Gershom, xiii, 72, 116–117, 120–121, 141, 152n18, 156n27, 158, 199, 206, 208, 212, 213n11
Sexuality
  Sexual Subversion, xiv, 3
  Bedtrick, xi, 47, 75, 98n27, 239n46
  Feminine Deceit, Holy Deceit, 36, 79, 139, 184
Sin/Transgression, x, xi, xin1, xii–xv, xvii, 1, 3–4, 6, 8–9, 14, 18, 21, 23, 25–26, 28–29, 35–36, 38–39, 49, 51, 53–54, 61, 63, 66–67, 71–72, 75–77, 79, 85–92, 94–101, 103–104, 106–107, 109–112, 124, 126, 131, 133–134, 136–137, 139, 146, 198, 200, 210, 215–217, 223–224, 226–228, 231, 234, 251–252
Sabbatai Ṣevi, 220
  Sabbatean Thought, Sabbateanism, 87, 101-104, 143n56, 210, 215-217,
Shekhinah, xi, 220, 241–250
  Shechkinah as the Mother of the Messiah, xi, 220, 241–250
Shinan, Avigdor, 3, 55n87
Snake, 23, 156, 156n27
Sodom, 14, 28, 30, 32–34, 36, 47, 52, 59, 64–65, 91, 127–132, 134–135, 138, 141, 144, 228, 235
Solomon, xi, 1, 19, 29, 34, 41, 92, 94, 129, 183, 207, 213n11, 221
Son of God (divi filius), 20, 41, 67, 73, 130, 228, 239n48
Sublimation, 4n10, 40, 90n7, 125–126, 235

T

Taboo, xi, xin1, xv, 23, 35, 37, 39–40, 125, 127, 141, 141n53, 216, 228, 232n35
Tamar, x, xii–xiii, 1–8, 10–15, 17–20, 22–25, 27–30, 31n24, 32–44, 46–47, 51–56, 58–68, 70, 76–77, 81–83, 85, 88, 90, 90n7, 92–93, 98, 100, 110, 113–114, 115n8, 123, 127–128, 142–143, 146–149, 147n5, 149n9, 150–173, 160n37, 176, 177n9-10, 182–188, 204, 208, 211, 213, 215–216, 221–222, 229–232, 235–236, 239n46, 242–243
Trible, Phyllis, xv, 30, 34n32, 56
Turner, Victor, 20n31, 114, 214–215

Theurgy, 114n5
Trauma, 31, 31n24, 32n27, 33, 35, 39, 59, 64, 70, 70n112, 121, 128, 170, 196, 234–238, 251n82, 252
Ṭiqla, 112, 124, 132–145, 133n32, 184, 215–217
Tiqqunei Zohar, 1130–114, 118–120, 125n2, 173–175, 175n5, 180–181, 188, 192–201, 203–205, 208, 244n61
Twins, 43, 53, 55, 59, 65, 82n17, 92

V

Virginity, xvii, 51, 57–58, 215, 219, 221, 223–225, 227, 227n26, 229–230, 230n32, 231–233, 233n36, 234–237, 329, 241, 241n53, 242–244, 245n65, 246–248, 248n74, 249–252, 249n77

W

Wine and drunkenness, 2, 42, 44n58, 47, 64, 91, 95, 98, 130, 145, 228
Wolfson, Elliot, 101, 105, 109, 113, 117, 197, 211, 212, 247, 249
Women, Femininity, xii, 16, 25, 27, 80, 118, 164, 175, 208n80, 212, 231, 234, 249
  Sisterhood, 236, 238
  Strange Woman, 5n13
  Agency, xiv, 80n13, 192, 236
  Female Archetypes, xi, 25, 27, 29n14, 94, 100, 132, 141, 150, 154–155, 164, 224, 232
  Feminine narrative, 2, 8, 13, 16, 61, 76
  foreign woman, 3, 28, 31, 56, 62, 72, 88, 93, 154

Y

Yael, 83, 88, 90, 90n7, 92–93, 96, 98–101, 103–104, 106, 110
Yalkut ha-Makhiri, xii, 1, 11, 72, 77, 79–82, 217, 238–239, 239n46
  David's mothers in, 73–77

Z

Zakovitch, Yair, 3, 3n9, 10n7, 45n62, 55n87, 68n110, 76–77, 79, 177n10
Zohar, x–xiii, xvii, 2, 49, 63n102, 101n38, 112–115, 115n8, 116, 116n13, 117–124, 118n20, 132–136, 138–149, 147n5, 150–155, 157, 156n28, 158–159, 160n37, 161, 164, 166–170, 173–174, 174n2, 179–181, 181n22, 185n32, 186–1891, 197, 202, 204–213, 213n10–11, 215–217, 241n53, 242–250
Zoharic Circle, 132, 132n30

www.ingramcontent.com/pod-product-compliance
Lightning Source LLC
Chambersburg PA
CBHW052014290426

44112CB00014B/2237